AF713066

A New Approach to Psi

This book critiques conventional parapsychological viewpoints about extrasensory perception (ESP) and psychokinesis (PK), collectively referred to as 'psi'.

Since the 1930s, an over-arching view on psi has been built on J. B. Rhine's research and theories at Duke University. The author argues that there are fundamental problems with the psi paradigm, and offers solutions based largely on Jung's Theory of Synchronicity, treating the subject matter in a rigorous scientific way. The synchronicity concept speaks to ambiguous psi terminology, the narrow methodological approaches in psi testing, and limited interpretations of psychic experience that do not consider the pivotal role of meaning. This book considers problems with terminology, findings, and the psi construct from a Jungian synchronistic standpoint, which gives credence to issues such as archetypes, meaningfulness, and numinosity.

An important new contribution to the understanding of psi, this book will be of interest to practitioners and researchers working in the disciplines of psychology, parapsychology, consciousness studies, and physics, especially quantum mechanics.

Lance Storm is a Visiting Research Fellow at the School of Psychology, University of Adelaide, Australia. He has over 20 years of post-doctoral research experience as a theorist and designer of funded experiments in parapsychology. Storm has published in major journals including *Psychological Bulletin*, *Journal of Parapsychology*, and *Journal of Scientific Exploration*. He is a full member of the AIPR, and Chief Editor of the *Australian Journal of Parapsychology*.

A New Approach to Psi

Re-Envisioning Paranormal Experience as Meaningful Coincidence

Lance Storm

Routledge
Taylor & Francis Group
LONDON AND NEW YORK

Designed cover image: The Flammarion Engraving. The original black-and-white version can be found in *The atmosphere: Popular meteorology* (1888, p. 163) by Camille Flammarion (1842–1925), published by Hachette (Paris). Colorized version owned by Günther Schöll, Germany. Used with Permission.

First published 2025
by Routledge
4 Park Square, Milton Park, Abingdon, Oxon OX14 4RN

and by Routledge
605 Third Avenue, New York, NY 10158

Routledge is an imprint of the Taylor & Francis Group, an informa business

© 2025 Lance Storm

The right of Lance Storm to be identified as author of this work has been asserted in accordance with sections 77 and 78 of the Copyright, Designs and Patents Act 1988.

All rights reserved. No part of this book may be reprinted or reproduced or utilised in any form or by any electronic, mechanical, or other means, now known or hereafter invented, including photocopying and recording, or in any information storage or retrieval system, without permission in writing from the publishers.

Trademark notice: Product or corporate names may be trademarks or registered trademarks, and are used only for identification and explanation without intent to infringe.

British Library Cataloguing-in-Publication Data
A catalogue record for this book is available from the British Library

ISBN: 978-1-032-91098-7 (hbk)
ISBN: 978-1-032-91097-0 (pbk)
ISBN: 978-1-003-56132-3 (ebk)

DOI: 10.4324/9781003561323

Typeset in Times New Roman
by KnowledgeWorks Global Ltd.

To the memory of a psi explorer, Michael A. Thalbourne (1955–2010)

Dedicated to truth-seekers everywhere

Special thanks to Helen and Madeline for their curiosity

Contents

Preface

> ... there is a capacity for acquiring knowledge that transcends the sensory functions.
> (J. B. Rhine, 1947, p. 204)

The word "psi" is used "either as a noun or adjective to identify paranormal processes and paranormal causation" (Thalbourne, 2003, p. 92). Psi works as a shorthand term for *extrasensory perception* (ESP) and *psychokinesis* (PK) as *processes*, but the word is also descriptive (e.g., a *psi* effect). ESP and PK are considered paranormal because ESP is defined as the "acquisition of information about, or response to, an external event, object or influence (mental or physical; past, present or future) otherwise than through any of the known sensory channels" (Thalbourne, p. 40), and PK is defined as "the direct influence of mind on a physical system that cannot be entirely accounted for by the mediation of any known physical energy" (p. 98). But then we come to *meaningful coincidence*, or as Jung called it, synchronicity—a "coincidence in time of two or more causally unrelated events which have the same or a similar meaning" (Jung, 1952/1969, para. 849). Conventionally, the meaningfulness in synchronicity differentiates it from psi which tends not to be regarded as meaningful. Going a little further, and in keeping with conventional views, Palmer (2016b) notes that psi is regarded as "an ability" whereas synchronicity is held to be "a principle of nature" (p. 193). Both claims may be saying too much because some people see a degree of overlap (Mansfield et al., 1998), as did Jung, who regarded psi as a form of synchronicity: "These [ESP] experiments and the whole experience of ESP are sufficient proof that meaningful coincidences do exist" (1968, para. 1198).

As to the actual reality of paranormal phenomena, we are treading a fine line because parapsychologists have not arrived at any firm conclusions about the so-called 'extrasensory' process (if it is *extra*-sensory), and the limits of ESP have not been demarcated. In other words, ESP may either be an extended form of information gathering, or something that only looks like information gathering. To put it another way, it may turn out that ESP means nothing more than opening the door to reality (inner and outer) somewhat wider than usual by way of *expanded* consciousness—a modest variant of *extended* consciousness—opening our minds to what is within us and all around us, but all the time working within the isolating parameters of spacetime (the mathematically determined four-dimensional construct).[1] So-called paranormal 'information acquisition' may be a process more like osmosis or infusion, or merely the manifestation or recognition in consciousness (or awareness) of correlates, just as our sensory modalities (seeing, hearing, etc.) facilitate the creation of correlates—processes that build up pictures of the world, but we must note that these pictures would indicate *correspondences* only, for it can never be possible to witness and describe reality exactly as it is, though we have hints, most of which are probably ineffable.

Likewise with PK, parapsychologists are not sure to what extent the human will or consciousness itself can *manipulate* matter in the physical environment (if that indeed is what is taking place). In other words, PK may not be limited to mental *influences* on living and non-living systems, but may actually include the *creation* of physical substance (i.e., matter). Alternatively, too much may have been claimed for PK, which may prove to be a misleading term for convenient psychophysical 'arrangements', and certainly psychophysiological phenomena should not be (but often are) thought of as PK. We are free to speculate on these limits, and arrive at our own definitions of, and theories about psi—and our speculations either rein in or go beyond conventional understandings of ESP and PK—but currently we are nowhere near a solution. Nevertheless, such speculation can open the door to broader concepts like synchronicity that embrace ESP and PK, and add extra psychological and psychophysical dimensions to psi. And I regard that expansion as a likely and important step.

Many of my colleagues might not be surprised to read these remarks as it is becoming quite the trend in parapsychology to think in these ways, as polarizing as they may be. But all would agree that the paranormal (at least at face value) is no weirder than Einstein's "spooky action at a distance," which quantum physicists call "entanglement" (i.e., non-classical correlations of separated but related particles). In fact, Filk (2014) suggests that entanglement is possibly the closest physical parallel to Jung's synchronicity. And it helps some psi theorists to know that Einstein authoritatively gave spacetime a 'relative' foothold, having once said "the distinction between past, present and future is only a stubbornly persistent illusion."[2]

In this book, I endeavour to explore the phenomenon of psi from all angles; its ambiguities and its paradoxes, but more than that, I will consider its inconsistencies and even its inadequacies, many of which are clearly stated even within the field of parapsychology itself. While I cover not only psi but also synchronicity in some detail in this volume, the reader will find a more detailed attempt to merge the two concepts in a subsequent book (Storm, 2025).

Conceptually, work on this book began in 2008 with an anthology I edited called *Synchronicity: Multiple Perspectives on Meaningful Coincidence* (Storm, 2008e)—I will be referring to chapters from that anthology quite often throughout this book. I thank again those who contributed to that anthology. Some of them are no longer with us: Victor Mansfield (1941–2008) passed away suddenly only months before the anthology's release, Berthold Eric Schwartz (1924–2010) passed away two years after publication, William Braud (1942–2012) passed away four years after publication; James Hall (1934–2013) passed away five years after publication; and both F. David Peat (1938–2017) and Lila L. Gatlin (1928–2017) passed away nine years after publication—my posthumous thanks go to those magnificent scholars. No doubt the works they leave behind are seeds from the past growing in the present and into the future. I also extend my posthumous thanks to two contributors Kenower Bash (1913–1986), and John Beloff (1920–2006), both of whom had passed before I had given even the slightest thought towards compiling a collection of synchronicity articles that became the *Synchronicity* anthology. I must also thank the other contributors Robert Aziz, Joseph Cambray, Marialuisa Donati, George Hogenson, Roderick Main, John Palmer, Sally Rhine-Feather, Shantena Sabbadini, and Charles Tart. Influences from all these authors are apparent in my three summing-up chapters in *Synchronicity*; indeed, the works of these same authors will quite often be cited in the pages to follow.

In practical terms, as far as producing the manuscript that became this book, I did not actually start tapping away on the keyboard until 2017. My thanks go to all those just mentioned, as well as my newfound colleagues, students, and friends who, in many discussions on the topics of psi and synchronicity, set me thinking that it was time for another *look* (at the psi problem), and another *book* (on synchronicity), even when none of us expected it at the time. Those people include Laurence Browne, Tony Jinks, Madeline Kretschmer, Colin Mitchell, Dominic Gill, and Robb Tilley.

—Lance Storm
2024

Notes

1 To avoid evoking 'classical' or Newtonian ideas of two separate constructs (space + time) working in tandem, I use the term 'spacetime', which is in current use in physics to indicate the inseparability of the components comprising the four-dimensional continuum that depicts gravitational and relativistic (observer-relevant) effects.

2 Einstein wrote a letter of condolence to the Besso family after his old friend Michele Angelo Besso passed away. The alternative translation of the relevant passage is: "… the separation between past, present and future has only the importance of an admittedly tenacious illusion" (Venning, 2019).

Introduction

> … if psi is hidden, it is hidden in plain sight and everywhere.
>
> (James C. Carpenter, 2012, p. 7)

Is parapsychology running low on grand ideas that might help us understand the paranormal? For that matter, have we exhausted the past of these ideas? Many parapsychologists might point to a range of theories,[1] and argue that they have enough to be getting on with as not all theories have been refuted and discarded. But parapsychologists might also be stuck in their old ways and not really advancing. American philosopher Thomas Kuhn (1962) spoke to this problem by claiming that science, when stuck in an old paradigm, and finding itself short on answers, cannot progress unless and until there is a complete shift to a new paradigm that answers a host of new questions. These sorts of shifts have happened in other disciplines; for example, biology (Darwin, 1859/2004) and physics (Heisenberg, 1949).

Whether parapsychologists are ready or not, parapsychology may also be heading for a paradigm shift given that some extant parapsychological theories seem due for retirement; it is more than mere opinion that parapsychologists have, for too long now, been grappling with outmoded concepts like extrasensory perception (ESP) and psychokinesis (PK)—terms which I defined in the Preface. For example, there is a move towards 'nonlocal' explanations away from old 'energy' and 'informational' models whereby ESP was formerly conceptualized as a signal buried in noise. Similarly, where PK is thought to be a direct influence by mental exertion on animate (physiological) and inanimate (physical) matter, others argue that retro-causation suffices in explaining the so-called 'influence'. Yet even when there are attempts to synthesize a range of parapsychological theories, the approach is still very much grounded in old (conventional) forms of parapsychological thinking (e.g., Nahm, 2019).

One grand idea that may help us understand the paranormal in a very different (paradigm-shifting) sense is C. G. Jung's Theory of Synchronicity (Jung, 1952/1969, para. 916–946). Jung defines synchronicity as a "coincidence in time of two or more causally unrelated [acausal] events which have the same or a similar meaning" (para. 849). A good example of synchronicity is the well-documented

DOI: 10.4324/9781003561323-1

Stockholm fire incident as reported by Jung (1952/1969, para. 912, 915). In 1759, at a dinner party in Gothenburg, Swedish religious leader, scientist, philosopher, and mystic, Emanuel Swedenborg (1688-1772), while in an agitated state, had a vision of houses on fire nearly 500 kilometres away in Stockholm. Jung writes:

> When … the vision arose in Swedenborg's mind of a fire in Stockholm, there was a real fire raging there at the same time, without there being any demonstrable or even thinkable connection between the two.
>
> (para. 912)

An account of this fire, including such details as the time of the fire, and when it was put out, was given by Swedenborg to guests at the party held by a Mr. William Castel. Though the fire had consumed 300 houses, Swedenborg was relieved that the fire had stopped three doors from his own house (a fact which was confirmed later). The same account was given later to the Gothenburg city authorities. It took two to three days for news from Stockholm to reach Gothenburg by courier. Jung makes a point about the meaningfulness of synchronicity in that the fire "was in a sense, burning in him [Swedenborg] too" (para. 912), and he hails this psychological fact as being a prime ingredient of the synchronistic event. This revelation of Jung's is derived from details in Swedenborg's biography in which is indicated the likelihood of a psychological state Jung describes as an "inner fire"—an inner manifestation or representation of fear and anxiety.[2] The archetype of fire is often taken to be symbolic of intense emotional affect, frustration, turmoil, and so on. Therefore, Swedenborg's "inner" (or spiritual) fire is of particular meaningful (i.e., psychological) significance. As an aside, C. A. Meier (2001) relates a similar event involving inner and outer fire which took place outside the Café Odeon in Zurich where physicist Wolfgang Pauli was seated, "pondering over his inferior function (feeling-color red)" (p. xviii):

> There was a large, unoccupied car parked outside the café. [Pauli] could not take his eyes off it, and then it suddenly caught fire and burst into flames.
>
> (p. xviii)

This example gives further evidence of the experient's psychological (inner) link to the physical (outer) event without the need to assume the link is causal—that is to say, Pauli did not *cause* the car to catch fire, which can be explained in any number of normal ways. In fact, relatively speaking, acausality *per se* is not the mystery; the real mystery is how Pauli managed to get himself into these situations! (For more on Pauli's synchronicities, see Chapter 2.) Note too that for the more common type of synchronicity to be effected, we need (a) an inner *and* outer condition (acausally connected), and (b) meaningfulness (i.e., an *equivalence of meaning*, or a meaningful parallel). If we do not have these two conditions (a) and (b), we only have a meaningless coincidence, or a cluster of meaningless coincidences, which Jung calls "meaningless chance groupings" (1952/1969, para. 846).

Yet synchronicity theory has not been embraced by the parapsychological community as a viable proposition (for a refutation, see Beloff, 1977), though ironically it does seem that synchronicity is a phenomenon academics and lay-persons quite often experience and talk about amongst themselves (and practice, for example, in the *I Ching*). Indeed, parapsychologists overlook it, unlike their stock-in-trade ESP and PK, which I will argue are, for the most part, ultimately the same thing as synchronicity. In fact, Jung (1951/1969) implied a parallel between psi and synchronicity when he says that Rhine's experimental results rule out the possibility of "transmission of force" or other causal factors, leading him to assume that "improbable accidents of an acausal nature—that is, meaningful coincidences—have entered the picture" (para. 979).

Perhaps synchronicity is thought to be too loosely and inconsistently defined (conceptually speaking), and therefore too multi-faceted for controlled experimentation in the laboratory; or too 'psychoanalytic', and therefore too much owned by analysts and psychiatrists; or too 'metaphysical' so that it is only really appreciated by philosophers, theologians, or those in the New Age movement (Hocoy, 2012). Indeed, Jungian psychotherapist Ira Progoff (1973) refers to the seeming "conflict" in Jung's merging of "the rational scientific and the nonrational esoteric" (p. 10). Or maybe the label 'acausal' has put researchers off—this is evident in John Beloff's (1990) resistance (see Chapter 3), and Jule Eisenbud's tirade of 1977 against synchronicity (calling it a "cosmic copout"), quoted at length by author and psychic Alan Vaughan in his book *Incredible Coincidence* (Vaughan, 1979, pp. 220–222). Or maybe the above reviews were too negative for synchronicity to rate as a solution to parapsychology's ultimate question, What is this "anomaly in need of an explanation", to borrow from Jessica Utts (1991, p. 377).

As parapsychologists know, Utts's "anomaly" goes by the name 'psi'—a convenience term used "to describe paranormal processes and paranormal causation" (Thalbourne, 2003, p. 92). For parapsychologists, evidence of the paranormal is primarily statistical in nature, though it is far more than that when viewed phenomenologically (i.e., as a lived experience in subjective consciousness). Synchronicity is more phenomenological than statistical (the latter of which best describes lab-psi, or at least that is how it has come down to us). And the reason anything paranormal has come down to us as *primarily statistical in nature* is because psi (unlike synchronicity) became a laboratory specimen; there was (and is) much one can do with it in the laboratory in the sense of controlling it, and there are countless examples of this (skeptics should take note of that point). But in the process, psi has been stripped of its natural status (i.e., it has lost its ecological validity); small wonder it looks nothing like synchronicity.

However, I suggest the time is right for a re-consideration of Jung's theory. While that may take some intense effort, theorists may be emboldened by the justifiable fact that parapsychology is riddled with ambiguous terminology requiring an assessment (or re-assessment) aimed at resolving problems that are not merely 'semantic' in the vernacular sense but even go beyond meaning and understanding and connotation (on these problems, see Braude, 1998, 2020). In Chapter 1, I will show that much of the culpability for those problems stems from J. B. Rhine's legacy, for it is Rhine who furthered the use of the terms extrasensory perception, psychokinesis, telepathy, clairvoyance, precognition, and so on. Telepathy refers to the "paranormal acquisition of information concerning the thoughts, feelings or activity of another conscious being" (Thalbourne, 2003, p. 125). Clairvoyance is defined as "paranormal acquisition of information concerning an object [or symbol] or contemporary physical event; in contrast to telepathy, the information is assumed to derive directly from an external physical source" (Thalbourne, 2003, p. 18). Precognition is defined as "a form of extrasensory perception in which the target is some future event that cannot be deduced from normally known data in the present" (Thalbourne, 2003, p. 90). To continue that point on 'culpability' (for want of a better word), the classic error we are all warned against—namely, *reification*—has a far bigger retarding influence on the field's progress than playful *speculation* about the substance, the reach, and the potential of the paranormal, the former of which (reification) many parapsychologists use as a protective shield and a justification for the latter (speculation), and *vice versa*. Psi in any of its manifestations will serve to illustrate this point.

The state of play right now? Parapsychologists continue to reel from long-held accusations disguised as explanations that putatively rid skeptical society of this psi spectre (a fine example of this bias manifests in the polemic by Reber & Alcock, 2020).[3] Still in vogue are the usual suspects that explain away psi: publication bias, fraud, methodological errors and misconduct (e.g., sensory leakage, optional stopping), dodgy handling of the data (e.g., data-mining)—all now captured by the more general term, *questionable research practices* (QRPs).[4] The list goes on (more on these and related issues can be found throughout the book; especially Chapters 2 and 3). In those two chapters, I will show some of the effects of the Trickster, mainly from the parapsychologist's point of view, and we will see psi as synchronicity in fine form. It will also be seen that some so-named psi effects deserve the claim of 'anomalous' (or even "paranormal"), but other related effects have over-stayed their welcome (in particular, the chronological decline effect and possibly the experimenter effect in certain laboratory situations).

Where accusation fails, but denial still persists, I have begun to think that the refusal to even admit the possibility of so-called psi phenomena is not sufficiently explained by any one of the following factors working alone: (a) the extraordinary 'unbelievability' of the phenomena (their 'woo-woo' aspects); (b) violation of Broad's (1949) Basic Limiting Principles;[5] (c) crippling fear of the phenomena; or (d) social, philosophical, and/or religious prejudice. Many (maybe most) disciplines get singled out whenever *at least* one of these factors is evident, especially (d), but they always bounce back and the public invariably maintains its trust in them.

It is worse for parapsychology—it never had a problem 'bouncing back' because it never had a respected or recognized place in a disciplinary context. Broadly speaking, parapsychology is *too different* when compared to the other disciplines, simply because *all* these factors (a) to (d) work in tandem against it, and that is enough to place parapsychology in a class or domain of its own; namely, Trickster territory—the mainstream world sees parapsychology as being in violation of the natural order, and it does not like it when the rules get broken too often and in too many ways, and things that should not happen, do so.

There is, however, also the likelihood that traditionally oriented psi pundits hold a (misconceived) view that coincidence, even the meaningful kind (as in synchronicity), cannot possible explain psi—especially in psi's most varied, detailed, and inspirational forms; and in its capacity to predict; and in its accuracy and precision (though I must add all of these are *occasional*, ironically making psi *often* unpredictable and only *relatively* reliable). There is a little more to synchronicity than coincidence, and only some informed parapsychologists are aware of the contingent factor of 'archetypes' in synchronicity (see Chapter 1). Jung tells us that archetypes are like ground-plans or blueprints, and *when they constellate* their overall effects in normal and paranormal events will carry with them characteristic pre-defined meanings, the key archetypal process of which we are only beginning to understand as the operative factor underpinning synchronicity.

Speaking from my experience as an empiricist, my feeling is that the whole idea of seemingly uncontrollable archetypes playing a crucial part in synchronicity, and the extension of this concept to ESP and PK, puts off experimenters who are set on gaining as much control over psi as is humanly possible (to do that, they need psi to be a *caused* effect; an expressed ability). I suspect too that those and other experimenters might simply say contingent factors are the same as those variables which (if not unknown) are *thought* to be, or *are* psi-conducive, or psi-permissive, or necessary, or sufficient in bringing about a psi effect. All very fine, and they may indeed have archetypal links, but I make two points on the issue of control: First, the aim of gaining as much control over psi as possible is generally restricted to the confines of the laboratory, not the real world, and since lab-psi and real-world psi are so polarized, we do not assume that lack of control in the latter (so true of naturally occurring synchronicity and spontaneous psychokinesis) must extend to the former. It follows that synchronicity, if it could be brought into the laboratory, would have every right to be treated like laboratory psi. Second, it never occurs to the majority of those in the experimental community that, for example, the replication problem, so ingrained in parapsychological thought, and bemoaned by parapsychologists, is a failing that might be resolved by a much-needed broader vision such as is offered by synchronicity theory and its inclusion of archetypes—as classical Jungian scholar, mathematician and colleague of Jung, Marie-Louise von Franz (1992) has stated: "… something synchronistic might happen when an archetype is constellated" (p. 27).

As I see it, the archetypes—or more accurately, failure to identify and elicit (*constellate*) archetypal situations in the laboratory, or even posit their presence) may be at the root of our *main concern* (which is the sporadic nature of psi) in experimental parapsychology (these issues will come up in Chapter 4). However, testing synchronicity should not be any more difficult than testing ESP and PK. Indeed, I suggest throughout this text that experimenters are already doing that, but do not realize it—for example, they only need to consider the content of their targets in terms of their numinosity (e.g., their emotional charge) and their relevance and meaningfulness to participants. John Palmer (2008), although a parapsychologist with a long history of following the Rhinean paradigm, nevertheless suggests as quite feasible the possibility of creating laboratory-based situations where archetypes and archetypal situations may be invoked.

The fact that a paranormal factor seems to be involved in psi and synchronicity justifies the comparison, but so little is known about both that we really have no notion of what is going on when either happens, or how and why they happen—as Brian Millar (2012a) says "those who talk about Psi without a theory *literally* don't know what they are talking about" (p. 11). Elsewhere he argues that signal-based (Rhinean) theories "offer unlimited possibilities for psi technology", but if "psi consists exclusively of nonlocal correlations it can hardly be of more than theoretical interest" (Millar, 2015, p. 175). I hope to show that none of these statements can be entirely true. In Chapter 4, I necessarily look at an array of theories that touch on synchronistic ideas to see if any of them might justify the claim that parapsychologists do at least have an *inkling* of what they are talking about. And throughout the book I will argue that anything 'signal-based' certainly has limits, but the *parapsychological* idea that there is no upper limit to 'nonlocal effects' is far from proved, regardless of what physicists say about nonlocality. This idea will be picked up in Chapter 5, and in pursuit of even spookier parapsychological ideas, I will necessarily shift my focus to the world of physics, and consider one of the biggest hopes parapsychologists have for an answer to the psi riddle: Quantum Mechanics (QM).[6] As physicist and parapsychologist Dean Radin has said:

> We'll see what happens when experience is viewed from the perspective of quantum theory, and in doing so we'll find a surprise: Certain phenomena previously thought to be impossible might, in fact, exist.
>
> (Radin, 2006a, pp. 5–6)

As I see it, Radin is not wrong in saying "we'll find a surprise", but what form might that "impossible" surprise take? Speaking against this idea, Millar (2015) argues that "the coherent quantum state upon which the psi effect is supposed to depend" (p. 175) would decay as soon as one tried to apply psi to the world. But nobody knows for certain if this is true, and the debate continues.

Psychologist and psychiatrist C. G. Jung (1875-1961), together with Nobel Prize laureate and physicist Wolfgang Pauli (1900-1958), came close to a QM answer of sorts in the mid-20th century. They tied psyche and matter together conceptually (especially in their anomalous modes) by demonstrating how archetypes influence scientific thinking. But in a real sense, they argued further that archetypes were related to a single principle underpinning and uniting psyche and matter (Jung & Pauli, 1955), such that a schematic philosophy has sprung from its suppositions (Atmanspacher & Fuchs, 2014; Meier, 2001). (These far-reaching but dubious ideas are developed in Chapter 5.) It is true that most of the quantum phenomena we know about were at least proposed, if not demonstrated during the period Jung and Pauli were working—they were not speculating about future possibilities—but still the idea of unification of psyche and matter did not catch on. Coming close to a union of sorts, a number of major players in the field of QM in those early days turned towards esoteric ideas that would encapsulate their sentiments about the reach of consciousness in the physical domain, but Jung and Pauli were far more *avant-garde* in their approach. Perhaps that is why these two great minds of the 20th century hardly made a stir with synchronicity. Note that in Chapter 1, I discuss a humbler version of unification (of ESP and PK to be specific), and we shall see that fall short of expectations as well.

Let us, however, consider the issues more closely: Everton Maraldi (2017) suggested: "… much of the evidence available is not sufficiently understood or is merely suggestive of certain paranormal claims" (p. 900). Commenting briefly but with sobering concision, Maraldi was referring to the parapsychological limits of consciousness (the relevant literature of which was reviewed by Daher et al., 2017), but Maraldi's point (as he makes clear) necessarily applies equally and more generally to psi. It is a fact that the assumptions that extend from the parapsychological findings are *often* poorly conceptualized, *largely* unfalsifiable, or *overly* dependent on metaphysical associations, much of which traces to cultural biases—this general truth (albeit too conservative for some) will become more and more cogent throughout this book. And since the pragmatic subset of physicists have given up trying to understand QM phenomena (as noted by Campbell, 2007; Tom Campbell, 2014), and even frown upon theoretical excursions into its 'fundamentals' (Becker, 2019), what would the juxtaposition of one mystery (e.g., psyche) against another (e.g., matter) mean to a baffled public? By extension, how unlikely is it that the general public might be interested in, let alone be able to conceive of a fundamental unity underpinning psyche and matter?

While it is true the public, then and now, are incredibly naïve about QM phenomena and synchronicity, the more open-minded in society tend to be predisposed to an interest in one or the other based on assertions held about psyche and matter. That is, the two communities seldom if ever come together simply because a unified conception of the two, psyche and matter, into some automatically implied but not justified mysterious 'third thing' is impossible to imagine; that no less would be the reason many people valorize one over the other, and are even happy to latch onto the appropriate 'ism'. Parapsychologists must be careful they do not buy into this bias, but of course many have. They must realize that selling parapsychology like one would a religion or a political cause, by making belief-based, philosophically-derived declarations, or careless appeals to what may in some cases only seem to be empirical proof, is a monumental *faux pas*, made no less true by the fact that the alleged QM interactions and associations between psyche and matter are far from proved, and currently look more like mythological motifs (again, see Chapter 5 for details).

That being said, I hope some of my more speculative claims are proved valid, or will at least be shown to bear some degree of truth, but even if the more naïve propositions I put forward are proved false, they will at least work as a caution to others. Again, for those ideas that are invariably true or are proved true, my wish is that they assist in paving the way towards constructive ideas about psi and synchronicity, and their unification (an aim I pursue further in a companion text—see Storm, 2025).

Notes

1 For a review of the more prominent theories of psi, see Chapter 8 in Irwin and Watt (2007).
2 A fire case was described by Icelandic researcher Erlendur Haraldsson, who noted the similarities with the Swedenborg case. Haraldsson (2011) reports on Icelandic physical medium Indridi Indridason, who channeled a once-living man named Emil Jensen. In November 1905, Jensen claimed, through Indridason (in Reykjavik), that a lamp factory fire was burning in Copenhagen at that very moment, which was later verified. Jensen had lived near the site of the Copenhagen fire, but had died in 1898.
3 The article by Reber and Alcock (2020) has been comprehensively rebutted by Williams (2019).
4 Some proportion of allegedly paranormal effects can be explained normally, such as by QRPs, but my focus is on the unexplained component.
5 Philosopher C. D. Broad (1949) introduced four major basic limiting principles (though other examples are given) thought to be self-evident and generally taken for granted: there can be no backward causation (i.e., no future-telling), no action at a distance (i.e., no mind over matter), no perception unmediated by the senses (i.e., no mind-reading, no distant seeing), and mind depends on brain (i.e., consciousness cannot engage in nonlocal functions).
6 Quantum mechanics (QM) describes sub-atomic phenomena at odds with the Newtonian cause-and-effect paradigm that currently and sufficiently explains the material world that we experience in everyday life (for examples of QM phenomena, see footnote 1 in Chapter 5).

Chapter 1

The Rhinean Revolution and What It Did for Parapsychology

Instead of knowledge of what we are, we have beliefs.

(Joseph Banks Rhine, 1947, p. 4)

For many parapsychologists, the biggest leap forward in parapsychology came in the form of a life-time's work of one man, J. B. Rhine. Arguably the first major academic parapsychologist with global influence, Rhine set the agenda for psi research and got the ball rolling for serious investigations at universities across the world. This chapter describes some of his work, but deals mainly with Rhine's theoretical perspectives on psi. There are numerous problems with the terms used in parapsychology, and we meet with these problems both in the field and in the laboratory. Psi phenomena can be viewed from a synchronistic perspective that broadens our understanding of the nature of psi.

Who Was J. B. Rhine?

If you are a parapsychologist, Joseph Banks Rhine (1895-1980) would be one of your heroes or major influences, and speaking for myself, that is no exaggeration. Rhine is considered to be the grandfather of parapsychology in the Western world; indeed his influence from the mid-1930s onwards extended beyond the English-speaking world to universities and other research institutions the world over. Right up to the time of his death in 1980, Rhine laboured to keep the parapsychology ball rolling.

Rhine's earliest memories are of his father telling him to dismiss "beliefs and tales" about clairvoyance, and all things 'psychic', as "superstitious nonsense" (1937/1950, p. 13). However, Rhine's influences also include a story told by his university professor of a woman who dreamed of her brother's suicide by a pistol shot to the head. These and other details in the woman's dream were later confirmed in real life. This account, and others like it, left Rhine with a strong impression that there was more to these sorts of 'beliefs and tales' than mere superstition. Indeed, Rhine did do some dismissing of his own, but only of those folk theories that explain such puzzling occurrences as chance or coincidence.

DOI: 10.4324/9781003561323-2

Rhine concluded that "systematic experimentation" would be the best way to confirm whether the human mind can "know things in a psychic or extra-sensory manner" (p. 21). It was at Duke University in 1930 that Rhine started his formal investigations.

Rhine's educational grounding included a Ph.D. qualification in botany and plant physiology, courses of which at the time gave him a solid statistical training that proved helpful in experimental design and data analysis. Fortunately for Rhine, his work was noticed by William McDougall (Head of the Psychology Department at Duke), who gave him a teaching position in psychology that ultimately led to a professorship, thus elevating his prestige and credibility.

One of Rhine's noted modifications to ESP testing was the abandonment of the standard 52-card deck for the so-called Zener card deck of five symbols (see Figure 1.1). The problem with the 52-card deck is that ESP effects can be determined statistically in a number of ways (i.e., by suit, by face value, by colour), giving skeptics the opportunity to accuse experimenters of "hypothesis saving" (Irwin & Watt, 2007, p. 52). Rhine's innovative approaches led to card-testing clairvoyance in various ways, such as participants calling Zener symbols in a shuffled deck that had not been sighted by the experimenter, thus eliminating telepathy as an alternative hypothesis.

Figure 1.1 The Zener card symbols: star, wavy lines, square, circle, and cross. The deck of 25 cards has five of each symbol. (*Source:* © 2024, L. Storm)

Rhine gave serious attention to sensory cues such as subtle tell-tale folds on cards, or poor-quality printing that leaked information through to the reverse sides of the cards. It was also necessary to make sure the experimenters did not give themselves away with unconscious facial expressions and vocalizations any time a correct card was called because that would give the participant a slight clue as to the identity of subsequent cards. Rhine also designed PK experiments using dice, first by hand-throwing, and then using cages to eliminate the possibility of subtle outcome-biasing manipulations, otherwise known as sleight of hand.

These and other Rhinean innovations, as well as those of other experimenters who exemplified Rhine's pioneering spirit with experimental developments of their own, suggest a 'revolution' in science started by Rhine. It was he who established parapsychology as a university sub-discipline that incorporated the scientific method at a peculiar time in world history when behaviourism in psychology in particular, and the materialist agenda generally, were gaining a collective foothold in university campuses. Indeed, there is much more about Rhine and his influence that needs telling, and in the next section, I will go into more detail about his role as a scientist, and his contributions to parapsychology.

What Rhine Did for Parapsychology

Rhine's contribution to parapsychology is inestimable. He coined the term 'extrasensory perception', and popularized the term 'psychokinesis' (coined by Henry Holt), as categories for describing two seemingly different paranormal phenomena (Rhine, 1934). Extrasensory perception (ESP) includes telepathy, clairvoyance, and precognition (defined in the Introduction). Psychokinesis (PK) includes (i) bio-PK (a.k.a. 'direct [or distant] mental influence on living systems' [DMILS]; Braud & Schlitz, 1991); (ii) macro-PK, denoting PK on systems at the 'greater-than-molecular' level (e.g., metal-bending, table-tilting, materialization, apports, levitation, psychic healing, and thoughtography [i.e., psychic photography]; some researchers add poltergeist phenomena to the list); and (iii) micro-PK, denoting PK on systems at the 'molecular' level using, for example, random number generators (RNGs), but more generally defined as "minute influences on inanimate, probabilistic systems, producing effects that can only be detected through statistical means" (Varvoglis & Bancel, 2015, p. 266). Therefore, some parapsychologists consider dice-throwing and coin-flipping to be examples of micro-PK (for a critique, see Braude, 2015).

Even though by the 1940s, Rhine (1947) regarded ESP and PK as "one single fundamental two-way process" (p. 130), both terms have made it into everyday speech, and these days most dictionaries carry definitions of one or both terms.[1] Parapsychologists have grown accustomed to the terms ESP and PK, and generally believe there are arguably clear distinctions between them despite the occasional overlap. Rhine's earliest work was focused on finding evidence for the two phenomena. Many card-guessing and dice-throwing studies showed Rhine going to great lengths to test ESP and PK, respectively, in people from all walks of life and levels of psychic ability, and these are featured in an early series of books, including *Extra-Sensory Perception* (Rhine, 1934); *New Frontiers of the Mind* (Rhine, 1937/1950); *The Reach of the Mind* (1947), and *New World of the Mind* (1953).

Rhine opened the door for contemporary and future parapsychologists, and in a short decade or two after Rhine's work began, there was an explosion of research that looked at ESP in dreams, as well as the influence of meditation, relaxation, and hypnosis on PK outcomes.[2] (See also Alvarado, 2011, to get an idea of the diverse approaches taken in ESP and PK research during the period 1937-1947.) This research culminated in the ganzfeld paradigm that has been running successfully in laboratories all over the world since the 1970s (Honorton, 1985; Storm & Tressoldi, 2020; Storm, Tressoldi, & Di Risio, 2010; Williams, 2014).

In the case of PK, Rhine's dice-throwing work paved the way for contemporary and future scientists to take the mental influence on matter seriously. His pioneering work led to the two classes of PK defined above; macro-PK and micro-PK. Given these two sub-classes, two types of meta-analysis emerged in the 1980s and

1990s—those on macro-PK studies, and those on micro-PK studies: For macro-PK, dice-throwing studies conducted over a fifty-year time span (1935 to 1987) were meta-analyzed by Radin and Ferrari (1991);[3] for micro-PK, studies on RNGs (a.k.a. random event generators, or REGs) were meta-analyzed by Radin and Nelson (1989). At a later date, studies were conducted on biological systems (bio-PK or DMILS). Significant cumulative effects were found in all these meta-analyses.

As early as the 1930s, Rhine also began taking note of the types of individuals who seemed to give the best performances on ESP and PK tasks. He found repeated evidence that the more enthusiastic, curious and motivated participants would more reliably score above chance than did other types of participants (Rhine, 1937/1950; 1947). These observations did not pass the scrutinous eye of Jung (1952/1969) who noted that

> lack of interest and boredom are negative factors: enthusiasm, positive expectation, hope, and belief in the possibility of ESP make for good results and seem to be the real conditions which determine whether there are going to be any results at all.
>
> (para. 838)

On that basis, Jung also noted that Rhine was right to test large numbers of participants rather than small samples with the same number of total trials (which means more trials for fewer participants), because the latter group, being overtested, would tire and lose interest.

Given that ESP and PK were considered by Rhine to be a single 'two-way process' at some fundamental but indiscernible level, the Rhinean model nevertheless gave parapsychologists tools to work with, especially in terms of nomenclature. From that perspective, parapsychologists were able to work under a common banner, with a common objective, because they had the same tacit understanding about any given paranormal phenomenon in question. But in reality, Rhine (1974) recognized a serious problem as paraphrased by German parapsychologist Eberhard Bauer (1984):

> … a large number of parapsychological research topics, such as out-of-the-body experiences, the survival problem, retrocognition, psychometry [token-object reading] and even telepathy are basically insolvable problems which cannot be studied empirically as it is impossible to eliminate clairvoyance as a potential alternative hypothesis.
>
> (p. 143)

These and similar problems are still prevalent and relevant today. For example, Millar (2015), whom I quoted earlier, has added to the list of hypotheses: "Telepathy could actually be clairvoyance, precognition could actually be psychokinesis", and for that matter, just about "any experimental result could be a form of PK" (p. 165). In the next section I will show how some of these problems manifest, and detail the implications for modern parapsychology.

Rhine's Ideas under Scrutiny

Some might find it hard to believe that in the 21st century, many parapsychologists still seem to think it possible to avoid any conceptual confusion over the terms ESP and PK by *not* using them interchangeably when they think they have identified the paranormal effects in question (e.g., ganzfeld vs. metal-bending). And since ESP and PK are often referred to as a *unitary* phenomenon known as *psi*, those same parapsychologists go further by referring to both effects as the *operation of psi* or *psi at work*. This option also makes it conveniently possible to avoid any ambiguities (e.g., when parapsychologists do *not* know which of the two, ESP or PK, will better serve to describe or explain an RNG effect). Despite such assumptions, a number of theoretical, conceptual, and practical difficulties have come to light, and it might prove helpful here to identify them and their origins, and assess their impact.

To borrow from Rhine (1947, p. 4), it often seems more accurate to specify what we collectively believe about a phenomenon rather than what we know of it. Given that Rhine himself said this, it is perhaps not surprising to learn that Rhine's legacy is a mixed one—even after reading a single reputable book or journal article about the history of parapsychology, one is likely to come across criticisms of the man and his pioneering science, particularly criticisms concerning his methodology and, in the case of the science, its scope, and these are not just criticisms from skeptical authors like James E. Alcock (1981), but come from well-meaning and psi-supportive parapsychologists like Jan Ehrenwald (1947) and G. N. M. Tyrrell (1946). These parapsychologists pursued their own lines of research in a virtual vacuum, given Rhine's disinterest in, and criticism of (for example) case studies and the survival question, much to the chagrin of traditional institutions like the Society for Psychical Research (see Alvarado, 2011, for other criticisms on Rhine's opinions and approach).

Certainly, Rhine shaped the direction of parapsychological research just through his constant presence in the research journal he co-founded, the *Journal of Parapsychology*—in the first decade of its publication, Rhine dominated a considerable 29% of its content in papers he either authored or co-authored. This legacy, combined with his many published books, makes Rhine a foremost authority on parapsychology. In this section, therefore, I will focus specifically on how Rhine modelled ESP and PK.

The Problem of Unification

Even given his ardent work and very focused approach to the identification of types of paranormal phenomena, Rhine (1946a, 1947) was more than open-minded about an ESP/PK convergence ('unification'), and he appeared to embrace the proposition of a *unitary process* underlying ESP and PK. Rhine's position extends from his philosophical standpoint that ESP and PK do *not* lead to dualism. Having disavowed "absolute dualism" (acknowledging only a "relative" form; see Dommeyer, 1982, pp. 122–123), Rhine then resisted other "older *isms*" like monism, but we shall see that his argument suggests (as indeed philosopher Frederick Dommeyer claims) the logical solution to the mind/body problem *is* 'double-aspect' or 'dual-aspect' monism: "body and mind are two aspects of some underlying factor" (Dommeyer, p. 122).

We might wonder what this 'underlying factor' meant to Rhine and how it relates to a unitary paranormal process. We have to back-track first before we can get to Rhine's ultimate point. First, the two (ESP and PK) seem poles apart: As would be clear to the reader by now, ESP is generally characterized as 'informational', 'receptive', and involves 'incoming' ('afferent') influence, whereas PK seems like a 'motor' function, responsive or expressive, and involves outgoing ('efferent') influence. Second (and consequently), ESP is traditionally considered a *mental* function or experience (though there can be physiological correlates), while PK acts on the *physical* world.

In spite of this dichotomization, it appears ESP and PK must at least work together; indeed Rhine went to great lengths explaining how "PK implies ESP, and ESP implies PK" (1947, p. 129). For example, PK on (say) a die must involve the "mind of the subject … operating upon it" (p. 128); not just to cause a physical effect, but to make the PK process "intelligible" (p. 128). Thus, PK is 'dependent upon ESP". While Irwin (1979) finds "PK and ESP belong to the same phenomenal dimension" (p. 127), he also finds there are some information processing differences (sometimes incompatible), and resists the idea that "PK requires [ESP] guidance of the sort originally envisaged by the Rhines", arguing that "there is little empirical evidence" for it (p. 118; see also Irwin, 1985). However, as Rhine (1947) explained, the capacity to monitor the extent of a PK effect via feedback ultimately goes beyond the limits of "sensory perception" (p. 129), suggesting ESP is a very fast process. As we shall see, there is more to it than that.

In stating that "the relationship holds the other way" (p. 129), Rhine (1947) meant ESP is dependent upon PK: "some physical effect [PK] has to take place on the object, or upon some intermediating physical system, when the object is perceived [ESP]" (p. 129). It is not entirely clear what Rhine means here, though we could argue that both mind *and* brain have to interact during telepathy. Perhaps a similar rationale applies for clairvoyance and precognition. Relevant experimentation is not entirely convincing, and what is also clear is that Rhine was proposing effects that are purely causal ('energic') in nature. For example, very early on, a perhaps somewhat over-confident Karlis Osis (1953) argued that it was relatively easy to demonstrate ESP during PK action, but the reverse (PK action during ESP) was only ostensibly demonstrated much later (Osis & McCormick, 1980).

In the former case, where Osis's (1953) participants were blind to pre-selected targets (die faces) in a dice-throwing task, the generally significant outcomes indicated a "close relationship between ESP and PK" (p. 298). While a 'two-step' process possibly explains the dice-throwing effect (first, ESP to determine the target; then PK to effect the desired outcome), Osis believed a one-step ("diametric") process was more likely with ESP knowledge *and* concordant PK reaction occurring in a single step. Even so, Osis could not elaborate on how this one-step works—that is, he could not say *how* ESP and PK were "two different aspects of the same process" (p. 298). For Rhine, a diametric process *might* explain the 'PK' effect as long as "diametric" means constant (reiterative) ESP monitoring *from start to finish*—it will not be enough to identify the target up front via ESP and leave the rest to PK.

In the case of PK action during ESP, Osis and McCormick (1980) reported higher levels of a PK effect (strain-gauge activation) associated with target picture identification (ESP), but it was not clear what the PK had to do with the ESP. Osis and McCormick conceded that their combined effect could not be "holistically regarded as a composite of ESP and PK action" in the sense Rhine (1947) meant where the PK effect "exists at the surface of stimuli" (p. 327). It is also possible (under the psi hypothesis) the test subject (psychic Alex Tanous)—"out-of-body" during testing, but 'methodologically' blind to the fact that there was a PK component—may have gained unconscious knowledge of the experimenters' broader aims, and responded accordingly; arguably producing a redundant PK (spill-over) effect.

Returning to Osis's (1953) point about the insoluble one-step process—*how* ESP and PK might be a single diametric process—we see that Rhine (1947) is both tactical and astute: ESP only *seems* to be a mental process, and PK only *seems* to be a physical process. Rhine argued that we can only see a proxy reality filtered by our own mental/physical apparatus that masks the unitary experience (i.e., it is only a relative or epistemic form of dualism that demarcates subjective experience). Hence, "the facts of parapsychology not only do not require one to be a dualist—they do not *allow* one to be" (p. 179). These points have been largely ignored.

As we can see, mainstream parapsychological thought (but not practice) is undermined by Rhine's 'deep' thinking, but dual-aspect monism is not, even when we consider the following: PK does not always seem to require extrasensory guidance (e.g., psychokinetic metal-bending [PKMB] can easily be guided—initiated and halted—by visual inspection and feedback alone), and ESP does not always seem to involve a PK component (e.g., there is no evidence to date that clairvoyantly perceiving an object means also that the object has to, or must, undergo a psychokinetic change or influence). While Rhine (1947) would say that there has to be an element of one (e.g., ESP) in the other (e.g., PK), this dual aspect may escape detection by scientific (experimental) means for Rhine admits that the 'perceptual' (ESP) or 'kinetic' (PK) effect is a result of what the "test was designed to measure", and we "would expect one end of the reaction to be obscured when the other is being demonstrated" (p. 130). Unfortunately, that means the principle of unification may remain a theoretical supposition, and mainstream parapsychological practice remains unaffected. Interestingly, the fact that synchronicity aligns with dual-aspect theory was not enough to convince Rhine of Jung's (1952/1969) theory. Jung argued that synchronicity was an *acausal* phenomenon, so that rather than a link being drawn between two events by making causal associations, the connecting principle in a synchronistic event was entirely through meaning—hence, the terms meaningful coincidence and synchronicity are often used interchangeably. Though he did not give any strong reason why, Rhine's doubt probably springs from the causality/acausality dichotomy about which, after lengthy correspondence with Jung, "Rhine's concept of causality remained conservative" (Mansfield et al., 1998, p. 14).

Rhine's embrace of unification is reinforced by his acceptance of the ideas of Thouless and Wiesner (1947), who used the Greek symbol Ψ (psi) to designate "the entire ESP-PK process" (Rhine, 1947, p. 179), which is to say ESP and PK are different aspects of one process. Thouless and Wiesner demarcated ESP from PK, naming them Ψγ (psi-gamma) and Ψκ (psi-kappa), respectively, in order to indicate that the two were different aspects of the same process. That demarcation aligns with Rhine's viewpoint. Rhine accepted the term psi, and it has been used ever since in parapsychology to designate "paranormal causation" and "paranormal process" (Thalbourne, 2003, p. 92). Having entered the lexicon, Thalbourne defined the term 'psi' in his *Glossary*, where he describes it as a "single process", and not "distinct and essentially different processes" (p. 92). Rhine not only used the expression psi as a blanket term for both ESP and PK "phenomena", but he also acknowledged "psi" as a "process" (p. 131). But later, he conceded psi is a "device of convenience and does not imply that it is *known* that there is only one basic underlying type of process" (Rhine & Pratt, 1957/1974, p. 9). Similarly, Ballard (1986) reminds us that ESP and PK tell us "nothing about the essence of psi" (p. 146).

None of the points in previous paragraphs completely undermines the possibility of a single underlying psi process, but that process is even more of a conundrum when we realize that, "strictly" speaking, the term psi also applies to "survival of death" (Thalbourne, 2003, p. 92), raising issues to do with "discarnate psi" and 'living-agent psi' (see Braude, 2003, for an in-depth analysis of these options). As an alternative to both, there is also the notion of a 'psychic reservoir' where only information survives *post mortem* and seems to require paranormal access. Far from facilitating an understanding of psi as a process, these possibilities invoke conceptual extensions to psi that only confound—that is, disambiguating the phenomena found within the working limits we seem to think are reasonably applied to psi is problematized by the very fact that we do not know what the actual limits are. We can see why Ballard (1986) claimed "Psi does not work well as a concept or a construct" (p. 146). Perhaps Ballard, and Palmer (1986b) too, had the right idea about psi, and we should be using the term nominally. Ballard called out the difference between a "nominal definition" (i.e., "an assignment of meaning") and a "real definition" (that which is, or can be, "affirmed to exist"; p. 146):

> Our definitions of psi appear to be nominal, not real.... Are we not simply giving a label to something unknown, be it a process, capacity, or something else? ... The problem is we have taken this summary term and reified it as a unifying concept. (p. 146)

One would think that confining the term psi to descriptive (adjectival) or operational usage only (as in 'psi scores', 'psi phenomena', and 'psi hypothesis') would catch on and that would be the end of it, but many in the parapsychological community still use the term 'psi' so extensively and indiscriminately it has, with lasting repercussions, created and perpetuated the working hypothesis of a single underlying *process*. For example, many a parapsychologist, when confronted with the age-old dualistic problem of how *intangible mind* (e.g., as reified consciousness) can affect organically separate *tangible matter* (e.g., dice or spoons), feels confident that the issue is easily and obviously resolved once it is understood that the *cause* underlying this effect is *psi* (clear evidence of reification, and as far from *descriptive* usage as one can get). Of course, the effect has *not* been explained. This conundrum over psi 'influence' applies just as much to discarnate consciousness as it does to incarnate (embodied) consciousness. Palmer (1986b) has noted how the use of the term psi in such ways tends to confound an "explanatory" principle with parapsychology's "subject matter", leading to statements like "parapsychology is the scientific study of psi" (p. 140).

To conclude, having noted the overlap between ESP and PK, Rhine acknowledged a possible unitary psi process underlying the two, but a convincing argument and proof remain elusive. Thus, the demarcation is maintained: Since disparate observable experimental outcomes and spontaneous phenomena *do* suggest more than one process afoot, it has become difficult to bridge the ever-widening phenomenological gap and convincingly argue for a single process. Rhine and his ilk have been categorical to a fault: With the utmost integrity, these pioneering parapsychologists pursued the standard aims of the scientific enterprise, which is par for the course, but the apparent evidence for two major categories of psi compromises the notion that psi is a unitary (not dichotomous) process, and even the idea that psi is a *process* has come into question. The reason for the underlying self-deception appears to be phenomenological in nature. In other words, subjective experience—the *as ifs*, and *what it is like*—has decided the matter. It is perhaps not surprising that few raise these issues in a manner sufficient to change the collective mindset, and some might argue there is little to be accomplished in trying, though I suggest it might shift people to a synchronistic mode of thought in which unification is a metaphysical endpoint, but the psi construct is more a projected intuition of that idea. Instead, decades later, psi is now more than a 'term of convenience' (as Rhine called it). More than a means to an expedient (operational) end, psi has gained (or more accurately, been given) unwarranted explanatory power (i.e., it has been *reified as a unitary construct*). Psi has been elevated from an epistemological idea or belief to a pseudo-ontological fact, yet we do not get a sense in which its component parts (ESP and PK) are one and the same process.

This situation is not to fault Rhine, or Thouless and Wiesner, and in fairness to Rhine, he knowingly contributed to the epistemology of psi, but simultaneously, perhaps only half-knowingly, put a question mark over its ontology via his philosophical inspection of the mind/body problem. Indeed, he acknowledged the fact that "no one can conceive of the interaction of the two systems [mind and body], except by supposing that there are properties common to both" (1947, p. 178). In trying to discern this interactional "common ground", he set down two extremes: either it is something almost material as represented by an "underlying order of neutral substituent energetics … a substrate", or it is something merely conceptual in the form of a "transition point, an abstraction" (p. 179). And with that, the "common ground between mind and matter" remains "completely obscure" (p. 179). We might therefore suppose that psi—the 'common ground' between ESP and PK—is equally 'obscure' and ultimately unworkable as a construct.

While these issues will come up again in later chapters, the next subsection focuses even more on psi and the ESP/PK dichotomy as manifested in the problems parapsychology has with process-driven terminology.

The Psi Process and Parapsychological Nomenclature

Notwithstanding this unresolved problem with psi as a unified process (and we will see how it is almost impossible to talk independently about process and nomenclature),[4] we must wonder what drives the reductive attempts towards unification raised above. I would like to think it is an intuitive response that speaks to some kind of fundamental (perhaps metaphysical) truth that the psi process is a single process acting the same way no matter the manifestation. Indeed, it may be more than a mere intuition: From his research findings, Rhine observed that ESP and PK necessarily overlap and interact, as argued above (see his extended argument in Rhine, 1947, pp. 128–131). While he argued his case quite well, he could not (and nor has anyone been able to) devise the means by which ESP *and* PK are evident in a single psi event with both components crucially 'diametric' in the overall effect, and perhaps that is because the interactions as a composite effect cannot be tested—recall the problems raised by Osis (1953), and Osis and McCormick (1980). This outcome is exactly what we might expect when ESP and PK are not *phenomenologically* reducible (Rhine even makes this point). That is, humans might get hints of a single process, but the mind/matter distinction is insurmountable.

The following series of modern studies highlights the problems that arise when trying to test whether a performance distinction between ESP and PK is demonstrable, or indeed whether ESP and PK converge to a single process (Roe, Davey, & Stevens, 2003, 2004, 2005, 2006). At the start of the first paper in this series, Roe et al. (2003) pointed out a range of interpretations of this unitary phenomenon, none of which have been demonstrated:

> ESP and PK [is] unitary with neither primary (Schmeidler, 1994), unitary with PK as the basic phenomenon (attributed by Schmeidler, 1994, p. 229, to Helmut Schmidt), or unitary with ESP the basic phenomenon (as captured for example in decision augmentation theory (DAT): see, e.g., May, Utts, & Spottiswoode, 1995[a]), through to a view associated with William Braud (e.g., Braud, 1985) that sees ESP and PK as complementary phenomena that have quite distinct characteristics and thrive under differing conditions.
>
> (pp. 343–344)

Roe's team ran four conditions (true-ESP, disguised-ESP, True-PK, and disguised-PK) in a greyhound racing game where participants could use either ESP or PK to effect a win. Half the trials in both the ostensibly true-ESP and true-PK conditions were actually disguised-PK and disguised-ESP, respectively, so participants never really knew which psi function they were using. Results were inconclusive across the four studies, although in the second study, the disguised-PK condition (pseudo-ESP where participants *thought* they could use ESP) yielded significant psi-hitting (Roe et al., 2005); and in the fourth study, the disguised-ESP condition (pseudo-PK where participants *thought* they could use PK) yielded significant psi-missing (Roe et al., 2006). However, of the remaining conditions (all 14 of them), none were significant. The upshot is that there was minor evidence that *different* psi outcomes were possible, but these seem more to do with deception (autosuggestion effects) than two different types of psi because the two disguised conditions gave participants no conscious clue about what they were to demonstrate—that is, the instructions gave those participants the wrong intentions in those two conditions. And when there *was* a chance to demonstrate two genuine effects (ESP and PK) to see if performance levels were the same across *known* conditions (i.e., participants were told truthfully which faculty was being tested), evidence was not forthcoming. Such a minimal number of significant findings, and even the suggestive correlations, were not sufficient to determine either a performance distinction, *or* convergence to any kind of unitary effect. To put it another way, Roe et al. could not show that ESP and PK *in any form* were related.

Findings like these and Rhine's fail to convince that the psi process is fundamentally unitary, but one also wonders how the problem is helped when such concerted efforts on Rhine's part were made to disambiguate and consolidate the two distinct categories of psi, ESP and PK (see Chapter 3 in Rhine & Pratt, 1957/1974). Rhine and Pratt even defended clairvoyance, precognition, and PK as "experimentally isolated" (p. 45). Perhaps Rhine realized that he had no choice but to work as a relative dualist and a phenomenologist. But Rhine's earlier statements pointed in a different direction: First, he argues that even the 'experimental isolation' of ESP effects must still include a PK component embedded in clairvoyance and precognition (Rhine, 1947); and second, 'perceptual' (ESP) and 'kinetic' (PK) effects are really the result of what the "test was designed to measure" (Rhine, 1947, p. 130). Thus, a dilemma emerged over how psi manifests, but it did not end with the Rhines. Bauer (1984), who was briefly mentioned above, spoke to this issue:

> It is safe to assume that this dilemma is not simply a semantic one. It reflects principally different theoretical models which have of course consequences for the empirical testability of the hypotheses derived therefrom.
>
> (Bauer, 1984, p. 143)

Sobering thoughts indeed—the various psi modalities (clairvoyance, PK, etc.) may imply different forces or laws at work, and therefore a number of theories explaining the diverse phenomena might be in order (in this section, and the section to follow, we will see how theorists have grappled with this problem). But when we reflect, we see again (as Rhine noted) that the dilemma is at least partly attributable to *methodology* (or *circumstance* in real-world scenarios) so that any given psi phenomenon may merely be a bi-product of how it is tested—which is to say, ESP and PK may be drawn out (identified, isolated) disproportionately purely because the test favours one psi aspect over the other. Or that is what we are led to believe *given the psi hypothesis*.

Only two decades after Rhine made his point public, Scottish philosopher and parapsychologist, Clement Mundle (1967) sought to resolve the "notorious problem" in psi theories where it is taken for granted that the "substratum is mental" (p. 205). Thus, after some considerable deliberation, he came to define telepathy as "ESP whose source is the mind or *brain* of another person" (pp. 206-207); he thereby felt he "must then define clairvoyance" as "ESP whose source is physical objects *other than another person's brain* [emphasis added]" (p. 207). But where does telepathy end and clairvoyance begin (and *vice versa*) when dealing with the mind/brain complex and the physical body associated with that complex? How can it be that the act of psychically reading the physiological state of a brain (and detecting, say, a brain tumour) is *not* clairvoyance, but *is* telepathy, whereas reading (say) the state of someone's liver *is* clairvoyance, but is *not* telepathy?

One sees here the same kinds of problems raised by Robert Morris (1975) when he observed that terms like "telepathy, clairvoyance, precognition, and psychokinesis have lost some of their capacity to define distinct concepts or even distinct operational procedures" (p. 179). Morris was not merely referring to the phenomenological aspects (how they appear to us) and their associated nomenclature. We thus have an oblique reference to the ontological problem associated with psi: "What is psi, basically?" (p. 181). Of course, the real issue here comes down to the *situation* in which Morris finds himself (i.e., *circumstance*). Morris draws attention to an unfortunate distinction whereby, for example, psi between 'like' organisms of matched evolutionary development is *telepathy*, whereas psi between two dissimilar species (e.g., a human and a fish) is probably going to be regarded as a test of *psychokinesis*, with the species 'higher up' on the evolutionary scale trying to influence the behaviour of the less complex organism.

Any reasonable person would see a dilemma of sorts if two ostensibly different types of psi (two different processes) can be tested by essentially the *same procedure*, with no means of differentiating the nature of the effect (Braude [1998, 2020], and Rabeyron [2020] both make reference to such problems). It could even be argued that Morris (1975) expressed a philosophical prejudice in assuming that fish do not have minds (thus ruling out telepathy), but *do* have rudimentary brains and nerve ganglia that can be influenced psychokinetically by a human mind or brain. And let us not deceive ourselves—the effect of interest in the human-to-human case is just as likely to be PK for the same reason (even if it be called telepathy) with one subject seeking *to influence*, or having his/her cerebral processes *influenced by*, the cerebral processes of another. However, in a really unusual scenario we can imagine a baffled individual physically responding in a way he cannot explain because his motor cortex and/or central nervous system (CNS) are being influenced covertly and *psychokinetically* by an agent, but his mind is not being influenced *telepathically* (as far as he knows). At first blush, personal testimony might be a clue to psi modality, but we can see that introspection has its limits. And as already implied, Morris's (1975) reference to the difficulty of isolating the psi modalities alerts us to the likelihood that the approaches to "testability" (Bauer's term) are deceptively reaffirming of what they find in terms of nomenclature, as Rhine (1947) noted earlier (for a similar line of argument, see d'Espagnat, 2006; Roe et al., 2006; Schmeidler, 1988).

Are our definitions at fault? We have already seen that may be a problem. In his *Glossary*, Thalbourne (2003) gave us standard definitions that almost avoided the mind/brain conundrum by referring only to *paranormal acquisition*: clairvoyance is the "paranormal acquisition of information concerning an object or contemporary physical event; in contrast to telepathy" (p. 18), where telepathy is "paranormal acquisition of information concerning the thoughts, feelings or activity of another conscious being" (p. 125). He avoids saying these can be mental or cerebral events, but he defines PK as "the direct influence of *mind* [emphasis added] on a physical system that cannot be entirely accounted for by the mediation of any known physical energy" (p. 98). And Thalbourne uses the term 'paranormal', but renowned parapsychologist Charles Honorton (1993) recommended abandoning the term because he regarded it as an "anachronism" (p. 210), and he implied that the terms ESP and PK were speculative by nature, preferring "anomalous communication and energetic processes", respectively (p. 211).

As will be seen, the problems with these terms are still unresolved in parapsychology as it stands today, for terms like 'paranormal acquisition of information', 'anomalous communication', and 'anomalous energetic processes' seem to describe the phenomena only passably—they introduce biases (for starters, much is assumed about what information is, where it is, and how it can be accessed, and/or energy is needed to power these processes). It may be wiser to view them in a figurative (or hypothetical) sense rather than a literal sense.

As mentioned above, the problem of nomenclature is tied to the problem of process—the very terms ESP and PK imply different processes, but there are reductionist attempts that aim for a kind of unification (even if only in a relative sense); some with an extra-sensory twist—for example:

- Under his Mental Realism model, Keith Chandler (2001) did not think clairvoyance was possible (see also Taylor, 2019, p. 15), and reframed it as telepathy (either real-time or precognitive) since inanimate objects are not conscious (i.e., they do not have minds);
- Edwin May and Sonali Marwaha reclassify some forms of PK (e.g., RNG effects) as outcomes you can demonstrably generate using run-of-the-mill precognition (Marwaha & May, 2015, 2016), but all other ESP forms also reduce to precognition;
- As indicated in the examples above, Thalbourne (2004) necessarily dropped the Rhinean categories altogether and opted for his own term 'exosomatic psychopraxia' for ESP/PK as a merged or unified paranormal phenomenon (see Chapter 4).

Some reductionist attempts have a psychokinetic twist—for example:

- Under Observational Theory (OT), Houtkooper (2002) notes that "the various paranormal phenomena, psychokinesis, telepathy, clairvoyance and precognition, can be unified into one basic mechanism" (p. 179). This mechanism is a kind of retroactive causation (retrocausation) known as "retroactive PK" (a.k.a. 'backward PK', time-displaced PK', 'retrocausal-PK', or *retro-PK* for short);
- Millar (2019) prefers the term "trans-temporal coupling" rather than retro-PK, because the psi effect is a "quantum correlation";
- Mishlove (2000) suggests that "precognition and psychokinesis are not discrete phenomena" (p. 149). Both involve anomalous interaction with the physical world—one draws information from it; the other, manipulates it. They are "two sides of the same coin".

None of these bids has reached broad acceptance, and certainly ESP and PK are still not thought about much differently since Rhine's time. While neutral terms for ESP and PK have been suggested—namely, 'anomalous cognition' and 'anomalous perturbation', respectively (see May, Spottiswoode, & James, 1994)—these terms do not suggest unification,[5] and they are arguably inaccurate and misleading (for criticisms, see Braude, 1998, 2020). Braude (2020) notes that 'anomalous cognition' and 'anomalous perturbation' can too easy apply to "phenomena falling outside the domain of parapsychology" (p. 219). Anomalous cognition could describe the many skills demonstrated by gifted savants like Daniel Tammet (2007), whose skills are not necessarily psychic *per se*, and anomalous perturbation could include any of the peculiar and unexplained cosmic phenomena (galactic rotation and orientation), whereas at least it was always understood that ESP and PK (blunt as they are as terms) were about what people could do paranormally. Conversely, Honorton's (1993) terms 'anomalous communication' and 'anomalous energetic processes' naturally suggest two distinct processes, even if that was not his intention—regardless, they are not yet proved to be mutually exclusive. Whether or not the researchers mean to use these terms only in a *nominal* sense (until better terms come along, or until unification is proved), they all use the term 'psi' as a collective term and overlook the fact that it was always meant to describe "the entire ESP/PK process" (Rhine, 1947, p. 179) as a "single process" (Thalbourne, 2003, p. 92; see also Thouless & Wiesner, 1947). When we come back to the Thouless-Wiesner demarcation of ESP and PK as Ψγ (psi-gamma) and Ψκ (psi-kappa), respectively, in order to indicate that the two are *different aspects* of a *unitary process*, we see a philosophical outlook that binds one to the notion of a single underlying reality (psi) that is yet 'Janus-faced' in its manifestations, to borrow from Austrian parapsychologist Peter Mulacz (Parapsychological Association, 2022).

One possible reason for the failure to adopt a workable unifying paradigm may have its source in Rhine's influence, which has been extensive to say the least. As I pointed out previously, Rhine paradoxically edged towards unification *and* differentiation. Over many decades, he had justifiably and painstakingly set the agenda for how parapsychological research should be conducted and how the results thereof should be interpreted. This influence has been, and still is, culturally broad-ranging, but the problem with the ambiguity inherent in the Rhinean differentiation is that it has poor diagnostic utility or capability (as I have suggested, Rhine probably half-suspected the ambiguity emerges *sui generis* from a differentiation forced upon us by subjective experience). Nevertheless, and as a consequence, researchers like Jule Eisenbud have slavishly followed the Rhinean model, such that his views on synchronicity are a classic example of this over-adherence: Eisenbud (1980) argued that we should not only interpret synchronicity in terms of psi, but also look for a causal agent (i.e., find someone responsible for the psi). However, attempts to interpret synchronicity that way kick-start further problems due to the Rhinean subtleties. Certainly, using conventional parapsychological terms, we could (for example) label Swedenborg's synchronicity (vision of the Stockholm fire) as clairvoyance being outside the range of Swedenborg's normal sense perceptions.

We might also consider telepathy as a possible solution—Swedenborg may have reached out telepathically to someone in Stockholm who was an eye-witness to the fire. Equally, Swedenborg's vision could be explained as 'future' knowledge (i.e., precognition). In other words, the vision Swedenborg experienced could have been a mental construction built around future newspaper coverage and reports of the current situation in Stockholm—the vision as images of the actual fire did not have to come to Swedenborg *in real time*.

Let us not forget 'physical' explanations—the material reality of the burning houses in Stockholm may have perturbed Swedenborg's brain in some way via a "psi field" or similar (see Roll, 1966). We come back to Eisenbud (1983) who would not dismiss the possibility that Swedenborg started the fire using his own PK (this he calls 'active analysis' because the effect centres on what Swedenborg *did*; not on information Swedenborg passively *received* or *perceived*). In fact, Jung, playing devil's advocate, also raised the possibility that "Swedenborg's unconscious staged the Stockholm fire" (1952/1969, para. 915). And I could go on: We could opt for hybrid forms such as *telepathic precognition* (a.k.a. *precognitive-telepathy*). That is, Swedenborg could have read the *future* state of mind of a well-informed eye-witness, or even someone who would only later read newspaper reports of the events that transpired in Stockholm. Or opt for *clairvoyant precognition* (a.k.a. *precognitive-clairvoyance*) in order to get an overall picture of the full and total damage wrought by the fire (i.e., the after effects). We could even propose a combination of any of the above if one single process seems inadequate in 'explaining' different aspects of the event. All of these options are attempts to reduce synchronicity to types of psi, rather than the other way around, but rather than any of these explanations being clear-cut, they seem riddled with ambiguity.

Other cases provide similar ambiguity due to terminological inadequacy: For example, British soldier, aeronautical engineer and philosopher, J. W. Dunne

(1875-1949), in his classic work *An Experiment with Time* (1927), reports an "unusually vivid and unpleasant dream" (p. 34) of a catastrophic volcanic eruption on the island of Martinique in 1902 (the event started April 23 and continued into early May). Dunne did not give an actual date for his dream, but says it was during "Spring", which starts in mid-March. There is a disparity over the final death toll that has (as we shall see) implications for the ESP process *per se*—Dunne (1927) reported a dreamt figure of "four thousand … unsuspecting inhabitants" perishing due to the eruption of Mount Pelée (p. 34), whereas the *Daily Telegraph* reported a "PROBABLE LOSS OF 40,000 LIVES" (p. 35). For 15 years, Dunne adhered to his dreamt figure of 4,000 until he discovered his error of being "out by a nought" (p. 36); probably due to Dunne's unconscious and conscious misreading (see Jung, 1952/1969, para. 852). From this point on, speculation runs rife:

First, if there was a misreading, that suggests Dunne's dream did not take place *before* the catastrophe in Martinique (in fact, Dunne [1927] initially regarded the dream as "clairvoyant"; p. 37). Instead, the dream may have happened while the newspaper carrying the tragic story was on its way to Dunne, who believed the 4,000 came to him "*because of the newspaper paragraph*" (p. 37). While that view might still suggest clairvoyance of a sort, Dunne's realization led him to arrive at a different conclusion (more on that shortly). Indeed, this error is not surprising as Dunne habitually misreported names and details, and even admitted to his inaccuracies.

Second, Millar (2015) argues that Dunne's error proves the "ecological validity" of "precognition/retro-PK" (p. 174) because real-time ESP (e.g., clairvoyance) is impossible in the Observational Theories (OTs). The OTs are derived from the quantum mechanical notion that conscious intention (actually observation) brings about all psi effects and these are retrocausal and psychokinetic (PK), such that all forms of ESP have a retro-PK explanation. Millar argues that the actual event could not have been the source of the information, whereas the 'substance' of the newspaper itself (i.e., *feedback*) is the more likely source, with the information that served the dream coming from the future time when Dunne had the actual paper in his hands and was only then able to view and read it! In that respect, Millar's assumption has some degree of parsimony, or we can at least give it the benefit of the doubt. But the OTs are far from proven, so many parapsychologists would not dismiss real-time ESP just yet. However, I note that Heilprin (1903) puts the figure at around 25,000. This figure also entered into print right after the event, *and in Dunne's lifetime*, but Dunne (1927) never mentioned the figure, perhaps because *it never came to his attention*. This omission puts conventional precognition in a bad light, but the OTs are off the hook (for now).

The third explanation is rather anticlimactic: Dunne (1927) almost dismisses the whole event as the result of "Identifying Paramnesia … *false memories*", though he finds it an "extremely unpleasant notion" that he had "never really had any such dream at all" (p. 37). This occasion is not the only time he describes a paranormal dream as being "of the same character" (p. 37). No doubt this comment refers to his dream of a group of soldiers telling him they had successfully crossed continental Africa. The following morning, Dunne discovered this same news—once again in the *Daily Telegraph*—in an article describing a successful Cape-to-Cairo expedition in 1901, led by journalist/explorer Lionel Decle. Dunne at first concludes that these dreams "had been induced, either by the readings of the paragraphs, or else by telepathic communications from the journalists in the *Daily Telegraph* office who had written those accounts" (p. 38). Dunne later rejected both conclusions for no strong reason: Instead, he 'proved' to himself his dreams were precognitive from a later series of dreams, the many details of which he "carefully recalled" (p. 40), and "closely studied or carefully memorized" (p. 47), prior to any form of objective verification. Later, the "written record" (p. 63) also enjoyed special status for Dunne. Of course, careful rehearsal and/or data-logging helps establish the order of events, but Dunne's logic is not *deductive*; it is *inductive*—his current actions are deemed precognitive, so he assumes it was ever thus. A very unsatisfactory conclusion.

So what modality do we opt for if we must classify Dunne's psi experiences? Clairvoyance? Retro-PK? Telepathy? Precognition? (For convenience, we might rule out false memories as an explanation.) Dunne was satisfied with his conclusion of precognition, though he would not have had the option in 1927 to consider synchronicity. We actually cannot dismiss the synchronicity assumption, and Eisenbud's (1983) *active analysis* hardly fits the bill in the instance of both Dunne's dreams—unless it is reasonable to assume that an all-seeing and omnipotent Dunne brought about a large-scale PK effect with him causing a volcanic eruption, *and* he psychically nudged Decle and company in their trek across continental Africa!

Most skeptics, and even the innocent and curious, would balk at the flexibility of the various interpretations and assumptions just made, seeing them as typical evidence of a fringe science in desperate need of some good housekeeping, which includes whipping up some precisely defined terms. Indeed, parapsychologists would be happier if the various psi events could be more easily and unequivocally labelled. But we have seen that this is impossible, and any of five currently available labels (telepathy, clairvoyance, precognition, psychokinesis, and synchronicity) continue to be seen as reasonable (workable) according to one's particular parapsychological camp (although the term synchronicity is rarely used and maintains little favour).

As is the case in science generally, it would seem the only way to get to the crux of the matter and find valid labels is to test the various types of psi in the laboratory. In fact, I have already started the ball rolling as far as 'lab-psi' goes, although the studies featured in the last two sections were aimed at experimentally testing whether ESP/PK was a unified process. Of course, for laboratory work, appropriate controls must be implemented, though that would also require surmounting the interpretive bias introduced by methodology (a point already made; for an example, see Mossbridge, 2023, where some apparent differences between presentiment and precognitive Remote Viewing [RV][6] are due purely to methodological approach). Notwithstanding this *caveat*, modern parapsychological practice would still seem to be the preferred approach to isolating effects since *spontaneous* cases of synchronicity (like Swedenborg's) and psi (like Dunne's), by their very natures (if we have to differentiate), resist conclusive Rhinean-type classifications.

Laboratory Psi and Parapsychological Nomenclature

When it comes to nomenclature, anecdotal accounts of psi experience show us that specific paranormal effects remain elusive when we try to identify their specific nature by name. In the specific instance of laboratory testing, where controls might help us, we shall see what can be gained in using current parapsychological nomenclature. In this section, I will consider the viability of telepathy, clairvoyance, precognition, and psychokinesis as constructs under the psi hypothesis.

Telepathy. We have seen that nomenclature only serves the purpose of accurately describing effects if those effects can be isolated. In his optimism, Rhine (Edwards, 1983) indicated there was "firm proof" for three types of psi: "clairvoyance, precognition, and PK" (see also Rhine & Pratt, 1957/1974, p. 45), necessarily excluding *pure* telepathy. As L. E. Rhine (1971) had noted, telepathy might be "a special kind of clairvoyance" based on observation of "*brain activity*" (p. 43). Pure telepathy is indistinguishable from clairvoyance if the targets are on record during the trial, *and* it is indistinguishable from precognitive-clairvoyance if the targets will go on record at some future date (recorded in both cases for the sake of independent data checking and objective confirmation of effects).

The "hardest of the psi types to isolate" (Rhine & Pratt, 1957/1974, p. 40), pure telepathy is nevertheless possible amongst honest, trustworthy, astute individuals who keep no physical records of their targets, although Rhine and Pratt, and Schmeidler (1969, 1977), suggested pure telepathy has been adequately proven based on methodologies involving secretive coding of targets (e.g., Birge, 1948; McMahan, 1946). Schmeidler (1977) explains how the agent (i.e., sender) can go through a series of digits from a random numbers table, and secretly link these digits with (say) Zener symbols (e.g., "three will translate as a circle … five will translate as a cross …"; p. 145). After the run, a count of hits (i.e., run score) can be toted by checking symbols against the digit series (which the agent should never reveal). If there is any active clairvoyance, it will be of no use as that will only help 'see' symbols and/or ambiguous arrays of digits in the tables. It is thought best that the experimenter record only run score, as any more detail than that may provide sufficient information for the percipient's precognitive clairvoyance to be effected during the actual runs. Other provisions may be necessary, which I will not discuss here—suffice it to say, the protocol requires honesty from the agent. But things get tedious when a second observer is brought in to work with the agent/sender for the sake of objectivity, because the coding secrets have to be conveyed almost by innuendo.

However, the problems do not end there. Rhine and Pratt (1957/1974) pointed out that certain psychophysiological processes (many yet to be unearthed, but see Williams, 2015) do not indicate "direct thought transference" *per se* (p. 56), but may indicate clairvoyance if physiological traces in certain organs (the brain, nervous system, vocal chords) can be read. I already implied this dichotomy in the previous subsection where I discussed the flaws in Mundle's (1967) assumptions about human organs. We simply cannot say clairvoyance never facilitates or replaces telepathy. It is thus the case that parapsychologists sometimes have to resort to the "non-committal technical term" General Extra-Sensory Perception (GESP) when labelling ESP arrived at either by "telepathy", or "clairvoyance", or "both sources" (Thalbourne, 2003, p. 46). Yet this psi hybrid is not assessed in the meta-analyses because it is too blunt an effect. It is merely assumed that telepathy is the likely effect because there has been apparent (or presumed) evidence for it in the past. In fact, the evidence is poor, and merely operationally and conventionally consists of 'transmissions' of images (a limitation of the ganzfeld design); not actual thoughts, so the effect should hardly be alternatively referred to as mind-reading *per se*. So a question mark hangs over the working hypothesis put forward in any meta-analysis that refers to a sub-set of studies that tested so-called telepathy (Storm & Tressoldi, 2020; Storm, Sherwood et al., 2017; Storm, Tressoldi & Di Risio, 2010). Fortunately, however, these meta-analyses do allow one to reach certain conclusions about the psi modalities (see the next subsection *Rethinking Psi as Synchronicity*), but parapsychologists do need to ask themselves if they are taking the kinds of precautions advocated by the earlier researchers (e.g., Schmeidler, 1977).

Clairvoyance. If we consider the nature of pure (real-time) clairvoyance, we seem to be on relatively safer ground because we only have to isolate a single individual in a pure clairvoyance condition by confining all possible psi sources to *targets only* to rule out agents and/or experimenters as sources, lest telepathy become possible. Also, post-trial feedback is disallowed so as to rule out any kind of precognitive interaction, though it seems run-scores can be presented and kept for statistical purposes.

In the early days of psi research, Tyrrell (1936) conducted a series of clairvoyance experiments to control for telepathy and precognitive-telepathy by using a five-box array with a concealed lamp in each box.[7] The aim in each trial for the sole participant (psychic Miss G. M. Johnson) was to identify which light-tight box contained a lit lamp, and then open the box, which thus gave her direct post-trial feedback. Johnson's hits were recorded as parallel lines on moving tape, with misses as single lines—the lines, however, did not reveal the actual box, thus ostensibly prohibiting precognitive-telepathy. Tyrrell was satisfied that telepathy had been excluded, and clairvoyance (the aim) was possible only after the trials. Strangely, he suggested the outcomes had the "appearance of precognition", but he also suggested "combined clairvoyance and telepathy" might explain the effects (p. 149).

Other tests of clairvoyance have been conducted. Rhine and Pratt (1957/1974) describe the "chute" series of card-sorting tests conducted by Humphrey and Pratt (1941). Zener cards were used. Cards were dropped into openings marked by five key cards forming five disorganized piles. Without going into tedious methodological detail, Rhine and Pratt were convinced pure clairvoyance was isolated because they assumed an experimenter tallying the results could not keep a conscious or unconscious mental record of card sequences that a participant could exploit using precognitive-telepathy. Many parapsychologists regard the case for clairvoyance as proven by this kind of work, but today we know astounding feats of memory are possible as evinced by card-counting in gambling scenarios. While these kinds of performances involve conscious rehearsal, the cognitive unconscious can record lengthy sequences even without conscious intention and rehearsal (Bergström, 2011; Flegstein et al., 1998). Thus, we could not rule out precognitive-telepathy.

In the modern era, experimental designs run on computers cannot control for other precognitive interactions. For example, Schmeidler (1964) used computers to test for specific effects—namely, clairvoyance, precognition, and precognitive-clairvoyance—but her studies produced results that were ultimately inconclusive, not simply because she did not control for precognitive-telepathy, but also because she did not control all the factors pertinent to the computer itself as a psi source. Computers may well be programmed to generate each target in real-time, and then present *run scores only* on-screen as feedback, which can be recorded for statistical purposes, but the computer's calculation of hits and misses will have an electronic presence, thus allowing for precognitive-clairvoyance. As Kennedy and Taddonio (1976) note: "ESP allows proper responses to targets that exist only as complex algorithms and electromagnetic pulses" (p. 26). That statement applies equally to future algorithmic computations of hits (not just to targets in real-time). Thus, modern parapsychological experiments featuring computers, even as far back as the 1960s, have never resolved the extraneous psi source problem. Surprisingly, in the new century, even the most recent meta-analyses treat clairvoyance (more out of convenience) as if it was a viable construct in spite of the fact that it has nothing more than face validity (Storm & Tressoldi, 2020; Storm, Sherwood et al., 2017).

A case for clairvoyance might still be made by considering the successful remote-viewing (RV) studies, but we have to take a closer look at the influence of feedback because under the OTs, clairvoyance is not possible, and only precognition is possible in the form of retrocausation (mentioned in the previous section). In keeping with the main principle of the OTs, the "active element in the future influences the past by PK.... [T]o be able to PK or precognize something you must later see how it turned out" (Millar, 2015, p. 167). Opinion over the value of feedback persists in the RV community (Targ, 2019)—I can even throw in an evaluation of my own: In a study by Targ, Targ, and Lichtarge (1985), using free-response[8] Remote Viewing (RV) targets, two out of two feedback conditions (precognition and clairvoyance) found only chance results, but clairvoyance was demonstrated in the 'no-feedback condition'. In other words, there was no support for retrocausation, but it seems the take-home message was not just that feedback is *not* necessary for successful RV, but that feedback might even be detrimental to the RV effect (see also May, Lantz, & Piantineda, 1994).

Generally speaking, many in the RV community will claim that feedback is not essential for RV effects, thus saving the clairvoyance hypothesis. For example, a study by Targ and Tart (1985) offered evidence against the OTs (which demand feedback) in favour of pure (no-feedback) clairvoyance of 'computer-chosen numbers'. Conceivably, their design would rule out the ability of percipients to "precognize the future state of their brain" (p. 485), simply because there would be no feedback about the target order (i.e., there would be no evidence of retrocausation). Three significant individual performances in a non-feedback condition corresponded to beliefs about feedback and non-feedback (e.g., one percipient, who believed feedback was essential, psi-hit; one who believed feedback was *not* essential, also psi-hit). But the authors failed to report the hit-rate for the combined data in the feedback condition, which was significantly greater (13.06%) compared to the non-feedback condition (8.33%, where MCE = 10%). Even if the odd occasion of psi-hitting *without feedback* presented itself, this study was a back-handed proof that the OTs might be correct about the need for feedback (i.e., clairvoyance is more like precognition).[9] Millar (2019) actually dismisses the design for it allows for experimenter effect (one presumes he would not be swayed from this opinion had these statistics been made known to him). Note, as will be seen, in uncontrolled situations in the field where real-time RV is being tested, target-related information can come from the past and/or the future (theoretically), even if it was not *consciously* taken on board by the test subject. Of course that argument is not in the spirit of OT—the RVer has to *receive* direct feedback at some stage; not *perceive* the actual event retro-cognitively or precognitively, though that is entirely acceptable in some psi theories such as Psi-Mediated Instrumental Response (PMIR) and Decision Augmentation Theory (DAT; see Chapter 4).

We can see an example of trans-temporality without feedback in renowned remote-viewer Patrick H. Price's landmark remote viewing of 1974. In that viewing, Price sketched an aerial view of Rinconada Park in Palo Alto, California, at a time when the site was a swimming pool complex, but Price described the site as a "water purification plant" (Targ & Katra, 1998), and he sketched in "nonexistent water-storage tanks" and related machinery (p. 42). One definition of RV suggests we not overlook psi from multiple temporal sources, given that it is regarded as "acquisition of information that is blocked from the known senses by shielding, distance, *or time* [emphasis added]" (May, 2014, p. 314). This definition leaves open the possibility that real-time information can be supplemented by time-displaced information that cues the RVer, whether they know it or not. As it happened, in the mid-1990s, evidence of a waterworks was discovered (long gone at the time of Price's viewing). It was built on the same site in 1913, with a photograph to prove it (see Targ & Katra, 1998, p. 43). Price, who died July 14, 1975, possibly 'viewed' the original source via retrocognition; indeed, Targ and Katra seem to think so—"he [Price] had looked back fifty years in time" (p. 44). The OTs cannot account for Price's successful hit (he never received feedback), but as far as we know, Price never said he looked back in time, and it was never proved that he did. Given RV, Price could have either remote viewed *in real time* the photograph on file (say) in the city's records office, *or he precognized the photograph* that was later reproduced in the *Annual Report of the City of Palo Alto* in the city's centennial year of 1995. In short, we cannot isolate a clairvoyance effect.

Time-displaced RV can be demonstrated another way, for Price also showed possible evidence of precognition rather than real-time viewing (clairvoyance) of goings-on at a Soviet site of great interest in Kazakhstan, formerly part of the

Soviet Union (Targ, 2012). Price described possible bomb construction at the site. This remote viewing was also in 1974; Price died *without ever receiving personal feedback* on his performance (again ruling out OT). In 1977, the publication *Aviation Week & Space Technology* gave a report on 'sphere-fabricating activity at Semipalatinsk'. Targ (2012) regarded the whole RV session as feedback-free "*direct experience of the site*" (p. 55), but seven years later, he opted for an RV effect caused by "direct access to *any point in space-time* [emphasis added]" (Targ, 2019, p. 590). That change of opinion is a kind of concession on Targ's part because any kind of psi (except retrocausation requiring feedback) would have been as good as any other *while Price was alive*, even 'viewing' future contents in that *Aviation Week* article, irrespective of the fact that he had died before the issue came out. The word 'feedback' that Targ resists so much may not apply, but the spanner in the works is the fact that RV cannot be isolated as pure clairvoyance.

In these two RV cases, we are led to believe that Price primarily received *real-time* information. Advocates of RV do not deny trans-temporality, but the problem is that successful RV trials can never be proof of pure clairvoyance as long as the experimenter has not (or cannot) control for trans-temporal (retrocognitive and precognitive) sources (and retrocausation if we admit the OTs).

Precognition. In the previous paragraphs, the *possibility* of precognition was raised as an alternative to clairvoyance, but what can be said of specific laboratory attempts to isolate precognition? After his series of clairvoyance experiments, a successful follow-up experiment led Tyrrell (1936) to conclude that "there is evidence pointing strongly in the direction of Precognition" (p. 164). Tyrrell gave Miss Johnson *delayed feedback*, requiring her to make her choice by opening a lid, and *only then did the light come on*, which would rule out clairvoyance and precognitive-telepathy, but perhaps PK cannot be ruled out. There is no strong argument against Johnson psychokinetically controlling *in the present*, and throughout a sufficient number of trials, any of the mechanical or electro-mechanical processes taking place in the rather archaic devices Tyrrell constructed that are very much of their era. And Tyrrell concedes that the trials tested precognition only "because they appear to be so" (p. 149). Consequently, Tyrrell never really made adjustments that proved any kind of pure psi effect. Taking the problem a little further, we must consider the possible role of the 'delayed feedback' Tyrrell gave Johnson, in the spirit of the OTs. Although the tape was of no use to Johnson, those future events and Johnson's real-time actions might be regarded as "composite actions" resulting in *retro-PK* under the OTs where the present (i.e., Johnson's behaviour) is *influenced* by a future condition, rather than anything actually *being changed* (i.e., no physical influence on the apparatus). Conscious feedback is therefore necessary for retro-PK to work.

At a much later date, Broad (1962/2011) discussed the various complications in Tyrrell's experiments, arguing that they had limited controls, including lack of control over paranormal effects besides those Tyrrell thought had (or might have) taken place. There are other examples like this where controls are limited, or much is assumed: Mangan's (1955) *pure* precognition tests using sure-fire procedures (generating targets by so-called 'fixing events' based on dice throws and random number tables) amount to very little because their credibility rests on the assumption that we can set limits to psi—that we can constrain and control it as we please—so that fixing a target in a sufficiently complex way must mean the participant "would not know what to do *even via ESP* [emphasis added]" (Morris, 1982, p. 329; see also Morris, 1968). Rhine and Pratt (1957/1974) were just as confident in their so-called "weather cut" (p. 57)—a method using published temperature readings to decide how a pack of cards should be cut, therefore thought to be beyond PK capability if it meant influencing a thermometer or the actual weather. However, Rhine and Pratt never entirely eliminated alternative explanations outside the precognition assumption, and they even gave a few examples.

At a much later date, using a similar complex method (involving future stock-market prices and temperatures) to rule out real-time ESP and PK, Fiona Steinkamp (2000, 2001) was unable to demonstrate precognition effects. We are also led to believe that apparent real-time psi (clairvoyance) has been successfully demonstrated in extremely difficult precognition tasks that rely on complex mathematical calculations to generate future targets (Morris, 1968). Still, Steinkamp (2000) tested the two hypothesized modalities, clairvoyance and precognition, using a free-response design, while participants did not know which modality was being tested, and she was able to demonstrate a significant clairvoyance effect, but not a significant precognition effect. We have a serious problem if it is only the complex operational procedures that account for the failures in the latter, coupled with the fact that clairvoyance (if that is what it is) can creep in irrespective of that complexity. In a follow-up study (Steinkamp, 2001), results were not significant in either condition. An earlier meta-analysis on forced-choice studies (Steinkamp, Milton, & Morris, 1998), that compared clairvoyance and precognition, did *not* show a significant difference between the two modalities, although each set produced a 'statistically significant cumulated overall effect" (p. 193). These results suggest: (a) clairvoyance and precognition effects may be as strong as each other (Steinkamp, 2000, agrees); and (b) clairvoyance may sometimes be easier to elicit than precognition, but again, that may be a methodological issue. And given the possibility that clairvoyance could contribute to precognition, there is no case to argue for precognition as a pure effect.

Looked at another way, as proposed above by Houtkooper (2002) and Millar (2015), perhaps all psi is precognition as a retrocausal effect. While Irwin and Watt (2007) suggest test results on the OTs are "inconsistent" (p. 128), their conclusion flies in the face of the generally non-significant set of forced-choice precognition studies that *did not* provide feedback (15 studies) in contrast with those that *did* provide feedback (89 studies) and were overall significant (see Honorton & Ferrari, 1989, p. 297). In fact, the non-significant pool of studies had a combined negative hit-rate suggesting psi-missing (target avoidance). However, the break-down of the feedback findings is even more pertinent, and gives away a key point—feedback is not just *informational* (if at all), but it does seem to be *motivational*, and therefore affects performance on trials by keeping the participant interested, trail after trial. Feedback may well maintain participant interest and dedication to the task at hand via continued encouragement, anticipation (the *hope* of guessing right), and reward (hitting). To demonstrate this assumption, 'trial-by-trial' feedback produced the strongest mean performance of the three feedback types ($z = 6.98$), followed by 'run-score' feedback ($z = 4.74$), followed by "delayed" feedback (usually by mail; $z = 2.11$). So a key issue affecting performance is the *immediacy* of the feedback. The best performing group receives the motivating feedback at the most optimal time as far as subsequent trials are concerned when the *motivational* effect is expected to be at its strongest. If psi was entirely dependent upon the *informational content* of the feedback, effects would be consistent regardless of the time feedback was given—argued here is that feedback keeps participants motivated.

A related effect—time interval—proves the point. Time interval is the time between response and target selection (ranging in milliseconds to months): Feedback cannot be given until after the target has been selected/generated (target selection is not to be confused with participant response). So, the greater the time interval, the more delay there is in getting feedback. Not surprisingly, Honorton and Ferrari (1989) showed that so-called precognition goes into decline the longer the time interval. Since the immediacy of feedback is so important for motivation, late feedback means the motivating factor for subsequent trials, and even runs, may come too late as well. As it happened, and just as I have argued here, Honorton and Ferrari made the point that the decline was possibly due to a "motivational" factor; not an "intrinsic physical boundary condition" (p. 299).

Jon Taylor (2019) states: "Precognition is more likely when the temporal distance to the future experience is short" (p. 14). Taylor, in his "strictly materialist" brain model, argues that where there are declines, it is a matter of "neuroplasticity" (p. 16)—as the time interval increases, the "synaptic connections forming the pathways change constantly" (i.e., the resonance between the current brain state and the future target weakens so matching goes into decline also). Importantly, Taylor also argues that "feedback about the target (or result of the experiment) must be given to the participant in the future" (p. 15), and precognition is "more likely when the experience of the event in the future produces strong emotional impact" (p. 16). So for Taylor, personal relevance of the experience motivates (i.e., the task is incentivized) and is therefore *arguably* a causal factor (it is a conducive condition), but feedback is *definitely* a causal factor (it is a necessary condition), but there is no mention of the motivational role underlying feedback. The irony in such a position is that the "strong emotional impact" cannot come without the feedback.

Taylor's (2019) theoretical leanings also rule out the possibility of 'clairvoyance contacts' (they "do not occur") and 'telepathy contacts' (they are "difficult to produce"; p. 15). On the evidence, I would agree that solid cases for *pure* clairvoyance and *pure* telepathy have not been made (and possibly cannot be built on experimental evidence), but Taylor then argues that these so-called *real-time* psi effects are primarily precognitive—"many telepathy experiments are explained as precognition of the percipient's future knowledge of the target … [and the] significant results of [clairvoyance] experiments are attributed either to precognition or to precognitive telepathy with a person who has knowledge of the target information"

(p. 15). While Taylor leaves open the question of pure telepathy, he does make a case for hybrid modalities, which works against the Rhinean agenda that seeks to prove three basic and pure, mutually exclusive forms of ESP. That of course is not Taylor's problem, but feedback-dependent theories like Taylor's have a serious downside, as we shall see.

I must note that the rationale behind time gaps and variable feedback delays is that it creates (even perpetuates) the premise that precognition is a linear and causal effect that can be modelled—and the model just happens to be open to temporal contingencies and even violations. Indeed, time symmetry is *the* fundamental premise underpinning precognition (see Bierman, 2010). Given the way the modern mind is built and shaped culturally, it seems reasonable to assume that knowledge *about* the future, that cannot be gleaned from any clues in the present, must come *from* the future, which explains the special status of feedback. Yet it is puzzling how the not-yet fully understood fundamentals of quantum mechanics (QM) has helped to give substance to the OTs (for a review, see Millar, 2019), with feedback taking a pivotal role in the psi function. I will consider the inadequate psi/QM relationship later (see Chapter 5), but given the aims of this section, I must look at the OTs from the point of view of those who dispute the claim that *all* ESP reduces to precognition which reduces to feedback-dependent retro-PK.

Feedback-dependence gets to the heart of arguments about the nature of psi when the OTs come into the picture, but experimental research with feedback in the laboratory cannot fully reveal that nature. The problem centres on real-world situations where psi is tested. Targ and Tart (1985) illustrate the problem with an oil-drilling scenario: They argue that it makes sense to drill for oil if the future feedback is positive (i.e., oil will be discovered), but they note that the answer could also be "No, do not drill" (p. 486). Unfortunately, knowing not to drill via feedback *from the future* can only be found out the hard way—one actually has to drill.

We could consider the problem from a different perspective; that of 'multiple worlds' (Carroll, 1990). Suppose for the moment that all these hypothesized worlds provide different kinds of feedback about locations (some with oil where one plans to drill, some without), and one could always find oil no matter where one drilled as long as one was able to enter the right world for that location. But are multiple worlds like that? It may be more likely that the presence of oil (or not) for that location is an established fact *across all worlds*. The OTs tell us that feedback is only possible *provided* the event (drilling) is carried out *to completion*—one drills, not because the outcome is only ever positive, but because one wants feedback (good or bad), which is only available *after* the drilling has been done! As Millar (2019) says: "What can be affected/seen by psi is curtailed to the feedback available". Under the OTs, feedback and selection constitute one event, so one cannot change anything; not the future, not the world, and not the feedback:

> Because a past state is connected to the psi source via the feedback channel the past cannot be *changed* by psi: what is done is done – effectively graven in stone.
>
> (Millar, 2019)

If the OTs are viable and must replace clairvoyance, Targ and Tart state "a potentially productive oil well might be skipped, for there would be no future feedback information for a valid psychic prediction to be based upon" (p. 486). This is a critical point—clairvoyance would more likely give a bigger picture of the presence of oil that feedback from one single drill operation might miss—but a greater problem prevails: Since feedback is contingent upon drilling, there can be no psi advantage for the hypothetical oil company if the OTs truly describe reality. And that should be reason enough for Rhineans to champion clairvoyance and drop the OTs altogether. In fact, since it is claimed that mining companies do employ RVers, and do not do as well without them (Jenkins, 2017; Playfair, 2015), it is quite probable that RV must be clairvoyance.

More broadly, the fate of the OTs is sealed—it is all very well that the OTs might make sense in the laboratory, and they have had some success there, but the laboratory sets a limiting case. Beyond that, the OTs cannot tell us how precognition works. The real world (as macrocosm) does not consist of random events remaining in indefinite states until they are observed—quite the contrary and for the most part, that world is decidedly deterministic, even for long periods of time, as in the example just given (like Einstein's Moon, oil is only where you find it, whether you do or do not intend to look). But it also now looks as though successful lab-psi is not necessarily attributable to feedback. I do not, however, discount the value of feedback—as I suggested above, motivation coupled with emotional impact brought about by ongoing feedback incentivizes *subsequent* effects. But in spite of there being a good case for clairvoyance in this instance, we have already seen in the previous subsection that the more general case for pure clairvoyance is not proved. More to the point of this subsection, the case for retrocausation is also limited. Whatever precognition may be, it does not have to be retrocausal.

Synchronicity is a solution that bypasses these considerations. Here the role of archetypes is pivotal, as Jung sees them as contingent factors in synchronicity. Jung (1952/1969, para. 841, 847) describes archetypes as nodal points or structural components of the collective unconscious (deep in the mind) that govern or influence our "patterns of behaviour" (para. 841). In other words, archetypes play a pivotal role in how we think, feel and act. They are innate and inherited. From an evolutionary or hereditary point of view, archetypes have become so distinct and well-defined as human factors that govern whole ways of being, they can be depicted and observed as motifs or idealized characters in a cultural product (*though these are only ever representations*)—examples include Hero/Heroine, Wise Old Man/Woman, Child, and contra-sexual components of the hero and heroine (i.e., *anima* and *animus*, respectively). Other psychological constructs include the persona (one's social mask or public image), natural numbers, the ego, and the 'central archetype' or Self (Jung also spells it as "self"), which is sometimes referred to as 'higher self' to avoid confusion. While archetypes are indeterminate in number, one assumes there must be an upper limit.

Going further, Jung (1952/1969) sees archetypes as providing a "foundation" or "a direct connection" to synchronistic experience (para. 845, 912). An archetype forms the substructure of a synchronicity, giving it its common theme, and acting as a defining quality throughout the experience, thereby, intensifying the meaningfulness. To return to the oil-drilling example; it is not a matter of psychically detecting the presence (or lack) of subterranean oil in real time or in the future, or needing time-slippery feedback to make a decision. Instead, it is a matter of whether an *archetypal situation* can be set up based on *the psychology of the particular individual* (ostensibly in the role of psychic), in conjunction with other factors, including the drill site, the *proposed* action to drill there, and the presence of oil (or not). This scenario must then be played out in the mind of that individual; even better if we capitalize on such an unpredictable situation by having (say) three psychics on the job, in the hope of getting a majority report. I say 'psychics' are suitable for the job because those people we consider to be 'psychic' *per se* (i.e., by convention, they demonstrate psi to a sufficient or marked degree) also happen to be prone to archetypal effects that go with synchronicity. Again, to quote Jung (1975) there are people whose 'supranormal faculty consist[s] in their already being in, or voluntarily putting themselves into, a state corresponding to an archetypal constellation—a state of numinous possession in which synchronistic phenomena become possible and even, to some extent, probable" (p. 542). For such people engaged in an oil-drilling endeavour, there is either archetypal resonance pertinent to the task at hand, or there is nothing to that effect. Provided an archetypal situation is constellated, the person(s) sensitive to it could intuit a favourable outcome based on the archetypal pattern that will be played out.

Psychokinesis. Noting key points made previously, and harking back to the Tyrrell (1936) studies, we can see that if ostensible ESP effects were demonstrated, there is the theoretical possibility that the experimenter and/or participant had unwittingly used PK (real-time or retroactive) to manipulate the allegedly random process of target selection, which can explain ESP effects like clairvoyance and precognition (see Eisenbud, 1982; Mundle, 1964). Not only may PK have occurred in Tyrrell's experiments, but many experiments, before and after, using dice or RNGs, and other physical apparatus to test ESP (e.g., precognition), may really be tests of PK.

Of course, some parapsychologists are now fairly certain that PK (a.k.a. anomalous perturbation) is generally a weaker effect compared to ESP (a.k.a. anomalous cognition; see Cardeña, 2018), although a few experimental domains challenge that assumption. For example, human and nonhuman 'noncontact healing' (often thought of as forms of macro-PK), and studies that fall under the Global Consciousness Project (Nelson, 2015) using RNGs, produce impressive effect sizes (.33 as of 2015/2016) exceeding those for most ESP domains (except Remote Viewing at .39; see Cardeña). However, the noncontact healing studies are only *nominally* PK, and some forms of noncontact healing could merely involve *telepathic* connections with living organisms. Based on many decades of healing research, William Bengston (Australian Institute of Parapsychological Research, 2022) makes it quite clear that psychic healing involves information, not energy transfer, and "the healer is not the driver of [psychic healing]; it's not a PK effect". Generally, however, effect sizes for a good half dozen experimental ESP domains are stronger (larger) than the best the PK domains have to offer (see Cardeña, 2018, Tables 1 and 2). In particular, RV, ganzfeld, presentiment (predictive physiological anticipation), and dream-ESP, take the lead over most PK domains.

But PK implies ESP, as pointed out above by Rhine (1947), so if Rhine is correct, what would account for the apparent difference, with PK a generally weaker effect? On the one hand, perhaps the *merely apparent* physical strictures and demands of some PK experiments (i.e., the perceptions of complexity and difficulty) are psi-suppressive and intimidate some participants,[10] whereas the same conditions are not thought to be present in ESP experiments (for a discussion of these issues, see Roe et al., 2003; Storm & Thalbourne, 2003, also raise the issue).[11] The disguised-ESP condition (pseudo-PK) that yielded significant psi-missing (Roe et al., 2006) and the disguised-PK condition (pseudo-ESP) that yielded significant psi-hitting (Roe et al., 2005), are good examples of this possibility. Rhine's point about methodology applies here, where the effect can turn out to be the result of what the "test was designed to measure" (p. 130), and by 'test' Rhine means methodological aims and hypotheses.

On the other hand, if Rhine is wrong and one submits that PK is independent of ESP, *pure* PK should surely primarily result in null effects in micro-PK tasks for it is difficult to imagine how a pure PK effect could be brought about precisely and accurately without ESP guiding the process, particularly in micro-PK processes—without ESP, how would one know one deviation from another? In fact, some parapsychological theories (PMIR and DAT) hang on this supposition despite what other remarks these theories suggest about ESP and PK (see Chapter 4). Regarding PMIR, Stanford (1974b) holds that "implicit extrasensory guidance" is "part and parcel" (pp. 326–328) of many PK events. Regarding DAT, a conventional PK effect in the RNG case is effectively reduced to an ESP effect (see May, Utts, & Spottiswoode, 1995a). Since results tell us otherwise, and since significant micro-PK effects *are* reported, perhaps Rhine cannot be wrong. Of course in principle, and as discussed above (see *The Problem of Unification*), macro-PK (e.g., PKMB) might be effected with only a watchful eye providing the necessary feedback (no ESP guidance necessary). But again, we simply cannot be sure ESP guidance is not involved in even that kind of PK, and as stated earlier there may be no way of proving it.

As with the muddle over psi *as a process*, it is indeed a hindrance to parapsychological progress that we maintain (on theoretical, hypothetical, and operational grounds) a few seemingly robust and seemingly mutually exclusive paranormal classifications or modalities, when attempts to isolate them have proved frustratingly difficult, or even impossible. We have seen—just as Osis (1953) discovered—that unification is not simply a matter of identifying two inseparable effects (ESP and PK) buried in psi. The crux of the unification problem is that we cannot control and draw out the two forms in one event; nor can we see a pure effect that could not be explained in various ways (i.e., as one or another modality). The next subsection will consider the consequences of this conundrum, and offer an alternative view.

As will be seen, the assignation 'synchronicity' would be a preferred term because it eliminates the problems that come with nomenclature that speaks to various psi modalities thought to have differing mechanisms.

Rethinking Psi as Synchronicity

Although Rhine's (1934) two categories, ESP and PK, met with Jung's approval,[12] Jung also tried to move theoretical parapsychology forward somewhat by proposing more than a 'fundamental similarity' between the two. Indeed, he suggested their 'parcelling' under the rubric of synchronicity that implied broader connotations not envisioned by Thouless and Wiesner (1947). However, the only way of determining that ESP and PK might not only be a unitary process, but synchronistic as well, as Jung's theory suggests, is to show how the coincidentiality[13] seen as ESP effects and PK effects is contingent upon synchronistic factors such as archetypes and meaningfulness.

Thus far, the evidence is growing only slowly, the findings are not always significant, and research has been conducted by only a handful of experimenters across a number of different laboratories worldwide (Braud, 1983; Houran & Lange, 2012; Roe, Martin, & Drennan, 2014; Storm, 2008b; Storm & Rock, 2014a; for research on archetypes specifically, see *On Model Building* in Chapter 4). But certainly the experimental approach to synchronicity does not require that ESP and PK terminology be invoked, even if some parapsychologists cannot resist the temptation. That aside, it is not usually helpful to try to explain to naïve participants, using Rhinean terms, that either ESP or PK, or even both proportionately or disproportionately, could underpin a given psi process and subsequent effect (if one is forthcoming), as that is quickly perceived as unenlightening, and thereby often fails to impress. This failure is avoided in synchronistic experiments which *cannot* isolate psi causes (see Appendix A for examples). In the interests of public relations, the experimenter might even be advised to explain that a meaningful coincidence is being sought (which one may couch in terms of, say, an *as yet unexplained selection bias*), and avoid using standard parapsychological terms altogether, including associated acronyms.

As we have seen, the naïveté (or incompleteness) of conventional psi interpretations *and* Eisenbud's (1980) Rhinean approach is apparent for two reasons: (i) synchronicity cannot satisfactorily reduce to ESP or PK given that this nomenclature is ambiguous and leaves us with a practically and theoretically incomplete science of which a range of mechanisms and modalities are proposed that may not pertain; and (ii) there cannot always be (as Eisenbud would have it) a causal agent (an "observer") responsible (at least in part) for the "elements in a multiple coincidence" (p. 26), with remaining uncaused elements left to chance.

Regarding (i), notwithstanding the issues with the terminological problems discussed, the meta-analytic studies highlight quite an important issue, for Storm et al. (2010) found no significant effect-size difference between the three ESP modalities; telepathy, clairvoyance, and precognition. The same finding tends to be reported elsewhere (e.g., Howard, 2018; Steinkamp et al., 1998; Storm & Tressoldi, 2020; 2023; Storm, Sherwood et al., 2017). These studies suggest that ESP either (a) takes three different forms, and each is generally of equal strength (a point made above in regard to clairvoyance and precognition; endorsed by Steinkamp, 2000); or (b) is a single phenomenon operative each time across three provisional psi modalities (subcategories) awaiting unification.

However, there may be extenuating factors—the pools of studies may be impure (i.e., the groupings may be contaminated). For example, possibly some number of studies (if not all) are only nominally testing telepathy for clairvoyance, or *vice versa*. Other studies may not be testing precognition as 'future-telling', but simply testing real-time PK on its own, or in combination with some form of real-time ESP (telepathy, or clairvoyance, or a combination of the two). It may be that all ESP effects must have a critical PK component as Rhine (1947) suggested. More generally, as we have seen, there is the added complication of other hybrid modalities, and since these 'conflations' do seem to exist, but cannot be controlled adequately, (a) and (b) would be confined to the theoretical realm, and all bets would be off.

Some parapsychologists are optimistic that a single theory will one day suffice in explaining some or all forms of psi (see Chapter 4 for examples). Previously, I said we are at the mercy of a conceptually poor (nebulous) construct; namely, psi. I noted that the concept does not bridge the gap between its ambiguous extra-sensory and psychokinetic aspects. Of course, the suggestion has been made to test performance differences on ESP and PK tasks (see Irwin, 1985), but no concerted effort has been made; at least not until the series by Roe et al. (2003, 2004, 2005, 2006) was run. However, recall my conclusions above (see *The Psi Process and Parapsychological Nomenclature*). I state again that if psi manifests as mutually exclusive modalities or forms, we cannot seem to be able to isolate them.

Regarding (ii), no observer or agent is omnipotent (as will be seen shortly when I consider the case of Ted Owens, the so-called 'PK Man'). Eisenbud (1980) insists on there being a "considerable range of conceivable latent psi powers of the observer" (p. 25), but by what measure does he set this hypothesized range of surely limited 'latent powers'? Any given limit of psi necessarily limits causality on the observer's part, yet we know that many cases of synchronicity are too complex structurally (temporally, spatially, agentively, and contextually) for us to accept that a causal agent/observer was completely or even mostly responsible. For an example, see Tart's (2008) case, the excerpt of which is reproduced in full in Appendix B. An even more impressive example of multiple synchronicities, that would only be *tortuously* reducible to Rhinean/Eisenbudian psi, is Dean Radin's (2018) 'quadruple synchronicity' described in his book *Real Magic*. Indeed, Radin loosely opts for 'magic' as his preferred explanation, describing it in more scientifically accessible terms as "intense intention [that] warps or distorts aspects of reality" (p. 86).

Along similar lines, is an incident that took place some years ago—I found a Seven of Spades blown into my drive-way (I still have the card). Some time later, I went out to dinner with my sister and her family when they were in Adelaide.

After the dinner, I went up to the counter to pay. No one was serving at the counter, but there was a single card on the counter laying face-down, so I flipped it over. It was the Seven of Spades. I wondered why it was that card, why me,[14] and why it just happened to be waiting for me. How long had it been sitting there? And besides all that, where were the other 51 cards, on both occasions? NB: the odds by chance of replicating the effect (i.e., getting the same card a second time) is a significant 1/52, where a chance result is usually set at 1/20.

Even attributing only *partial* responsibility to the agent/observer, as Eisenbud prefers, then requires a leap of faith from those who wish to believe that the many uncaused but necessary elements of the synchronistic scenario conveniently fall into place by chance (as Eisenbud suggests). Maybe some synchronicity pundits *are* prepared to accept that synchronicity has a chance-like quality *because* chance seems to be involved, but for all we know (or do not know) about psi, why does the Rhinean model not treat garden-variety (uncontrolled) psi in the same manner, requiring the same leap of faith? Eisenbud does not go there because the Rhinean model (probably to its detriment) was never set up to accommodate or explain the many (chance-like) elements of the general 'architecture' (the so-called 'macrocosmic' structural elements)—this perspective may give parapsychology the vital shot in the arm it so desperately needs (more on this macrocosmic aspect shortly).

Many a parapsychologist may say that one advantage of the Rhinean approach is that psi is spotted and explained well enough without the clutter of mandatory chance parameters helping the effect along. That is a very naïve view: No psi experimenter yet has discovered a way to identify and count *only* the non-chance hits; and no parapsychologist yet is sufficiently well informed to say with certainty that there is no need for a broader approach that helps identify the (problematic) *capitalization of chance*, as Eisenbud would call it. Superficially, that failing might even explain why cases like Ted Owens are so puzzling (reviewed in the next subsection). My argument here is that if Eisenbud's claim legitimately applies to synchronicity (i.e., chance has an important role to play), then it applies even more to psi.

The fact that synchronicity can happen in a complex, profound, even grand manner, does seem to introduce complications that do not burden garden-variety psi. Even given the above criticisms, some commentators still feel there is no other recourse but to continue with an Eisenbudian variant of the Rhinean model, and reduce synchronicity to a "refined, extensive, and potentially very intimidating form of large-scale psychokinesis" (Braude, 2007, p. xiv). While that approach might imaginatively address the grander synchronistic issues, Braude concludes the move is "controversial", but "unavoidable." But forcing synchronicity to fit any of the available Rhinean categories, even large-scale PK, is only 'unavoidable' if the synchronicity concept *has to be avoided.* And we might wonder why defaulting to a Rhinean model is an improvement since the fallibility and futility of that move has been demonstrated. As will be seen, the demands made by synchronicity are minimal by comparison, and less of a strain on our credulity. It may therefore prove fruitful that synchronicity remain as a working hypothesis rather than have it relegated to the side-lines, or even dismissed out of hand.

In viewing *psi* as a special kind of *coincidence* (meaningful coincidence to be precise), and collapsing these two concepts into one, we must wonder how the idea would be received by the various communities. While it does seem that a contingent of parapsychologists are not averse to the idea, it is not just a matter of winning a degree of tolerance for a modified (souped-up) version of psi; there is work to be done. This work includes the measurement of meaningfulness (requiring an understanding of the personal dynamics of the individual), and (perhaps the most challenging of all) the development of ways and means to gauge the activation of archetypes; their limits and situational contingencies.

We might also acknowledge the importance and advantage in informing participants they may have a numinous experience, which is to say, we must seek to measure *numinosity*, or factor it into our experiments (e.g., in the targets), because it ties in with the affectivity (emotional response) that is evoked during an archetypal experience. Numinous experiences give one a sense of mystery in the moment. Jungian scholar Aniela Jaffé (1967) explains that the numinous experience is "awe-inspiring" and "usually accompanies the experience of synchronistic phenomena" (p. 272).

It is understood that the main reason laboratory-based psi research is successful is because human intention is introduced without which chance fluctuation would remain within its usual parameters. However, intention on its own will not suffice (it is not a cause); the presence of intention is only a first step towards pushing the limits of those parameters. With a sufficient number of 'intending' participants, extrachance exceptions may occur, which allows the hit-count to reach significance, due to the presence in the count of *realized* coincidences, which implies that synchronicity is likely present in the mix and with it, the three factors just mentioned (namely, meaningfulness, constellated archetypes, and numinosity). Whenever intention is thought to be involved in a correspondence, the experimenter must be aware that whatever the will intends, the emotional system may be free to support and that may link to the archetype. I stress again that intention is not causal; it is merely part of a contingency arrangement.

Moreover, the use of homogeneous (unpatterned) environments (as in ganzfeld), or guided imagery (as in imagery cultivation; see Storm, 2023a), certainly help the individual relax and concentrate, but rather than altering the 'signal-to-noise ratio', by giving the signal clearer presence against a subdued background of environmental, physiological, and mental noise, these treatments more likely give the imagination a *freer* rein—more aptly applied to imagery cultivation than ganzfeld. Besides which, proponents of the idea that peripheral or inconsequential noise can be reduced, have not adequately explained how noise is attenuated *as well as* irrelevant psi signals which are also noise, but the desired psi signal *can* get through just because it is unlike those noises just mentioned. Even some kind of 'filter theory', whereby specialized areas of the brain take on the task of identifying the 'good' psi, will not explain how 'bad' psi does not get through (Ehrenwald, 1975). Generally, we are led to believe that successful psi signal reception ultimately comes down to intention effects, as implied, suggested or stated in the various psi theories (see Chapter 4). The preferred view is that in telepathy (to use conventional nomenclature), the imagination meets archetypal processes half-way and, by the capacity of the archetype to 'extend' (not being limited to the individual psyche), or "transgress" (to use Jung's word), a "doubling of a thought content in two physically separate persons" is enabled (Jaffé, 1967, p. 278), without the need to conclude that anything was 'transmitted'. Similarly, in the case of clairvoyance, precognition, and PK, we have an object of interest instead of a second person. Outside the laboratory, concerted efforts by von Lucadou (2015) and his associates (e.g., von Lucadou & Zahradnik, 2004) are good indications that meaning is becoming a fixture in paranormal experience and research, and the idea of a psi signal can be seen as redundant.

One of the weaknesses of the ESP/PK paradigm is that it has not generally or seriously been viewed in these contexts, but a synchronistic turn of mind would shift research to issues related to the imagination (individually, and in a collective human-wide framework), and away from "consciousness and the mind-body problem", and away from the notion of freewill acting entirely alone to produce a psi effect—at least "in certain contexts" (Greatrex, 1999, pp. 5–6)—because synchronicity is a broader, more *holistic* construct.[15]

These ideas of Greatrex (1999) need amplification, but they are basically the same as those already stipulated by Jung (1952/1969), who saw synchronicity, with its "causeless order" and "meaningful orderedness" (para. 948), as a seemingly paranormal inner/outer link—a link between the psychological and the physical, or between "psyche and physis" (para. 948). In essence, both are saying synchronicity implies that these factors (consciousness, mind, body, freewill, and their interactions) are broadened or extended—not in themselves directly, but indirectly (i.e., they are relativized) because of this synchronistic principle that has archetypal roots. In certain moments, we are not tied down absolutely to our limited functions; we are relatively freer than that, but may only see examples of that in manifest form under appropriate conditions (these conditions are evident in typical synchronicities such as described in the case of Swedenborg). There is no great or critical need to factor into our parapsychological theories the personal notions of psi ability, extended consciousness, unlimited mind, and untethered freewill where intention and volition are given a free rein without consequence. It may seem to be the case that each of these plays a pivotal role in psi. While the idea has some allure, as it suggests agency and cause, the synchronistic view is wary of such ideas since it goes beyond the rules and restrictions of causality. I find in Ted Owens a fine example of a man occasionally caught up in a web of synchronicity, whereas conventional parapsychological paradigms offer limited explanation for his plight.

Ted Owens: The Synchronicity Man?

The failure of such categorical efforts at consolidating psi nomenclature and describing the psi process is well illustrated in the case of Ted Owens (a.k.a. the PK Man), whose extraordinary paranormal feats are still not explained (or at least not fully, or not to everyone's satisfaction; see Mishlove, 2000). Ted Owens (1920-1987) claimed he was the cause of UFO appearances, lightning and thunder, plane crashes, power outages, turnarounds in sporting events, and even the Challenger space shuttle disaster of 1986. Braude (2001) has disputed some of Owens's 'predictions' (notably the weather forecasts), but the 'too-hard basket' is not yet emptied, for the argument from precognition is fairly pitted against the argument from PK—neither can be ruled out entirely. But nor can 'cherry-picking': Jeffrey Mishlove is on record for stating that about one third of Owens's predictions never eventuated, and he notes:

> … the account presented [in *The PK Man*] has failed to provide a complete reporting of all of the many statements made by Owens. Perhaps there are tens of thousands of incorrect claims that have been hidden from the readers. If one had a complete picture, one might see that the unusual coincidences were just "lucky hits."
>
> (Mishlove, 2000, p. 138)

If that were true, there would be no point continuing with this case. However, giving Owens the benefit of the doubt, and assuming some proportion of paranormality in the cumulative record of "hits" reported by Mishlove, most researchers do seem satisfied to attribute such effects to psi (e.g., PK). But nobody has seen the need to suggest synchronicity as an explanation for Owens's predictions, when even his failures would be accommodated under synchronicity theory for failure is inevitable without the contingent archetype, and to be frank, archetypes do not volunteer their services. Instead, under the psi paradigm, the usual explanations offered for failures are mainly methodological and no one pins the problem on how psi or psychic ability *per se* is inadequately conceptualized (for examples, see Harary & Targ, 1985; Schlitz et al., 2021).

Ordinarily, going after methodology is an appropriate approach to take, but on occasion researchers remain trapped in a cycle of frustration when studies fail to replicate with no apparent reason. For example, Schlitz et al. (2021) attributed their failures to "some aspect of the current studies [that were] … impossible to falsify …" (p. 82). Even nearly 40 years earlier, Harary and Targ (1985) said much the same thing, blaming the failures on 'displacement" (p. 84).[16] And if Owens had been in a controlled psi study and his so-called PK ability failed him, the usual excuses would be offered, but his successes would no doubt be due to his exceptional PK ability. In short, we would be no wiser no matter the outcome (we shall see that even Owens himself offered alternative explanations for his psi outcomes that no ordinary parapsychologist would swallow). Yet Owens's mental (disturbed) state has all the hallmarks of a man who was markedly sensitive and susceptible to synchronicity (and many would regard him as an egotistical man in serious need of change, psychologically speaking—a change he seemed incapable of initiating let alone acknowledging). Perhaps Owens's bravado (for want of a better word) made Owens prone to synchronicity. But notice how *his* 'effects' are always about drawing attention to himself; they are invariably about doing damage; and they are often about winning and losing (i.e., tilting fate in one direction or another, and not to everyone's advantage). For all that, as we shall see, the synchronicity explanation minimizes the culpability of Owens's actions (though perhaps not by much).

Owens is a special case that illustrates these points for there is no question that his psychology contributed in large part to his unique paranormality. In fact, we can make an example of Owens, and use his case to illustrate more general principles of synchronicity. If all those uncanny phenomena, insofar as we wish to treat them as paranormal, really are correlated with Owens, we do not necessarily have to accept that he is always culpable, despite appearances to the contrary (as we are always reminded in science: correlation does not prove causation). Owens himself effectively disavowed *his own agency*, and he constantly pointed the finger at "Space Intelligences" (SI's; Mishlove, 2000, p. 20) whenever he was questioned about his psi feats. Owens apparently felt that he had to cooperate with the SIs to bring about these sometimes horrifying events, so that his involvement appears to amount to not much more than *consent* and *participation* of a sort (so there is only some complicity).

Even with SIs as a *root cause* for Owens's effects, can we not regard 'consent' and 'participation' as more than 'impartial observation' from someone who identifies as 'co-author' of unfathomable processes he cannot (and occasionally does not) claim to have completely orchestrated himself? That is, Owens is more than complicit in his actions; after all, an accessory, before, during, and after the fact still bears considerable guilt. Mishlove seems to thinks so—he calls these SIs a "polypsychic extrusion from Owens' own psyche" (p. 20), and suggests that SIs are unconvincing psychological "crutches" invented by Owens to assuage his guilt. But Mishlove seems to contradict himself, for he then compares Owens to Nature as though his destructive actions were like those of the sky gods of Olympus and they (Nature, gods/archetypes), and especially Owens himself, cannot be judged by human moral and ethical standards. Braude (2001), however, does not excuse Owens so easily—Owens *is* a "monster", and Mishlove is making a "category mistake" (p. 186) by suggesting that Owens can act with impunity.

Perhaps culpability, and likewise impunity, extend only so far. Thus, it is one thing to spot the agent/observer (and attribute blame), but quite another to trace agency/causality when it is spread so far afield (hence, the impunity), which combine to create a dilemma difficult to unravel in a world where black-and-white interpretations are demanded. Nevertheless, a middle position is tenable, though it may be hard to fathom. Owens, in positing these manifestations (these SI's), was as close as a person can get to recognizing archetypal forces, and cooperating with them without those same forces destroying him (indeed, it may have been the case that they did destroy him in the end through liver failure, psychosomatic or otherwise). But it is quite a stretch to say that Owens has godlike powers, or the 'gods' (archetypes) lent Owens their power unconditionally. Indeed, his many failures prove they did not (this problem is not so different from the sporadic nature of psi in the laboratory). We are often led to see (or assume) fervent, unwavering intention on his part, when we consider his posturing, his bluffs, his bravado, and his hits. But he did tend to relent and defer to outside agency. This is more than modesty or a deeply disguised morality at play. Guilty he may be of "overt vindictiveness", and he may not be "altogether admirable" (Braude, 2001, p. 183), but his is no mere ploy, misdirection, cop-out, or denial. On the contrary, Owens has a very real but tacit stirring in him—an understanding of sorts—that tells him his paranormal machinations are not his own, which otherwise would be *completely* attributing to him (and tantamount to forcing him to accept) total responsibility—something he would have been emotionally and intellectually incapable of handling (at least, for the more damaging incidents that he blamed on the SI's).

It is true, for the most part, that if Owens was responsible for holding the *idea* of destruction (wherever the idea came from), he may have been morally guilty as well, but there does appear to have been an intuition (albeit ever so slight) that the dramatic, even catastrophic events surrounding him, belonged to a wider sphere of events in motion, each with their own causal chain, with him acausally connected to all of them, though he may have liked to believe (on those occasions when his ego *did* grip him) that his participation facilitated events. These images bring to mind Goethe's *The Sorcerer's Apprentice* (Zipes, 2017), which depicts an undisciplined student of magic who thinks he, and he alone, is in total control when wielding supernatural power, which ultimately gets the better of him. Synchronicity in Owens's case presents in just such a way.

Had he known better, Owens might have seen 'his' actions as similar to the "magic causality" that Progoff (1973) describes and parallels with synchronicity, though the parallel with 'magic', being inaccurate and misleading, is somewhat over-stating the facts. That is because Progoff, in calling archetypes "effective factors that bring about processes of change at profound levels of the human psyche" (p. 105), seems to imply an infallible and absolute readiness on the part of the archetype to participate at call (on demand) and to effect a change. All evidence is to the contrary. However, as sporadic as they are, when archetypes do manifest to full effect, the experient's psyche is impelled to ride out that "magic effect" like a surfer rides out a huge wave, not knowing where it will go and what havoc it may wreak. The Jungian analyst Robert Johnson once compared archetypal energy to the high-voltage electric current that should not be carelessly accessed from the domestic wall socket (Segaller, 1989). Archetypal forces are very powerful; they go beyond the parameters the psyche might like to set, and cannot be controlled let alone successfully summoned entirely at will. Owens might have been aware of the risks involved because he warned that SI's are extremely dangerous and can be life-threatening. He even appealed to individuals (including Mishlove) to intervene on his behalf in the hope that tragedy could be averted; again distancing himself from the false assumption that he might be taken as the agent. Whenever Owens was in-tune or aligned with these archetypal energies, he would have seen manifested effects which most observers would have attributed to Owens (not knowing any better), and when there was never going to be an alignment with archetypal energies, he would have failed and looked like a phoney.

These archetypal energies are not to be mistaken for intrapsychic forces only; they extend to the environment thus giving the observer the sense that the environment yields to the agent's wishes, or cooperates with the agent, by psychokinetic means. As Jung says:

> You can never say with certainty whether what appears to be going on in the collective unconscious of a single individual is not also happening in other individuals or organisms or things or situations.
>
> (Jung, 1952/1969, para. 912)

Owens's psychological state merely reflects the archetypal forces of the transpersonal, or better, macrocosmic order, which thus invoke the synchronicity concept—as Progoff (1973) says: Synchronicity is

> a principle functioning in the macrocosm as a whole.... [H]owever, we have the individual beings who participate in the pattern, whose lives and actions express it.... The individual microcosmic life is an aspect of the larger general pattern of the macrocosm. Nonetheless, the individual who is engaged in expressing the macrocosmic pattern that encompasses him is doing so by actions in his life that are apparently decided rationally.
>
> (pp. 128-129)

That last point explains why psychic functioning is not only thought to be an ability, but is also thought to be completely controllable by human reason (but then Progoff does say 'apparently'). We do know, however, that many psychics and mediums never make such claims.

Putting it in simpler terms, Peat (1987) describes synchronicity as "a microcosm which reflects the dynamics of the macrocosm as it unfolds simultaneously into the mental and material aspects of a person's life" (p. 187). Jaffé (1967) is even clearer when she describes the archetype as arranging or manifesting itself in the facets of the synchronistic event:

> we are dealing here with an unusual manifestation of its [the archetype's] 'emergence into consciousness' by means of a split [that underlies] the process whenever something comes into consciousness.
>
> (p. 276)

Without this kind of perspective, it is easy for Mishlove to say Owens is the cause of the uncanny phenomena, while SI's are seen as an excuse. However, SI's—those *manifested archetypes* that even 'talk' to Owens (see Owens, 1969)—might be better thought of as part of a contingency set, another part being Owens's *desire* to set up (or, more likely, align himself with) a certain inevitable (archetypal) outcome. If Owens is sufficiently aligned with those energies, he tends to get a result, but we must recall the above analogy of the surfer riding a wave. That understanding tells us something far more meaningful than the garden-variety (causal) psi of the Rhinean paradigm. And why should we be compelled "to throw up our hands at the unfathomability of the universe" (Eisenbud, 1980, p. 25) if we dare embrace synchronicity, but not feel equally befuddled and dismissive of psi? As Vaughan (1980) says, an explanation that appeals to psi "does not take into account that the how and why of psi are unknown" (p. 21).

The Rhinean model simply does not address the holistic nature of psi phenomena; it was never designed for that purpose. Instead, it remains conceptually narrow (just as Ballard intimated), the implications of which, from the above, should now be clear: Rather than being the sole author and culpable agent of occasional paranormal feats due to an extraordinary ability, Owens's intentions (images, ideas) may align with archetypes that 'transgress' and coincide as equivalences in the external world. In either case, no effect is guaranteed, but with psi it is thought the external world is beholden to human whim, whereas synchronistic outcomes are indeterminate and statistically dependent upon archetypal and environmental factors. Archetypes can "go beyond their frame of reference… and the psychic sphere" (Jung, 1952/1969, para. 964), and while synchronicity theory rules out causal connections, a claim which may not satisfy every theorist, we do have inklings that archetypal rather than chance factors are at play.

As we also learn, Mishlove (2000), like Eisenbud, did not make a distinction between chance effects (lucky hits) and 'chance-like' (archetypal) effects, or at the very least they could never be sure which was which. Unfortunately, one may appear as the other, which prompted even Jung to speak of synchronicity as if it occurs by chance: "synchronicity … consists essentially of 'chance' equivalences" (para. 964). But as Jung also notes, we can anticipate related but unknown outcomes and make predictions based on the synchronistic elements. That is what Jung means when he talks of "sifting chance events and separating the acausal ones [synchronicity] from those that can be causally explained" (para. 823). A definitive example is given in Jung's (1952/1969, para. 844) 'birds' case. A woman reported a gathering of birds at the time of her grandmother's death, and then later, her mother's death. When a flock of birds appeared outside her house a third time, the woman had an anxiety attack for she 'knew' intuitively that her husband's life was in danger, as she was to discover later when he was brought home dying from a heart attack. Jung notes that "the flock of birds evoked the corresponding memory-images and consequently her fear" (para. 857), but "the death and the flock of birds seem to be incommensurable with one another" (para. 845). Nevertheless, the dead are identified with birds; Jung points out the archetypal references and historical antecedents for that association (para. 850–851). Some cases of synchronicity can be difficult to decipher when the main elements are abstract or symbolic (consider my Seven of Spades example). In other words, the woman was not only conditioned to react in a certain way to flocks of birds, but she was also privy (had she but known it) to the workings of a particular archetypal process underscoring her emotional reactions.

It is ironic that Eisenbud, for all his resistance to synchronicity, proposed that psi might be governed by an ordering principle of nature (to keep it lawful and structured); a notion which is almost a push towards a "general acausal orderedness" of which synchronicity is a part (Jung, 1952/1969, para. 965). This quote surely gives us a clue:

> What we know narrowly as psi may thus be construed as in some way an indispensable part of the executive arm, so to speak, of the laws of probability and as such plays an important role as a guardian of various 'givens' which can be deviated from only within more or less given limits.
>
> (Eisenbud, 1983, p. 162)

Eisenbud sees the psi effect as caused within a probabilistic framework, but the archetype too functions probabilistically though not causally but coincidentally (and therefore synchronistically) through meaning; synchronicity is purposeful for that reason. As Jung has said of the archetype, it is "a special psychic instance of probability" (Jung, 1952/1969, para. 964). By proposing certain stochastic limits to psi, Eisenbud has actually moved the conventional understanding of psi towards something holistic like synchronicity even if that was not his intention. And even the 'darker' aspects (that may be evident in *active analysis*) that Eisenbud attributes to psi are no less true of synchronicity; the personal quotient being part-and-parcel of a transpersonal experience with all the forces of the psyche (the ego, conscience, conscious and unconscious desires, the archetypes) acting like arbiters or enforcers, often on opposing sides of the ontological fence, seeking "cosmic balance" and even "destruction" and "self-destructiveness" (points raised by Braude, 2017, in discussing Eisenbud's ideas on psi). Arguably, when it comes to matters of conscience, some individuals (like Ted Owens) will have a struggle on their hands matched in scale only by the mayhem in which they find themselves but, for a little insight and a sizeable dose of contrition, change might have been possible.

All this leads to another important point about the apparent schism (i.e., the psi/synchronicity dichotomy); namely, 'causes'. Palmer (2016b) differentiates psi and synchronicity in standard fashion (as do others, as we shall see shortly), but he also devises relevant hypotheses concerning the testing of both, all set in place by weighing up both the conventional (Rhinean) view on psi on the one hand, and a standard synchronistic understanding on the other. As I said in the Preface, Palmer (2016b) reiterates the conventional view of psi as "an ability" (i.e., the psi source and therefore the cause can be isolated) whereas synchronicity is "a principle of nature" (p. 193). The four relevant hypotheses Palmer constructed looked at participants' attitudes to chance (a form of locus of control) as a "trait that … would influence success in applying [psi] ability" (p. 195), but not synchronicity. None of the four hypotheses were significant, except for a marginally significant negative correlation between chance scores and ESP scores ($p < .07$), taken to mean psi, not synchronicity, explained the effect—psi scores tended to improve the more chance was not thought to affect the outcome. There was no evidence the so-called 'principle of nature' was involved or not involved.

I suggest one cannot separate the individual from the effect, psi or synchronicity, but that does not mean any trait or state is causal just because it correlates or predicts outcomes. Like the sciences generally, parapsychology has made too much of the cause *per se*, even stretching the definition in its hunt for explanations (see 'The Trick of the Cause in Parapsychology' in Chapter 3). However, being aware of acausality as an underlying principle of synchronicity, Palmer (2016b) suggests certain human attributes or influences cannot underpin synchronicity because these can be taken as causal factors. He recognized this point earlier when he posited that "synchronicities might accompany conscious intent [i.e., volition]" (Palmer, 2008, p. 181) in reference to card-guessing, which could "activate an archetype" (p. 181). Surely this means card-guessing could involve psi, or synchronicity, or both. And that could be true of divinatory practices (e.g., the *I Ching*), a few studies of which were reviewed by Palmer (2016b, p. 194). Yet he includes the *I Ching* effects as "evidence of psi" (p. 195), whereas the synchronistic alternative was not suggested. Palmer may have shifted his position, and assumed that the *I Ching* process in those studies *depended on* (as if to say *was caused by*) participants' conscious intentions, and therefore could not be synchronicity by definition, whereas Jung (1951/1969) thinks intention is an initiating or contingent factor: "The *I Ching* presupposes that there is a synchronistic correspondence between the psychic state of the questioner and the answering hexagram" (para. 986; see also Jung, 1989).

These kinds of situations are confusing. How do we draw the line between intention/volition merely acausally *accompanying* an effect, and intention/volition actually *causing* an effect? I regard the problem as a false dichotomy. More generally, all Jung's cases suggest that the psychology of his patients were crucial aspects of their synchronicities, but he did not make causes of his patients' hidden (and probably measurable) predispositions. If we do not recognize Jung's position, we should expect synchronicity to happen to everyone constantly, regardless of their psychology. This we do not see. We must also not be too doctrinaire about this 'acausal connecting principle' in the synchronistic context, lest typology and characterology (beliefs, attitudes), measures of intention (volition), and so on, be seen as irrelevant in synchronicity. There is good reason to investigate them as potential correlates, but not as causes. For example, Jung (1975) certainly classes intent as contingent, not causal, in synchronicity, and says as much when he speaks of archetypes not being "evoked by a conscious act of the will" (p. 541). And Jung also argues that the more astute psychics and mediums, who *seem* to have ready access to their own psychic function, only do so because they actually put themselves in "a state corresponding to an archetypal constellation" (p. 542). But there can be no demands placed upon archetypes. Of course, there is the possibility that effects may still only be occasional, as befits the probabilistic nature of archetypal processes.

The consequent error is that allegedly causal factors or influences can be drawn into the psi process. In my research, I always viewed psychological and other variables as *correlates* of psi, and nothing more. I suggest the same reasoning should be applied to synchronicity. Individuals, through their psychological states and traits, merely attempt to align themselves with synchronistic outcomes as Owens did, even if they do not know they do this, and if they do align, then archetypal factors may tip the scales of chance in favour of an effect. We must view synchronicity as something more than psi but less than an absolute principle of nature like inviolable constants. We can see how there is an interplay between what the individual wills (intends) and something 'other', and this interplay paints a bigger, more dynamic (synchronistic) picture of psi.

Yet Broughton (1988) expressed his resistance to the idea that psi can be both "a type of mental faculty or ability" *and* "our participation in a transcendent consciousness" (p. 190), by which he means in the latter case, "a higher reality, another dimension of existence that goes beyond the confines of the individual" (pp. 189-190)—that is, a 'principle of nature'. This anti-complementary view described by Broughton is a predominant one; it reflects a broadly felt opinion in parapsychology and in some philosophical circles today. For example, philosopher Richard Tarnas (2007) thinks the same way (see his Notes, p. 498). He sees psi as a "perceptual or cognitive faculty", but synchronicity has metaphysical links to a "meaning-embedded world" (p 498). Both views are inaccurate. A *transcendent* experience could be in the 'backyard' of the deeper realms of the unconscious with individuals clearly but merely occupying roles, meaning that many decisions they make will be governed by that state and will only be *thought of* as acts of volition (Jung, 1964/1970).

In case my analysis of Owens does not illustrate my point well enough, another example might help here, and again Jung (1975) comes to our aid—he gives an account of two sisters who had been left out of a Will involving a mansion with attached title and estate that instead went to a distant cousin. One night, out of spite, they made a doll in the cousin's image and threw it onto the fire. The mansion burnt down that same night. Outside the chance factor, Jung says: "Either the doll set fire to the mansion (but how?), or the fire kindled the fantasy of the sisters (but how?)" (p. 539). The case is extraordinary (mind-boggling) *if we think causally*, and rare *if we think statistically*, but these ways of thinking are only confrontational from those standpoints. Synchronicity theory, however, addresses the meaningful connection whereby "the outer event *occurs simultaneously inside the psyche*" (p. 539). Both events have their own causal pathways, but are not causally connected. Note too that we have already encountered this 'fiery' symbolism (recall the Swedenborg case and similar examples given earlier). Such 'heated' exchanges, interactions, and emotionally intense scenarios are thus not so isolated in human history and they seem to be aligned with archetypal themes and forces. As I also said earlier, there are situations in human affairs that are typically archetypal and we have seen that archetypes do come into effect in synchronicity.

***

Rhinean categories are not helpful—especially in spontaneous cases. Notwithstanding the fact that these categories (ESP, PK, and their sub-categories) served as working models for many decades, all parapsychologists are aware of the problems with psi process and nomenclature, but none have resolved these problems. Following on from that point, the Rhinean paradigm does not conceptualize all aspects of psi (its range, its limits), and therefore lacks explanatory power—we find we must call it out (the Owens case serves that process well). Yet, still we see the Rhinean paradigm is let off the hook—anything outside the norm for which a human agent appears responsible *is* psi, or becomes promissory psi until further notice.

The difference with synchronicity is that Jung effectively extended the source of psi beyond the person, so that even the most 'gifted' (afflicted?) person does not have unlimited power, and certainly does not get to fulfil all his/her intentions (see Jung's model, Chapter 4). Rhine did not make this extension—he never really went beyond the personal quotient, and that is perhaps one reason why so many Rhinean parapsychologists resist a more holistic view of psi. Rather than seeing psi as a synchronistic attunement or alignment contingent with the macrocosmic order, they prefer to see psi as the outcome of an 'ability'.

Having brought attention to the draw-backs in the Rhinean model, let us proceed to the next chapter which looks at Trickster phenomenology as it is often manifested in the practice of parapsychology. As an archetype, the Trickster has a pervading presence in human activities and its particular character is generally disturbing and misleading, and even extends beyond normal realms to the paranormal.

Notes

1 My massive tome, the *Webster Universal Dictionary* (Wyld & Partridge, 1968), reads as follows for 'extrasensory perception': "Perceptive powers (as in telepathy) not yet scientifically explained" (p. 495), which is a tacit acknowledgment of the phenomenon. There is no entry for 'psychokinesis'.
2 For example, Rhine (1946b) showed that participants' PK results were significantly improved when they were hypnotized and instructed to act "in a spirit of fun and relaxation" rather than "try very hard" (p. 126).
3 On macro-PK in dice-throwing: If we acknowledge Braude's (2015) argument that dice are "observable systems", then the kind of PK that can affect that system can be regarded as occurring at the macroscopic level (p. 260).
4 I prefer the term *nomenclature* because it is a formal rule-bound system for naming phenomena in a profession or field, whereas *terminology* can be seen as a set of terms that have not necessarily emerged systematically but have been inherited and can be applied loosely. Parapsychology has a *vocabulary* that is a mix of both (e.g., 'ghost' vs. 'apparition' vs. 'discarnate entity').
5 For further points about the ESP/PK dichotomy, see Roe, Davey, and Stevens (2003).
6 In Remote Viewing a percipient "attempts to describe the surroundings of a geographically distant agent [or location]" (Thalbourne, 2003, p. 107).
7 Stokes (1985) tells us the early stages of Tyrrell's (1936) experiments did not feature a "formal randomization procedure" (p. 403). When G. W. Fisk pointed out the oversight, Tyrrell then used random numbers, but effects were still significant. All well and good, but for our purposes the question is: If psi was operating in Tyrrell's tests, what specific psi modality was tested?
8 Free response is a term that "describes any test of ESP in which the range of possible targets is relatively unlimited and is unknown to the percipient [perceiver/receiver]" (Thalbourne, 2003, p. 44).

9 Note too that the review by Targ and Tart (1985) of earlier pure clairvoyance tests is inconclusive.

10 In a similar vein, some might prefer to speak in terms of 'dissonance', which is implicated when explaining the difficulty of eliciting psi effects, especially PK (Tierney, 2020).

11 A range of other effects can be explained this way, including treatment differences. For example, in the present vs. future Coordinate Remote Viewing performance comparison, the real-time effect was stronger than the future-telling effect (see Müller & Wittmann, 2021). The general finding in the meta-analyses is that precognition is no stronger than clairvoyance (Steinkamp, 2000; Storm & Tressoldi, 2020; etc.; see also *Rethinking Psi as Synchronicity* in this chapter).

12 The precognition category, in particular, is regularly evoked by Jung due to the implied effect of "foreknowledge" as a common phenomenological concomitant of synchronicity (see Jung, 1952/1969, para. 973-978).

13 The term 'coincidentiality' is defined as "the underlying principle, or state or condition indicating a concurrence of events or circumstances with no apparent causal connection" (Storm & Thalbourne, 2018, p. 64). I note the use of the word "coincidentiality" in the study by Johansen and Osman (2015, p. 41), where it is undefined but appears to be used in the same sense. Storm and Thalbourne independently coined the term to describe a single factor resulting from factor analysis. This definition is a catch-all (neutral) term for coincidences that fall into two categories: (i) meaningful coincidences—i.e., synchronicity (Jung, 1952/1969, para. 850), implied in the words 'underlying principle'; and (ii) "meaningless chance groupings" (para. 846), which are covered by the terms 'state or condition'. Beitman (2022) would expand on (i) above to include serendipity, seriality, and simulpathity, as these are meaningful coincidences.

14 One website source on cartomancy (divination by cards) says of the Seven of Spades that its "central meaning is certainty" (https://cardarium.com/7-of-spades-meaning-in-cartomancy-and-tarot/). Another source suggests those who draw this card "make excellent psychologists"—a *convenient* coincidence if nothing else as it does confirm my career choice (https://www.metasymbology.com/templates/cards/sevenofspades.html). Still another suggests people under the influence of this card "work quietly – often secretly – and [are] usually willing to remain behind the scenes"—true of me, and appropriate for a parapsychologist who likes to avoid the spotlight of skepticism (https://www.sevenreflections.com/cards-of-destiny/cards/seven-of-spades/).

15 I take 'holistic' to mean "intimately interconnected and explicable only by reference to the whole" (https://www.lexico.com/definition/holistic). The word 'holistic' also means "dealing with or treating the whole of something or someone and not just a part" (https://dictionary.cambridge.org/dictionary/english/holistic).

16 Thalbourne (2003) defines displacement as a form of ESP "shown by consistently obtaining information about a target at one or more remove, spatially or temporally, from the actual target designated for that trial" (p. 31).

Chapter 2

The Trickster in Parapsychology

Part I. Secret Weapons

… it is the Trickster who is most associated with chance and synchronicity.
(Allan Combs & Mark Holland, 1996, p. xxxix)

The Trickster is a meddling progenitor of misdeeds. Its modern equivalent stands behind inexplicable psychosocial anomalies and disturbances, and even over-interpretations and misinterpretations of findings even though these may not be outrightly ambiguous. Individuals working in the sciences, and especially parapsychology, are not immune to these effects. Some (perhaps all) of these effects may be resolved through vigilance and an unbiased approach to data and findings.

Who Is the Trickster?

Archetypes play a pivotal role in synchronicity (Jung, 1952/1969, para. 963). But to what extent? Jung seems clear on the matter when he said that the equivalence (commonality, similarity, parallels) we see in synchronicity "rests on the psychoid factors" he calls "archetypes" (para. 963). That is a general statement that seems to suggest that an archetype has to figure in some way in a synchronistic event, and it can be any archetype. Overall, we can only claim synchronicity if certain contingencies are met, leading to the following schema (not necessarily in this order though the end-product is always the same): archetype → affect → numinosity → meaningfulness. Or to be formulaic: archetype + affect + numinosity + meaningfulness = synchronicity. Failing this structure, we merely have a meaningless chance grouping, and so it would seem an archetype is pivotal (contingent) in a synchronistic arrangement. Formulaically, we could assume an archetypal influence if the presence of affect, numinosity, and meaningfulness are discernable. Like most fields of inquiry, key elements inherent in an effect are sometimes not easily identifiable (if at all), while others do not go unnoticed. The same can apply to archetypal elements.

There is one archetype known as the Trickster (Jung, 1959/1968), and if we are to put stock in Jung's theory, we have to concede an occasional place for it in synchronicity. We have seen this factor arise in the preceding chapter in issues to

DOI: 10.4324/9781003561323-3

do with psi, its process, its nomenclature, its interpretation. So who is the Trickster? And what is so important about 'him'? To write part of this chapter, I have to admit a certain dependence on a controversial book by George Hansen, *The Trickster and the Paranormal* (Hansen, 2001). Occasionally in his writing, Hansen himself is evidently prone to Trickster phenomenology and he has to be read with due caution, but his message is nonetheless sobering, and should make serious parapsychologists think hard about their positions in the field, no matter how entrenched and safe they think they might be inside or outside academia. Likely as not, that 'entrenchment' and apparent safety might underlie a naïve system of belief set up by the parapsychologist to help create a false sense of security.[1] Ultimately, parapsychologists can find themselves marginalized, which is one of the main issues Hansen deals with in his book. However, this chapter aims not to explore those issues; of greater interest is finding out how the Trickster archetype relates to psi and synchronicity. I will add that it is likely the Trickster archetype is behind some spurious research findings in parapsychology, which puts an even bigger burden on the parapsychologist's shoulders. As I hope to show, readily identifying signs of tricksterish elements in psi research can help us avoid the pitfalls of the Trickster archetype.

Hansen (2001) describes the Trickster as a personification of a "collection of abstract properties that tend to occur together," such as "disruption, deception, … psi phenomena, and marginality" (p. 427). Further details can be found in Jung (1959/1968, para. 456–488). The Trickster is a personality of "no fixed shape, form or image" (p. 427), but 'he' seems more than a personality, and a changeable, fickle one at that (cf. Hermes/Mercury, Pan, and Loki for Western mythological equivalents).[2] Outwitting the gods of the various pantheons for his own sake (sometimes just to make a point), or for the sake of humankind, he (or it) is best described as a process, and is activated (i.e., the archetypal qualities that it embodies are constellated psychologically) when a liminal phase is entered into. This liminal phase or condition can lead the individual, or a social group, to acts of subversion or deconstruction of binary (i.e., oppositional) systems whereby "there is a reversal of the positions of privilege or a blurring or collapse of the line dividing the pair [of opposites]" (p. 62). Such opposites include God/Human, Heaven/Earth, Male/Female, Life/Death, rational/irrational, normal/paranormal, and so on. For example, rational behaviour may become irrational.

The Trickster, then, is activated under circumstances where conventional, privileged structures are criticized, threatened, or indeed attacked and subverted (these criticisms can be seen as liminal or as the embodiment of liminal phases). Thereby, the Trickster challenges the rationalistic assumptions uncritically laid down and maintained by our institutions. These conventional structures are embodied in academia—specifically our universities and other public institutions, including our political and bureaucratic structures, corporate and business enterprises, and orthodox religions (and let us not forget the media who are never impartial when it comes to controversy). Ironically, we also see situations in our institutions where the Trickster overthrows convention and takes root in the form of (say) new policy, and either way, consequences such as reduced status, relationship and/or career failure, etc., can threaten those who transgress by not adopting the new perspective.

What *does* the Trickster have to do with the paranormal (psi/synchronicity)? The simple answer is the paranormal too easily threatens conventional privileged structures. Historically, the supernatural, and therefore the paranormal, emerged and evolved alongside the hegemonic tradition of the various privileged structures, and since the paranormal is anything but normal, it is immediate fodder for mainstream attack, persecution, and ostracization. Jung (1959/1968) was strongly aware of these negative tricksterish forces (para. 457, 469) and their sociological impact—hence, his hesitancy to introduce synchronicity formally to the world, as indicated in his Foreword to his *Synchronicity* essay (Jung, 1952/1969, para. 816), publication of which was delayed by 20 years for fear of the negative reception his theory might elicit.

Most people who have read even a little history are aware of dichotomous or dualistic schemas (even prejudices) that are age-old, and part of the human condition. The gender divide and the Reformation are classic examples, the repercussions of which have echoed down the proverbial corridors of time, and are still with us. Hansen (2001) gets more concrete when he takes other examples from the real world. For example, in the world of the paranormal, the Trickster is activated in the relationship between UFO sightings and psychic ability—a relationship noted earlier by journalists (e.g., Keel, 1978) and researchers (e.g., Basterfield, 2001; Basterfield & Thalbourne, 2002). This relationship is not coincidental, but destined nonetheless to activate the Trickster quality of marginalization. The likely consequences? Public ridicule by the media; loss of vocation, ostracization by friends, family, and loved-ones; and even early death.

Patterns of events like these occur over and over again, and they seem to have beleaguered parapsychologists since the late 1800s. Hansen (2001) points out that the Trickster is also constellated as a result of attempts to institutionalize parapsychology and psychical research because *organizing* the paranormal is antithetical to the Trickster. Hansen gives examples to show how success in parapsychology, in the form of establishing laboratories, research output, and journal circulation, is generally short-lived (other researchers have commented on this problem—Schlitz, 2001; White, 1994). J. B. Rhine is a case in point. Rhine set up a long-running and successful on-campus parapsychology laboratory in Duke University's Psychology Department. According to Duke University rules at the time, J. B. Rhine had to retire at age 65 and would not be allowed to run the laboratory. Upon his retirement in 1962, he set up (off-campus) the Foundation for Research on the Nature of Man, which included The Institute for Parapsychology which eventually became the Rhine Research Center in 1995. Hansen paints a rather grim, inaccurate, and misleading picture of those events, but the fact remains that changes in the discipline of psychology (e.g., the major shift to Behaviourism; lack of support for parapsychology) during and since Rhine's time at Duke, and other administrative issues (e.g., the unpredictable new leadership of the on-campus lab), were a deciding factor in the move to go off-campus. Rhine was always highly respected at Duke, but the move off-campus gave Rhine the advantage of personally overseeing the expansion of parapsychological research free of Duke's administrative influence (J. G. Kruth, personal communication, January 27, 2022). Still, we see here a good example of how the system invariably pushed a controversial field to the fringes of academia. Two of my own short-lived parapsychology laboratories (one at the University of Adelaide co-founded with M. A. Thalbourne, and the other at Deakin University co-founded with A. J. Rock) were officially shut down for administrative reasons mainly to do with outright prejudice (bureaucratic protest) against our aims.

Even successful runs of psi experiments are destined to meet with deceptive Trickster phenomenology in the form of *apparent* experimenter effects, decline effects, and other biases that make psi elusive and 'mercurial' (i.e., tricksterish)! For the rest of this chapter, I will focus on these phenomena and show how they may be physically real but can also be mere phantoms, in both cases generated by the Trickster archetype.

The Trickster in the Laboratory

The issue over experiments with psi (including synchronicity) requires elaboration for there is one place where the Trickster is unwelcome—the laboratory. The Trickster constellates during specific moments when events and outcomes hang in the balance—these moments mark the critical phase of an experiment when probabilities of outcomes shift so that unlikely and unwelcome results (e.g., accidents) may be likely. Notably, these may be as rare as we expect them to be, thus evoking chance as a causal factor, but that does not necessarily lead to a satisfactory solution; especially at the stage when data and patterns in the data are to be interpreted. Jung (1959/1968) warns of the types of "accident," "gaffe," "slip," or "faux pas" that can thwart one's will and one's actions which are naïvely "chalked up as defects of the conscious personality" (para. 469). Jung wants it understood that the Trickster is like a personality in its own right working behind the conscious personality, and these "defects of the conscious personality" themselves can open the door to trickster phenomenology.

There are well-known incidents where this problem has been demonstrated. Wolfgang Pauli is a case in point. As the story goes, Pauli had such a unique but destructive psyche that experimental physicist Otto Stern banned Pauli from his Hamburg laboratory. There were other occasions at the physics laboratory in the University of Göttingen, Germany (an expensive measuring device stopped working), and likewise at Princeton University, New Jersey (a particle accelerator sustained serious fire damage). Pauli seems to have had an affinity with fire and the damage it can cause. His peers even coined the term 'Pauli Effect'—jokingly, a second Pauli "Exclusion Principle,"[3] according to which "a functioning device and Wolfgang Pauli may not occupy the same room" (Burri, 2005).

The Pauli Effect, which is markedly synchronistic in nature, may have been exacerbated by the fact that Pauli drank to excess, and he was noted for his irritability when giving seminars—his students dubbed him the 'scourge of God' and 'the terrible Pauli' (Peat, 2008, p. 17). Synchronistically, the breakages in the laboratory are mere physical correlates (accidental parallels) of Pauli's fractured mental state. It is worth noting as a relevant factor that Pauli entered into Jungian therapy with Marie-Louise von Franz whose toils with him have been made public (Gieser, 2005).

But what does the Trickster have to do with Pauli? Does it mean Pauli played tricks on people? No, of course not. At least, not out-rightly and certainly not consciously—when it comes to the slippery concept of the paranormal, we never really learn the source of the mischief (for want of a better term), even if we have our suspicions. Notwithstanding the fact that even scientific equipment can fail, and quite dramatically, and there is the possibility of incompetence on the part of Pauli's peers who might have been looking for a scapegoat to cover their own ineptitude, the Pauli Effect might still be referred to by some as Pauli's psi. But 'psi' could be a misnomer—as was the case with Ted Owens (the PK Man). Mishlove (2000) was never sure that chance could not account for some of the seemingly paranormal feats attributed to Owens. In the real world, though we may convincingly rule out causal connections, we still do not know how to rule out chance factors completely, apart from the fact that we often have inklings that something (probably archetypal) is afoot. As I said above in regard to Pauli at the Café Odeon involving the car that burst into flames (Chapter 1), mechanical devices and equipment can also fail of their own accord, and since the phenomena are rare and surprising, and seem to happen in the presence of certain people, our interest and attention should by rights switch to those persons rather than the phenomena (see Braude, 2007, pp. 148–149). As already noted, acausality *per se* then becomes less of a mystery compared to the greater mystery of how it is that Pauli managed to get himself into these situations. In the laboratory, we must note that Pauli was not welcomed as an experimenter or collaborator; quite the opposite—he was uninvited, a *persona non grata*—which speaks volumes.

Any experimenter can be a 'Pauli-type,' though most would say they were just 'having a bad day' (such phenomena are referred to elsewhere as "experimental miscarriages," and can include "various accidents such as equipment failure, procedural error, inappropriate randomizations, etc."—Kennedy & Taddonio, 1976, p. 10). Of course, the Pauli-type *in reverse* also exists so we can expect positive outcomes. Though nobody really knows if it is psi, whose it is, and whose is the strongest (the experimenter's or the participant's), psi from the experimenter has come to be known as the 'psi experimenter effect' and many parapsychologists make hypotheses about it, they discuss it, they argue about it, and they even expect it (more on that later).

Given these few points, let us now consider the Trickster in slightly more positive aspect (some might say 'Trickster in reverse')—an arguably favourable effect. In another synchronistic case, we have trickserish phenomena at play in Jung's (1952/1969, para. 872–915) research into astrology. Jung conducted a series of studies in the 1940s in an attempt to test his theory of an underlying meaningfulness that would connect causally unrelated events. Jung was trying to establish empirical (statistical) evidence of a "psychic equation" between external events (astrological aspect) and inner experience (choice of marriage partner). Results suggested the presence of synchronicity in the form of three Lunar aspects of special interest to Jung (i.e., Moon/Sun, Moon/Moon, and Moon/Ascendant), each of which appeared in three respective subsets of data (para. 902), formed seemingly randomly "just as the post brought them in" (para. 873). The corrected statistics calculated on the pooled data were first regarded by Jung as "inconclusive" (1951/1969, para. 989), but not to "a degree which one could have described as probable" (1952/1969, para. 906), meaning the results were too improbable to be attributable to chance alone. Yet he still referred to "the chance nature of the result" (para. 909). The upshot of the whole effort is that Jung first found something, then he wasn't sure, then he was, then he wasn't!

The story, however, does not end there. Of particular relevance, synchronistically speaking, are three smaller experiments that Jung himself instigated. Three experimenter/subjects were instructed to select sub-samples randomly from the larger sample of natal charts used in the main analysis. The type of conjunction that appeared more often than any other in each sub-sample exactly described the psychological profile of each of the relevant subjects who selected that sub-sample:

1 The first subject was "in a state of intense emotional excitement." Mars is the "emotional" planet, and the sub-sample was dominated by Mars aspects (para. 897).
2 The second subject was a female patient "whose main problem was to realize and assert her personality in the face of her self-suppressive tendencies." Her sub-sample featured the ascendant-Moon conjunction, which has a passive (suppressed) influence in the chart (para. 898).
3 The third subject was a woman "with strong inner opposition whose union and reconciliation constituted her main problem" (para. 899). Sun-Moon conjunctions dominated her selection, symbolizing the union of opposites.

Statistically, the results were not considered significant, but the variances in the data, which indicated the featured conjunctions of each sub-sample, corresponded with the psychic state of the subject. Serendipitously, Jung had found a variant of what he was looking for—suggestive evidence of meaningful coincidence; not once, but three times.

Seemingly in denial, Jung later made this unwarranted remark to a friend: "what an excellent joke was made with the use of astrological statistics; people have even thought I wanted to prove something in favor of astrology. It is hardly worthwhile to deal with all this pack of nonsense" (J. Kirsch, 1972, as cited in Progoff, 1973, p. 137). In truth, Jung *was* seeking a proof of sorts for *meaningful coincidence* as an *astrological effect* (1952/1969, para. 867). As a side issue, he refers to the three above-listed effects as synchronistic demonstrations of the "secret, mutual connivance" (para. 905), and definitely claimed his co-workers' psyches were connected to the physical material (natal charts) by way of their apparently random selections that demarcated outcomes as nothing other than meaningful coincidence. While those 'selection biases' were not categorical proofs of astrology, it can be conjectured that the human psyche was involved in the synchronistic process.

A similar case of serendipity occurred in Christopher Moreman's (2003) aim to show that a so-called cross-correspondence effect could be fabricated.[4] Using pseudo-scripts (randomly selected portions of text from 15 randomly selected library books) and pseudo-mediums, he showed how very easy it is for investigators to concur that similar (meaningful) patterns can present across unrelated texts from different books. Parapsychologists and statisticians might wish to muse over the implications of Moreman's finding, but I also make the point that in the very same study, Moreman spotted a "surprising coincidence": One of his randomly sampled texts was by Rudyard Kipling whose sister Alice Kipling Fleming (as 'Mrs. Holland') was a medium involved in the original cross-correspondences work. Moreman was prompted to note "how often strikingly meaningful coincidences actually occur" (p. 232). While Moreman shows how cross-correspondences can be fabricated and therefore can be meaningless, the irony and meaningfulness of the Kipling correspondence did not escape Moreman.

These trains of events indicate Trickster phenomenology at its most surprising, or even frustrating if one wants to view it that way, as most people will see that these timely interferences get in the way of the so-called objectivity of science. Speaking of Jung's study, Progoff (1973) even noted that Jung thought there was some "trickster element at work" (p. 137). Slightly appropriate in this instance, it is interesting to note how Jung describes the Trickster in a person's behaviour whereby the person "manages to achieve through his [*sic*] stupidity what others fail to accomplish with their best efforts" (para. 456). But I am certainly not insinuating incompetence on Jung's part (only impatience as he freely admits), or implying it is a characteristic of anyone working in fringe or mainstream science. And we have to take note of the second part of the quote—that our best intentions can still result in failure or misunderstanding. I will not elaborate on these aspects here—more importantly, the point I want to convey is that the Trickster plays out in a process that 'turns the tables' on us (as Jung and Moreman noted), and like all archetypes, it concludes with a shortlist of possible outcomes, all of which are predictable, and it is up to experimenters not to allow themselves to be deceived (the usual outcome) merely because they are swayed by what they perceive to be insurmountable evidence (for or against) that may later prove to be premature and/or not all that convincing upon closer inspection.

Jung (1959/1968) notes that the Trickster would be viewed with skepticism in civilized society (for example, Parker & Millar, 2014, wish to avoid the anthropomorphic aspect the concept entails), but many of us would still describe our slip-ups as "fate playing tricks" or "things being bewitched" (para. 478) as if some outside entity *was* at work. And if we upscale, and propose that the Trickster might manifest in a subtler guise, anything that happens worldwide to large groups of researchers, over extended periods of time, might be naïvely viewed as good science when it was merely tricksterish science all along. That is a most important lesson to learn, and highly relevant to the rest of this chapter.

The Trickster's Secret Weapons: Experimenter Psi and the Decline Effect

In this section, I will speak of two major problems that are, to varying degrees, the bane of the psi experimenter's existence—the experiment psi effect and the decline effect. These problems are not unique to parapsychology, and they are not necessarily as bad as each other—experimenters can expect to come across one or both of these problems on occasion. Of course, experimenters will disagree with each other over which is worse. The point of this section is not to settle that score, but demonstrate the relevance of each problem to psi experimentation in the context of Trickster phenomenology, and show how subtle and tricksterish elements can be involved in the interpretation of experimental results.

The experimenter-psi effect (a.k.a. 'E-psi') refers to "unintentional psi which affects experimental outcomes in ways that are directly related to the experimenter's needs, wishes, expectancies, or moods" (Kennedy & Taddonio, 1976, p. 1; for a discussion of E-psi, see Palmer & Millar, 2015, pp. 295–299).[5] This definition is limited, as we cannot rule out the experimenter's intentional (i.e., deliberate) psi, implied in the fact that some experimenters/investigators arguably try to "psychically influence their results" (Palmer & Millar, p. 296). Also, those needs, etc., could be pro-psi or anti-psi. Either way, the experimenter is likely to have more motivation than participants so the assumption of E-psi seems not only plausible, but also seemingly confirmed in some instances. However, this motivational bias does not mean E-psi is always present; and nor should we assume any outcome from E-psi is necessarily in the direction favoured. E-psi is well documented, but tends only to be discussed as a within-study effect (Kennedy & Taddonio, 1976). Sometimes related to E-Psi, is the so-called decline effect (DE), which is defined as "the tendency for high scores in a test of psi to decrease, either within a run, within a session, or over a longer period of time" (Thalbourne, 2003, p. 27). The DE is also well documented (Colborn, 2007; Rhine, 1969).

I must clarify my position on E-Psi and DEs. First, I am sure E-Psi will always be a problem as long as there are experimenters,[6] although I only see it as a problem *within* studies (if only because we cannot accurately determine participants' psi contributions let alone those of experimenters), but not so much a problem across studies (i.e., *between* studies). A solution to the problem of E-Psi is unlikely, but it is likely that E-Psi across studies (i.e., between-studies E-Psi)—as can be shown in the meta-analyses—is a pseudo-problem anyway.

Second, Thalbourne's definition of DE indicates there are two kinds of decline—'*within* study' and '*between* studies.'[7] In this chapter, my main focus is on the between-studies DE, which is a steady decline in psi across studies conducted by a broad range of experimenters and laboratories. My reasons for this focus will become evident throughout this chapter, but basically, within-study DEs are mostly caused by boredom, lapses in interest, and loss of motivation (I do not dispute these reasons), whereas between-studies DEs require more sophisticated explanations such as improvements in study quality over the years, or deliberate changes in experimental design (from simple and fun, to complex and tedious) because theoretically oriented experimenters want to understand the psi *process* rather than merely *prove* psi's existence. To varying degrees, Bierman (2001) disputes both explanations for DEs, as I do. I argue that *if* there appears to be a between-studies DE, that decline is *more than likely* an artefact. However, mistakenly accepting the DE artefact as a genuine effect (this happens, and often) illustrates how Trickster phenomenology can hold unwarranted sway over a community. I will make the same argument for E-Psi.

Types of Experimenter

Millar (2012b) argued that "parapsychology's elite are themselves particularly endowed with psi ability: they attribute scoring to subjects, in line with the psychological tradition, while it actually comes from their own psi" (p. 1). The 'elite' are the experimenters, and 'subjects' are participants. Under the assumption that experimenter psi (E-Psi) exists (albeit to varying degrees), there are only two mutually exclusive ways it might manifest: Either exactly as Millar proposes—Hypothesis 1 (H1): Experimenters cause *all* the psi and participants do not have any psi—or Hypothesis 2 (H2): Experimenters can combine their psi with their participants' psi (this is the more conventional view).[8] Whichever is the case, it is the custom for psi researchers to seek support for the psi hypothesis by finding a significant effect as psi-hitting, but E-Psi can sometimes manifest as psi-missing, and intentionally so (more on psi-missing later).

Having stated H1 and H2, I find I need to consider both in the light of the "distinct groups" conceived by Palmer and Millar (2015), who classify experimenters as "Virtuoso" (one who "*regularly* produces clearly significant results"), "So-So" ("occasional significance"), and "Psi Challenged", a group who "(almost) never reports significance" (p. 298).[9] Parker and Millar (2014) argue that there are some star experimenters or 'Virtuosos' (e.g., Helmut Schmidt, Rupert Sheldrake) who do well on their own (i.e., they produce significant results when they self-test), which explains why they produce significant results in studies with participants (under the premise that participants have no psi), whereas less-gifted ('Psi Challenged') experimenters who do poorly on their own prove unable to replicate Schmidt's and Sheldrake's results ('So-So' experimenters are somewhere in between). But to argue that virtuoso solo-experimenters must bring their psi to their experiments *because they are virtuosos* is not a valid assumption, as it is based on inductive logic (not straight-forward deduction). After all, I am not entitled to say there must be a black cat on my roof, and I need not check, because looking through my windows I can see black cats on both my neighbours' roofs. Granted there may be *some* ideal scenarios as outlined, but perhaps 'Virtuosos' are merely good at encouraging psi in their participants. 'Psi Challenged' experimenters, however, may discourage psi in their participants. It is also possible that participants use psi to pick up the 'vibe' of their assigned experimenter to give them what they want. Despite the seemingly adequate measures to control such overt and covert psychological effects, something like this may have occurred in the landmark study by West and Fisk (1953) where West was notably psi-inhibitive and Fisk was notably psi-conducive: West's participants produced chance results, but Fisk's produced psi-hitting (see also Wiseman & Schlitz, 1997). As Palmer noted: "each hypothesis can explain the results of the other" (Palmer & Millar, 2015, p. 297).

We must also consider intention, which manifests in the sheep-goat effect,[10] as well as outcomes in systems of divination, such as *I Ching* (Storm & Rock, 2014a) and Tarot (Blackmore, 1983). The unique divinatory outcomes (as feedback) are pertinent (meaningful) as far as participants are concerned (see Storm & Rock, 2014a), but the best Millar would offer is that E-Psi is used to probe individual minds to determine their beliefs and/or mental states, and outcomes are E-psi-adjusted accordingly. But surely these are virtuoso performances of a capacity far beyond Schmidt and Sheldrake. And because the effects are so obviously synchronistic (not garden-variety psi)—that is, outcomes are *meaningful*—the participant, as an individual, surely deserves all bragging rights if they produce a significant effect. It is perhaps hardly surprising that common-sense prevailed, and Parker (not so much Millar) made a concession, admitting that participants must have their own agency: "if there are psychic experimenters then there have to also be psychic participants" (Parker & Millar, p. 45). So, as a matter of convenience, the problem of E-Psi invariably confines itself to the premise put forth in H2 above, and we have to abandon the idea that experimenters can maintain E-Psi consistently *and* do it without participants.

To add to the argument, Palmer and Millar (2015) argue that the "influence of the experimenter" could be found in a "large scale meta-analysis" (p. 298). While it is arguable that the Palmer and Millar classifications are transferable from solo-based to participant-based studies, we can agree that meta-analysis may tell us something more substantive about the limits of E-Psi. As it happened, Parker and Millar (2014) had earlier pointed out that the ganzfeld meta-analytic results (in Storm, Tressoldi, & Di Risio, 2010) are "relatively independent of the experimenter" (p. 48; for other examples, see the next subsection). Those results indicate that at least *some* ganzfeld psi (arguably most) *must be coming from participants*. I note, however, that the 'E-Psi isolation problem' is born of the nature of psi itself as an hypothesized effect that has virtually no limits—theorists can always conceptualize and re-conceptualize psi parameters to meet any theoretical contingency, so we cannot exclude H1 absolutely, but on parsimonious grounds H2 is preferred so I will take that into consideration as I now look at the meta-analyses more closely.

The Meta-Analyses: I. Experimenter Psi

Given H2, participants must be regarded as doing most of the psi work, and must account for most of the psi variance, but to a lesser extent E-Psi has variance of its own, which is to say, it too has positive or negative influence, but sometimes fails, and has no influence at all (even Millar would agree about E-Psi variance given his part in forming the above-listed classifications). I reach this conclusion about participant-psi and the limited role of E-Psi on empirical grounds: the meta-analyses I have co-authored (Storm & Tressoldi, 2017; Storm et al., 2010, 2012; Storm, Sherwood et al., 2017) have found no significant investigator/laboratory differences in the following domains: free response, ganzfeld,[11] forced choice,[12] dream-ESP,[13] and sheep-goat effect (SGE). I find the same patterns in other researchers' meta-analyses dating back decades (NB: the following meta-analyses were conducted on databases comprised of many dozens, or scores, or even hundreds of studies):

- Ganzfeld: "… the significance of the overall effect is not dependent on one or two investigators" (Honorton, 1985, p. 61);
- Forced-Choice Precognition: "The effect is clearly not due to a few major contributors" (Honorton & Ferrari, 1989, p. 285);
- Dice Throwing: "the overall effect does not appear to be due to a few exceptional investigators" (Radin & Ferrari, 1991, p. 68);
- Sheep-Goat Effect: "these data provide strong evidence against the view that the results … are attributable to a few 'lucky' major contributors" (Lawrence, 1993, p. 78);
- Free Response: "… no significant difference in effect size between studies with different principal authors" (Milton, 1997, p. 289);
- Extraversion/ESP Forced Choice: "… the impact of ESP/extraversion testing order is consistent across investigators and is not attributable to idiosyncratic research styles or other characteristics of a single prolific investigator" (Honorton, Ferrari, & Bem, 1998, pp. 264–266);
- Extraversion/ESP Free Response: "the ESP/extraversion relationship is consistent across investigators" (Honorton et al., 1998, p. 267);
- Direct Mental Interaction: "… no significant difference among the mean effect sizes obtained in these labs ["San Antonio, Las Vegas, Edinburgh, and Freiburg"]" (Schmidt, Schneider, Utts, & Walach, 2002, p. 12).

The parapsychological community had these facts about experimenters and laboratories before the end of the 20th century—that is, quite some time ago.[14] There appeared to be no convincing evidence of long-term E-Psi, yet it seemed that virtually no one noticed. One could argue that these experimenters may mostly be psi-believers, and that is why the meta-analyses produce significant overall effects, which also tend to cluster (hence, no experimenter/lab difference), even though there may be a few psi-nonbelievers conducting studies. In fact, one comparison (Storm et al., 2012) included the very successful psi-believing experimenter Rupert Sheldrake who was highly praised by Brian Millar (see Palmer & Millar, 2015), but he did not excel (was not an outlier) when compared to other experimenters, and neither was the skeptical experimenter Richard Wiseman an outlier in the opposite (psi-missing) direction.

Most authors of the relevant meta-analytic studies seem rather casual (or quietly confident) and merely reported their findings in a perfunctory way, and only a couple downplayed the concern that had been generated by such critics as Akers (1987). For example, Honorton and Ferrari (1989) made the point that Akers was wrong in claiming that "successful parapsychological outcomes are achieved by only a few investigators" (p. 285). Lawrence (1993) also dismissed Akers's remarks. Overall, to maintain that between-studies E-Psi is a serious impediment to parapsychology is perhaps not the most productive attitude to hold—the meta-analysts should certainly agree. Yet many parapsychologists still appear to be overly concerned by E-Psi, and still express this concern (e.g., Hövelmann, 2015; Palmer & Millar, 2015; Parker & Millar, 2014). Irwin (2014), in his survey of members of the Parapsychological Association, stated:

> The possibility that parapsychological effects on experimental psi data may stem from experimenters themselves has been recognised for nearly 30 years. Nevertheless, many contemporary parapsychologists continue to be mindful of our failure to resolve this dilemma and see it as one of the major problems facing parapsychology today.
>
> (p. 158)

Pertinent here is the earlier effort taken by Parker and Millar (2014) to identify the source of psi: They profiled some key figures in parapsychology based on psi-conducive style and manner that may have worked favourably on participants to elicit their psi, at least as much as E-Psi, if not more so. Other factors to be noted included laboratory ambience, motivational factors such as experimenter attitude, history effects over the duration of testing, prior experiences of success (and failure), and what is even more revealing, the "morphing" effect (an admitted "trickster effect" where the psi effect changes its guise across time and situation; p. 48). Despite this broad-based approach, they demonstrated that controls and manipulations have never been good enough to isolate E-Psi.

While some academic curiosity concerning *within-study* E-Psi may be warranted, parapsychologists should perhaps entertain less tricksterish notions and not be so dismayed by the pseudo-dilemma of *between-studies* E-Psi. Irwin (2014) noted that only one respondent "seemed prepared to accept experimenter-psi effects as intrinsic to the modus operandi of psi" (p. 159)—in the respondent's own words: "*Experimenter effects are expected if consciousness has nonlocal properties*" (p. 159). We might take that to mean most other respondents are still bothered by E-psi nearly two decades into the 21st century. Of relevance, another respondent said there was "*Not enough consideration of the effects of … the 'Trickster archetype'*" (p. 155). Some degree of awareness might be all we need—just enough to kerb our concern and limit our credulity. I must remind readers that the Trickster, as an activated archetype, is a psychological proneness to err in our thinking when a liminal phase is entered into—that borderland between doubt and certainty—that provides the trigger to err.

I suggest the Trickster archetype has been at play over many decades, giving us one big paranormal headache, but it has been found out. We cannot completely bury the phenomenon; it is reasonable to expect it to turn up in any given experiment. That is equally our problem; E-Psi will not go away entirely, but its global effect across studies looks more like a mere phantom than anything else. All that aside, the time spent looking for E-Psi was not wasted—parapsychologists found something worth knowing and, if they can adopt appropriate levels of *warranted* confidence and (not false) certainty commensurate with that finding, they are one step closer to relinquishing the doubt that triggers the Trickster that subsequently leads to the creation of spurious beliefs and findings.

Where the Trickster still rears his ugly head is in the insistence on E-Psi being a ubiquitous effect, occurring both *within* studies and *between* studies. As usual, the skeptics are our nemesis. Wiseman over-generalizes in dismissing E-Psi as the "get out of a null effect free" card (Wiseman, 2009, p. 37), when he should know that the string of meta-analyses cited above yield no evidence of between-studies E-Psi. At the very least, Wiseman should change his argument and tell parapsychologists to confine their argument to within-studies E-Psi only, for Wiseman knows *from personal experience* that within-study E-Psi has been demonstrated (see Wiseman & Schlitz, 1997). Wiseman even managed to have his cake and eat it too, having gainfully used the so-called "Wiseman experimenter effect" (O'Neill, 2001, p. 5) to facilitate a nonsignificant result (Wiseman, 2001). Reference to later failed attempts to demonstrate E-Psi (as experimenter differences) only furthers my point (Parker & Millar, 2014).

Finally, Alcock (2003) says the psi-experimenter effect is really just "a lack of consistency, a lack of general replicability" (pp. 38–39), so we can take his comments as generally referring to within-study *and* between-studies E-Psi. Like Wiseman, Alcock is wrong on two counts: (a) long-term consistency and replicability *have* been demonstrated in the meta-analyses; and (b) only within-study E-Psi exists (see West & Fisk, 1953; Wiseman & Schlitz, 1997). This refinement on the limits of E-Psi is an issue that will need more focus in the future.

In terms of synchronicity, how should we interpret all of the above? There appears to be no real threat of E-Psi in the *between*-studies scenarios. As already suggested, we should assume participants are doing a great deal of (if not all) the paranormal 'heavy lifting', and can thereby legitimately claim the lion's share of effects as psi. The effect may be better demarcated as synchronicity if we can witness and quantitatively gauge affectivity amongst a sufficient number of participants. The synchronistic aspects primarily concern the meaningfulness of targets, but the degree to which interest can be encouraged in the various paradigms has a definite sway on outcomes (e.g., forced-choice targets are not expected to raise interest as much as free-response targets).

Insofar as there is a risk of E-Psi occurring *within*-studies, normal social interaction with participants should be encouraged, so that the right-minded experimenter can be seen to motivationally influence participants (i.e., by raising their affectivity or emotional commitment to the task), which appears as interest and motivation, resulting in enthusiastic responses that may then lead to a synchronistic effect, albeit intentional in the same way that the individual makes a worthy and focussed effort when using a divinatory system like the *I Ching*. Parker and Millar (2014) even concede that ESP is not 'extrasensory perception' but may be "extraordinary synchronous phenomena" (p. 50).

The Decline Effect

The decline effect, generally speaking, is a complicated multi-factorial affair manifesting in many and varied guises, depending on how the psi effects and the decline effects themselves are defined, and how they are tested (for a review, see Colborn, 2007). Nevertheless, the common understanding is that psi goes into decline over a given time period (Colborn, 2007; Kennedy, 2003). Rhine, for example, said:

> We destroy the phenomena in the very act of trying to demonstrate them. Evidently the tests themselves get in the way of the abilities they are designed to measure.
> (Rhine, 1947, p. 190)

However, Alcock (2003) and Wiseman (2009) both argue that the psi-decline is just another excuse for failure to replicate. Like E-Psi, I find no conclusive evidence for psi-decline in the long run (i.e., *between* studies), though I allow for the possibility in the short term (i.e., *within* studies, including the natural attrition of *recurrent spontaneous psychokinesis*; RSPK; see Roll et al., 2021, pp. 94–98). Colborn (2007, p. 2) refers to these two types of decline as "chronological" and "episodic," respectively. As will be seen, the argument for declines is complicated by issues to do with study quality, but my meta-analyses tend not to show long-term declines—the distributions are generally flat, or even *inclining* in one instance (i.e., forced choice).[15]

Contributors to Wolman's (1977) classic handbook spent very little time discussing the decline effect—the word 'decline' is not even in Wolman's Index—and furthermore, although it was somewhat of a talking point amongst Rhineans (Pratt et al., 1940/1966), that was only in the context of within-study declines. Some have made passing reference to the possibility of broad-ranging (but still limited) declines (e.g., Beloff, 1994; Pratt, 1978). Like between-studies E-Psi, long-term (between-studies) declines seem to have come to our attention in the 1980s and 1990s via the meta-analytic literature but, like between-studies E-Psi, these meta-analyses gave us early warning that the declines were probably aberrations.

While chronological declines can reasonably be expected (and explained) in single studies (e.g., for the psychological reasons already given), the problem with declines spanning many years or decades is that we need some kind of historical or methodological change to explain it. After all, it could be argued that, when we find such declines, it possibly indicates *improvements* in study quality over the years (i.e., psi effects are artifacts of poor experimental design), and psi effects would diminish or vanish with the flaws. As will be seen shortly, there is no support for that hypothesis. The other possible reason was given above—shifts in experimental designs to complex and tedious tasks that demotivate participants and thus lower psi responses (for the ganzfeld anyway; see Radin, 2006a). Demotivation would not be the case in earlier studies, but nobody has tested this claim, and Bierman (2001) refutes its likelihood across a number of paradigms anyway. Bem, Palmer, and Broughton (2001) presented a similar argument for the ganzfeld—deviations from the standard protocol tended to result in failure, but they did not stipulate what is inherent in the deviations that inhibits psi (e.g., what is so offensive about a musical target compared to a visual target?). Thus, we never did find convincing explanations for these alleged declines, yet continued to believe in them based on well-meaning articles that highlighted the effects (Bierman, 2001; Colborn, 2007; Kennedy, 2003).

The Meta-Analyses: II. Declines and Inclines

As it happens, the earlier meta-analyses (forced choice [precognition only], free response, dice throwing) give us some evidence to dispute the between-studies DE or chronological decline effect (a.k.a. CDE) in the form of an array of correlations that are easily interpreted. In those same meta-analyses from the 1980s and 1990s referred to above, we find that methodological quality *improves* significantly over time (using publication date as the time measure),[16] while effect sizes are *constant*[17] over time (Honorton & Ferrari, 1989; Milton, 1997; Radin & Ferrari, 1991).

Alternatively, in other earlier meta-analyses (extraversion-ESP, sheep-goat effect), when methodological quality is *constant* over time, effect size is either *constant* over time (Honorton et al., 1998; Lawrence, 1993), or in *decline* (Honorton et al., 1998), although that one decline refers to extraversion/ESP forced-choice studies only (not extraversion/ESP free response), and the authors attribute the decline to an artifact due to administration of the extraversion measure *before* the ESP task in earlier studies. In these cases, we could have an artifact caused by poor-quality, but there is little to go on.

Furthermore, in these and other meta-analyses, the relationship between study quality and effect size was also investigated (a negative relationship would also suggest that psi effects are artifacts). Overwhelmingly, the relationships were not significant (Honorton, 1985; Honorton & Ferrari, 1989; Lawrence, 1993; Milton, 1997; Radin & Ferrari, 1991;[18] Radin & Nelson, 1989; Schmidt, Schneider, Utts, & Walach, 2004[19]). Again, no evidence of artifacts can be claimed.[20]

For the ganzfeld domain, significant declines over time have been observed (see Bierman, 2001; Milton & Wiseman, 1999), but ostensible declines[21] existed long before Hyman and Honorton (1986) implemented guidelines that focussed on qualitatively improving the ganzfeld methodology, so it cannot be assumed that study quality was single-handedly responsible for those declines. As Palmer (1986a) pointed out, it should not be assumed that declines result from removal of flaws, just as it is presumptuous to claim that past ganzfeld successes were due to the presence of flaws. Furthermore, Bierman (2001) does not present an overwhelming case for declines, as he also found a so-called rebound effect (i.e., U-shaped curve) in the ganzfeld effect-size distribution, suggesting a "recovery from the decline effect" (p. 5), and he found a rebound effect in the RNG domain, but no proof either way for a decline in the Remote Viewing domain (see also Utts, 1996).

Taken together, the above meta-analyses do not provide conclusive evidence for CDEs, and the argument for quality-based CDEs is simply not convincing. This is a subtle issue, and it is easy to overlook, or just brush aside as frivolous, but we have to realize that it becomes more and more apparent, as we dig deeper, that a major ongoing (many decades long) state-of-play in parapsychology has been this phantom of chronological declines. Critically, parapsychologists had the evidence to hand *at the time* to dismiss the effect outright (just as they could in regard to E-Psi).

While the occasional commentator has not been convinced by the claims for CDEs (Utts, 1996; Walach et al., 2002), the effects seem to have been taken at face value. Thus, many parapsychologists and skeptics spoke of chronological declines in real terms. Bierman (2001) states:

> … it soon became clear that apart from sequential effects within a run of trials it was quite difficult to exactly 'replicate'… the results of original studies: a sequence of similar studies tended to show a decline of effect size from study to study.
> (p. 3)

It is a peculiar response from Bierman, given he found those rebound effects. Bierman even saw the need for a "radical change in world view" to explain failure to replicate. Perhaps parapsychologists need not go so far just yet—not until they know what it is they are supposed to be explaining. Yet other parapsychologists have followed Bierman's lead, and taken the effect seriously:

- Stokes (2007) declared: "… most investigators are not able to obtain reliable and replicable experimental evidence for psi …" (p. 80). He puts the initial significant findings down to fraud (more on that shortly);
- In regard to the ganzfeld studies, Radin (2006a) rightly disputed the skeptical claim that the "decline [over time] is due to improving methodologies" (p. 122). However, he does attribute the decline to "changes in experimental goals" (p. 122)—a worthy rationalization possibly or partially befitting the facts, but not really called for at the time if the databases (i.e., the meta-analyses) had been examined more thoroughly. And evidence of declines in other disciplines does not get us off the hook (assuming there is a 'hook')—*two wrongs don't make a right*;
- Kennedy (2003) also spoke of "widespread declines in psi effects" (p. 58), concluding that "psi effects are unsustainable" (p. 69);
- Despite Colborn's (2007) own warning not to reify declines out of credulity, he still reviewed, and considered the likelihood of a range of empirically related causal factors for declines (I am particularly focussing on chronological declines here). For theoretical reasons, that is not necessarily inappropriate, but it implies a problem that was poorly substantiated in the first place. Colborn does however list "counter-advocates" who also do not believe in long-term declines (e.g., Walach et al., 2002).

Have we reached that point where we should drop the whole idea of CDEs as we find more and more evidence justifying that move? For example, similar patterns to those described above emerged in later ganzfeld and forced-choice meta-analyses, in an RNG meta-analysis (Bösch, Steinkamp, & Boller, 2006), and in a meta-analysis by Mossbridge et al. (2012) on presentiment. (Note that *ES* = effect size in the list below):

- Ganzfeld: there is "a linear decline in [effect-size strength] over a 34-year period … [but] a rebound effect is also indicated" (Storm et al., 2010, p. 478);
- Ganzfeld: "… the correlation between mean quality scores and *ES* values … was extremely weak and not significant" (Storm et al., 2010, p. 475);
- Forced Choice: "We note that the correlation between year of study and *ES* is positive and significant for the database … indicating an incline, meaning that *ES* values increased over the 24-year period" (Storm et al., 2012, p. 257);
- Forced Choice: "The correlation between mean Quality Scores and *ES* values … was very weak, negative, and not significant, …, suggesting that effect size was not an artifact of poor experimental design" (Storm et al., 2012, pp. 251–252);
- RNG: "… the quality of studies was high" (Bösch et al., 2006, p. 507); and "study quality was also positively correlated with year of publication" (p. 508);
- Presentiment: "the higher-quality studies produced a higher overall ES and level of significance than the lower-quality studies" (Mossbridge et al., 2012, p. 7), whereas the correlation "between quality score and ES was not significant" (p. 8).

In spite of these new findings, coupled with the earlier findings, explanations for CDEs still persist, resurrected in the form of a slightly modified argument from fraud—"fraudulent experimenters" in the early stages of research are replaced by newer "nonfraudulent experimenters" at a later date (Stokes, 2015, p. 47). Hence the decline. In other words, Stokes was still arguing the case for fraud, as he did back in 2007. Yet he knew well enough that

> Many meta-analyses have found no evidence for a positive relation between methodological flaws and the size of reported psi effects.
>
> (p. 44)

This problem is simply explained away as more fraud!

> … people who report fraudulent results may also report more perfect methodology than was actually used (assuming that the experiment was even conducted).
>
> (p. 44)

Unsubstantiated statements like this prove beyond a doubt that the Trickster knows no bounds. Again, the mud-slinging only starts when doubt and suspicion arise: "My newfound skepticism regarding the existence of psi *is not based on any new concrete evidence for fraud among parapsychologists* [emphasis added], but rather on a general lowering of my respect for all scientists" (Stokes, 2015, p. 45). What are we to make of a science where empirical evidence can be trumped by opinion?

Contemporaneous contrary findings from other researchers may help steer a reasonable course for parapsychology (Baptista, Derakhshani, & Tressoldi, 2015), while more recent meta-analytic evidence gives even more justification to dismiss the CDE:[22]

- Ganzfeld update: "There was no statistical evidence for an effect-size decline in the ganzfeld domain …" (Storm & Tressoldi, 2020, p. 213;
- Ganzfeld update: "The correlation between mean Quality and *ES* was weak and not significant ... so we claim that effect size is not likely to be an artifact of poor experimental design" (Storm & Tressoldi, 2020, p. 200);
- Remote Viewing: "Looking at the *ES*s … we can affirm that there is no sign of decline in almost 40 years" (Baptista, Derakhshani, & Tressoldi, 2015, p. 203);
- Sheep-Goat Effect (SGE): "The relationship between the sheep-goat CR(ES) [critical ratio effect size] values and year of publication is positive and significant.… In other words, the SGE has increased across the span of about 20 years …" (Storm & Tressoldi, 2017, pp. 93–94);
- Sheep-Goat Effect (ESP): "ESP effects [over the years] generally have not increased significantly [in a two-tailed test, but the ESP effect is marginally significant in a one-tailed test]" (Storm & Tressoldi, 2017, pp. 93–94);
- Sheep-Goat Effect (SGE & ESP): Storm and Tressoldi (2017) state "in both cases [SGE and ESP] … increases in effects have been independent of study quality" (p. 94);
- Dream-ESP: Storm, Sherwood, et al. (2017) report "no significant decline in *ES* related to quality, …, but quality control in experiments has improved over the 49-year period" (p. 130).

We actually see an *incline* effect for the SGE, while the ESP effect is stable (Storm & Tressoldi, 2017). The presentiment effect is also stronger in the better quality studies (Mossbridge et al., 2012). Regarding the dream-ESP meta-analysis, Storm, Sherwood, et al. (2017) did find that the correlation between year of study and effect size was negative and significant, but they also found suggestive evidence that "illustrates the complete opposite of the sceptical hypothesis that improvements in quality necessarily mean *ES* must plummet" (p. 130). Although it was found that two dream-ESP databases (Maimonides Dream Laboratory [MDL] studies and post-MDL studies) were not significantly different from each other in terms of mean effect size, the difference did approach significance. Though not reported in the paper (Storm, Sherwood, et al.), I tested both databases separately for effect size declines over their respective periods, and neither DE was significant.[23]

Ramifications of Claimed Experimenter Psi and Chronological Decline Effects

We now come to the ramifications of these findings in the context of the Trickster, but first, here is how the Trickster has manifested itself: On the evidence, the parapsychology community argued the case for the E-psi effect—it argued a similar case for CDEs. This went on for decades. Most parapsychologists accepted the 'evidence' for both effects based on single studies, or small sets of studies, and then larger sets. The propositions seemed valid, reputations were at stake, time and money had been invested; reasonable explanations had to be proffered to the wider community to save face. The mainstream (largely skeptical) community took and ran with the parapsychologists' arguments and, *in their opinion*, saw them as mere excuses used to explain the failure to reject the so-called Null hypothesis (i.e., the hypothesis of no effect). That gave cause for embarrassment; even ridicule (trickster outcomes). True to Trickster form, however, there is a twist—perhaps parapsychologists spoke too soon: E-Psi and DEs do seem to occur in a number of studies, but these apply mainly to short-term (within-study) effects, whereas no (or debatably too few) long-term (between-studies) E-Psi and CDEs are demonstrated in the various meta-analyses comprising many studies that are considered representative of the respective experimental domains (i.e., free response, forced choice, etc.). Given the evidence, chronological manifestations of the effects appear to be unfounded, but episodic effects look genuine (the evidence persists).

It is important to note that my argument here is not that the Trickster lies behind E-psi and CDEs, in the sense that it actually causes them. These two effects could occur, but it would not be the Trickster that caused them if they did occur, and if they did not occur, it would not be the Trickster that prevented them. Instead, I have asked (and answered) the question, Was there evidence for these effects, and if there wasn't and it was thought there was, what is behind that mistake?

If we were somewhat myopic, we could argue that the parapsychological community might have spared itself some embarrassment if it had waited a little longer, but how long is a little longer? Science is an accumulative enterprise, and scientists make discoveries and present them in fits and starts; the point being, science is an ongoing process of continual revelation. Truth be told, parapsychologists, singly or as a community, simply did not know better, and can only work with the best data available at the time. So it is easy to argue that hindsight has 20/20 vision, whereas science does not. But that is to ignore the clues. The earlier literature should have helped ameliorate the negative exposure caused by E-Psi and CDEs, and perhaps both issues could or should have been downplayed given that there was not a lot to go on—indeed, some investigators did that.

Interestingly, Radin (2006a) gives an appropriate metaphor that conveys more than is first realized. He refers to the Pygmalion effect which he parallels with the experimenter expectancy effect (i.e., E-Psi). The Pygmalion effect owes its origins to the myth of a Greek sculpture Pygmalion who fell in love with a statue he carved from ivory, and subsequently named Galatea. Aphrodite, the Goddess of Love, rewarded his fervour by bringing the statue to life—as Radin says: "This myth reflects the concept of a self-fulfilling prophecy" (p. 285); a classic cautionary tale warning us to be careful what we wish for (although Pygmalion seems to have done well out of it for the couple lived happily ever after).

While Radin directly acknowledges the point that sufficiently motivated experimenters can use their own good manner and/or psi in the laboratory, the less direct point is that the myth also warns researchers not to make too much of anything they *think* they find because that gives it reality—parapsychologists have to be careful they do not talk an effect into existence; and this *caveat* applies to CDEs, not just E-Psi. Indeed, Colborn (2007) makes the point about the decline effect: "we might call it into existence via reification" (p. 3). I would argue that parapsychologists have made too much of these long-term effects—they appealed to them too often (again I emphasize I am not discounting *within*-study declines). I give the final word to physicist and parapsychologist Roger Nelson who said my findings are matched by his experiences exactly,

> … in the lab, in meta-analysis, and in long-term programs of research. EE [i.e., E-Psi] explanations are too easy, and need (as we often say) prospective research to really establish bona fides.
>
> (personal communication, August 21, 2017)

And the same can be said of chronological decline effects.

***

At the beginning of this chapter, I considered the presence and influence of archetypes in synchronicity. I adopted Jung's theoretical position on that issue, but even Jung himself did not delve too deeply into the reach of the archetype as far as the field of parapsychology was concerned. Thus, one question in particular needs special attention: How does the archetype have bearing on psi in particular, and parapsychology in general? One special archetype—the Trickster—gives us indication of the archetype's reach. Trickster phenomenology permeates deeply into the sciences. It is not a simple matter of dismissing the Trickster as mere superstition, and calling out its anomalous effects as the result of delusional states or chance. Certainly supernatural agency is not proposed as a cause though some phenomena are so bizarre, it is hard to resist.

In the modern era, however, we have learned we must take responsibility for our psychological aberrations, but we still often fail to see that when they are our own, and we thus dismiss them as attributable to 'other' (external) sources. Renaming the Trickster does not rid us of it. It not only manifests directly in the laboratory (as Pauli may have discovered), and in how sets of data are collected and collated (as Jung may have realized), but also it has a unique way of clouding the issue and rendering effects that can confuse and lead to false understanding, as is the case in parapsychology—specifically in relation to E-Psi and CDEs.

We must be careful we do not over-reach, even when the evidence looks conclusive, but what is to be said when evidence is ignored or not seen for what it is? Avoiding these pitfalls successfully calls for constant vigilance, based on a clearer understanding of the human factors in psi research. Researchers make a virtue of their conservatism (implying they take a cautious approach), but that does not entirely rid them of their preferences, prejudices, cherished hypotheses, and entrenched notions and beliefs. This chapter suggests that interpretations and positions can be hard to shift despite the findings. We could almost say that some archetypes are not welcome in parapsychology, particularly the Trickster, though we will never escape the fact that archetypes still play a necessary role in synchronicity and, by logical extension, psi.

Given the Trickster effect, parapsychologists' experimental designs and explanations of outcomes highlight limited agendas that did not take into consideration the broader (archetypal) picture of synchronicity as it plays out in our lives. Naïvely, parapsychologists' inadvertently focused in too limited a fashion on that one factor we have called "psi" (for want of a better term), which is only one aspect of synchronicity. Had there been a clearer understanding about psi—that it is a small part of a bigger whole—and had that been noticed and acted upon earlier, the decades of research that bracketed the end of the 20th century would have culminated in a very different picture of the field of parapsychology and its findings.

Notes

1 That sense of security is a naïve position to hold because of the unresolved prejudice faced by parapsychologists, especially in academia. The scene is changing for the better in some parts of the world (noticeably Europe, especially the UK), but I (writing in Australia) have personally experienced institutional career-threatening prejudice (twice in fact), and I know a number of parapsychologists overseas who have similar stories to tell. This prejudice extends beyond centres of learning to the media and mainstream society.

2 Jung (1959/1968) equates the Trickster with the alchemical Mercurius which is the equivalent of the Greek god Hermes (see Combs & Holland, 1996). The mythological parallels are too complex and interwoven to go into detail here.

3 Pauli's Exclusion Principle (for which he won the Nobel Prize) is so-called because matter is explained as occupying its own space to the exclusion of other material objects, such that one cannot pass through the other. Specifically, "(1) no more than two electrons can occupy the same orbital, and (2) two electrons in the same orbital must have opposite spins" (Singh, 2015, p. 116). Light and radiation are given exclusive exception to this rule. This principle is fundamental to our understanding of the nature of matter as, for example, in its formal presentation in the periodic table of elements.

4 In the original Cross-Correspondences work (see Saltmarsh, 1938/1975, for a review), members of the Society for Psychical Research found correspondences hidden within messages from different mediumistic communications. The messages in these communications were singly meaningless and only seemed to make sense once the contents were cross referenced. The findings were considered evidence for survival, though others argued that ESP would explain them.

5 Eisenbud (1963) is probably one of the earliest researchers to bring E-Psi to the attention of parapsychologists.

6 A survey of members of the Parapsychological Association (Irwin, 2014) reported that many parapsychologists regard experimenter psi as a major problem for parapsychologists, and many refer to the need to disentangle participant and experimenter effects.

7 Between-studies DEs might also be called "*chronological declines*" (CDs; Irwin, 1999, as cited in Colborn, 2007, p. 2), but I will not use that term because CDs can be either across experimental paradigms (e.g., ganzfeld), or over the lifetime of an individual, and I only want to focus on the paradigms. CDs contrast with "*episodic declines*" (EDs), which are "within an experimental run or within a session" (Colborn, 2007, p. 2)—I refer to these as within-study DEs.

8 As I am focusing on E-Psi, I will not be discussing the third (unlikely) option that experimenters do not have E-Psi, and all effects come from participants only.

9 Palmer and Millar (2015) do not dwell too much on participant-psi. It appears they regard participants' psi as constant (and inconsequential?), and prevalent within and between studies. It also appears they take "significance" to mean psi-hitting, since they state that parapsychologists are "rigorously" selected (even self-selected) "for success in their experiments" (p. 298), and success usually means significant psi-hitting.

10 The terms "sheep" and "goat" (applied to psi-believers and psi-skeptics, respectively) were adopted by Schmeidler from a New Testament simile that describes how a shepherd "separates the sheep from the goats" (Matthew 25:31–33). It is claimed that sheep tend to score significantly above mean chance expectation (MCE) on psi tasks, whereas goats tend to score at or below MCE. A sheep-goat effect is evident if there is a significant scoring difference between sheep and goats.

11 The ganzfeld is a "special type of environment (or the technique for producing it) consisting of homogenous, unpatterned sensory stimulation" to the eyes and ears of the participant, who is usually in "a state of bodily comfort" (Thalbourne, 2003, p. 45).

12 The forced-choice design is so named because the target-guess is "one of a limited range of possibilities which are known to [the participant] in advance" (Thalbourne, 2003, p. 44).

13 Dream ESP involves ostensibly paranormal communication while in an altered state of consciousness commonly known as dreaming. Pioneer research into the telepathic nature of dreams was first conducted at the Maimonides Dream Laboratory in New York during the 1960s and 1970s.

14 The Schmidt et al. (2004) study was in fact started well before 2002 (an abstract was published that year and results presented at a PA Convention). They used a database of studies up to the year 2000 so I include Schmidt et al. as indicative of DMILS research around the turn of the century.

15 We can make the argument that E-Psi is responsible for these declines—experimenters (like participants) tire and lose motivation, focus, and interest, as they get older. We might also argue that aging "star" experimenters eventually retire, and perhaps they are not replaced by younger "star" experimenters. Then we could expect DEs. However, since I find no convincing evidence of long-term declines in the meta-analyses, all experimenters (assuming E-Psi) must, *on average* and *on occasion*, be putting in equal amounts of their own psi across the decades (a pretty tall order), or they put in none at all.

16 Note that Schmidt et al. (2004) did not look at quality over time (footnote 14 explains this study's inclusion).

17 Schmidt et al. (2004) may loosely be considered an exception; they report two significant declines over time (DMILS and Remote Staring [RS]). However, date of study (year of publication) dropped out in a regression analysis (DMILS), and for RS, it was shown that N (sample size) correlated significantly with date—thus, the earlier smaller studies tended to "overestimate the true effect size" (p. 13); besides which, there were only 15 studies in the sample.

18 At first, Radin and Ferrari (1991) found that quality correlated negatively and significantly with effect size, suggesting that design flaws present in low quality studies were contributing to the success of earlier experiments, but further analysis of a homogeneous subset of data (i.e., outliers were removed) revealed no suggestive evidence of decline in psi effect due to poor quality.

19 For DMILS, I used the revised non-significant "*overall study quality* and *effect size*" correlation (Schmidt et al., 2004, p. 244). For Remote Staring, the effect-size/quality correlation was positive and non-significant.

20 In some studies, we cannot draw any strong conclusions because findings were limited—that is, patterns over time were not checked for quality (Schmidt et al., 2004), or were not checked for both quality *and* effect size (Honorton et al., 1998).

21 Surprisingly, Honorton (1985) did not test the correlation between effect size and year of study—if he did, he would have found a weak negative (albeit crucially nonsignificant) relationship for his 28-study database, $r(26) = -0.20$, $p = .155$ (one-tailed).

22 Declines over time have not been reported in the more recent RNG meta-analyses (Bösch, Steinkamp, & Boller, 2006; Radin & Nelson, 2003).

23 MDL studies: $r(12) = -0.02$, $p = .943$ (two-tailed); post-MDL studies: $r(34) = -0.20$, $p = .238$ (two-tailed).

Chapter 3

The Trickster in Parapsychology

Part II. More Secret Weapons

> … Psi phenomena, including synchronicities, … respond to, and are shaped by, the ideas, beliefs, and anxieties of the observers.
>
> (George Hansen, 2001, p. 216)

This chapter continues from Chapter 2, with further depictions of the Trickster in parapsychological practice. The sciences generally will always have their ups and downs, and parapsychologists too must learn to ride these out. That ride is part of the big picture view of science which incorporates the human aspect—that means more than just how scientists must deal with unpalatable glitches in their findings, for it goes deep into the psyche to the archetypal core of our being. The problems of dealing with false positives and false negatives, spotting questionable research practices, and not getting carried away with magical ideas, philosophical 'spins', and our fears, are all challenges set against us by the Trickster. All these issues are discussed in this chapter. But we find the Trickster extends beyond the psychological core of our being; let us not be deceived into thinking he is a foe that can be met on a level playing field: As I said previously, his defeat requires constant vigilance, but above all, it requires honesty.

False Positives and False Negatives

There are two more tricksterish 'weapons' that are somewhat minor in status when compared to E-Psi and chronological decline effects (CDEs). They are the false positive and the false negative. These are legitimate problems in psi research, but as will be seen, the Trickster may be detected in the shenanigans people get up to when they evoke their presence. The false positive is, as Colquhoun (2017) so simply puts it, "a 'significant' result when there is nothing but chance at play" (p. 2), so logically the false negative is a *non*significant result when there is *something more than* chance at play. From what we know about chance, it is not a cause *per se*, but it does suggest causes—if we have a genuine false positive or false negative, there must be real causes at play. The bigger problem, however, is that both can be used as modes of attack or defense, even to serve an ideological

DOI: 10.4324/9781003561323-4

position. Thus, it is not too difficult to see the relevance of these falsities to Trickster phenomenology.

As we can see, false positives and false negatives are a different kettle of fish from E-Psi and DEs (chronological and episodic). E-Psi and DEs differ from false positives and false negatives in that the latter two are alternative (e.g., non-psi) interpretations of statistical outcomes, but they are not explanations *per se* (i.e., they have to be explained), whereas the former two generally stand as higher order explanations in themselves (or go some way towards an explanation) by referring directly to experimenter influence (E-Psi) or to trends in data (DEs) as sources of the problems. In this section, I will show how the Trickster gets in through the back door if the meanings underpinning the false positive and the false negative are misinterpreted, or the impact of each is not fully explored.

Statistically speaking, the false positive is also called a Type I error—it is the result (theoretically) of *unduly* rejecting a true Null hypothesis (e.g., a significant effect was found, but the effect is an artifact). As for the false negative (a.k.a. Type II error), it is the result of failing to reject a false Null hypothesis (e.g., the effect was not significant because the sample was too small, or an inappropriate statistical test was used).

In one sense, the false positive (e.g., convicting the innocent) might be seen as worse than a false negative (e.g., failure to convict the guilty), as illustrated in Blackstone's (1783/1978) formulation: "It is better that ten guilty persons escape than that one innocent suffer" (p. 358). Likewise, we might wonder which is worse—that we think we have psi or synchronicity when we do not (false positive), or we fail to find it when it *was* there (false negative). It depends on the person. Thalbourne (1995) argued that it all depends on whether you are an 'Expansionist' (you prefer to make Type I errors) or a 'Conservative' (you prefer to make Type II errors). On the one hand, Expansionists

> prefer to spread their net wide in the hope of discovering novel phenomena and thereby conquering new territory for science. As Louis Lasagna (1984) puts it: "I'd rather err occasionally than miss a real live miracle" (p. 12). Expansionism is an essentially liberal scientific attitude.
>
> (p. 355)

On the other hand, Conservatives

> are more apprehensive about – or see as more costly – their making the mistake of saying that an event was psychic when in reality it turns out not to be so. They would rather occasionally miss out on the real McCoy than approve a fake. Better to have an incomplete catalog of nature than one bulging with interlopers.
>
> (p. 355)

Thalbourne adds that neither is wrong. But in parapsychology, as in science generally, both types of error are tricksterish, and it is difficult to argue that one is worse than the other. But like Blackstone, I would tip towards false positives being worse, and I shall explain why here (NB: the problem comes up repeatedly in the next section). The false positive does parapsychology considerable damage when findings are scrutinized from the outside by mainstream critics—it simply looks like parapsychologists are too keen to latch onto anything psi-like, to their embarrassment when it does not replicate, whereas the false negative does lesser damage because, although the very effects parapsychologists seek may elude them, that is *only in the short term* for the long-term cumulative record of multiple meta-analyses trumps the short-term effect (see Cardeña, 2018). Critics, however, do not see it that way—it is unfortunate that the benefit of the doubt is never forthcoming, whatever is found (see Reber & Alcock, 2020). Critics will say that appeal is made to both errors as proof that parapsychologists are 'hunting snarks'; which is to say, sometimes parapsychologists only *think* they have it; sometimes they *think* they've missed it. In a nutshell, the critic prefers to say parapsychologists *always think wrongly* whatever they find.

But parapsychologists did not invent the Type 1 error and the Type II error, and it goes without saying that appealing to one or the other is fair practice when justified. Yet Alcock (2003) wonders why parapsychologists do not "give the Null hypothesis a chance" (p. 49) *as if* parapsychologists never do this. In fact, that is precisely what they do as often as they must—for example, former Editor-in-Chief of the *Journal of Parapsychology* (*JP*), John Palmer "adopted a guideline for *JP* papers that all significant results that are not replications should be declared as tentative pending replication" (Krippner et al., 2021, p. 2), implying that significant first-findings could be Type I errors. In other cases, parapsychologists do at least brave the implications of failing to find support for the Alternative hypothesis by publishing in journals that have a policy of publishing non-significant findings (see the next section for details). Also, even when it is made clear that a certain experimental design may not have been appropriate for testing psi, the skeptic will not accept that the design had anything to do with the non-significant outcome.

Alcock might say I have misread him, but he is quite clear: His position is that *support* for the Null hypothesis means the "observed results" come about "naturally", and have "nothing to do with psi" (p. 31). In his mind, he is only asking parapsychologists why (when they fail to reject the Null) they never own up to the possibility that there is no psi, *and never was*. Conceptually, my previous comments are the correct way to respond, but there is another important conceptual point to be made here: For Alcock, accepting the Null is the same as *proof of no psi*,[1] but this is not what a parapsychologist should ever have to accept for that is an abuse of the conservatism inherent in the limited principle of the Null. The Null cannot speak to the possibility of an effect not ever happening *at any time* as if it does not exist; the Null does not give an effect a deadline, or dismiss an effect if a specific number of tests have failed to find significance.

Alcock (2003) implies even more—giving the Null a chance means parapsychologists must never claim Type II error (a false negative), even though that is the parapsychologist's prerogative. And there is a double-standard here: Given

Alcock's position, it would never occur to him to give the *Alternative* hypothesis a chance. It is almost as if his special pleading (pp. 30-31) sufficiently relinquished any need for that option. Worse still, Alcock argues that parapsychologists err in proposing hypotheses that might explain the lack of replication—these hypotheses are: "experimenter effect" (pp. 38-39), "sheep-goat effect" (p. 39), "psi-missing" (p. 39), and "decline effect" (p. 39). Alcock believes the Null hypothesis "is not given a fair chance when data that are consistent with it are explained away in this manner" (p. 39). In fact, all four of these counter-hypotheses are reasonable and testable and have some support (as shown above). It is ironic that Alcock never mentions the fact that the so-called 'usual suspects' skeptics throw in to debunk a psi claim (e.g., fraud, sensory leakage, improper randomization, or other design flaws) actually help them avoid giving the Alternative hypothesis a chance. Let's call his oversights blatant and obvious Trickster effects and leave it at that.

Parapsychologists, of course, have to be on their guard when they do fail to reject the Null and accept the Alternative (i.e., they claim an effect nominally called psi). I am not saying Type I error should be assumed for the entire dataset, but interest needs to be taken in addressing the problem of occasional false positives in the dataset. Parapsychologists' decisions are based on a general statistical finding but, because I equate synchronicity with psi, the effect requires a little more than a so-called 'significant p value' to indicate its true merit. From this point onwards I will focus on the false positive only as I wish to contrast psi and synchronicity, and to do that, I need to examine *effects we have or think we have*; not *effects we may have missed*. (There are ways of dealing with false negatives that concern design issues, sample size, etc., but they do not interest us at this point.)

Schmeidler (1964) and Rao (1968) were amongst the first researchers to take a serious look at so-called 'error phenomena' (also called 'artificial positives' or 'false positives'), and they noted the 'coincidental' nature of these phenomena. It seems as though insufficient attention has been given to these effects, which is surprising given that false positives can never be classed as psi, so they stand as exactly the kind of pseudo-effect one would think parapsychologists would want to nip in the bud *tout suite*. In other words, if we take it as read that false positives do occur, then parapsychologists must find some way to exclude from their counts those outcomes that arise by chance (insofar as false positives are purely random hits).[2] There have been attempts to determine the real level of the psi effect (see Boerenkamp & Schouten, 1983; Timm, 2000), and draw it out from mean chance expectation, but generally the 'real' psi hits are not separated from the chance (random) hits, mainly because no one seems to knows how to do it. Hence, parapsychologists just take the overall hit count, find the p value, and if it is significant, claim a psi effect.

However, under the assumption that psi *is* synchronicity, more can be done to identify false positives. Specifically, the be-all and end-all of a trial should not simply be the outcome, even if it is a hit. If the outcome image or text contains sufficient information that could be personally relevant, these could be rated for meaningfulness by participants (see how this can be done, and has been done with the *I Ching* in Appendix A). Jung (1952/1969) made the distinction that some incidents could be 'pure chance', but there are some whose "chancefulness" is "open to doubt" (para. 826). It follows that the discernment of meaning is a critical factor that decides whether a hit really and truly should count as a hit rather than a false positive.

Along similar lines there is a need to re-envision target sets (perhaps only necessary for some free-response designs). For example, Watt (1988) had earlier drawn the theoretical conclusion that the best psi targets are meaningful, have emotional impact, and contain human interest. I will make similar points in Chapter 4 (see *Towards a Synchronistic Understanding of Psi*). Researchers must give participants the opportunity to find meaningfulness in the experimental outcomes, otherwise the threat to laboratory psi-testing is that it may be finding "a sterilized, depotentiated form of synchronicity—it being stripped of its greater value, namely, meaningfulness in its fuller or richer capacity" (Storm, 2008c, p. 281). Note Tart's (2008) view on this same issue:

> Some parapsychologists … who have been discouraged by years of research that does not seem to lead to any reliable understanding or control of psi, are beginning to think of paranormal events as synchronistic.
>
> (p. 121)

It is probably no coincidence that the experimental domains in parapsychology that yield the strongest effect sizes also happen to feature designs that offer the most meaningful outcomes, though more could be done. Ganzfeld (see Cardeña, 2018) and Imagery Cultivation (IC; see Storm, 2023b), and more generally the free-response designs with their visual targets, yield the strongest effects, whereas the weakest effects are found in the dice-throwing and RNG studies, simply because outcomes are not very meaningful.

Following from these demonstrated differences, the participant's right to a meaningful experience is one of the reasons I have given so much attention to the *I Ching* over the years because it is a system of divination that offers meaningful outcomes (for examples, see Storm, 2008b; Storm & Rock, 2014b). My one major misgiving about the *I Ching* tests is that 64 choices and the ranking thereof can be overwhelming for participants to the extent that differentiation becomes increasingly nuanced and therefore arduous as the session proceeds, which can have a negative impact on selections and ultimately overall effect size.

More recently, as results seem to be indicating, IC seems more ecologically relevant than ganzfeld in the sense that it encourages the imagination to a greater extent. It seems logical that adopting synchronistic methodologies would help create a synchronicity-like experience for participants, which would thus increase effect sizes, especially if the experiments approximate real-life scenarios. No doubt chance will always be a factor that can inflate as much as deflate an effect, but it is reasonable to propose that the number of false positives can be reduced, while that number could be offset by an increase in genuine hits due to the ecological validity of the design. One other distinct advantage is that we can expect the various correlations will be more accurate as the false positives in a dataset go into decline.

Another important step would be to offer feedback to participants. Meaning and purpose is garnered from feedback. Research shows that feedback is best given to participants at the very end of a task or a trial run as it helps if they receive the information when it is most relevant (most meaningful) to their mental state (for a review of studies that support this claim, see *Precognition* in the subsection *Laboratory Psi and Parapsychological Nomenclature* in Chapter 1). If immediate feedback is motivational in itself, and may have positive effects on the subsequent trial or trials, experimenters may see effect-size inclines. Another variable to look at is numinosity, to be described, for example, in relation to Schwartz's work in the study by Krippner et al. (2019) (see *Towards a Synchronistic Understanding of Psi* in Chapter 4).

Declaring Type I or Type II error as the need arises is fair practice, yet some critics seem to think it is also fair practice to call out parapsychologists for that practice as if they are only doing it to save a cherished hypothesis, or even cover up some unforgivable crime. Assertions like that are not only biased; they are underhanded. But the certainty of a significant effect can deceive experimenters into thinking the false positive at the trial level is not an issue. Experimental designs can always be improved, and to think otherwise is a deception. Usually in a psi study the participant is given an 'aim' and a 'target' as if some kind of marksmanship was under scrutiny. By reconceptualizing the psi task as an opportunity for synchronicity, participants might see the personal relevance of task success. The chance hit and the meaningful hit might then be differentiated.

Questions About Questionable Research Practices

The Trickster knows no bounds, and in scientific research, a researcher can follow up a number of leads based on the complexity of ideas, approaches, and findings, while the wide scope for interpretation leaves many doors and windows open in a house of meaning that we would rather see secured from outside threats. We can spot the Trickster at work when researchers massage the facts, or twist vital information, or tell half the story, or adopt questionable methods, or avoid conducting analyses that might turn things around—in fact, these actions are part of a set of 'tricks' that we could call the Trickster's *modus operandi*. Though the Trickster may be hard to spot, we do not have to assume we are always dealing with deliberate deception—after all, the primary objective of most researchers is to put things right, so one should at all times give them the benefit of the doubt, and assume their hearts are in the right place. It is on that note that I need to review a paper by Bierman, Spottiswoode, and Bijl (2016). The major problem with this paper is that it is very loosely guided by a paper by John, Loewenstein, and Prelec (2012a), who at least went to the effort of actually sampling a population of psychologists ("5,964 academic psychologists at major U.S. universities"; p. 525). They had some real data to evaluate, whereas the analysis by Bierman et al. consists primarily of guesstimates based on John et al.'s statistics.[3] It is for this reason that the approach taken by Bierman et al. needs to be addressed.

Bierman et al. borrowed five questionable research practices (QRPs) from John et al. (2012a), and came up with another two, and entered so-called 'prevalence intervals'[4] into simulations of the ganzfeld database from Storm et al. (2010). Bierman et al. suggested that the ganzfeld database is considerably less significant (but still significant) if these hypothetical QRPs were present (for a more sophisticated treatment but similar finding, see Bancel, 2018). These QRPs are:

1 *confirmation-to-pilot* (a confirmatory experiment is prematurely halted if results are negative; trials are dumped, the protocols are adjusted, the experiment is restarted);
2 *pilot-to-confirmation* (a 'test-run' study, data of which are included in a confirmatory experiment if there are no problems);
3 *optional stopping* (stopping short of a specified number of participants as soon as significance is reached);
4 *optional extension* (testing more than a pre-specified number of participants and only stopping once significance is reached);
5 *publication bias* (not publishing studies that produce only chance or negative results);
6 *deciding to exclude data post hoc* (removing participants who are unsuitable); and
7 *fraud* (Bierman et al., 2016, pp. 8–10).

If present in the ganzfeld studies, these seven QRPs can inflate the ganzfeld psi effect (e.g., by polluting the data with false positives), but of course evidence of QRPs have to be found. While few would doubt that tightening the reins on parapsychological practice is a worthy idea if it identifies sources of artifacts, the problems with the rationale underpinning that intention are manifold, and Palmer recognized this fact when he said Bierman et al.'s (2016) paper was "a monumental waste of time (and journal space)" (2016c, p. 143), given the authors ostensibly implied the whole venture was hypothetical. Palmer, however, even disputed that implication, pointing out that he (Palmer, 2016a) previously had argued that Bierman et al. had every intention of proving that the ganzfeld database was "inflated by QRPs" (Bierman et al., 2016, p. 1), so that their study was not hypothetical at all. In their own words, they aimed to demonstrate the ganzfeld database "would be a good example of how purely random data can be distorted into the appearance of significance" (Bierman et al., 2016, p. 2).

I will consider each of these seven QRPs and question the rationale adopted by Bierman et al. (2016). First and second—confirmation-to-pilot (CtoP) and pilot-to-confirmation (PtoC); the first starts as a confirmatory study, and the second starts as a pilot study. These two effectively suggest that trials are sometimes excluded *just because* they are misses, or sometimes included *just because* they are hits, when the decision to exclude or include should only hinge on technical issues to do with experimental design protocols. Bierman et al. claim that excluded data contributes to the file-drawer problem (i.e., publication bias), whereas the inclusion of questionable data (showing a promising hit rate) is inflationary. While the latter is quite correct for both CtoP and PtoC, one of the reasons for halting an experiment is that protocol adjustments may be needed, so there is good reason to dump trials even if there seem to be (or are) excessive misses—under those conditions, that data should not be part of the file drawer. Bierman et al. may have allowed for that eventuality, but it is not clear in their paper. Another of their problems is they (allegedly) borrowed for their simulation a CtoP prevalence estimate from John et al. (2012a), who never featured CtoP—the figure of "40.7%" (see Bierman et al., 2016, Table 1, p. 8) seems to have come from Table S2 (John et al., 2012b, p. 15) which is for optional stopping.[5] And there is no prevalence figure for PtoC; only prevalence intervals that seem to be stabs in the dark.

Third and fourth—optional stopping and optional extension. These can push a study into significance; all the experimenter has to do is designate a certain number of participants to test, but then keep an eye on effect size and stop short when, or extend testing until, significance is reached. Palmer (2016c) keenly observed that any study that had committed optional stopping or optional extension could be identified from *N* (i.e., the number of trial counts)—specifically, "nonround *N*s" (p. 143). The two-fold hypothesis of optional stopping and optional extension following Palmer's assumption has not been conducted as an exercise, but I present one here. Since researchers rarely state that they stop short, or extend testing, one has to be ruthless and exclude any study that seems to have an unusual number of trials, which means the innocent suffer with the presumed guilty. Nevertheless, on that basis, I reduced the same 102-study database used in my ganzfeld meta-analysis (Storm et al., 2010) to 52 studies (these 52 had *N*s of 10, or 20, or 30, and so on, up to the largest *N* of 120). Multiples of ten are as round as one can get, so I have been extremely conservative (the results of my original study, and the new findings for the reduced 'rounded *N*' database, can be found in Appendix C). Even for a database almost half its original size, little has changed statistically for the crucial values. Also, about 1/4 of the studies in both databases are independently significant (about the same for the original database). These results tell us all we need to know about the efficacy of the ganzfeld treatment. So, *as an exercise*, if we ruthlessly adjust for optional stopping and optional extension, on the hypothetical assumption that these options were present as QRPs in some ganzfeld studies, we end up with a purified database with consequent effects that are even more unquestionable than before. (NB: In Appendix C, I also reduced Bierman et al.'s "S1 Dataset" of 79 studies in the same 'ruthless' way—the results are comparable.)

Fifth, regarding publication bias, parapsychology journals (unlike mainstream psychology journals) go to great efforts to publish studies with nonsignificant results—they tend *not* to end up in the 'file-drawer'. That is because the Parapsychological Association (PA) Council adopted a policy in 1975 of opposing the *exclusive* publication of studies with *only positive outcomes*. Thereby, "negative findings have been routinely reported at the association's meetings and in its affiliated publications" since that date (Bem & Honorton, 1994, p. 6; see also Honorton,

1985, p. 66). Bierman et al. (2016) actually mention this publication policy, and they state that "a non-significant outcome is not a danger to the career of the parapsychologist" (p. 8). However, they argue that parapsychologists "may be driven by a non-materialist or spiritual worldview that they try to defend" (p. 8),[6] implying that the policy would be ignored. Therefore, in order to be "cautious", Bierman et al. "assume that the prevalence values of the use of QRPs in parapsychological research *are similar to those measured in experimental psychology* [emphasis added]" (p. 8). Bierman et al. seem not to realize that experimental psychologists also have worldviews to defend, but the same experimental psychologists do not have a publication policy like that of the PA. Thus, there is no level playing field. In fact, it may be argued that all the QRP prevalences and prevalence intervals used in Bierman et al.'s model are inflated.[7]

It is possible to test the likelihood of publication bias using various statistical tests. In Storm et al. (2010), we chose two methods to demonstrate statistically whether publication bias was likely. The first test, using Rosenthal's (1979) so-called Fail Safe File Drawer (FSFD) formula, had been used by a number of parapsychologists since the 1980s, so we used that formula for comparative purposes, whereas the other test from Darlington and Hayes (2000) is more conservative. Focusing only on the result using Rosenthal's formula, Bierman et al. (2016) observed:

> Storm et al calculated that 2,414 unpublished studies were required to eliminate the overall [significant] results of the GF [ganzfeld] database. Storm et al argue that this number, given the limited resources of the field and the acceptance of publishing negative findings, is unreasonably large.
>
> (p. 9)

Bierman et al. (2016) then point out that researchers who calculate these numbers "generally assumed incorrectly that the decision not to publish is unbiased", and they also argue that the same researchers err in thinking "that the unpublished studies have zero effect size" (p. 9). It *is* true that Rosenthal's (1979) method is misleading "because it treats the inherently biased file drawer as unbiased" (Scargle, 1999, p. 22), and falsely assumes an overall effect size of zero. That is why we also presented a more conservative estimate of 384 unpublished studies that *does* assume bias; not only can these unpublished studies have a 'zero effect size', they can have negative values (Storm et al., 2010, p. 477). Bierman et al. focused on the least conservative result, thus making Storm et al. look like they were unjustifiably downplaying publication bias to the extreme, having based it on a figure so inflated that it made the ganzfeld database look too good to be true. Any reader not familiar with the Storm et al. meta-analysis would assume that Bierman et al. discovered a critical flaw in the meta-analysis.

Sixth, an experimenter's decision to exclude data *post hoc* in the ganzfeld context means unsuitable participants are removed (removal could be based on the fact that the participant fell asleep, or complained, or was late, or vexed, or uncooperative, etc.). However, if a participant produces a result that "conforms to the desired hypothesis [i.e., is a hit], the experimenter may be non-consciously less inclined to remove the subject [participant]" (Bierman et al., 2016, p. 10). Bierman et al. argue that this practice is tantamount to "fraud" (p. 10) if removal of "subjects with misses" gets *too high* (nominally over 5%)! Irrespective of whether it is fair to simulate this QRP in their model, setting an arbitrary frequency of 5% to demarcate fraud from legitimate practice is itself questionable.

Seventh (fraud), Bierman et al. (2016) have little to go on, so they rely on John et al. (2012a, 2012b) to inform them. They refer to John et al.'s 'admission' figure of about 4.4% (actually it should be 4.34%—John et al., 2012b, p. 16), and adopt an apparent 'guesstimate' for parapsychology of 3.4% which, it turns out, is based on one case (i.e., "one senior researcher in the 80 studies post-1985 database [who] might be guilty of deception" because he or she "had been implicated in errors in the randomization procedure"; p. 10). This one case is from a database of 29 principal investigators (1/29, or 3.4%), which yields an inflated fraud rate because they could have taken the "two studies" by the "senior researcher" out of the "80 studies" (thus, 2/80, or 2.5%). What is 'questionable' is (i) how "errors in randomization procedure" translate as fraud; (ii) why only the principal investigators represent the 'persons of interest' and not all the researchers (e.g., research assistants); (iii) why 3.4% is considered a fair and valid indicator of parapsychological fraud merely because it is 'close' to John et al.'s 4.34%; and (iv) why the equally valid 2.5% is not preferred.

QRPs basically translate as many different ways to commit fraud when the QRP is deliberate—otherwise, they only indicate carelessness on the part of some researchers. However, the practice of assessing QRPs is questionable in itself when coupled with various oversights, errors of commission and omission, misrepresentations, and so on. The accusing finger points to the Trickster, even to the degree that some researchers, in obeisance to a higher cause, interpret conservatism a little differently to the rest of us. When things like this happen, it is hard not to see an agenda that ignores the objective aims of a science that should tell all; an aim that also lets the pieces fall where they may. John et al. (2012a) are correct in saying "QRPs can waste researchers' time and stall scientific progress …" (p. 531), but we do have to be mindful, when checking for QRPs, that we do not punish the innocent with the guilty.

Magic, Reliability, and Six Sigma

From the point of view of the Trickster, we might wonder what to make of magic, which in the past has included shamanism, alchemy, herbalism, and related practices (and even their revival in modern times). In this section, however, I confine my inquiry to magic in such forms as 'ceremonial magic', 'sympathetic magic', 'chaos magic', and so on, but not phoney stage magic. Magic clearly involves intention, which recalls the pertinent factor of "*dirigibility*" (Pratt et al., 1940/1966, p. 319), where the participant can guide the psi process, which happens to parallel intentional synchronicity mentioned earlier (for details, see Storm, 2025). I raise these issues here because magic, and ideas associated with it, do play a role in Trickster phenomenology in the form of the unhelpful cluttering effects of misguided ideologies and worldviews. However, some aspects of psi, synchronicity, and magic do seem to overlap. For instance, the idea of 'sympathy' (from the Greek *sympátheia* = 'same emotion') implies a symbolic connection or correlation between a ritualized action or object and a matching targeted event or individual. This idea brings to mind successful outcomes in synchronistic and psi correspondences where stimuli match responses. The 'matching' implies the 'sameness'.

The principle of magic is best explained by Scottish social anthropologist and folklorist Sir James George Frazer in *The Golden Bough* (1889/1922), whereby either "like produces like" or "effect resembles its cause" (p. 11). Frazer, however, is highly critical of magical practice—he goes on to say that these principles are 'misapplications of the association of ideas', and he describes two types of magic: homoeopathic (the association of ideas by similarity) and contagious (the association of ideas by contiguity):

> Homoeopathic magic commits the mistake of assuming that things which resemble each other are the same: contagious magic commits the mistake of assuming that things which have once been in contact with each other are always in contact.
>
> (p. 12)

Put this way, we may agree with Frazer, who happens to have been speaking about 'correspondences', but he sees them as coincidences in the casual sense. But let us not discount the parapsychological hypothesis that an individual intent on doing psi can help structure an 'imaginal' framework that may align with a desired effect (e.g., a healing or gambling success). While that too might sound like homoeopathic magic, this is not necessarily so (as will be seen). Yet psi is thought to be 'real magic' by some theorists who do not see a difference. They essentially argue that psi is 'old wine in new bottles', and claim that parapsychology is the study of magical processes (see Radin, 2018; Roney-Dougal, 1991/2010).

While Roney-Dougal (1991/2010) generalizes to the magic in science and technology, Radin (2018) focuses mainly on parapsychology, and thus defines magic as "mental influence of the physical world, perception of events distant in space or time, and interaction with nonphysical entities" (p. 1). That definition could cover some technological advances and findings in QM, but Radin mainly intends it to cover PK, ESP, and life after death, respectively. Trouble is the commonalities between psi and magic do not rid us of the disparities.[8] My focus here is not merely to assess the presumed psi/magic parallel, but to see where synchronicity fits in.

If we equate real magic with psi, does magic come about through information transmission and/or energy exchange? Not if psi is synchronicity, and what applies to psi, will apply to magic (assuming there is a case for the parallel). But nor can synchronicity be seen as homoeopathic magic or contagious magic where 'sameness' (correspondence) is the all-important effect of interest—alarmingly, many people (including parapsychologists) make the same mistake so it is no wonder that psi might be thought of as magic. Fortunately, most do not believe they live in a world where imagined conjunctions (through prayer, invocation, or whatever) alone suffice in bringing about magical effects. If the world was like that, not only should these effects happen in abundance, we would not have cause to attribute any of our magical successes to chance or accident, or the general flux of things in nature (e.g., entropic processes), or random fluctuations. Common sense and reality testing could never hold sway, since there would only be meaningful coincidences; never "meaningless chance groupings" (Jung, 1952/1969, para. 846) as mentioned in the Introduction.[9] We know skeptical arguments can be made in the attempt to *reduce* the former (meaningful coincidences) to the latter (meaningless chance groupings) because certain statisticians and psychologists, with our best interests at heart, do not want us to make the same mistakes made by primitive minds; but just as bad is the *elevation* of the latter to the former—that is, seeing all meaningless chance groupings as meaningful coincidences. None of these problems are resolved as long as parapsychologists and magicians fail to think *synchronistically* and therefore fail to apply the protocols that differentiate meaningful coincidence from meaningless chance groupings.

Alternatively, if theorists insist that psi and magic do involve information transmission and energy exchange, then neither psi nor magic can be synchronicity. We would then expect to see psychic/magical outcomes as the direct *causal* result of protocols/rites. But in what sense are the causal processes evident in those protocols/rites? And as before, should we not see these effects frequently, albeit for different reasons? Ultimately, one draws a very long bow when equating psi with magic: When Radin (2018) claims that religious rites are magic, we are to assume he means the rites are magic and therefore psi. But in the science of parapsychology, one likes to see evidence. If verifiable magical outcomes are not forthcoming in the practice of magic, the claims made for such practice are hollow. In fact, that is exactly where we stand with religious practice—we never see the claimed effects in spite of countless millions of repeated trials.[10] I am specifically thinking of so-called Holy Communion as just one example, and as practiced in many Christian churches—by ritualistic (magical) process, the bread and wine are supposedly transubstantiated (transformed) into the body and blood of Christ. Calling the process 'magic' is either a misnomer because no objectively proven magic happens (because the bread and wine remain as so-called 'accidents'), or if mere ritual counts as magical practice what is its objective, objectively speaking? It does not even suffice to *believe* magic took place (belief does not guarantee an effect; even a placebo effect) no matter what satisfaction parishioners may say they gain from the rite. Of course, there may be some kind of gain, but it is evidently religious, spiritual, or psychological, which is arguably the true purpose of the ritual. But failing the presence of any *substantive* evidence, we are compelled to see Communion as purely symbolic—it is *sublimated* "ritual anthropophagy" to be precise (Jung, 1942/1954, para. 339)—which is to say transubstantiation is not a literal transformation. Other religions hold similar (magical) beliefs, and conduct many similar practices that effectively reduce to magic without objective proof of effect.

It is noted that practitioners of sympathetic magic try to bring about effects by *intentionally* creating (imagining or acting out, with or without paraphernalia) the first half of a 'coincidence' in order to bring about (encourage, draw out, or attract) the desired second half; the *final cause*, as Aristotle would call it. This is to think in terms of the '*if* A, *then* B rule', which is 'scientific causality' by any other name, and in that guise has great appeal. In all truth, we lack a firm knowledge base that allows us to say with certainty that conscious intention is a necessary and sufficient cause or condition in any practice involving paranormal goals. Storm and Thalbourne (2005a), however, did show that change in so-called 'pro attitude' (effectively intention) resulted in a shift from a nonsignificant psi hit-rate (20%) to significant psi-hitting (30%). It should be noted that this study involved the experimental manipulation of pro attitude (intention) as an independent variable. But if anyone thought that intention could overcome all psi-inhibitive obstacles, the high 'miss' rate in parapsychology indicates otherwise (see any of the parapsychological meta-analyses listed in the previous chapter). Granted, in most studies, intention on the part of the participant and/or experimenter is only *assumed* (i.e., it may have been absent in many trails), but when intention in the form of pro attitude has been *demonstrated*, effects were sporadic (Storm, 2006, 2008b; Thalbourne & Storm, 2014). In some cases, effects are even opposite to those intended (Carpenter et al., 2021; Storm, 2022).

Going further, should we not exclude as magic any kind of paranormal effect that is nonintentional? A suite of studies looking at 'implicit anomalous cognition' (Palmer, 2015) does not suggest actual magical effects are involved since participants do not have conscious engagement in the aims and outcomes (though some might argue the experimenter does). One could also mention studies that look at implicit PK effects such as those investigated under the banner of the Global Consciousness Project (GCP; Bancel & Nelson, 2008; Nelson & Bancel, 2011). These effects are examples of an ostensibly synergistic relationship between human mental activity and environmental or societal events, although recent findings limit the effect somewhat (see Bancel, 2017a, 2017b; May & Spottiswoode, 2011a, 2011b; Nelson, 2011). Large populations are reputed to have their attention and/or emotional responses brought into focus on a single world event, and these responses are objectively recorded as correlated deviations on devices such as RNGs. Some examples of events that caused "small but statistically significant deviations" include Lady Diana's funeral in 1997, and the 911 attacks in New York City in 2001 (Nelson, 2022). But what exactly was intended? Nelson only refers to actual intention in limited cases such as laboratory testing and consciously "shared moments" (e.g., "social media gatherings for shared prayer"), but for the most part testing in the field involves protocols that do "not specify a directional intention" (Nelson). So on occasion where GCP effects are nonintentional, how are effects limited to the designated RNGs to the exclusion of other devices? What kinds of other devices might be affected, and should we be concerned? Above all, as already asked, why would magic include nonintentional psi which are covered by theories such as PMIR ('conformance behavior'), DAT, and even RSPK (discussed later in Chapter 4)? Magic as a *practiced* art surely requires intention. If, however, we concede the existence of unconscious (nonintentional) magic and equate it with implicit psi, we cannot call magic only a *practice*, and we can make the same claim for psi—any further discussion in this context is pure semantics. Of course, one's thinking might change if only those in charge of the RNG hardware in the GCP case are responsible for the effects. In that case, we might well posit orchestrated intentions from the operators.

As described, we could consider GCP outcomes (and other forms of psi for that matter) from the point of view of consciousness extension (nonlocal consciousness) which may go some way towards supporting the third proposition given by Radin (2018); namely, magic as "interaction with nonphysical entities" (p. 1). This proposition would require a proviso—'extension' *per se* has to imply more than an altered state of consciousness. There is no doubt that some theorists might say post-mortem survival is implied in extended consciousness (i.e., as a discarnate or a non-physical entity) in having psychokinetic influence or extra-sensory capacity outside the physical body (as in NDEs and OBEs). However, we cannot say whether it is magic or psi since the causal and correlational factors involving the brain and its neurophysiology during these allegedly paranormal experiences are not fully understood (see *Expanded and Extended Consciousness* in the subsection *On Model Building* in Chapter 4; see also Valencia & Froese, 2020). While better evidence for post-mortem survival is thought to come from sources that describe far more explicit effects (as indicated, for example, in mediumship research; see Braude, 2020), that evidence does not resolve the survival vs. living-agent psi debate.

Thus far, the upshot here is threefold: First, it is difficult to make a convincing case for psi as a magical process that may or may not involve information transmission and energy exchange; second, the driving principle of magic—intention—is probably no more reliable *generally speaking* than it is in psi research; and third, magic cannot account for all paranormal effects, and certainly not those outside the intentional sphere (that is, without inviting in uncontrollable, experimentally untestable, supernatural forces). On that second point, we have no experimental evidence indicating how well practitioners of magic perform in tests of magic (or psi) compared to control groups (see Ventura, 2020). But if magic is somehow different from psi (even if there is some overlap), how do we test magic *as magic* without it also being a test of psi? Those who argue for the psi/magic parallel, will say we cannot. All things being equal, however, if the psi-performance record in the extant scientific literature is any indication, then real magic must fail as often as psi fails, and for the same reasons (i.e., insufficient focus, training, or preparation, or negative influence from skeptics, etc.). Those deficiencies affect how humans do many things, not just psi and magic, so these commonalities are not a defense of the parallel. In short, we cannot expect practitioners of magic to perform beyond the natural limits that we have already seen apply to psi. This brings us to the problem of reliability.

Early on, parapsychologists became aware that psi effects always seem contingent upon one variable or another, or a cluster of variables, which spurred the hunt for moderators, modifiers, correlates, and predictors, as a means by which effects might be manifested or even strengthened. By name, many of these factors can be seen as sophisticated psychological concepts (e.g., extraversion, low neuroticism, good social adjustment, motivation, enthusiasm, sensation-seeking, transliminality,[11] etc.) that go far beyond the imaginal, thereby falling outside the scope of older (magical) discourses. From an academic standpoint, progress in this area has been highly productive, with chapter after chapter in voluminous tomes dedicated to the search for various psi-related factors (see Cardeña et al., 2015; May & Marwaha, 2015a, 2015b; Wolman, 1977). Clearly though, something is amiss, for advances have been slow. The evidence from the findings—the small (or weak) effect sizes, the relative inconsistency, the sporadic nature at the trial level in even the most successful experimental domains, and the rarity of unique spontaneous cases—makes that quite clear. Even the anecdotal cases of large-scale psi and synchronicity, and here we must also include magic, no matter how impressive (see Mishlove, 2000; Radin, 2018), do not prove the general reliability of these effects, notwithstanding the isolated exceptions (for example, see Schwartz, 2009). Thus, it is misleading and irresponsible of paranormal practitioners to claim too much for their effects, *except* that these outcomes, and their frequencies, are exactly what we can expect of synchronicity.

Unreasonable claims placed upon the paranormal originate in the *fallacy of omnipotence*—it is age-old and never better illustrated than in all forms of divination (i.e., foreseeing or seeking sanction by supernatural agency), including a whole range of practices that reduce to the reading of omens. Let us take *haruspication* (reading entrails) as an example: It was believed in Ancient Babylon, Rome, and other parts of the ancient world, that the condition of a sacrificed animal's internal organs could portend a future outcome—if the animal's bodily organ was healthy, the gods give sanction; if the animal's bodily organ was unhealthy, the gods did not give sanction. One could argue that haruspication, like magic, is an attempt to set up intentional synchronicity on the premise that 'things that are alike happen together', but the persistence of fruitless ancient practices, merely shows that practitioners of the various arts,[12] when they are overcome by powerful but misinformed beliefs and superstitious urges that cloud what reason they have, seem to have no clue about natural limits, and could care less for them (as evidenced by their rhetoric). Practices that hold their own on traditional grounds, but lack sound methodological controls and bank on chance outcomes, can translate as bilking the system, whether the practitioners know it or not.

In real terms, and to be less negative, chance (here meaning 'true randomicity') may, now and again, seem to be subverted by psi or synchronicity, but it is anybody's guess whether and when that 'subversion' will take place (and it is worth noting that we cannot be sure that 'subversion' is the mechanical process we might think it is). In short, nobody can know that moment when a 'hit' is likely (after all, psi effects, like QM phenomena, can only be determined probabilistically for large clusters of events, but cannot be determined for the unique case; more on this issue in Chapter 5). As parapsychologist Richard Broughton (2018) has said of the Remote Viewing program run by the US government and its agencies, and equally applicable to private research establishments,

> … psi could be useful.… Psi does not enter the picture as some sort of magic power … The take-home message is that *psi isn't magic.*
>
> (p. 3)

Broughton's sobering statement ("*psi isn't magic*") means paranormal research does not come with a guarantee of its hypothesized outcomes, but the quote can also be taken in a pejorative sense. Broughton could also mean that the psi effect *per se* cannot be bolstered *mechanistically* by magical practices (i.e., through the deployment of rituals and oaths, with or without the use of aids such as amulets, talismans, sigils, etc.). At best, these are more likely to induce knock-on psychological (placebo) effects rather than hold causal powers in their own right. Indeed, the somewhat postmodern spin of so-called 'chaos magicians' prioritizes the role of belief, and puts little stock in supernatural force *per se* (Carroll, 1987; Hine, 1993). To some extent, this understanding even aligns with the parapsychologist's findings that paranormal belief (e.g., the sheep-goat effect)[13] has a noted influence on psi outcomes. As an aside, the pivotal, psi-conducive role of paranormal *belief*—the very embodiment of intention—puts a question mark over the literature that finds paranormal believers need clinical attention (e.g., Lilienfeld, Ammirati, & David, 2012; McLean & Miller, 2010). It is as good a place as any to raise this issue here, for although *some* paranormal believers may *tend* to have poor working memory (Dudley, 1999), or schizotypal ideation (Hergovich, Schott, & Arendasy, 2008), or may even *tend* to suffer from delusions, psychosis and schizophrenia (Cella, Vellante, & Preti, 2012; Houran & Lange, 2004), these findings are not always confirmed (Irwin, 2009). And it should be noted that when there are viable (significant) associations, they are often only slight, meaning it can be a stretch to claim paranormal believers have these 'tendencies' (for an evaluation of such issues, see Thalbourne & Storm, 2019).

Ultimately, one needs to go further than arguing whether the 'psi = magic' equation has any merit for parapsychology (or it is a tricksterish folly) for, as much as we would prefer otherwise, human will-power (e.g., wishful or magical thinking) ultimately cannot raise psi outcomes to the same levels of reliability found in the manufacturing industry, and I come to this reliability issue for good reason because of the critical misunderstanding about reliability when related to statistical dispersion. These days, refined production processes ensure extremely low rates of product defect (a.k.a. 'nonconformance') based on specification limits set to six-sigma (6σ) deviations from the optimal standard of quality.[14] Six Sigma processes are highly accurate (e.g., 99.9997% accurate or 3.4 defects per million opportunities if a control limit is set to 4.5σ).[15] These values are determined using various statistical techniques and production procedures too detailed to go into here. That aside, the 6σ performance criterion, which translates as approximately one defect in a billion, is effectively hypothetical (only realistic in the short term, whereas 4.5σ is normative for the long term). Needless to say, such standards border on the unattainable, and have attracted heavy criticism (Bartok, 2018; Crosby, 1996, 1999; Tennant, 2001).

The pertinence of 6σ to parapsychology comes from the fact that (for example) meta-analytically determined values as extreme, and greater, across many different experimental domains, are touted as proofs of psi beyond dispute.[16] These values certainly indicate rarity (see again, Rawlette, 2019a), but if one did not know better, one might think that reports of '6σ plus' in psi research puts parapsychological findings on par with industry standards, giving rise to the impression that psi is reliable and even replicable on demand, with seldom a failure. To think that way is fallacious, and certainly not simply because it might be argued that a sample only needs to be sufficiently large to produce psi effects. It is clear that psi effects are taken seriously by many mainstream scientists (see Cardeña, 2014), and practical applications have been demonstrated in the field (Harary & Targ, 1985; Schouten, 1994; Schwartz, 2000, 2005), but reliability levels fall short of expectations, inside and outside parapsychological circles (Irwin, 2014), which is not the problem faced by industry. This is because 6σ in industry has an entirely different meaning than it does in parapsychology. In industry, for all practical purposes, the value can be viewed as indicating an extreme *failure* rate (i.e., acceptable *defect* rate) never likely to be reached, thus guaranteeing a high degree of reliability; in parapsychology, 6σ represents the opposite and implies a *success* rate, or (to be more precise) a result so extreme that a chance explanation can be ruled out in favour of an anomaly (presumed to be psi), but which has nothing to do with its reliability.

As an example, meta-analysis of the successful ganzfeld design for the period 1974 to 2018 reached a monumental 8σ (Storm & Tressoldi, 2020). The hit rate was 31% (where chance would be 25%), calculated from a multiple-study (accumulated) hit rate of 1188 out of 3885 trials. The 8σ estimate comes from a so-called Binomial Exact *Z* score for that ratio of hits across a total of 114 ganzfeld studies that used a four-choice design. The figure is not a reliability indicator at the study-level, or a warning to researchers to expect very rare psi-missing, but it is a strong statistical justification for a conclusion that cannot be given for any single study on its own (i.e., multiple cases of weak evidence are combined to yield strong evidence). Statistician and parapsychologist Jessica Utts (1999) explains the problem at the single study level in terms of repeatability: "ganzfeld experiments of the size typically conducted should not be "successful" very often, even if the true effect is that the target can be correctly guessed about a third of the time" (p. 631). The same reasoning applies at the trial level, but in regard to studies (the more important criterion in parapsychology), we see that 28% of ganzfeld studies were independently significant, meaning 72% produced purely chance results and, as far as trial counts are concerned, sample sizes vary from under 10 to well over 100 with no clue given as to ideal sample size or ideal number of trials (although some specific recommendations have been made; see Baptista, Derakhshani, & Tressoldi,

2015). It is due to outcomes like this that psi and synchronicity should be equated because psi is not as “constant and reproducible” (Jung, 1952/1969, para. 965) as we would like to think (see also Palmer, 2008, for similar opinions). Ganzfeld psi is more like synchronicity in its sporadic and unpredictable form at the trial- and study-level, but the main lesson to be learnt here is that typically low *success* rates in psi research cannot be legitimately contrasted with an industry standard like 6σ (one-in-a-billion), which refers to an extremely low *failure* rate, and therefore a very high degree of *reliability*.

Of course, in protest, parapsychologists might argue that the comparison was never meant in that sense. Conventional thinking in parapsychological circles is more in line with that of physicists who very much depend on their ‘discovery’ criterion of 5σ. As if to break their own rule, they frequently make headline news claiming discoveries of new particles at 3σ or 4σ that sometimes prove to be nothing more than “statistical fluctuations” (Sabine Hossenfelder, 2021, gives examples). Early in ganzfeld research, sigmas were at those levels. Physicists and parapsychologists do put great faith in the idea of big numbers (extreme sigmas) being too big to ignore and declare they must stand for some kind of legitimate discovery. They would also be quick to claim they do *not* use the sigma criterion to suggest their disciplines have adopted industry standards, but it *is* a standard of sorts where bigger is seen as better. It is all very misleading for, in parapsychology, mean effect sizes are not increasing; only the sigmas increase as data accumulates. We have to keep in mind that sigma is used purely as a reference to a chance result if the Null hypothesis of no effect was true. That is the correct interpretation of sigma, but the misleading side effect of a very large sigma is not simply that it eliminates chance as an explanation; it makes rarity (intermittency) look good.

In fairness to parapsychologists, they explain intermittency as being due to generally small effect sizes (or *vice versa*), and why should that be a problem? There are examples in medical research where much smaller effects are taken very seriously, and have profound social impact. For example, on ethical grounds, the National Heart, Lung, and Blood Institute (DeMets et al., 1984; Kolata, 1981) discontinued a propranolol study nine months ahead of schedule because of the clear benefits of propranolol on patients with a recent myocardial infarction, even though the effects were reported to be weak (for other examples, see Spencer, 1995). Cases like this cast parapsychological research in a justifiably comparable and favourable light, but the ambiguity in the various figures (highly significant but weak effect sizes due to low success rates, which translate as high failure rates)—quite common in the psi-research meta-analyses—sends out a mixed message. Actually, it is a two-pronged message, the first, subtler message being that psi (as just mentioned) is more like synchronicity than many might care to admit. Certain defining characteristics of synchronicity also define psi, but little to no attention is given to them; specifically, affectivity (i.e., the emotional factor) is an important criterion, and it ties in with motivation and enthusiasm, all of which are triggered by anticipated (hoped-for) meaningful outcomes. Underlying that entire process is the possible constellation of the archetype. These contingent factors are difficult (though not impossible) to implement—so psi (i.e., synchronicity) remains weak due to its natural rarity and its cousin the high fail-rate.

The second, more salient message concerns the way in which one *views* the findings of the experimental domains—increasingly larger datasets might boost sigma, but nothing changes at the study level or the trial level. In the end, one's *view* will be contextually dependent on whether one habitually sees the proverbial glass as half-empty or half-full (or about 1/3-full and 2/3-empty in the ganzfeld case). But viewpoint or context alone cannot resolve the pragmatic (methodological) issues of parapsychological practice. These practices, though they have some limited applications, have not reached that stage where psi, *as a product*, meets industry standards in the formal sense. Some psi-pundits will think otherwise, and for that reason, we see the Trickster in full force once again. To shore-up this point, see the examples from Associational Remote Viewing research in Storm (2025).

The Trick of the Cause in Parapsychology

If we are to avoid steering science in a direction it does not need to take we have to be cognizant of the fact that mixing personal or consensus biases with objective findings must surely make science more mythological than it has to be. In science, including parapsychology, there is a burgeoning need for the concept of causality; it does not suffice to find evidence of an effect without knowing what caused the effect. Take, for example, the persistence of, or even the obsession with, Rhine's causative concepts ESP and PK right up to the present day that leaves a number of parapsychologists looking askance at such a thing as an *acausal* connecting principle (i.e., synchronicity). In this regard, Irwin and Watt (2007) make a good point about many scientists being "so wedded to explanations in terms of physical and mechanical causes that the teleological [goal-oriented] approach is unlikely to appeal …" (p. 133). Indeed, the skepticism, indifference, and even prejudice, is evident over the decades in the meagre synchronistic research output mentioned in the Introduction, coupled with a sporadic stream of commentaries, reviews, and theoretical nut-cracking (e.g., Beloff, 1977; Braude, 1979; Eisenbud, 1977, as cited in Kelly & Tucker, 2015; Nachman, 2010; Stokes, 1987; Vaughan, 1979). For all their sincerity, some of it advances our understanding very little if at all, even when it is pro-synchronistic (e.g., Vaughan, 1979), while others conveniently preserve the status quo (e.g., Beloff, 1990). In this regard, Beloff hides nothing:

> … *if* Jung is right in subsuming all paranormal phenomena under the principle of synchronicity, then experimental parapsychology becomes a contradiction in terms. This seems to me to be a good enough reason for thinking he must be wrong.… synchronicity is a concept which has wandered by mistake into psychical research.… meaningful coincidences … make little sense applied to real life …"
>
> (Beloff, 1990, p. 23)

Beloff may be dissuasive to some, but he is clearly uninformed, even in 1990 when there were four studies I can find (Braud, 1983; Jung, 1952/1969; Rubin & Honorton, 1971, 1972) that might have given him cause to rethink his position.[17] And therapeutically, the examples of meaningful coincidences making profound sense in 'real life' are manifold (indeed, I have given a number of examples in previous chapters).

Oddly, Beloff seemed sympathetic to synchronicity at an earlier time when he spoke of its contribution to parapsychology in positive terms (1977, pp. 581-582). Yet Beloff (1990) seems very much consumed by the philosophical problem of synchronicity—on the premise that synchronicity is acausal, he did not think it could be tested in the laboratory. It seemed, at least at some point in time, that his aim was more than to wrench ESP and PK away from synchronicity. He is partly correct in finding Jung in error, for Jung naïvely saw synchronicity *and* psi as concepts that jarred with the harsh reality of "mechanistic causality" (p. 22)—and Jung *was*, after all, in a quandary over some spurious empirical differences between psi and synchronicity (Jung, 1952/1969, para. 965). These issues may have fed Beloff's criticism, but his concern over the word 'acausal' should have subsided at this stage. Instead, Beloff (because of the way he argues) prejudices synchronicity by fitting only psi into a *scientifically causal* model (i.e., psi is an effect with a cause). In such a schema, psi would equally be described as having functional causality in the sense Russell (1953) means where there is not necessarily a deterministic causal law at work. Beloff accepted this 'post-Humean' necessity, especially because it happens to work conveniently for parapsychology: A "sufficient condition" is all that is needed; psi follows the '*if* A, *then* B rule', so psi is causal (Beloff, 1990, pp. 22–23).

Beloff (1990) could have embraced synchronicity, by (ironically) taking what he calls a "post-Humean" (causal) view as his launch point; all he needed to do was bend a little, for what that would have been worth, which is not a whole lot. For a start, causal terminology in the modern scientific sense is often hardly clear or specific; and can certainly have no explanatory power—even the associations it furnishes are only helpful in prompting the right questions as to *process*. For example, few would disagree that synchronicity requires the right conditions (the contingent archetype) for it to happen, just like psi with its various conditions. But synchronicity (and psi for that matter) still remains unexplained; its under-riding phenomenology, its fundamentals, remain obscure, and that is why no theory in parapsychology has cracked the problem of psi or synchronicity because causes *per se* have never been identified, and nor can they be if what we *think* is happening is not what is *actually* happening. When we speak of a 'functional cause', all we mean is we *might* be able to replicate or reproduce the effect if we do exactly what we did last time because the '*if* A, *then* B rule' works so well. So why fight it? But the situation is the same for psi which Beloff accepts so easily. I suggest Beloff thought of synchronicity in terms of the acausal unique case, but he did not see the bigger picture and give synchronicity the same degree of leniency he gave psi. Beloff would never have endorsed a unique psi event on its own merits (especially an ambiguous one); he would never have vouched for a psychic's psi claim on the mere say-so of that psychic; he *would* have demanded repeated testing in a controlled environment.

It is here that my point above about bias becomes relevant. For scientists, causes are all-important in the various fields; so much so that they must always try to find ways to make acausal phenomena manageable, and one way they do this is to change the definition of 'cause'. For example, Physicist Roger G. Newton (1967, 1970) runs a correlational argument: "the only foolproof method of scientifically testing a *causal connection* between *A* and *B* is "wiggling" one of them and watching the response of the other" (p. 1571). He also noted:

> The notion of cause and effect is defined by invariant (or statistical) correlation of the latter with the former.... The temporal order of the two is an *observational* fact. We may not believe that new experiments will ever find effects that precede their causes, but if they do causality itself is not thereby endangered.
>
> (Newton, 1967, p. 1274)

So a proven correlation *indicates* causality? Not so; at best, it may only *imply* causality, and ideally a search should be made for same.

While Jung wanted to treat acausal phenomena as a category in its own right, scientists prefer to describe some phenomena as 'indeterminate', or 'unpredictable' (e.g., nuclear decay in the single event), or 'spooky' (e.g., entanglement), but the word 'acausal' does not really serve a purpose. Of course scientists do test acausal phenomena (e.g., the discontinuities of modern physics, radioactivity), but they do it by grouping individual events in a large-scale statistical framework, thereby generating models, just as parapsychologists do when they test psi. Here I agree with Palmer (2008) on synchronicity:

> Any general, nomothetic principles one can glean from Jung's writings can serve as hypotheses to be tested by conventional scientific methods.
>
> (p. 188)

And Palmer describes ways in which synchronicity can be tested by parapsychologists. And that is where Beloff missed his opportunity. While Jung and Beloff held counter-positions, and each argued their own point of view, they both failed to see that *both* types of phenomena (causal *and* acausal) can be tested scientifically. As we have seen, physicists do it all the time.

The *principle* behind scientific causality is extremely accommodating, even to synchronicity (see Storm, 2008a, especially pp. 268-269), and Beloff (2008)[18] seems to have intuited this—he insisted synchronicity must be causal at some level (though again his bias shows): "... any system which admits of synchronistic correspondences tends to suggest, even if it does not logically imply, a causal origin for the system as a whole" (p. 102). This admission comes close to the idea that nondeterministic (acausal) relationships exist by being bound together *holistically*, but again (and somewhat tediously) the admission suggests for Beloff that synchronicity must ultimately have a cause. Thus, I see Beloff as missing the point again. Perhaps, to be gracious, a well-meaning Beloff, sympathetic to the idea of synchronicity by his own admission, thought it best to leave Jung alone with his 'big idea'—that synchronicity is underpinned *acausally* by archetypal arrangements that form part of a holistic, psychoid reality:

> As soon as [one] perceives the archetypal background [one] is tempted to trace the mutual assimilation of independent psychic and physical processes back to a (causal) effect of the archetype, and thus to overlook the fact that they are merely contingent.
>
> (Jung, 1952/1969, para. 965)

Although Jung sets causality and contingence apart, the word "contingent" might have set alarm bells ringing for Beloff, just as it did for Palmer (2008):

> "Contingent" means causal in the Humean sense. In this sense, synchronicities are causal virtually by definition.
>
> (p. 185)

However, I would suggest the 'Humean sense' can be over-applied in that typical scientific way already discussed—while the archetype is *contingent*, that does not make it a *cause*, but it could be seen as *correlational* in cases where its 'presence' is observed in the synchronistic 'mix'. The idea of testing archetypes in the lab may therefore be possible, but that will not make causes of them because they do not function like causes—put simply, they do not always deliver. On the one hand, the archetype by Jung's (1952/1969) definition (para. 965) cannot be elevated to the level of a cause: As von Franz (1992) has said: "... something synchronistic might happen when an archetype is constellated" (p. 27). On the other hand, by the very meaning of the word 'cause', a cause is always the reason something happens. As prerequisites or qualifiers for synchronicity, they provide a context that some might (mistakenly) read as a causal relationship, but as Flew (1953) noted, archetypes "show why certain concurrences are found striking, pointed, meaningful, even numinous" (p. 201). Like any effect, there are obviously *conditions* required for synchronicity to take place.

Ultimately, Beloff (2008) is slavish to his philosophical outlook and concludes: "If synchronicity is indeed a truth of nature then it is just one of those truths which may never be known to be true" (p. 107); so synchronicity has "wandered by mistake into psychical research" (Beloff, 1990, p. 23). Beloff's philosophical pigeon-holing of synchronicity, even if he thought it was appropriate, only served to marginalize it and certainly did not help to advance parapsychology.

Again, there is more than semantics at play over these words ('cause', 'contingency'), but it does seem the issue is largely over meanings. What may be difficult to settle is whether this semantic aspect is tricksterish nonsense or grounds for valid inquiry. One can look at the causality/acausality issue from other perspectives, and there are no doubt other ways to treat the problem. My past attempts to resolve the issue, was to play the same semantic game, and coin the term 'metacause' as a compromise between a 'scientific cause' *per se* and something merely *contingent* and *accidental* in the sense that Mansfield et al. (1998) use the terms ("the psychological and physical correlates [in synchronicity] are contingent and accidental"; p. 21),[19] so as not to commit the 'bad habit', as Hume calls it, of nominating *as a cause* anything remotely resembling a cause just to satisfy a scientific need (for further comment on this issue, see Storm, 2008a, pp. 264–265, 267).

For the reader's sake, and to expand on the causality conundrum, I present one final example from the literature—that same article by Mansfield et al. (1998), to which I refer out of convenience since I have previously highlighted some of its key points (see also Storm, 2008d). The Mansfield et al. article came many years after Beloff's 1963 presentation at the SPR (the latter of which ended up as a chapter in Beloff's book of 1990), and one might have thought the thinking would have changed since then, but it hardly budged. Mansfield et al. aimed to keep psi away from synchronicity, in agreement with Beloff, but Mansfield et al. do refer to psi as being part of Jung's general acausal orderedness. They go further and say synchronicity is *acausal* no matter what:

> since synchronicity is a sporadic, nonrepeatable expression of the *Unus Mundus*, the unitary ground underlying both matter and psyche, it is both historically acausal and "scientifically acausal." Thus, Jung appropriately emphasized the completely acausal aspect of synchronicity.
>
> (p. 15)

It is unfortunate that the debate here is centred on the unique case, but overlooks testing multiples of essentially unique cases within a statistical framework—that distinction might have helped settle the issue. Even so, the implication is there—Mansfield et al. differ from Beloff (1990) in that they turn their case on its head and concede the possibility of experimental synchronicity, and even claim that, with sufficient rigor and extensive consultation, it "would be done most convincingly" (p. 23), thus agreeing with Palmer, though Palmer equates contingence with cause (Mansfield et al. do not). But one wonders about Mansfield et al.'s conviction if they are able to make such a concession so late in their article—more to the point, and by their own admission, they clearly have no problem thinking *scientifically acausal* synchronicity can be tested experimentally (which I take to mean statistically)! What we see is Mansfield et al. undermining Beloff at a level so very fundamental to the latter's argument, while still agreeing with him on the necessary split between psi and synchronicity.

I shall now take a moment to reflect personally on the points I have made: Guided by my reading, and my work on the *I Ching*, I suggest only one of the following is correct: (a) Beloff is right to "eliminate" (p. 22) synchronicity from the laboratory because *acausal* phenomena cannot be tested; or (b) Beloff was philosophical *to a fault* and synchronicity *can* be tested in the laboratory because it is scientifically *causal*; or (c) synchronicity is scientifically acausal *but* is still testable.

Position (a) means I have never tested synchronicity (meaningful coincidence), and neither has anyone else. However, that reasoning and (a) are most likely untrue because large-scale statistical frameworks accommodate unpredictable single events when they occur *en masse*, as any parapsychologist or physicist will attest. Synchronicity thus fits the bill. Also, everything else I have claimed thus far about the psi/synchronicity parallel means (a) must be dismissed. That leaves (b) and (c).

Position (b) highlights the semantics involved in the pursuit of the truth about causality and acausality: The '*if* A, *then* B rule' necessarily means correlations can serve as the grounds for proposing scientific (functional) causes—the physicist already agrees with this rationale, and researchers like von Lucadou (2019) make prime examples of correlations in their MPI approach. But (b) misleads: There is always someone in research who will remind us that correlation does not imply causation; correlations do not even *point* to causes necessarily. Given my critique of Beloff's arguments, and in agreement with Mansfield et al. (1998) on experimental synchronicity, I necessarily abandon (b) because I feel the defense of synchronicity as necessarily scientifically causal (which, more broadly, is to defend scientific causality) offers very little if we are on the hunt for 'fundamentals'. That is why I aligned 'scientific causality' with 'magical causality' given that the pretences under-riding both lead to models but not explanations (see 'Magic, Reliability, and Six Sigma' in this chapter). The same goes for the 'fundamentals' in physics—scientific causality is a convenience that goes only so far. But I must be clear: Using the term *acausal* as I do is not done on ideological grounds or on the basis of a philosophical principle, for the term goes beyond ideology and philosophy—the kinds of acausal phenomena listed as part of Jung's general acausal orderedness substantiate that case, and apart from synchronicity and psi, these include astrological effects, microphysical phenomena (e.g., quantum discontinuities of modern physics—see Chapter 5), the ordering principles of the natural numbers (i.e., number properties), and the observable effects of the constants in nature (e.g., the gravitational constant G; the velocity of light c; and Planck's constant h).

Thus, I feel the only viable option is (c)—synchronicity is testable but scientifically acausal because it is built on the archetypes being contingent rather than causal, as Jung (1952/1959, para. 965) has said all along. This claim also eliminates the problem of regression to *magical causality* when we wish to explain synchronicity (see Palmer, 2008, p. 186). The same applies to psi—we must abandon the idea that people cause psychic effects with their special ability. While Palmer sees this as a tactical manoeuvre on Jung's part, Jung merely wishes to avoid ascribing to the psyche "a power that far exceeds its empirical range of action" (1952/1969, para. 915). Given all we know about the fallibility of psi and *intentional* synchronicity (e.g., the kind of synchronicity a 'knowing' individual *intends* when they use the *I Ching*), Jung is hardly speaking out of turn, but does describe the facts precisely.

Fear of Psi and Fear of No Psi

In 1775, the English essayist and moralist, Samuel Johnson, said "patriotism is the last refuge of a scoundrel" (Boswell, 1799, p. 348), by which is meant some people feel they have the right to say and do just about anything, no matter how abhorrent, in the service of a higher purpose, whether that purpose be driven by a belief in God and country, a political agenda, or good old-fashioned religious zeal. Some critics have argued that Johnson only had false patriotism in mind, which only begs the important question, What actions should be tolerated in the name of any kind of patriotism, true or false? The complex issue of deciding where the line should be drawn in defense of one's beliefs brings me to my point: When it comes to our deeply held values and ideals, the best, but often the worst, can be brought out in us in defense of these values and ideals.

In the context of psi, particularly belief in it (or not), we often see defensive volleys played out in the various electronic media manifesting as heated exchanges between opposing groups. And let us not forget the biased literature one would think mostly targets those already converted, given the arguments are often so gapingly flawed. On occasion, it would seem that a given party does not get a fair hearing; or blocks are put up to what would ordinarily be considered a persuasive argument. Thereby, parapsychologists (or at least those parapsychologists who believe) have every right to complain that skeptics do not give them the benefit of the doubt. But consider how skeptics see believers—they'd be right in wondering why cold-, warm-, and hot-reading,[20] and phoney spiritualism, fake mediumship, and sham metal-bending often get support from believers. And let us not forget that many an astute believer, who has little or no direct psi experience, seems easily convinced by paper after paper filled with statistics-based content (a large proportion of it *post hoc*), or inadequately argued theoretical musings. Granted, it is often observed that the most vocal of the hard-line closed-minded skeptics do not have a clue how science is done, and those who have some inkling still present distorted interpretations and lie about the facts by omission and commission (Gardner, 1981; Hansel, 1980; Randi, 1980). Yet in spite of all the problems and the biases, it seems both sides do often present a valid case.

I must acknowledge, though, the insurmountable evidence suggesting it is the "psi-censors" who would hunt down psi believers to conceptual extinction if they had half the chance, and we can gauge this from their various reprehensible actions in academia (Cardeña, 2015, covers this problem quite well). In this section, I am not going to argue who is off-side, skeptic or believer, though I have my suspicions—in fact, in a follow-up article to Cardeña's (2018) psi-supportive article, skeptics Reber and Alcock (2020) are negative to the extreme, mocking in their tone, and mostly misinformed (in fairness, where they may be right does little damage to the field). That aside, I am compelled to say there are none so blind as those who will not see, and both parties are often oblivious to their own unacceptable and unproductive attitudes and behaviours. Too often do we see the obvious signs of intolerance, ranging from vituperation and *ad hominem* attacks to open hostility, and we see it coming from both sides—from skeptics *and* psi believers (including afterlife believers). These volleys are not simply off-the-cuff verbal abuses and assaults that could be blamed on the heat of the moment; they are also matters of record painstakingly crafted by respondents, self-appointed critics, and aficionados who have had plenty of time to think about their remarks before they publish or post. In all truth, they really mean what they say, and they make no bones about how they say it.

In the academic world, where cooler heads supposedly prevail, one might have thought that these behaviours do not exist, or are rare. In fact, it is mostly academia that I am targeting, but I would wager their behaviours are just as frequent in the pseudo-intellectual and lay communities. Discretion prevents me from citing examples of both types, but a basic Internet search can lead the interested reader in the right direction. I will let Delin (1972/2002) summarize the two positions:

> The sceptic is accused of bolstering up a system in which he has high status, of pandering to the repressive demands of governmental authority, of willful blindness. The believer is accused of fabricating data; of pretending to believe in order to jump onto a financial bandwagon; of striking back at the scientific 'club' he has not been able to join; of being a deliberate agent for chaos. The atmosphere becomes charged with personal descriptions ranging from pig-headedness through stupidity to insanity.
>
> (1972/2002, p. 31)

There is some truth to all of these statements, and statements of that ilk not captured in the above quote. But what is the source of the outrage from both sides? In the case of skeptics, their reactions are usually thought to be drawn from their fear of psi. Indeed, for the Trickster, nothing works better than fear on so many levels—it clouds judgement; it disorients thinking; it drives prejudice; it encourages intolerance, and it propagates disharmony. Noticeably, fear can also destabilize certainty, but the best salve for doubt is a fanatical disregard of the facts. Fear of this type has received considerable attention (Carter, 2012). There are even autobiographical accounts of this fear (Mayer, 2007). Believers, however, also have a fear; it is fear of *no* psi, and the same tricksterish consequences apply.

But why is there so much fear? That depends on who you ask. For the skeptic, there's a lot to fear: if psi is real, how far can it extend? What if it cannot be controlled? How will the skeptic's deepest secrets remain hidden if psi is unleashed? What happens to the skeptics' worldview; their fundamental beliefs and philosophy, their science, their picture of reality if irrational forces like psi and superstition gain the ascendancy? For the believer, there is much to fear too: if psi is *not* real, how are those anomalous experiences to be explained—are they hallucinations, delusions, chance? What happens to their worldview, their fundamental beliefs and philosophy, their picture of reality if only cold reason and hard logic explain the world, and only rationalism and deterministic rules decide one's fate?

Fear of psi, however, also comes to some psi believers who fear they may become victims of dangerous irrational forces when they do experience psi (for an example, see Braude, 2008). Tart (1984) discusses this kind of fear, and recognizes it in parapsychologists as well, though they may fail to acknowledge it. Tart even offers solutions to this fear.[21] Of course, the skeptic would dearly love to put all these believers right because it is a fear they share: 'It's not psi', they may say, 'but believers *are* gripped by irrational forces alright; all of them in their heads!'

Surprisingly, not only can some skeptics have a manifested fear of psi; some may have a fear of *no* psi, but the fear of *no* psi lies dormant, for the most part, as a conflation of two kinds of unconscious doubt. I am not being unduly schematic here just to cover all four bases (say, in a 2 × 2 contingency table of believers and skeptics, some with 'fear of psi' and some with 'fear of no psi'), for it is a standard understanding in psychology (Jung, 1946/1979, para. 156; Schreiner, 2016) that extreme reaction ('fanaticism') tends to come from unconscious doubt, and where there is doubt, we might expect fear to grow. The first doubt, when manifested consciously, is seen as an inkling in the skeptic's mind that there might be some truth to the psi hypothesis (hence, ironically, the fear that psi might not exist), for something stirring in the depths echoes exactly the same sentiment as that of the believer; namely, that reason and logic are not sufficient to understand all aspects of the universe and all that it contains. We have discovered that quantum and cosmological facts defy reason and logic (and when I say 'we', I mean skeptics too). And we are discovering that certain aspects of human functioning may be no different: for example, Tressoldi, Storm, and Radin (2010) have given examples of "experimental evidence suggesting that some human cognitive abilities are better explained using quantum rather than classical formalisms" (p. S82). And since we are met with the impossible claim that no one understands (say) QM, and skeptics are beginning to discover all this, they begin to see that anomalous factors (even acausal ones) are real.

But following up with the second doubt, we can expect these skeptics to be disturbed by the consequences of an epistemological and philosophical gap if these anomalous factors do *not* exist, for unless that gap is filled, a full appreciation of reality can never be reached (in an imponderable universe even a questionable anomaly trumps a groundless superstition): Indeed researchers in the field of QM will tell us that this anomalous dimension of reality is here to stay; not only is there no getting around it, there is also no way of understanding it (see Campbell, 2007, for statements to that effect). These unconscious stirrings and scientific facts can create cognitive dissonance for skeptics, some of whom hasten to suppress it in order to save face with their less-aware peers. That is why the more vehement skeptics continue to behave as they do—the greater the denial of the anomalies, the greater the posturing, and we begin to see that they even "protest too much", to borrow from Shakespeare's (1601/1993) *Hamlet* (III.ii.239). Scratch deep enough, and all are believers under the skin—even truculent skeptics.

While these fears come from the consequences of how one processes the concept of psi, I suggest the one fear that stands out above all others (indeed, underpins them to some extent) is the fear of being wrong because so much of our self-image and even our ontological make-up is tied up in being right. This fear has a strong egotistical aspect, for to be right is to have the angels on one's side, to be favoured, to be chosen, but to be wrong is to be inadequate, to lack credibility, to be outcast, to be on the wrong team, to have backed the wrong horse. These attitudes should not impede the progress of science, but they do. All these fears, on both sides, embodied in those questions already asked, look like they are fuelled by good old-fashioned insecurity; the incessant desire to be right is an attempt to quash fear and insecurity out of existence in one fell swoop. Of course, neither the believer nor the nonbeliever believes they are wrong, and players hardly ever switch camps—rare examples of academics who started out as believers but became skeptics include Susan Blackmore (1985) and Douglas Stokes (2015); true skeptics who became believers include William James (1897), Carl Sagan (Schwartz, 2023), and possibly Wolfgang Pauli (as cited in Stapp, 2009, pp. 149–150),[22] but even well-known skeptic Michael Shermer (2014), publisher of *Skeptic* magazine, made concessions as only a believer would. Consider his response on the day of his wedding when confronted with a reinvigorated 'dead' radio belonging to his wife's deceased grandfather. On the big day, Shermer's wife Jennifer had wished her grandfather could give her away, but then the radio that Shermer had tried very hard to repair, started to play romantic music, this happened:

> That can't be what I think it is, can it?" she said. She opened the desk drawer and pulled out her grandfather's transistor radio, out of which a romantic love song wafted. We sat in stunned silence for minutes. "My grandfather is here with us," Jennifer said, tearfully. "I'm not alone."
>
> (Shermer, 2014)

Jennifer is just as much a skeptic, says Shermer, but importantly, he had no qualms advising readers of *Scientific American* that we keep an "open mind" and recognize the "significance" of such emotionally laden experiences; he even noted that "we should not shut the doors of perception when they may be opened to us to marvel in the mysterious."

I already made this point, but consider again the paradoxical situation where "the similarity between the two types [the sceptic and the believer] is far greater than either would care to acknowledge" (Delin, 1972/2002, p. 31). How does Delin justify this claim?

> The fact is that a position of scepticism is one that stands in need of justification as does a position of belief, and there is often as capricious a basis for the sceptic's disbelief as for the believer's credulity. In exactly the same way as the credulous person sometimes seems to go out of his way to find extraordinary

> things to believe in, the sceptical person often seems to be trying very hard to find things in which to disbelieve, and to modify his perceptions accordingly.
> (p. 34)

These actions, loaded with purpose and seemingly necessary, such as going out of one's way to "find extraordinary things to believe [or disbelieve] in", suggest a desire to stay convinced that one is not wrong, rather than be persuaded that the other might be right. To do this, one must amass evidence; and to do that, one must not only depend on the literature (which I comment on shortly), one must also be on the lookout for new forms and types of psi phenomena to believe in or debunk. And this staunch attitude, this tenacity and adamantine wilfulness, brings us back to doubt, and with it, the insecurity and the fear.

It may be possible to get to the crux of these fears by considering the issue of belief a little more closely. Since the time Delin first published his article, a great deal of research has been conducted into paranormal belief ostensibly suggesting that both types are not as similar as he proposed. Australian parapsychologist Harvey Irwin (1993, 2009) outlined four hypotheses that help explain paranormal belief as being attributable to one or any of these in combination: *social marginalization* (believers are isolated by age, gender, socioeconomic status, ethnicity, or culture, etc., whereas belief acts as a buffer to life's difficulties); *worldview* (paranormal belief is a subjective and esoteric aspect of a much broader picture of life, humanity, and the world in general); *cognitive deficits* (believers are said to have uncritical, naïve, and irrational thought processes based on deficits in education, low IQ, and poor reasoning skills); and *psychodynamic dysfunction* (paranormal belief fills a need for those seen as psychologically disadvantaged or maladapted, or socially deviant). Of course, if paranormal belief is validly explained or predicted by the correlates that come under these hypotheses, it logically follows that the same correlates explain non-belief (i.e., disbelief), under the assumption that believer and nonbeliever are polar opposites (see Irwin, Dagnall, & Drinkwater, 2017, for the same argument). However, these explanations for paranormal belief are not always tenable, and when there is statistical evidence, the effects are invariably weak to moderate in strength, meaning that the numerous correlates (so-called predictors) explain very little of the range in scores on the various belief measures.

What is good for the goose is good for the gander, and if belief cannot be adequately explained by these hypotheses, then neither can disbelief. While some degree of explanatory power *is* offered by these hypotheses, we still do not know the extent to which fear influences belief/disbelief—we only know the fears may be there. To put it another way, if the evidence explaining the sources of belief and disbelief is sparse, then there is not a strong argument for situating the various belief-related fears in those same sources. One can see how easy it is to be misled by research findings, and I have commented on this aspect of paranormal belief research when I drew attention to the fact that some paranormal believers are not necessarily following a cultural trend, or expressing easily exposed fanciful or popular notions (see also Jinks, 2012); they may be *sufficiently informed* and have a genuine understanding of paranormal phenomena not at all dependent on worldview, or for that matter, on the various hypothesized deficits, dysfunctions, and disorders. As my colleagues and I have said:

> Conventional procedures do not identify this [informed] type, possibly because the [experimental] designers do not concede its likelihood.… there may be subtle differences among paranormal believers, especially those who are high-scoring, but investigators do not seek out those differences.
>
> (Storm, Drinkwater, & Jinks, 2017, p. 224)

It may be a timely coincidence that the parapsychological equivalent of stalemate has been diplomatically proposed, at least in academia:

> many professional parapsychologists who believe in the reality of paranormal processes base their endorsement primarily on a reading of the literature on experimental psi research. There may be a key proof-oriented investigation they find persuasive, or the cumulative record of numerous independent psi experiments may be deemed to show such sound methodology and internal coherence that the reality of the paranormal is said to be an inescapable inference.
>
> (Irwin, Dagnall, & Drinkwater, 2012, p. 107; see also Irwin et al., 2017, for similar comments)

But,

> some sceptical academics may claim to base their *disbelief* in the paranormal on their own critical scrutiny of the very same literature. In either case, however, beliefs about psi would seem to be grounded, at least in part, in a careful rational analysis of available evidence.
>
> (p. 107)

These statements only speak to the surface issue of how believer and skeptic think because it looks to me like they are arguing over whether the glass is half full or half empty, but it is exactly how scientists think that gets to the heart of the more pertinent issue: the fears. It may be worth arguing for a stalemate, in that it might eventually lead to tolerance (i.e., acceptance of diverse multiple viewpoints), which may more easily be effected once those doubts and insecurities mentioned above are better managed, or even dissolved. That eventuality may allay the fears, but it seems more likely that a stalemate amongst academics will translate as intellectual ping-pong that society will see as indecisiveness.

Or perhaps it would be better to break the stalemate by changing our scientific thinking, which is tantamount to changing our epistemological perspective. We can draw a lesson from Nancy Zingrone's (2002) Presidential Address to the Parapsychological Association—she touched on this issue at its core by speaking of a "consensus" that is reached through an understanding of how science should be seen; not as a dialectic; either a "positivist, realist enterprise" or "a fictional construction", but as both a "positivist search for the truth" and an "interpretive soup of social, moral, cultural, and personal fashions, of obligations, understandings, [etc.]" (p. 24). To this mix must be added Progoff's "pre-scientific intuitive systems of thought" (1973, p. 11). Science will only advance by a re-consideration of what it has excluded; not by the constant valorization of what it has included.

That being said, Delin notes how scientific thinking "represents only a minority view" (p. 28). Given that is the case, we must assume the majority do not think scientifically. So, changing how the scientific minority thinks is a far cry from changing how the non-scientific majority thinks. Furthermore, even if there could be some kind of trickle-down effect of a new scientific truth, from the few to the many, science still only *presents* the findings; it is up to the various communities (i.e., institutions, universities, corporations) to weigh up the *meaning* and *consequences* of those findings, regardless of how encouraging, revolutionary, and world-changing they are.

Unfortunately, the communities, which represent 'establishment' values and principles (and our fears), put an inviolable priority on stability and control, or the word they prefer to use, security, over all other considerations, including any truth based on scientific findings. The trouble with that is the only security the establishment has in mind is the paranoid version gained by taking away some of our freedom, which means one automatically loses some of that hard-won tolerance. Result? Society sustains a barrage of abuses. The establishment, and anyone who represents it, has a natural aversion to honesty if and when presenting the truth may have dire consequences for the establishment and its representatives. At best, the truth will be massaged to fit that so-called 'security agenda'. As much as it hurts to say it, the very game we know our politicians play, is the same game played by the establishment generally. And as my proof, I come back to the examples given by Cardeña (2015). So, can a change in scientific thinking help tackle the problem of the fears that come from how we conceptualize psi? Only if our whole society changes and reaches that "consensus" that Zingrone (2002) mentions.

It is at this point, however, that the story takes a twist for I have focused on psi but not mentioned synchronicity in this section—the latter phenomenon puts a whole new slant on the issue over our various fears and how to overcome them. Earlier I said the demands made by synchronicity on people are minimal when compared with psi, whereas I have just given credence to the idea that psi propagates fears that could be regarded as unfounded, but nevertheless persist because of the theoretical suppositions made about psi. Meaningful coincidences, however, do not seem as impossible or unthinkable or as threatening as psi, and synchronicity's holistic nature is easily embraced insofar as people readily accept being a part of something bigger. Consider again the example from Shermer's own experience. Critically, while Shermer remains a skeptic to all things paranormal, he concedes the experience he shared with his wife—an experience we may call meaningful coincidence—served a purpose: "I have to admit, it rocked me back on my heels and shook my skepticism to its core as well. I savored the experience more than the explanation". What 'explanation' did Shermer consider? That Jennifer's grandfather made his presence known? That Jennifer used PK to power up a 'dead' radio? The denial is irrelevant; the experience is everything. By any other name, the simplicity of synchronicity does not necessarily conjure fear or raise as many doubts as does the theoretical speculations about the psi process.

We have thus learnt how definitions can do more harm than good for any phenomenon. In Storm (2025), I present possible scenarios of synchronicity's darker aspects but only when viewed in a certain light or lack of it. In the final analysis, and if the will is there, psi could easily be pitched in such a way that it could be seen as normal and become generally accepted, yet retain its paranormality (its mystery); *that* provided we re-envision the psi construct.

Overcoming the Trickster

I have covered a great deal in these past two chapters, yet more could be said of intentions. I did not bring into the foray (or I only touched upon) parapsychologists' home-spun beliefs, their deep-seated desires for change in science and society, their idiosyncratic philosophies, and just about every human trait that can be a strength or a weakness depending on the situation. Fear, as we have seen, is a particularly stifling and unproductive weakness, but we can acknowledge one strength when appropriately applied—namely, belief—which appears to be a motivating force with an empirically observable influence on the psi process. Belief brings with it a general desire to see an effect, or as Jung (1952/1969) says, an "unconscious readiness to witness a miracle, and to the hope … that such a thing may yet be possible" (para. 848). Thereby, belief is not a *causal* factor, although we do not know how deep (indeed how archetypal) belief might be as a *contingent* factor. It appears to be at the crux of an 'atmosphere', 'ambience', or 'environment' in which psi/synchronicity may occur. And although it can be changed, it is hard-won because it must involve over-riding a counter-belief; namely, doubt. The Trickster wins on doubt.

Similarly, hope is thought to engender the right kind of attitude, which is true of many psycho-social situations. The most Progoff (1973) can fathom from Jung's writings, and from his personal communications with Jung, is that "hopeful expectancy" or the "archetypal quality of hope" (p. 104), is activated in psi experiments where the participant is faced with the "impossible" (p. 105). We naturally extend this archetype to synchronicity, but need a little more than hope if we are to initiate paranormal processes. Parapsychologists test large numbers of optimistic 'young hopefuls', many of whom go away disappointed when they do not score a hit. Hope is a motivating force no doubt, but like intention, we cannot consider it a *causa efficiens* primarily responsible for bringing about the effect.

Jung seemingly moves the issue forward by preferring to speak, not of hope, but of the "archetype of the miracle" or the archetype of "magic effect" (p. 105). Progoff spends a little time trying to amplify these points—he speaks of the "expectation" of psi (the miracle) being associated with "uncanny" archetypal powers (p. 105); and ancient "belief" and "faith" in the ideas inherent in "*the archetype of magical effect*" (p. 106). He goes on to describe the shifting of energy within the psyche such that it clusters around one archetypal centre while simultaneously being drawn away from other centres (p. 108). Progoff even refers to the product as a "*complex*", and a "*dynamic balancing process*" (p. 109), whereby "specific kinds of cognition [are made] *directly accessible* to the psyche" without "the intervention of consciousness" (p. 110). While these archetypal factors may come into play as part of the dynamic range of psi or synchronicity, we do not know how much of that hope for a 'magical effect' might be false hope, and how much will be a prompt that constellates 'archetypal power'. The Trickster again? Most probably. The best advice is to be wary of our expectations.

Such clarifications from Progoff are appreciated, and we may even acknowledge the binding power and pertinence of the archetype, but we are no closer to conceptualizing the synchronistic process at the conscious end of the spectrum. Progoff does concede that this kind of detail cannot be supplied because every case is unique, and he ultimately relegates these uncertainties to the *transpersonal* and *psychoid* levels, and even notes that "personal factors are not significantly involved in the objectivity of the laboratory situation" (p. 106). Many experimenters would agree with that claim, but many would not. Surprisingly, it may be that Progoff's assumption is not far from the truth, though the laboratory *outcome* surely has something to do with personal factors insofar as intention is somewhat measurable albeit unreliable as a factor in consciousness related to psi/synchronicity.

These past two chapters should not be taken as a critical or disrespectful exposé of those who have contributed much good to the parapsychological cause, and there is no intention of making examples of my peers. In fact, most of what follows is true of scientists in general (recall the Pauli Effect); not just parapsychologists. The points expressed here should stimulate healthy debate—the fact is we have to be wary of what underlies our thinking when we try to answer scientific questions, and years of service, status, and respectability do not excuse us when we err. As Browne (2017) notes, the manipulations of the Trickster are "important lessons to people, particularly when they are caught up in rigid ways of thinking" (p. 13).

Some of those responsible for the research reviewed in these chapters, or even those who have not, will shrug their shoulders, and say that all of it is the business of science; there is no need for this Trickster character; science is rule-based, and scientists follow those rules, step by step. Scientists take the ups with the downs because they are human, and humans make mistakes. But that is precisely my point—*humans make mistakes*, and they *don't* always follow the rules; they get emotional; they procrastinate; *and they over-commit*. We cannot escape our humanness; who we are emerges out of basic (cognitive) processes, as well as biological, personal, and cultural pressures. Along with all our reflexes, drives, presses, patterns of behaviour (instincts), etc., we have certain modes of apprehension (archetypes), and it is one of these (the Trickster) that was the subject of these past two chapters for good reason—it plays such a big part in parapsychology as the opening paragraphs of the previous chapter explained. Recall that the Trickster is not some kind of supernatural being; it is an inherited psychological process that has mythological antecedents (i.e., the process plays out in age-old, specific, and predictable ways). But the Trickster goes further than that—hence its conceptual power: Like all archetypes, it draws in environmental factors in a way that no other psychological process does or can. Nevertheless, as the above examples indicate, the Trickster can be overcome by a readiness to spot and expose his tricks.

Sometimes the Trickster is so obvious we can foil him, but other times it is so subtle, it gets past us and damage is done. And we are disheartened when we discover our own weaknesses have misled us. Finding the trick is like exposing what a magician hopes his/her audience will never discover—namely, the truth—because exposure is disempowering for those who depend on concealment and misdirection. Other times, in regard to those with every good intention, and a genuine wish to further the sciences, finding the trick simply means honestly pointing out the dichotomies, the contradictory thinking, and the flawed arguments, and nothing will help that more than putting aside our biases (for an example, consider the conflicting interpretations of the DCQE results—see Chapter 5).

It is of interest to note that these warnings are not new, and have come in other guises. Nobel Prize winner for chemistry, Irving Langmuir, said very much the same thing in describing so-called 'pathological science' (his term), whereby scientific investigations are governed by the beliefs, desires, and personal philosophies I mentioned above at the start of this section:

> … there is no dishonesty involved but … people are tricked into false results by a lack of understanding about what human beings can do to themselves in the way of being led astray by subjective effects, wishful thinking or threshold interactions.
>
> (Langmuir, 1953/2002)

Langmuir describes some of the characteristic symptoms of pathological science:

1 "The maximum effect that is observed is produced by a causative agent of barely detectable intensity, and the magnitude of the effect is substantially independent of the intensity of the cause;
2 The effect is of a magnitude that remains close to the limit of detectability; or, many measurements are necessary because of the very low statistical significance of the results;
3 Claims of great accuracy;
4 Fantastic theories contrary to experience;
5 Criticisms are met by *ad hoc* excuses thought up on the spur of the moment;
6 Ratio of supporters to critics rises up to somewhere near 50% and then falls gradually to oblivion."

It is unfortunate that some of these can apply to parapsychological phenomena, but the reader may find it amusing that Langmuir visited J. B. Rhine's laboratory at Duke University in 1934, and mentioned these 'symptoms' to Rhine, informing him that they are characteristics of things that are not so. Rhine's response was:

> They are all characteristics of your thing too.... I wish you'd publish that. I'd love to have you publish it. That would stir up an awful lot of interest.... I'd have more graduate students. We ought to have more graduate students. This thing is so important that we should have more people realize its importance. This should be one of the biggest departments in the university.
>
> (Rhine, as cited in Langmuir, 1953/2002)

J. B. Rhine hit the nail on the head, but the crux of the matter is that the cock-sure Irving Langmuir had tricked himself—the very criticism he applied to marginalized research (fringe science) is the criticism he did not think to apply to the science he held so dearly. I will close this chapter by developing these ideas further.

The Trickster is as Jung (1959/1968) points out, "an approximation to the saviour" and the "saint" (para. 457-458). Not to be taken literally, Jung means that the Trickster, as a version of the so-called Shadow archetype, is the flip-side of the Hero archetype. This fact is important because of its relevance to, and broader meaning of, the Trickster's psychological function—for those with little background in Jungian archetypal theory, the Shadow represents all those aspects of ourselves that we repress and prefer to forget, but unfortunately they do not go away; they manifest in various behaviours and thoughts that we often cannot understand, or do not even realize are inappropriate (this can include choices and decisions we make in how we go about our business, negotiate relationships, etc.). Thus, we may be helpless in the face of the archetype (as Shadow, or as Trickster), but that is never more true than when we identify with it, or we are confronted by those who identify with it.

Identification with the Trickster assists the constellation of Trickster qualities which follow through to their inevitable end. How does one identify with the Trickster? By remaining unconscious to the truth about the Trickster. How does one break free of this identification? By *honestly* becoming more conscious which involves and actually *is* a transformation of personality. If the point is missed here, one can take as an example how it is usually the case that literature from both sides, pro-paranormal and skeptical, can be very persuasive, but persuasion is just another of those tools used by politicians, media, advertising companies, and even scientists, without it necessarily being a pointer to the truth, or our ultimate benefit. Here again is the trick of the Trickster in full force.

In the extreme worst-case scenarios (rare, but worth mentioning), those that identify with the Trickster—those that exhibit Trickster qualities—are unquestionably unconscious of what they could achieve legitimately but for a little more consciousness. However, like a fox (or similar animal—e.g., *Coyote* in Native American culture; Campbell, 2008), it is only through various sleights that many of their aims are achieved. In all truth, they are tempted by, and act on instinctual urges that clearly need refinement. Having read this far, the astute reader is probably reminded of many a politician, media mogul, or business tycoon, popular scientists, and even the odd 'psi warrior' (all of them false heroes), for those types tend to be sophisticated (relatively speaking), though nevertheless unsavoury, uncouth, unethical, unruly, or even immoral. In short, the activated Trickster in a person is marked by inferior behaviour driven purely by instinct. None of this necessarily means they cannot do their job, and do it well, but there are no limits to their shenanigans. Often it is too easy for parapsychologists to find examples in the defenses passed off as literature (peer-reviewed or otherwise), replete with personal slights, unsubstantiated allegations, fallacious thinking, and improbable evidence (as I will show shortly, certain magazines and websites are full of it).

While Trickster types are often associated with poverty (unemployment; lack of funds) and ceaseless struggle, some Trickster types have unprecedented success if only because they peddle a mainly mainstream agenda for which one can always be richly rewarded by those unscrupulous types just mentioned. However, this behaviour (and its consequent reward) is just as prolific in fringe fields like paranormal/UFO investigation groups, and alternate or independent news services, where credence is given to some conspiracy theorists who argue that disinformation agents flourish on all sides (including fringe areas). Consequently, disinformation is undoubtedly a Trickster tool *used by everyone*. Even so-called 'alphabet' agencies the world over (government initiated or controlled) knowingly use the disinformation tool because it serves at least three purposes (not always simultaneously): (a) to discredit or consolidate serious investigations (depending on the claims); (b) to dissolve the general public's apprehensions about official explanations, and (c) to feed 'believers' (i.e., dissenters, truth-seekers) the notion that they are supported. The ultimate aim is to control public opinion and reactivity (for examples where disinformation has been exposed, see Armonk, 2004; Church Committee Reports, 2014).[23] In short, we should question official reports issued by our government agencies just as much as we do conspiratorial theories; perhaps more so.

The Trickster can take a more subtle guise. One must be wary of the Trickster of misinformation or misunderstanding (or even self-deception) about the nature of things, as is propounded by amateur and professional paranormal researchers who mistake one thing for another, or are too easily swayed by half-truths or insufficiently developed theories and models (the same argument can be extended to conspiratorial ideation, which is not to undermine the truth-seeking objectives of its claimants). Yet for all that, the result can be an increased consciousness *provided one is open to being wrong.*

We also have the Trickster of serendipity (accidentally finding something of use while looking for something else), which can be mistaken for synchronicity (cf. Beitman, 2022). Then there is the Trickster of the anti-hero, who always lands on his feet and succeeds in spite of his bumbling (e.g., Maxwell Smart in the TV show of the same name, and Inspector Clouseau of the *Pink Panther* films; see also

Cambray, 2009). There are so many Trickster types, it is almost impossible to keep track of them all (e.g., Q in the TV Sci-Fi series *Star Trek: The Next Generation*, whose role is to mislead for higher, but often self-serving purposes). Of course, all these types are idealized versions to better illustrate the concept, but we can sometimes spot tricksterish activity before our very eyes, and even get caught up in it—the wise would do well to run! And just as it is possible to be a saint one day, and a sinner the next, tricksterish manifestations come and go, and it is that elusive unpredictability that catches the individual unprepared.

Delving into the study of psi and the supernatural, or having a passing interest in it, does not mean one need fear activation of the Trickster archetype in oneself. However, one may be a victim of the activated Trickster in someone or something else. For example, some Trickster individuals (e.g., the late James Randi), Trickster institutions (e.g., CSI; formerly CSICOP), Trickster publications (e.g., *Skeptical Inquirer*), and certain popular websites (e.g., Wikipedia), feel compelled to debunk all manner of paranormal claims without serious investigation, or (what is worse) even bring to a close, by devious practices, parapsychological research programs in university labs or units, and cause trouble for the members of those labs or units (for examples, see Thalbourne, 1995). These, I feel, are the parapsychologist's real threats—not so much activation of the archetype from within.

So, how does modern parapsychology resolve the Trickster dilemma? Thus far, I believe I have rendered aid just in identifying the types and situations of which one should be wary, and thus hinted at ways of dealing with the problem. But again, parapsychologists must become more conscious of their aims, their behaviours and methodologies, the way they interpret their findings, and the social ambience in which they are immersed. This is not to imply that a state of paranoia should be adopted—Palmer (2016a) warned that excessive policing of parapsychological research was enough to make one "paranoid" (p. 14)—but a healthy and vigilant attitude about the movements and changes within the social sphere is a must. An attitude like that can only help. Equally, the individual must develop a presence of mind to keep a low profile (or at least be choosy), for nothing is more inimical to the parapsychologist's ventures than exposure to the judgemental, disapproving, conservative, and naïve authority figures, who invariably seek out the aid of mass media to garner support from that subpopulation of the general public that laps up scandal.

Almost ironically, Felser (2001) sees parapsychology benefiting from psi itself, and recommends a kind of compromise that would help "facilitate the creation of a new, more inclusive form of consciousness in which second-order theoretical reflection is openly and explicitly informed and guided by first-order psi experience" (p. 79). Felser is worth quoting at length:

> Whether it is an insistent philosophical questioning that initially opens the psi portal, or else a spontaneous sensitivity that, once developed, opens up into a fully-flowering philosophical inquiry makes little difference. The time will come when the intuitive and the reflective are fast friends rather than wary

> antagonists. In the future, parapsychologists will be sensitives who openly and fearlessly plumb the depths of meaning of their own psi experiences.
>
> (p. 76)

Felser is not simply advocating more personal involvement from researchers—he is suggesting that parapsychology must attract a new type of researcher; maybe the 'synchronist' as Inglis (1990) uses the term. While that may be one way parapsychology goes, I do not feel (as Felser does) that this will only fully manifest sometime around 2550 AD. Still, if and when this change does happen, and it enters the arena of laboratory psi, parapsychologists may have even greater cause to be watchful of tricksterish phenomena (especially E-psi), but they will not be blind to it!

***

The message in the last two chapters concerning Trickster phenomenology is a bitter pill to swallow, especially when that message has to be owned. Insofar as the technical and scientific material described above has tricksterish components, parapsychologists must deal with a host of repercussions that translate as more than a matter of coping with unpalatable glitches in the various findings—we have to make decisions that have a strong social aspect.

Though I made brief mention of the influences of the Shadow, the Hero, and the Pygmalion effect, that major mythological (archetypal) Trickster figure shows most cogently of all how we interact with the world, and call into existence various anomalies, whether we intend them or not. Thus far, parapsychologists have made considerable gains over the decades—they have an informative (and constantly growing) series of meta-analyses, out of which have developed ongoing debates that may lead to much-needed solutions. But more work is needed—parapsychologists (and their critics) must tackle the numerous tricksterish problems (E-Psi, CDEs, false positives and false negatives, QRPs, magical ideas, philosophical 'spins', and our fears) and see them for what they are, and could be.

The above-mentioned 'bitter pill' generalizes to all the archetypes which, as we see from Jung's work, have replaced the gods. There is no longer a pantheon of capricious gods to appease or blame for our actions—particularly when things go wrong. Archetypal experience is an extra-dimensional experience. By the archetypes, we come to know ourselves, but to do that we have to learn how to spot them, and how to act appropriately in response. We can start by making a *study* of ourselves which requires close and honest scrutiny, and in my view Felser (2001) says as much. Synchronicity helps in that regard by drawing attention to critical life moments that can lead to meaningful and transformative solutions, provided those moments are understood correctly.

Let us now proceed to the next chapter where a series of parapsychological theories highlights a different kind of problem for the theorist. It will be seen that some of the basic premises underlying these theories speak to the problem of process, nomenclature, and associated empirical issues, and they endeavour to eliminate, rectify, or at least minimize the subsequent practical concerns and ambiguities.

Notes

1 NB: The Null hypothesis is merely a general statement (e.g., "There is no psi"), but one given incident of *accepting* the Null can never be the same thing as indicating that the Null *is proved true*. For a detailed discussion on this issue, see Nickerson (2000).

2 So the reader does not misunderstand me, it is only the *chance* (purely random) hits that I am calling false positives.

3 On this same point of getting 'real' data from the population in question, Palmer (2016a) notes that Bierman et al. (2016) did not need to make guesstimates; all they had to do was contact the authors of the ganzfeld papers to clarify with them whether certain QRPs were made.

4 A prevalence interval is a value range indicating how prevalent a QRP might be in parapsychological research.

5 The actual wording is "Stopping collecting data earlier than planned because one found the result that one had been looking for" (John et al., 2012b, p. 15).

6 Palmer (2016a) makes the same point about mainstream scientists (including "psi-skeptics") who defend "theories they identify with" (p. 7).

7 Apart from this major problem, Bierman et al. (2016) state that "JLP estimated the prevalence of [optional extension and optional stopping] to be 58% … and 22%", respectively (p. 7), but these are not prevalence figures—they are "Self-admission rate[s]" from John et al.'s (2012a) Table 1 (p. 521). Also, Table 1 in Bierman et al. presents five "JLP(%)" statistics that are supposed to be prevalence estimates, but are in fact "Admission estimates" from John et al.'s (2012b, Table S3 (p. 16). These are clear errors of commission for Bierman et al. state that their simulation will use prevalence intervals based on JLP's "*prevalence figure for each specific QRP* [emphasis added]" (p. 7). Bierman responded to these discrepancies by saying: "I think we took the admission rates as prevalence figures (as a lower estimate)" (D. J. Bierman, personal communication, December 6, 2017). Clearly, QRPs can extend to research on QRPs!

8 Readers can refer to Cardeña's (2019) review of *Real Magic* (Radin, 2018) for examples of the psi/magic disparities, but I take a different approach.

9 In one sense, Leibniz's pre-established harmony sets up the cosmos in the same mistaken way by thinking that a meaningful orderedness explains all correspondences so that causal orderedness is not needed.

10 While miracles might seem to be the exception, I argue that these are not magic.

11 Transliminality is defined as the "hypothesized tendency for psychological material to cross thresholds into or out of consciousness" (Thalbourne & Houran, 2000, p. 853). It is also the susceptibility to, and awareness of this material, which includes "imagery, ideation, and affect – these phenomena being generated by subliminal, supraliminal, and/or external input" (Thalbourne et al., 1997, p. 327).

12 A fruitless ancient practice in medicine—blood-letting, which continued for thousands of years and only died out in the Victorian era—is a classic example that shows how even 'normal' science is not immune to misinformed beliefs and superstition.

13 For a definition of the sheep-goat effect, see footnote 10 in Chapter 2.

14 'Six Sigma' methodologies were first formulated by engineer Bill Smith of the Motorola Company. Other trail-blazing companies that adopted 'Six Sigma' are Honeywell, General Electric, and Whirlpool. In a normal (Gaussian) curve of distributed values, sigma refers to the 'standard deviation', which is a measure of dispersion of values around a 'mean' (average) value. The larger the sigma, the more the value deviates from the average or optimal or expected value.

15 6σ is merely a *specification* limit, but experience has shown that an ideal *control* limit must be set, usually 1.5σ below 6σ, to ensure that production does not get close to the 6σ specification boundaries (Tennant, 2001).

16 I find no need to cite parapsychologists who report extreme sigmas because I do not wish to give the impression that they necessarily have the wrong intention.

17 The date 1990 refers to the updated chapter (Beloff, 1990) which was first presented as an SPR lecture in 1963, and then updated in 1977. Beloff (1990) states: "Rereading it now, after a quarter of a century, I am struck at how little my basic views on the nature of psi phenomena have changed since then" (p. 15). I assume his views on synchronicity had also changed very little.

18 Beloff's (2008) chapter is a reprint of his original article (Beloff, 1977).

19 Accidents come up frequently in this book. I have described literal accidents involving loved-ones, along with those accidents in the laboratory culpably linked to Pauli; synchronistic 'accidents' (psychological and physical) that are symbolic (in the same sense that the bread and the wine in the Catholic Mass are also called 'accidents'); and later (see Chapter 4) "objective accidental relationships" that describe coincidences (Diaconis & Mosteller, 1989, p. 860). In some cases, it seems as though there is an evolutionary (accident-avoiding) advantage to having paranormal ability (Broughton, 1988, 2015), although nature is clearly not egalitarian (i.e., we are not all blessed with psi ability—at least as far as we can tell). However, the function, as a peremptory alarm system, seems to fail dismally in many instances, and it might be better to acknowledge that, if and when there are accidents (so-called) or similar crises (e.g., sudden death) that *can* be spotted paranormally but not avoided, the reason for that kind of psi may be other than evolutionary (see Kennedy, 2000). Yet still the argument for evolutionary psi is not so easily dismissed—prior warning and avoidance (e.g., of danger) is often not possible in modern times only because we can so easily put great physical distances between ourselves and our loved-ones.

20 Cold reading is basically guess-work on the part of the psychic, helped by direct and indirect cues and clues from the unsuspecting client, and thus appears as ESP (i.e., telepathy between cold-reading psychic and discarnate entity). Some psychics also practice warm reading, which relies on broad statements true of most people. And then there is hot reading (information collected before the sitting through prior research and even clandestine interactions with persons known to the sitter).

21 Tart's (1984) solution to fear of psi is 'personal growth'. One discovers and accepts one's positive and negative sides, and becomes more "self-accepting and less fearful in general" (p. 141).

22 Other sources say Pauli had an interest in telepathy in the 1920s before he met Jung in 1930, and before he collaborated with Jung on synchronicity (Hermann et al., 1984).

23 Based on new evidence about JFK's assassination (and evidence ignored by the Warren Commission Report), the Church Committee findings prompted Erika Cheetham (famed interpreter of Nostradamus's prophecies) to drop her characterization of Lee Harvey Oswald as a "psychopath" (1976, p. 33) and adopt the neutral term "presumed assassin" (1989, p. 63) in her interpretation of Quatrain I.26 from Nostradamus's *The Prophecies*. Interestingly, she failed to regard Oswald as the accused "dead … innocent" in Quatrain VI.37 (1989, p. 343; cf. Hogue, 1987, pp. 96–100).

Chapter 4

Synchronicity and Related Psi Theories

> If you want to know how it works, first find out what it's for
>
> (Richard Broughton, 1988, p. 187)

In this chapter, I clarify some basic concepts about synchronicity. I will then compare synchronicity to some psi theories that are conceptually similar. I believe these theories share common ground with synchronicity, whether or not the respective theorists acknowledge the influence of synchronistic ideas on their theories. I return to a discussion of synchronistic principles giving more detail and justification for the use of the concept in parapsychology, showing how psi and synchronicity are too similar to be treated as disparate phenomena.

The Theory of Synchronicity

According to Jung (1952/1969): "Synchronicity … means the simultaneous occurrence of a certain psychic state with one or more external events which appear as meaningful parallels to the momentary subjective state" (para. 850). The fact that the occurrence is acausal is given by the rational judgement that it is inconceivable to imagine how a causal connection could be made between certain psychic (i.e., psychological) and physical events that only have meaning and meaningfulness as the common link, which spurs the comparison and gives rise to the question about causality in the first place. Jung suggests that the causality principle does not explain all phenomena, just as a theory of an 'acausal connecting principle' (synchronicity) would not be sufficient on its own to explain all phenomena. Acausal psychophysical events suggested to Jung a kind of 'meaningful orderedness' in the universe, which led him to hypothesize the existence of *a priori* meaning as given by "self-subsistent unconscious knowledge", or "absolute knowledge" of these events (para. 931). I would, however, suggest that absolute knowledge is more likely metonymic of the collective unconscious and its contents, the archetypes, which have spatiotemporal extension so that their characteristic qualities are not confined to one place (i.e., the psyche). Browne (2017) gives absolute knowledge an emotional layering and refers to the experience of it as a "*flash of total insight*"

DOI: 10.4324/9781003561323-5

(p. 105). This insight is surely triggered by one's intuitions juxtaposed against one's prior learning and knowledge, and these would provide a sort of grounding or reference point that helps differentiate the new contents in consciousness that do not seem to originate in the individual's life experience, and therefore give one a sense of its 'otherness'.

Jung (1952/1969) also saw synchronicity, with its "causeless order" and "meaningful orderedness" (para. 948), as a step towards resolving the mind/body problem, and a revision of psychophysical parallelism as conventionally understood in philosophical circles. Jung objected to Leibniz's pre-established harmony (the *synchronism* of "psychic and physical events"; para. 937) with its *acausal* and simultaneous 'interrelations' (though these cannot be called interactions). Where Jung is at odds with Leibniz is in the latter's idea that an "antecedent order" partially replaces the world of causes (para. 937), whereas Jung acknowledges causality—a point just made in the previous paragraph. This is a difference that makes the difference for Jung sees acausal events as part of the whole, but he insists *as optional* an interactional capability shared between mind and matter; not a Leibnizian mirror world where we can only see a 'parity' or isomorphism between all things but (in Leibniz's view) no capability of causal interaction. While this causal interactional option would seem to satisfy the Rhinean viewpoint, it seems to jar with the principal of dual-aspect monism and the acausality of synchronicity, but it makes sense if we think of *this* mind interacting with *that* matter, whereas there is no interaction between, say, this mind and its own brain because the two act as one.

For Jung, the idea of synchronicity is an intellectual necessity. In his Chapter 3 of the *Synchronicity* essay, Jung (1952/1969) invites readers to consider the parallels he makes of his concept with ancient ideas concerning the interconnections between things that are most noticeable when they are bound or unified by a particularly powerful, inter-penetrating and binding force or 'spirit', which can be read as a kind of structural or organizing glue. These interconnections manifest (are observed) as effects which Jung likens to correspondences or meaningful coincidences. The assumption that meaning is subjectively (even arbitrarily) determined is only relatively true in some socio-cultural circumstances, but there are, in those synchronistic circumstances, meanings that are objectively determinable and limited to the archetypes which are human-wide and extend into Nature. Atmanspacher's (2014b) reframing has it that constellated archetypal activity, necessary for synchronicity, "limits the range of possibly attributable meanings by 'objective', metaphysical constraints" (p. 192).

To avoid unending misconstrual, meaningfulness necessarily separates synchronistic events from events that are meaningless chance groupings, because the latter lack the activation of the psychoid archetype (the archetype is psychoid because it is neither purely psychical nor merely physical, and can therefore never be the subject of the psyche only). When Aziz (1990) refers to meaning at the "archetypal level" (p. 66), he means an archetype, evident at various levels of meaning, has been activated so its specific meaning follows, though the archetype itself is always 'irrepresentable' and can only be inferred (e.g., as images or ideas) from its effects in consciousness. At the basis of synchronicity, and from which comes its purpose and benefit (ranging from personal progress to evolutionary advantage), is the implied harmony of psychic and physical events as they interrelate. (These ideas are found to be best supported by a 'dual-aspect monist' metaphysics, as devised and discussed by Pauli and Jung, and presented further elsewhere—see Storm, 2025.)

We can understand synchronicity as two or more *event streams* that are *isometric* (i.e., having equal measure in terms of *equivalence*, *contingence*, or *meaning*). That is to say, the individual is able to recognize similar features and patterns when making a cross-comparison of the two event streams,[1] (comparable to Gatlin's *intersection* of *source lines* to be discussed shortly), and so is able to see the correspondence or 'approximate identity' (Jung, 1952/1969, para. 845). Interestingly, in describing synchronicity, Progoff (1973) refers to continuous lines of events, "each with its own causal chain" (p. 162), not causally related, and disconnected up until the moment when the "*transcausal factor*" (Progoff's term) "enters the situation" (p. 162). The transcausal factor is "the archetypal element that crystallizes the unity of a situation across time" (p. 162). The reason the individual is able to perceive the two or more event streams as being *equivalent*, *contingent*, or *meaningful*, is because the event streams have the same underlying archetype, so that each component of the event stream can be measured, one *by* the other; one *for* the other.

But one stream does not *cause* the other—each simply demonstrates that patterns repeat in nature, following the same archetypal rules, but not because any given 'time moment' has a specific quality—the constellation of a specific archetype imbues that moment with a certain quality. I suggest this 'quality' of a moment in spacetime is what Jung (1951/1969) should be taken to mean when he spoke of synchronicity being possible because of the "psychic relativity of space and time" (para. 978). That is why the synchronistic events can even be asynchronous with the 'later' component suggesting precognition merely because that already constellated component came into consciousness later. The individual's experience is inevitably limited and therefore outside the totality of macrocosmic event streams which are beyond the complete awareness of the individual.

The Synchronicity Quaternity

To account for acausal phenomena, and at the same time, allow the psychoid factor into the exclusively 'scientific' space-time-causality triad, Jung postulated the quaternity (a.k.a. *quaternio*) of space-time-causality-synchronicity (see Figure 4.1). According to Pauli (Jung's collaborator on the *quaternio*), this Synchronicity Quaternity (Version I) is inaccurate, so a second version was drafted. Jung adhered to the fourfold system, but Pauli informed Jung that classical physics had been upturned by the relativization of space and time to become the 'spacetime continuum', the antithesis of which is the 'conservation of energy'. The causality/synchronicity pole remained unchanged (see Figure 4.2).

There are four key concepts that pertain to the model depicted in Figure 4.2: (i) energy, (ii) space-time, (iii) causality, and (iv) acausality. The *'fourth'* (i.e.,

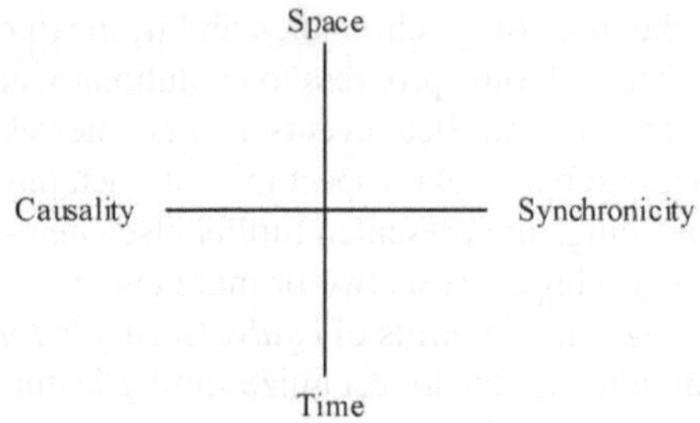

Figure 4.1 The Synchronicity Quaternity (Version I)—Jung. (*Source:* © 2024, L. Storm, based on Jung's [1952/1969, p. 96] original figure)

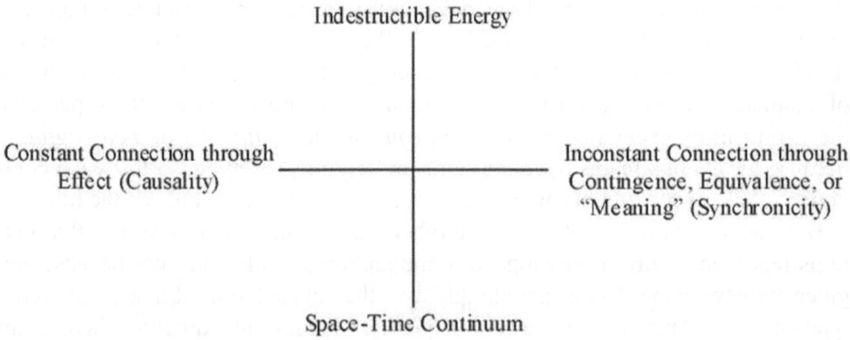

Figure 4.2 The Synchronicity Quaternity (Version II)—Jung and Pauli. (*Source:* © 2024, L. Storm, based on Jung's [1952/1969, p. 98] original figure)

acausality) that joins the '*triad of science*' is the inevitable chance-like factor that compensates the *non-chance*, or *certainty* factor of causality. The vertical axis represents a polarization of the two states that describe matter *per se* (i.e., matter invariably reduces to indestructible energy following German physicist Albert Einstein's formula $E = mc^2$; and matter has extension in the spacetime continuum), whereas the horizontal axis represents a polarization of the two principles that describe the ways in which matter can interrelate (i.e., causally and acausally). Thus, the difference between the vertical and horizontal connection is to do mainly with 'states' and 'relations', respectively.

Since Jung was intent upon broadening the synchronicity concept to embrace all acausal phenomena that idled away as part of the usual flux of Nature, this 'scientific' quaternio depicts a 'wider' form of synchronicity, which does not require the direct participation of an observing psyche, or the relevant presence of meaning (more correctly, meaningfulness). Thus, the acausal pole (synchronicity) accounts for all events that appear chance-like (random or acausal) in nature—they appear not to be predictable or deterministic—and are thought to have an archetypal substratum. And the model certainly legitimizes (gives objective status to) those first-hand experiences (i.e., synchronistic encounters) that touch upon the numinous and transpersonal through the meaningful elements in nature. So there does seem to be a need for some kind of quaternio: After all, Jung argues that three-fold (trinitarian) systems are incomplete and intellectually rigid, whereas his four-fold (quaternarian) system includes all relevant possibilities, and is therefore complete and flexible.[2] However, I refute the absolutism of this quaternio insofar as the wider (broader) definition of synchronicity is unworkable in practice (See Storm, 2025). I suggest Jung (1952/1969) is somewhat over-ambitious in regarding his expansive model as satisfying "the postulates of modern physics, and … those of psychology" (para. 963).

In Storm (2025), I point out how Jung found it necessary to posit an alternative (expansive) terminology that embraces so-called 'nonpsychic' synchronicities to divest them of human reference (for example, quantum discontinuities and radioactive decay do not require conscious observers and are not inhered of meaning, even though some kind of psychoid or archetypal substrate might be posited). While it is debatable whether the expansion avails the relevant disciplines of any more than is already accessible to them in the sense of how science is done, some do consider the move to be unifying: Donati (2008), for example, believes synchronicity (or at least certain of its elements) gives science a depth previously overlooked by allowing a place for psyche and its interactions in scientific pursuits, but this type of synchronicity surely is of the *narrow* form described by Jung (1952/1969, para. 965), and the interactions themselves will become a subject of investigation (to some extent, parapsychologists already do this). Some physicists argue that such inquiry is undertaken in quantum fields of study. Others dispute these interactions as unlikely (see Chapter 5).

Jung (1952/1969) also stated that "the archetype represents *psychic probability*" (para. 964), which schematically conforms to the nature of various synchronistic effects, such as their chance-like characteristics. The factor of "transgressivity" (para. 964) is thereby included in the postulation because archetypes "continually go beyond their frame of reference" (para. 964), manifesting in psychophysical events, the frequencies of which can only be determined approximately (though Jung had issues with some statistical treatments of synchronistic data; see 'The Trickster in the Laboratory' in Chapter 2). While I argue that statistical frameworks are possible in the synchronistic case, provided there is sufficient data (as in experimental parapsychology), Jung seems generally opposed, yet ironically gives the archetype a probabilistic dimension, as we have seen, and endorses psi as statistically demonstrable.

On Model Building: Consciousness, Psychophysical Reality, Archetypes, and the Self

As can be seen, there are many questions one could ask about synchronicity, and even Jung asked them. Probably the one that is most often asked is, How is it possible that an inner mental event and an outer physical event can align in such a way that the relationship is meaningful to the experient? We are now going beyond subjective assertions and validations of meaningfulness. That is, Jung (1952/1969) champions the notion of an acausal "*meaningful cross-connection*" between separate and unrelated events that have their own causal chains (para. 827). That still leaves us with a dichotomy. It appears Jung had come from a common-sense place of reasoning very much influenced by dualistic thinking, and one has to think in that mode to ask the above question. It was only later that Jung's perspective was influenced by the alchemical *unus mundus*,[3] yet even then, Jung's writings on synchronicity still maintain, for the most part, the 'synchronistic dichotomy' speaking, as he does, in terms of 'psychic relativity'. Some may be able to accept the ideology of a synchronistic principle that erases the dichotomy, but it leaves us with an epistemic split that derives from the same philosophical approach in parapsychology that yields two distinct categories, ESP *and* PK (see Beloff, 1978).[4]

Given that Nature itself (i.e., the nature of events) forces us into adopting a dualistic perspective (since we ourselves believe we enjoy both mental *and* physical realities and experiences), we see that the puzzlement behind the above question derives mainly from three common-sense assumptions: The dual (mind/matter) effect is (i) clearly demarcated; and therefore (ii) definable in absolute terms; albeit (iii) unexplained but clearly acausal.[5] Jung (1952/1969) has made this clear: "it is hard to see how chemical processes can ever produce psychic processes, and … one wonders how an immaterial psyche could ever set matter in motion" (para. 948). Even though synchronicity was supposed to be the bridge between two irreconcilables, we see that Jung has couched his argument for a synchronistic ontology in terms that are essentially epistemological: Specifically, mind and matter exist solely in the way they are perceived to be; the reality of the two distinct entities is a given; and no other viewpoint satisfies (which Jung later refuted). These views are based largely on ancient knowledge claims still endorsed today.

Epistemological short-comings ultimately let us down—that is, the phenomenon of synchronicity itself gives us no clue as to its actual mechanism if we couch our ideas and questions outside the ontological framework in which it should be situated. But any attempt to stay within that framework only proves to be a difficult exercise for the imagination when *meaning* must replace the *efficient cause* for synchronicity to make sense. Most attempts at explanation are sure to fail—they are merely descriptive, telling us how the world must be, or is desired to be, if it is to accommodate meaningful coincidence. Invariably then, another question also arises, Which philosophical framework best accommodates synchronistic phenomena; dualism or monism?[6] An answer to that question may go some way towards understanding synchronicity.

Ontologically, some commentators find a good-fitting philosophical argument for synchronicity in the Pauli-Jung version of dual-aspect monism. Oddly, Jung only hinted at this ontology in his major essay of 1952, and throughout the 1950s until Pauli's death in 1958, both Jung and Pauli discussed the basic idea of a 'neutral (unifying) language' for physics and psychology, with synchronicity at the centre of the construct (Meier, 2001). We cannot see that there is (or see how there could be) a unitary ground "between the observed and the observer" (para. 960), but that is the result of our 'epistemic split' from that unitary ground. Synchronicity merely presents *as if* two types of event, mental *and* physical, are occurring in three-dimensional space across the passage of time, but in dual-aspect monism one event occurs in a reality that manifests for us by way of its two aspects (one mental, one physical). Mind and matter form a complementarity. Within this unified reality, the aspects of mind and of matter are interconnected, and synchronicity reflects this interconnectedness.

To continue with this 'as if' model building, I *primarily* refer to synchronicity in neutral terms, and regard it as an *anomalous* phenomenon because we do not know how a conscious entity is able to tap (or slot) into an ordered and meaningful 'whole' as embodied in the idea of a holistic universe, or indeed for that matter, how it *might not, need not, or does not* tap (or slot) into anything *per se*, but is intrinsically a part of the whole. Perhaps the "whole universe is in some way enfolded in everything and that each thing is enfolded in the whole" (Bohm, 1986, p. 114). That is, everything *implicates* everything else. That might be called *thinking on an archetypal scale*. Bohm (1996) argues that spatiotemporally separated events *resonate* within the "implicate order", and sufficient resonance is identified as *similarity* (this resonance is supposedly a nonlocal quantum mechanical process). The similarity that results from meshing of inner (neuronal actions in the human brain) and outer (a 'distant' event in spacetime) is basically seen as meaningful; a kind of resonance. But I do not take literally the idea of resonance *per se* as in "resonance theories" (see Stokes, 1987, pp. 119–121). I do use the term 'resonance' in the context of a resonating bell or Warcollier's (1938) tuning fork (also used by Stokes), but only analogically (see the section 'The Deep Imagination, Memory Theories, and Emotion' in Storm, 2025).

Secondarily, I refrain from regarding synchronicity as a *paranormal* phenomenon demarcated from scientifically understood (normal) phenomena, since it may *only appear as though* synchronicity is physically impossible from the perspective of Broad's (1949) basic limiting principles (BLPs)[7] when there may be no actual violations. If so, the anomaly cannot be called paranormal. As Grattan-Guinness (1978) states, synchronicity "is more modest in its existential claims" (p. 954).

Though only a handful of researchers model the universe holistically, insofar as such a model *might* work as a scientific worldview with implied explanatory power (for examples, see Bohm, 1986; Deutsch, 2011), synchronicity depends on a holistic view.[8] That view accommodates certain postulates, or constructs, or concepts that contribute to the synchronicity model. Taking spacetime for granted (though I will return to the issue shortly), I focus here on four major constructs: *consciousness* (expansion and extension thereof), the *psychophysical reality* (i.e., the *unus mundus*; a unified, psychophysical, neutral background reality), *archetypes*, and *the Self*. All invoke intellectual resistance of one sort or another. The first construct ranges from the garden-variety *consciousness* possessed by living beings, as taught in textbooks (e.g., Kalat, 2011)—referred to as *awareness* in some textbooks (Bond & McConkey, 2001)—to its approximations such as 'perception', 'attention', or 'metacognition' (Davey, 2011). But I will discuss consciousness mainly in terms of its potential for expansion and extension. The second construct is the most speculative; the archaic notion of a psychophysical reality (the *unus mundus*). The third construct, Jung's (1952/1969) archetype, bears similarities to Sheldrake's (1981) "chreode" (= *necessary-path*) that underpins his hypotheses of *formative causation* and *morphic resonance*. The fourth is the Self (the totality of the psyche as ego consciousness + the unconscious). I will outline each of these four constructs in the context of synchronicity theory, and the reader may see how each is crucial in the synchronistic schema.

Expanded and Extended Consciousness. Koestler (1974) explains how our "biological equipment" limits us as to how far we can peer through the "keyhole of eternity" (p. 140), though he suggests a better view (i.e., a clearer picture of synchronicity) would come with an expanded consciousness.[9] This idea of expanded consciousness links in with Jung's idea of 'symmetry breaking' whereby "the balance of conscious-unconscious" is tipped in favour of consciousness; "toward greater differentiation of consciousness" (Jung, 1957, as cited in Meier, 2001, p. 168). Ordinarily, the development of human consciousness, the centre of which is a functional ego structure, is a natural maturational process, governed by evolutionary principles unique to human beings. There is no unnatural breakage or split that has to be healed or restored. The alternative is for the mind to remain in an immature childhood state. So-called symmetry breaking translates as striving towards greater consciousness. Limited 'working' consciousness is our first stumbling block, whereas the idea and known potential of an expanded consciousness connotes two things: First, the individual can gain greater awareness, inwardly and outwardly, and reach a greater understanding as a result of various disciplinary practices, learning, and increased knowledge, and second, synchronicity may occur more often (or be more readily detected) by way of an increased capacity to draw inner (psychological) and outer (sensory) data into one's field of consciousness. When these two combine, a more holistic view of the world might arise, which may be the key to an intrinsically intuitive understanding of synchronicity.

As it happens, ego consciousness, or the awareness one has of being a single, isolated entity in the world, is being relativized in research showing that objectively measurable interacting brain networks can result in dyadic (paired) and group consciousness that goes beyond unique personal consciousness, and even beyond expanded consciousness to 'extended consciousness' (Valencia & Froese, 2020). So-called 'self-other merging' results via *inter-brain neural synchronization* (a.k.a. inter-brain phase synchronization) during meaningful social interactions. As an example, shared and highly cooperative experiences between pilot and co-pilot in flight simulations during takeoffs and landings have been demonstrated, but the interconnection dissolves when the virtual plane is in cruise mode. Objective evidence comes in the form of a 'denser' pattern of EEG interconnections between the two pilots' brain activities during takeoff and landing compared to the 'noncooperative cruise phase'. Other tasks have been tested: 'playing guitars in duets', 'imitation tasks', 'visual search tasks', 'cooperation-competition games', and 'verbal or motor interaction' (Valencia & Froese, 2020, p. 3). It is important to note that "this phenomenon is not a general effect of a shared environment, but an emergent property of specifically social dynamics" (p. 2).

> This conclusion is reached by comparing the brain activity of 'real' pairs (pairs that did interact with each other during the task) with that of 'random' pairs (pairs that are created artificially after the experiment takes place, based on the role each had during the task). This way, all synchronization due to a shared environment or being exposed to the same or similar stimuli is discarded.
>
> (A. Valencia, personal communication, December 12, 2021)

I suggest, however, that many typically human (social) environments are archetypal situations, which may invariably constellate the same archetype within the dyad.

Connectivity is significantly demonstrated between real couples (friends, lovers), but is not as strong between random couples (strangers), and the synchronization is stronger if the exercise is cooperative rather than competitive. This shared capability may be traced back to prehistoric times when (say) a hunting party in a small tribe, consisting of members who have become genetically predisposed to think alike over many generations, needed to be alert to various dangers while on the hunt for wild game (i.e., they participated in the same social interactions).[10] Theoretically, synchronized spontaneous group behaviours that go beyond well-rehearsed actions and collective responses not induced by subliminal cues in the perceivable environment, may suggest telepathy, and even explain its wide acceptance, though that interpretation and understanding may be wide of the mark.[11]

Just to clarify, experimental work indicates that neural synchronization—the alignment of neural frequencies from various brain regions—is understood and experienced as such,

> when we become aware that 'we' are sharing a moment with someone else, it is no longer necessarily the case that we are fundamentally separated by our distinct heads—we could really be two distinct individuals sharing in one and the same unfolding experience.
>
> (Valencia & Froese, 2020, p. 5)

The relevant findings reported in the review by Valencia and Froese demonstrate the capacity for consciousness to extend beyond ego/Self parameters to dyads and groups, and show it to be objectively verifiable using, for example, EEG, fMRI, and many other objective methods.[12]

As a 'quester' amongst spiritual communities in countries far and wide (mostly Eastern and Middle Eastern), psi researcher Christine Hardy (2011) described her personal accounts of shared consciousness, suggesting she experienced 'self-other merging' via neural synchronization, though she does not speak in those terms. Meaningful social interactions are evident from her communing with like-minded individuals in group practices such as meditation and jam sessions using traditional musical instruments. Interestingly, Hardy interpreted her experiences as telepathic involving a "telepathic field" (p. 78). At this stage, we cannot say with certainty whether neural synchronization may involve a telepathic process (or indeed is that process), or is something only similar to a telepathic process. Speaking in synchronistic terms, however, neural synchronization does not have to involve a complex unconscious exchange and cross-checking of information (a 'dialogue' of sorts) to render a successful outcome. Rather, the shared environment itself, coupled with mutual prior knowledge, training, and understanding of the rules of engagement, may suffice in setting up a familiar interactional field for the dyad or group, and this environment in itself is functionally archetypal (indeed is an archetypal situation). While the protocols and the procedures of the shared activity (e.g., flying a plane, or playing musical instruments) may be novel, the capacity for inter-brain cooperation that stands behind them is ancient (i.e., archetypal).

As the same synchronization effects have been demonstrated in tasks such as "playing guitars in duets" and "imitation tasks" (Valencia & Froese, 2020, p. 3), the two authors conclude: "There is therefore no empirical reason to limit the basis of conscious experience to very fast neural activity occurring within a single brain" (p. 5). They even propose that

> the boundaries of the conscious mind could also be subject to constant renegotiation during an individual's interaction with his/her environment and with others, pointing to a mechanism that neurally binds us together and opens us up to an extended conscious mind in social interaction.
>
> (p. 5)

As I implied in the previous paragraph, the term 'extension of consciousness' may be a convenient and most obvious way of describing a very complex process that may be archetypal, albeit no less complex. Neural synchronization may also be evident in some cases of twin telepathy where the mind/brain complexes of twins are already predisposed to shared experiences at such distances that the normal workings of the sensory modalities are ruled out (for more on twin telepathy, see Playfair, 2002, 2017; Storm, 2025).

It would appear that induced extension of consciousness beyond conventional considerations and understanding has been demonstrated to great effect, but at this stage, inter-brain neural synchronization as "a mechanism that neurally binds us together" is not well understood (Valencia & Froese, 2020, p. 5). Therefore, though the possibility of extending consciousness seems not up for debate, we continue to speculate on the nature of consciousness.

Putting aside the person-person link, Koestler's (1974) point about expanding one's consciousness also implies 'growing into' a number of realms (mental, physical, metaphysical) as a tree grows upwards, downwards, and outwards. Taken figuratively, this growth refers to increased awareness of one's mental/psychological activity and one's environments, and how and in what sense this growth may be interpreted as expansion *per se*.

Psychophysical Reality (*the Unus Mundus*). We can incorporate the idea of a growing consciousness into the broader concept of 'psychophysical reality' (the *unus mundus*) because an expanding consciousness implies *expansion* and even *extension* into something, and the *unus mundus*, by definition, binds the various realms of the experienceable into a unified whole. The *unus mundus* should be our ultimate frame of reference, and synchronicity would be a kind of access point or Koestlerian 'keyhole'. Jung (1963/1970) says the synchronistic principle "suggests that there is an inter-connection or unity of causally unrelated events, and thus postulates a unitary aspect of being which can very well be described as the *unus mundus*" (para. 662).

The *unus mundus* appears to have coordinating properties which render correspondences possible. Taking a neutral position, the *unus mundus* would be underpinned by a kind of unified structural imperative that sets limits on what is possible throughout the universe, like the constants in nature that determine how matter may and may not behave, as exemplified by molecular rules that govern crystal formation, or number laws that determine, for example, physical patterns and limitations, geometrical configurations, and mathematical operations. Many of these are archetypal. Though the *unus mundus* might be taken merely as a metaphysical construct (e.g., a helpful aid to thought) originating in age-old ideas (see Jung, 1952/1969, para. 916-946), there is reason to assume it is as phenomenologically real as the universe which science and our senses have constructed for us, but which requires constant objectification.

Focussing purely on the human experience, the *unus mundus* would have its own 'underpinnings', structurally and formally (in the Platonist sense), and archetypally (given its link to the collective unconscious), as indeed Jung proposed. He noted that archetypes (like forms) have ordering properties that extend back in time, and into the future, and across the spatial divides, and we are the bearers of these. This is another way of saying archetypes seem to *transcend* spacetime—it looks like 'transcendence', but there would be no cause to say they *violate* spacetime rules. Rather, they function as contingent factors that bind, from moment to moment, both the contents of the psyche *and* the contents of the world because the latter have a psychoid component. The full experience of synchronicity emerges out of that overlap: Mayer (2018) eloquently puts it thus: "in synchronistic events the *timeless* sphere of archetypes would be connected to occurrences in the *timely* sphere" (p. 205).

We do need to be careful of our terms however: When von Franz (1992) says the "archetypal world is eternal", and therefore "outside time" (p. 121), we see how there is room for misinterpretation. So that there can be no mistake, she describes two very different but ancient concepts: 'timelessness' and 'time-boundedness': the former describes the world of the collective unconscious comprised of archetypes with their consistent and constant archetypal patterns and influences (and these have psychoid extension in the world)—they are immutable across the eons (*outside time*); the latter refers to our world of lived experience characterized by unfolding events *in time*. The former is locked in its own timeless domain, with no real means of determining their location (they are 'nonlocal'), but once constellated, an archetype does not suddenly bend the spacetime rules—its representations merely give the impression that space (distance) and time (past, present, and future) no longer constrict our experience.

One criterion that helps make the transcendent *unus mundus* conceptually viable and intellectually accessible is the intriguing idea that the classical constructs of space and time are not only relative, but are also dispensable under certain conditions. This idea is not new, and harkens back to the Einsteinian relativization of spacetime. While Jung (1951/1969, para. 984; Meier, 2001, p. 62) was quick to grasp the importance of that breakthrough, since it added weight to his argument about psychic relativity, mind and matter nevertheless remain distinct and relative to each other. In fact, the distinction is a necessity not only intellectually imposed *by* us; it is imposed *upon* us by Nature. However, the term psychic relativity is also relative, and should not imply that the psyche can literally bend or transcend spacetime and therefore access any event in time, at any distance, but we may be privy to what exists in timeless states (Jung's 'absolute knowledge'). I suggest that experience may disorientate; but may also give one a sense of advancing beyond the timeboundedness of the 'here and now'.

In the meantime, our continued extension in space and time contributes to our sense of being in the present, or better, in an ongoing present. Indeed, sheer experiential (phenomenological) force imposes this 'boundedness'—a sense of "witnessing from a psychophysical perspective" (Henry & Thompson, 2011, p. 247):[13]

> Prereflective bodily self-awareness comprises an experience of the basic distinction between one's subjective body and the phenomenal world.... [M]erely being a subject of experience involves a basic sense of self.
>
> (Henry & Thompson, 2011, p. 247)

Having a sense of self is to be 'bounded' through "self-appropriation or self-constitution [i.e., 'I-making']" (p. 248), but it is a sense of self that is not at all illusory as argued in some philosophical systems (often of an Eastern character), for even to have an illusion implies an ongoing sense of self. Also, "the felt boundary between subject and world is plastic and fluidly adaptive"; not "fixed and inflexible" (Henry & Thompson, 2011, p. 248). In view of these points, I suggest that we witness this plasticity or fluidity in those occasional, ostensibly transcendental experiences that have in the past been regarded as supernatural, mystical, or religious which, only in the modern era, are of parapsychological interest.

From our relatively limited (bounded) human perspective, we fail to see through and beyond a certain factor (actually the very condition that defines the synchronistic experience) which, if the process were fully transparent to us, would make possible an understanding of synchronicity that transcends mundane experience. That factor is the very occurrence of the mandatory mental and physical events, the distinction of which only exists because the bounded self rules it to be so (i.e., these events are differentiated as a result of the self's enforcement of the classical rules of space and time by which we are bound). In the true synchronistic sense, taking the correspondence as a given, meaning and meaningfulness become the primary criteria of interest because they unify and determine the relationship—actually, they are nested in the correspondence, and are given their specific form according to the archetype.

Archetypes. There is little resistance to the idea that 'universals' exist in the human mind/brain complex—indeed, there are hundreds of them, and many of these can be read as archetypal at that level (see Brown, 1991; McGilchrist, 2009; Pinker, 2002). And beyond those, there are theoretically and experimentally confirmed "deeper universals of mental structure" (Pinker, 2002, p. 435). They govern how we think, how we create identity, art, and tools, how we categorize, plan, express emotions, function in day-to-day living, and behave in isolation and in groups, and so on. These persistent principles account for the sense of continuity we experience as they force a certain consistency (even predictability) to all things, given that the same patterns repeat themselves, or are shared across experiences. We can parallel these 'deeper universals of mental structure' with archetypes, for both are especially noticeable in those mythic (archetypal) patterns of behaviour we see in social and relationship dynamics (Jung, 1959/1968).

There have only been a handful of studies that have objectively tested for archetypes in humans, if we do not include the experimental research on so-called 'deeper universals' (Pinker, 2002). These studies assumed Jung was correct in proposing that archetypal symbols carry implicit meanings. One of the first studies was by Rosen et al. (1991), who used a classical list-learning model to find "evidence of collective unconscious (archetypal) memory" (p. 211). For stimuli, 30 images (archetypal symbols) with associated meaning words were used (e.g., butterfly/soul). These were motifs that appear in mythology, as well as "works of art, and human artefacts," etc., all drawn from the Archetypal Symbol Inventory (ASI; p. 215). Participants were very poor at assigning their own meanings to the symbols. They were also poor at correctly matching symbols to *a priori* archetypal meaning words when the words were randomized. Apparently, conscious knowledge of the associations was virtually nonexistent, so if the associations do exist, it is probable they are largely unconscious. The third study was the 'acid test'—when meanings were matched and mismatched to symbols, matched words were correctly recalled significantly more often than mismatched words, leading the authors to claim "unconscious associations may positively influence the recall of symbol/word paired associates" (p. 223). Rosen et al. drew the conclusion that these unconscious associations were made possible because of our "unconscious (archetypal) memory" (p. 225).

Huston (1992) attained similar findings using fragmented word sets as archetypal cues to participants. For example, participants had to fill in the missing letters of a word fragment after seeing a symbol stimulus H_A_T_, which was matched with the ASI symbol Serpent (an ancient archetypal symbol associated with healing and common in many cultures), where the correct response was HEALTH. Matched symbols/meanings were completed at a significantly higher rate compared to the mismatched set.

Sotirova-Kohli et al. (2011) replicated the findings of Rosen et al. (1991), although they used Chinese *Kanji* symbols instead of the 30-symbol pictorial set.

They concluded that the meaning of the Chinese characters and the symbols were archetypal, as they appeared to exist as knowledge embedded in the unconscious. A later exact replication of Rosen et al.'s original design was successfully conducted by Sotirova-Kohli et al. (2013) using German-speaking participants only, thus demonstrating no language bias. We would expect that archetypes, given their primordial nature, would be laid down in the human genome long before language development.

The study by Bradshaw and Storm (2013) was also based on the study by Huston et al. (1991), but a few design parameters were changed, with the main change being the use of non-ASI images downloaded from the Internet (the meaning words were not changed). The reasoning here is that if archetypal images are truly universal, they must still be discernable even when their representations undergo modest morphological variations. Findings by Bradshaw and Storm still replicated those of the previous researchers. However, they made an important observation, which other researchers have not investigated: Specifically, we have to be able

> to draw some degree of distinction between two processes: (a) association based on *archetypal facilitation*; and (b) association based on *descriptive similarity* (which may not necessarily be archetypal at all).
>
> (p. 168)

Bradshaw and Storm (2013) made a partial attempt at differentiating archetypal facilitation from descriptive similarity. The full 30 word/symbol set was reduced to 23 due to evidence of conscious knowledge of seven word/symbol pairs. Oddly, of those 23, six words mismatched to symbols were recalled *more often* than 17 matched words. This effect could only be attributed to descriptive similarity in those six, as there could be no archetypal facilitation if words were randomly mismatched to inappropriate symbols (random mismatching was done for four different subsamples, data of which were pooled and analysed together, thus eliminating any chance of alternative archetypal pairings). It was concluded that the correctly matched set of 17 did have archetypal facilitation but descriptive similarity could not be excluded. Bradshaw and Storm did not test for further differences to see if they could find proof of archetypal facilitation only.

Taking this process one step further, two datasets can be formed, named after the implied effect suggested in two simple calculations: *Descriptive Similarity Only* based on the difference between the higher number of mismatched responses and the matched responses in the set of six mentioned above (a difference of 14.92%), and *Descriptive Similarity + Archetypal Facilitation* based on the difference between the higher number of matched responses and the mismatched responses in the set of 17 (a difference of 24.49%). Since large clusters of archetypes were assessed in these datasets, and the averaging effects of large subsamples diminishes individual response differences even further, the difference of 9.57% (24.49% – 14.92%) is a probable indicator of an effect above and beyond descriptive similarity; namely, archetypal facilitation. We see that studies using word/symbol pairs do suggest archetypes are inherently complex and pose a challenge to researchers—for example, as already pointed out, response rates varied greatly from archetype to archetype. And special attention needs to be directed towards differentiating archetypal facilitation from descriptive similarity.

There are other ways of assessing whether archetypal content in stimuli can activate appropriate responses (i.e., demonstrate archetypal facilitation). A study by Ivonin et al. (2015) used film clips featuring archetypal content. Participants were exposed to four archetypes (anima, animus, hero, shadow) and four explicit emotions (active-pleasant, active-unpleasant, passive-pleasant, passive-unpleasant). There was a specific film clip for each of these—a total of eight clips altogether. The authors' main aim was to determine whether physiological data was better at identifying archetypal experiences than introspective reports which were measured on the Self-Assessment Manikin (SAM; presented as arrays of human-like figures visually expressing a spectrum of emotions to which participants respond in accordance with affective states elicited by the stimuli). The physiological responses were cardiovascular and electrodermal activity, respiration, and skin temperature. The authors noted:

> When an archetype becomes active in one's psyche the individual experiences a complex of emotions specific to this archetype. For this reason, a possible approach for observation of archetypal experiences involves measuring emotional responses of individuals related to archetypes.
>
> (p. 3)

Their decision to use film clips as stimulus material is novel but appropriate given that film is a very effective medium for eliciting emotional responses from audiences, but the medium is also ideal for representing archetypes.

Ivonin et al. (2015) proposed that physiological data was better at reflecting archetypal experiences than introspective (emotional) responses because "archetypes are implicit and not readily available for conscious recollection" (p. 4). After each clip, participants gave their SAM ratings (the physiological measures were automatically recorded). The authors found that physiological data could recognize the archetypal experiences

> with an accuracy of up to 55 percent. The explicit emotion could be recognized [from physiological data] with an accuracy of up to 47 percent.... [whereas] the SAM data demonstrated that the archetypes could be differentiated with an accuracy of 33 percent while the explicit emotions were correctly predicted in 51 percent of cases.
>
> (p. 27)

The authors concluded that "physiological signals may offer more reliable information about archetypal experiences of the individuals than introspective reports" (p. 27).

A good example of archetypal facilitation outside the laboratory comes from Jung's (1989) memoir, in which he describes premonitory dreams and visions in the spring and early summer of 1914 about a "monstrous flood" covering parts of Europe, a sea of blood, many drowned bodies, and "the floating rubble of civilization" (pp. 175–176). Jung thought the imagined material was personal—he even though they indicated psychosis—until the First World War broke out in July of that year. It is a startling fact that many commentators regard these images as precognitive, and when asked of the world's political situation, Jung had no thoughts on the matter, although he did say he saw "rivers of blood" (p. 176). However, any reasonably astute individual can draw firm conclusions from the socio-cultural and political milieu, and we also know that Jung often described Europe at the time as a veritable powder-keg, with many newly formed nations struggling for self-determination against much resistance from other nations. Many politicians and common folk alike felt trouble was brewing. In other words, Jung had sufficient conscious and unconscious knowledge of the situation in Europe to dream of its future, even if he only half-consciously joined the dots, and did not fully realize until later what his prior experiences meant. In this particular instance, the martial archetype of war and its archetypal consequences were psychologically constellated well before their physical signs manifested. I see evidence of archetypal facilitation in the fact that Jung (1964/1970) anticipated these impending problems well before the war. Jung's inner ('warring') state of turmoil at this time (including his split with Sigmund Freud in 1913) is pertinent and crucially links the dream content with corresponding world events. If archetypes did not facilitate his 'premonition' (i.e., synchronicity), his guesses would have been stabs in the dark, but 'rivers of blood' hardly suggests relatively milder effects such as worldwide economic collapse or financial crisis—we have to see the dream metaphor as meaning wholesale slaughter and the deaths of millions.

A similar, personally relevant and precise case of archetypal facilitation can be made for Winston Churchill's intuitive response during the London Blitz of World War II. On one occasion, he chose to sit on the off-side of his vehicle rather than the usual near-side. He had never done this before, and his driver was perplexed. During transit on the Kingston by-pass out of London a bomb explosion raised the vehicle off its two off-side wheels (on the side Churchill was sitting), but seconds later the still rolling vehicle came down and continued on its way. Churchill was convinced that the vehicle, travelling at 60 m.p.h., would have surely rolled and killed him and his driver had he sat in his usual place. He reasoned that all his "beef" on the off-side made the difference, but he later claimed his actual decision came down to "something" in him telling him to "go round to the other side and get in there" (Fisher & Allen, 1964, p. 136).

During the Blitz, with thoughts of constant aerial threats at the back of his mind, Churchill made what *seemed* like a rash unexplained decision, but an unconscious image of a potential scenario probably guided his action to do things differently, even if it meant just a slight change in how he seated himself. We would not expect the same image to be activated in Churchill *before* or *after* the war, so we have a situational contingency, and these can often be archetypal. It therefore makes sense to see Churchill's decision as something like a plan (i.e., archetypal); sketchy but appropriate. Churchill could not have rationally deduced that a change in seating would give him some kind of protection against the immense force of an exploding bomb. Indeed, had the idea to change seating been presented to him by his driver, Churchill may have dismissed it as ineffectual and frivolous. But it can be argued that a complex network of facts unconsciously contributed to Churchill's decision (call it an intuition). He would, for example, have been well-informed about prior aerial attacks on London (locations and times), and he knew the route to his destination and the likely speed of his car. When intuitions result in seemingly fortuitous outcomes they are often seen as *premonitory* because there is no causal link, but an archetypal (crisis) situation can evoke a sense of foreboding and, in Churchill's case, a spontaneous reaction.

These sorts of immediate decisions are described in at least one psi theory; namely, Stanford's (1990) Psi-Mediated Instrumental Response (PMIR, explained shortly in this chapter). An anomalous (synchronistic) tone runs through examples of PMIR, in that the theory proposes that unexplained decisions can be driven by unconscious images that correspond with external events. Here we see an archetypal external dimension augmenting the inner psychological domain. Jung's collaborator, Wolfgang Pauli noted this extension, intimating the role of the archetype in synchronicity:

> The *ordering* and *regulating* factors [of archetypes] must be placed beyond the distinction of "physical" and "psychic".... [Thus] it would be inadmissible to define them [only] as contents of the psyche. The mentioned inner images ("dominant features of the collective unconscious" after Jung) are rather psychic *manifestations* of the archetypes which, however, would also have to *put forth, create, condition* anything lawlike in the behavior of the corporeal world.
> (Pauli, 1948, as cited in Atmanspacher, 2014a, p. 285)

Jung recognises these points when he speaks of "transgressivity" of archetypes (para. 964), whereby their constellations (fields of influence, so to speak) go beyond the individual psyche, taking the individual beyond an inner (psychological) experience to a psychophysical (inner/outer) experience. I refer to the archetype in this state as 'unbounded'.

We often question our habitual behaviours, altering our usual actions accordingly to see what eventuates. Archetypal facilitation can augment and enable our understanding, and help normalize premonitions and precognitions, seemingly taking the mystery out of psi, but we can also say that archetypal activations can evoke a degree of certitude about, and reliance on, our intuitions, fantasies, and dreams. Likewise, synchronicity does not have to be seen as entirely paranormal in the conventional sense, for many meaningful coincidences, even though their linked elements may be separated spatially and/or temporally beyond human understanding, do not violate the physical rules of our universe—they may be as logical and rational as anything that can be described in causal terms, yet still seem conventionally acausal. Pauli added to this overall understanding by stating that archetypes "extend the old narrower idea of 'causality' (determinism) to a more general form of 'connections' in nature ..." (Pauli, 1994, p. 164).

At another (biological) level, and to account for certain anomalies in species regeneration, reproduction, and regulation, Sheldrake's (1981) hypothesis of formative causation "proposes that morphogenetic fields play a causal role in the development and maintenance of the forms of systems at all levels of complexity" (p. 71). Morphogenetic fields order physical changes otherwise not conventionally explained. The constancy of forms is ensured through 'morphic resonance', whereby "the forms of previous systems influence the morphogenesis of subsequent similar systems" (p. 95). The 'chreode' is the resultant form as a (more or less) stabilized feature, instinct, or behaviour. There is research *for* and *against* formative causation, respectively (Dias & Ressler, 2014; Robbins & Roe, 2010). Though questions concerning morphogenetic fields and formative causation are not fully answered, the idea of consistent evolutionary patterns and order align with the fundamental ideas behind Jung's theory of archetypes.

Ordering principles must be bound by certain parameters (e.g., situational contingencies), so naturally they would act as boundaries for us. This would be true of archetypes. As is the case with anything lawful, we should necessarily entertain the possibility of a 'synchronistic limit' (constants work in similar fashion). This limit would account for failure as much as success (especially in experimental settings). This idea of a synchronistic limit does not conflict with the notion that some elements of synchronicity (mental or physical) may go unnoticed, and there may be many of these. That hypothesis is supported by examples of synchronicity that have multiple elements greater than the usual two, and a number of these have been (or will be) presented throughout this book. In this sense, the manifestation of a typical synchronicity may be analogous to the tip of an iceberg, for the way the *unus mundus* is described here and elsewhere (see Progoff, 1973), one would assume that it must be of a potentially abundant capacity, albeit ultimately finite.[14] We can imagine that innumerable inner and outer events (the elements of synchronicity) exist in potential in the synchronistic field like 'error terms' and 'unexplained variance' in scientific research (they are assumed to be there, given that they *do* emerge on occasion, usually unexpectedly). But just as a workable science is still possible under those conditions, we are not denied an adequate synchronistic experience despite the many unrealized potentials. Quite the contrary, and from the evidence, and in keeping with Koestler's (1974) point, an expanded consciousness opens the experient up to more synchronicity, as does an extended consciousness.

The more detailed a synchronicity, the more we might expect multiple archetypes to figure, which introduces multiple probabilities into the synchronistic equation, and therefore natural limits, in the sense that we cannot be sure which archetypes, or how many, may constellate. The constellation of multiple archetypes would suggest these more impressive cases of synchronicity are amongst the rarest, but it may be true that rarity is not always defined by the number of archetypes involved.

While frequency (rate of occurrence) may vary from synchronicity to synchronicity, they (and/or their details) may occur with such frequency that chance can be eliminated as an alternate explanation (Jung, 1952/1969, para. 967). However, we have also seen how statistical reasoning is only helpful to a degree, for it obscures Jung's point that individual synchronicities appear *as if* by chance and can only be evaluated on a casewise basis.

Some archetypes may represent in a single event or image, and may be short-lived, while others manifest in complicated scenarios that may consist of multiple synchronistic elements, and may be sustained for long periods of time (for an example of the latter, see Chapter 4 in Storm, 2025). The appearance in human relationships of these particular archetypes may be partly governed by genetic factors, so that a peculiar mix of biological, psychological, and chance-like (but not random) factors may be at play. The first two of these factors may in fact act as imperatives that suggest in very real terms a causal component, but these can only satisfactorily explain one component (one half) of the synchronicity—a point that has been made earlier, and will feature later in this chapter in Gatlin's (2008) theory of Meaningful Information Creation.

The Self. Returning to an earlier question, and to round out this subsection, if the *unus mundus* does not require management, or deliberation, or enabling by some unknown factor, we may wonder what the spur is for synchronicity to happen in the first place, and we may perhaps suspect that some degree of agency defaults to us. This is not to suggest that all synchronicity must be intentional at some level, but questions of this sort do resurrect the causality issue. As indicated, the natural suspicion that we are the causal nexus underpinning those synchronicities that revolve around our experience arises from the point of view of a 'bounded' self having a bounded (keyhole) experience. Notwithstanding the acausal nature of the archetype, Jungians may still see the 'Self' construct (our psychological totality; the 'Central Archetype')[15] as necessarily instrumental in synchronicity (a point which is hard to deny), and may note that synchronistic narratives are masterfully and uniquely executed, are personally relevant, are aesthetically dream-like (and rightfully owned by us like our dreams and fantasies), and spring into being as if from the imagination, yet are independent or semi-independent of the machinations of ego consciousness.

While this 'role' of the Self does imply human agency, we must be wary of the repercussions that ensue if a limited psychological structure is proposed to explain the whole synchronistic effect (or psi), for that would be tantamount to endorsing the arguments from 'magic' or 'large-scale PK' discussed in previous chapters. These can force an exclusively causal argument, over-rate egoic desire (and even need), and overlook the more crucial conditional and contingent arrangements. Like that other (smaller) 'self' or ego that witnesses "from a psychophysical perspective" (Henry & Thompson, 2011, p. 247), one must concede that the (bigger) Self is part of an *arrangement* (only from our limited egoic standpoint do we identify ourselves *instrumentally* as the central experient in the synchronistic play of events; after all, synchronicity is always for us and about us). And recall my synchronistic analysis of Ted Owens in Chapter 1. The Self, however, is the true centre—it encompasses in its sphere, or even embodies, a kind of microcosmic representation of the macrocosmic 'bigger' picture, or parts thereof.

The reader may recall that these points refer back to statements made earlier about the principles underpinning various systems of divination whereby it was proposed that actions at the human (microcosmic) level are undertaken in the *hope* that they mirror the larger macrocosmic picture of reality, knowledge or insight of which may give a fuller picture of reality and probable outcomes. But I stress again von Franz's *caveat*: (1992): "… something synchronistic might happen when an archetype is constellated" (p. 27). The reasons these points need to be emphasized is that it is a fundamental and irrefutable rule of life that even a right attitude, and our human needs (e.g., for love, or friendship, or success), cannot trump the vicissitudes of life as if it were a clockwork universe—there are no guarantees.

The Spacetime Factor and Archetypal Inevitability

The concept of spacetime was touched upon earlier. In this subsection, I seek to show that synchronistic phenomena do not violate spacetime rules. It might seem that synchronicity can appear as psi, thus exhibiting a certain paranormal dimension that does not follow the 'normal' cause-and-effect rules of information transmission, whereby thoughts or distant events become known that should not be known by ordinary means, or events are *effected* before they are *caused*.

For a phenomenon that is only supposed to be 'coincidental', it might seem inappropriate to describe synchronicity as operating by its own rules outside the constraints of spacetime. In fact, Jung (1951/1969, para. 984) has helped perpetuate that idea that it does by speaking of psi and synchronicity in the same way. Nevertheless, Jung also notes the *relativizing* factor or aspect of archetypes in synchronicity that gives a different, even contradictory perspective: Archetypal coincidence patterns, that underlie synchronicity experiences in humans, span the millennia and are highly consistent across spacetime, having been echoed, repeated, and refined down through the ages, and are carried by us and in us, so that a *prior* or *current* event (either of which constitutes the first element of a synchronicity) seems to 'anticipate'/ 'predict' a geographically *distant* or *subsequent* event (the second element), thus creating the coincidence (cf. Jung, 1951/1969, para. 967-968). This idea is borne out in the 'forecasting' principles underlying astrological processes (details in Storm, 2025), and mechanisms underpinning key actions in mythological material: For example, when a wizard or wise old man or woman can tell the hero or heroine of his/her past and present actions, and indeed is often able to prognosticate their futures in considerable detail, we are not surprised by the paranormality of the feat given its fictional context (i.e., we suspend our disbelief), but in real life, when a medium or psychic similarly informs a client, we must understand that the principle is the same—where we would ordinarily assume a paranormal process explains it, we need only defer to *archetypal inevitability*. Thus, it should come as no surprise that von Franz (1980) implicitly draws attention to archetypal inevitability in Pauli's explanation of precognition: "we in our psyche unconsciously know which archetype is now constellated and by that can predict what will come next" (p. 77).[16] This process seems so obviously aided by intuition and the imagination, there can be little reason to dispute it, so that it is not even a question of an ability to perceive potentialities (see Bohm, 1996, pp. 131–132), let alone receive backwards-travelling information, or experience retro-causality. There is no reason to assume telepathy and clairvoyance do not work the same way.

Invariably, we must turn (albeit briefly) to the initiating factors; the priming, cueing, or triggering mechanisms underpinning psi and synchronicity. Ecologically, some internal or external event provides a trigger (even if it is seemingly random); in the laboratory, some kind of cue (stimulus) is deliberately provided to elicit a psi response, or a protocol is executed (as in ganzfeld or imagery cultivation) which puts the participant in a state of readiness and thus gives them fair chance. (As an aside, forced-choice studies tend not to do this; consequently, the participant engages in little more than good guess-work, and perhaps occasional synchronistic correspondence, resulting in weak effects.) But in consideration of *knowing* "which archetype is now constellated" (to use Pauli's words)—though 'knowing' may be too strong a word—we do seem to rely on intuition and imagination once the process is initiated. Research has furnished good evidence that the human brain has an innate intuitive capacity to discern trajectories and future outcomes (Lufityanto, Donkin, & Pearson, 2016). The important role of the imagination is covered in Storm (2025).

With synchronicity, we tend to make a match or correspondence by comparing the first (mental) event with the subsequent (later) second (physical) event. We even feel, that we have predicted the *second* event stream based on observations drawn from the *first* event stream. But direction is actually inconsequential, and it does not necessarily matter which of the two event streams of the coincidence is to be the starting point for comparison of one with the other. If we did not travel 'forward' through time, from t_0 to t_n, but could reverse the flow of time, there may be occasions where we are able to predict or realize the *first* event stream based on observations drawn from the *second* event stream because the second event *manifested first* on our event horizon. For an example, see the comments made by Main (2004, pp. 41–42) about the *I Ching* process: "Users of the *I Ching* sometimes report that the textual image they obtain seems to correspond to their unconscious preoccupations ..." (Main, 2004, pp. 41–42).

Thus, meaningful coincidences are a conjunction of contents from two or more event streams because those contents are effectively isometric, archetypally speaking. Consequently, while Jung was quoted earlier in reference to one synchronistic element being a "normal, probable state (... causally explicable)", while the other is the "critical experience" that "cannot be derived causally from the first" (para. 855) that points to an objective (outer) experience at a later time, this heuristic should be understood as 'time symmetric', though only in a metaphoric sense, with no reference to any 'physical formalism'.[17] There are no causes involved; only archetypal contingence, so one event stream has no effect on the other. Both elements satisfy the condition of being "causally explicable", and both satisfy the conditions of being "critical" and not "derived causally" from the other. Consider Jung's (1951/1969) well-known scarab case: A female patient of Jung's could not make progress during analysis due to her intellectual resistance. Jung hoped for something unexpected. During analysis, the woman told Jung about her dream of a golden scarab in the form of a costly piece of jewellery. As she spoke, something tapped on the window-pane behind Jung—a large flying insect was knocking against the window-pane from outside. It was a common *rose-chafer* (a beetle of the *Scarabaeidae* family). The beetle was gold-green in colour resembling the golden scarab in the woman's dream. Jung said: "Here is your scarab" (1951/1969, para. 982). A simple shift of focus and accent shows that both the client's dream *and* the beetle on the window-pane can be *critical* elements, neither of which is derived from the other, and both, as single events, are normal, and probable, and *causally explicable*. Note that Haule (2011) takes Jung to mean only one of the events has a cause of its own ("one of the two linked events can be explained causally while the other cannot"; p. 72), which is not what Jung meant. Both events can be explained causally, but the link (the linking up; their coincidence) has no causal explanation.

It is easy to assume the relationship, as originally presented by Jung, is unidirectional or asymmetrical by force of contiguity (one event must come *after* the other). Indeed, it is the deception of a 'time-stamped' sequence, and our obeisance to contiguity, that contributes to the numinosity in synchronicity. But contiguity gets in the way of an understanding about the archetype as an ordering factor that binds the events *via meaning*; the archetype transcends subjective situational criteria and requires a more holistic view of the evident elements (what is known) as part of a broader whole comprised of what is sought in the unknown. By way of archetypal inevitability in the given moment, the intuitive individual (e.g., the wizard or medium), aware or not, identifies or infers the holism from the clues of a given moment much like knowing that a tree has roots without needing to inspect the tree. Even when no clue is present (as in psi studies), the appropriate archetype may be activated or constellated unconsciously from within, and not necessarily intentionally, but an intuition may suffice in triggering the appropriate response.

These principles may jar with the idea that there is a paranormal process underpinning synchronicity that is inviolable, invariant, and absolute. To be blunt, that interpretation is simply not required once one sees a world where event streams are multitudinous and omnipresent, and all one requires is predisposition or intention (i.e., capability of setting up an 'atmosphere' to use Progoff's word), and a sufficiently activated imagination that enables one to supply the missing piece of the puzzle. I venture to say there was some kind of deliberate intention on Jung's part to convey a sense of *paranormality* in synchronicity—he does link it to Rhine's findings, and his appeals to ancient worldviews can have a resonating effect on individuals that can trigger flights of fancy (1952/1969, para. 916-946).

To show how archetypal inevitability looks on the ground, I give account of a rather mundane episode concerning my bathroom ceiling fan, which suddenly, but all too late, came to mind while I was flying to Sydney from my home-town Adelaide. In my haste to get to the airport, the thought occurred to me on the plane that I may have left the fan running, and I wildly imagined that it might overheat, or set off sparks, and possibly start a fire. But I managed to convince myself that I had switched off the fan. I stayed at my colleague's place from Friday to Sunday for a conference held on the Saturday. It was hot in Sydney that whole weekend, so my host had placed a portable electric fan (albeit a very old one) in my bedroom that Friday night. Hours later, I woke up sweating, yet I could hear the fan motor running. When I switched on the room light, I discovered that the plastic fan blades had fragmented, and shards of various sizes were strewn about the floor and across my bed, though I was not injured. I immediately thought about my fan back home in Adelaide. The point here is that a 'fan' theme had been set—first, there was the initial experience with my Adelaide fan, then the emotional intensity of the inner image of a fan lurking in the back of my mind spelling out dire consequences, and finally a parallel event that manifested with potentially alarming consequences (the flying shards were potentially dangerous, but I slept through it all and woke up unharmed).

Saturday morning, after I had slept on it and thought about the synchronistic elements of the coincidence—how the Sydney event had run its course, but the Adelaide event was still unresolved in my conscious mind—a peace of mind was instilled in me as it dawned on me that *my relative safety* that Friday night might be reflected in the unresolved Adelaide event, given the equivalence of meaning (the take-home message being: 'no harm done!'). This interpretation is likely no more than an intuition, and there is certainly no need to propose precognition, even if the intuition is proved right. That Sunday afternoon, back in Adelaide, I discovered the fan had been turned off as I had half-suspected.

It is clear that an unconscious memory of switching off the Adelaide fan may have been lurking in the back of my mind, but to what degree could that memory have been a causal factor in the disintegration of the Sydney fan? Logically to no degree at all, other than it being part of the 'arrangement'. While I seemed to have gained an answer of sorts to a nagging doubt, why did it come in such dramatic form—why could I not simply have remembered (or tried harder to remember) that I had switched off the fan? One answer may be that our memories are never always recalled, fully or partially, as and when we wish, and even then they are simply not that reliable, whereas an archetype (or archetypes) provided the synchronistic tone for that series of events (probable archetypes such as 'energy', 'electricity', 'spinning wheels', come to mind; see Jung, 1959/1968, para. 68, 646). Of course, archetypes only idle away *in potentia* until there is a sufficient degree of affectivity in the experient so that the situation of *archetypal inevitability* can be enabled; only then may events of similar meaning occur (Jung, 1952/1969, para. 846). Had it been otherwise, I would not be telling this story.

As a final point, some critics, and even some hard-line synchronicity pundits, may regard the above postulates and schemata as inaccurate and flawed, or consider them irrelevant and redundant in view of the greater purpose and principles of synchronicity, though I find it difficult to see where I might have failed in applying them. Rather than care for the 'mechanics' of synchronicity, they may feel that only the developing human personality is key, and the paranormality of synchronicity as a 'principle of nature' is a proof that something bigger and external is looking out for them, though clearly not always, and often it is a case of 'too little too late' (for examples, see Rawlette, 2019b). I have often seen this notion that a supernatural 'intelligence' orchestrates synchronicity, with no recourse in Jung's essay to back up the statement, and no good reason to assume it (e.g., Mishlove, 2021; Window to the Soul, 2019; Young, 2023). Others may feel it preferable to posit a synchronicity model that follows the teleological principle of predestination (i.e., fate), thus ridding us of the paranormality problem altogether.

On the issue of fate, but in a broader sense that applies equally to a holistic, synchronistic worldview, American essayist and philosopher, Ralph Waldo Emerson made the following relevant statements in 1866:

> The secret of the world is the tie between person and event. Person makes event, and event person .... the soul contains the event that shall befall it; for the event is only the actualization of its thoughts .... The event is the print of your form ...
> (1957, p. 235)

It might be argued that Emerson was not thinking beyond mundane, everyday personal interactions and consequences, large or small, and cared not, or gave little thought to inexplicable or anomalous experiences, but the fact that he was a leader of the transcendentalist movement in the mid-19th century suggests otherwise. Transcendentalists saw how physical and spiritual experiences can be interconnected, which thus prompted the criticism that transcendentalism was "mysticism for mysticism's sake" (Ljunquist, 2002, p. 15). How a mystical turn of mind is supposed to be a flaw is anybody's guess if an intuitive outlook calls for it, and thereby leads to insights unattainable any other way. More to the point, Emerson clearly paved the way for a justifiable openness to anomalistic experience that did not come fully into its own until the 20th century, but which is certainly still overlooked or ignored. Even more to the point here, Emerson's thoughts on the nature of personhood and relationship with the 'soul' necessarily converge on the issue of fate *per se*; an end product familiar to the synchronistic mindset. Nowadays, the so-called soul might nominally refer to a psychological construct of considerable dynamism and power in the Jungian sense (as Jung suggests, one might call it an inner 'divinity', the psychological projection of which might explain the assumption of intelligence just mentioned). As stated in the quote above, one's fate (perhaps not the best word) can be seen as changes in psychological, behavioural, and attitudinal outlook resulting, at least in one way, from a synchronistic process that starts at a deep imaginative level of mind.

It seems the natural next step, having outlined the main parameters of synchronicity, is to mine the relevant theories in the parapsychological literature for parallels to synchronicity theory. By doing that we can test the timeliness and plausibility of synchronistic ideas, whether borrowed from Jung or arrived at independently.

Psi-Mediated Instrumental Response (PMIR) and Conformance Behavior

Decades after Jung proposed his synchronicity theory, Rex Stanford (1974a, 1974b) came close to a synchronicity schema in his psi-mediated instrumental response (PMIR) model by merging ESP and PK, although at that stage he did not see ESP and PK as quite the same process. In describing the PMIR model, Stanford (1974a) proposed that

> the organism nonintentionally uses psi to scan its environment for need-relevant objects or events or for information crucially related to such events, and when obtained, the organism tends to act in ways which are instrumental in satisfying its needs in relation to the particular object or event in question.
>
> (p. 35)

(Note that the "scanning component" was later discarded; see Stanford, 1990, pp. 57–59.) Stanford (1974b) extended the above definition to include PK phenomena. He then developed his *conformance behavior* model which "subsumes both ESP and PK" events under one model (Stanford, 1978, p. 198). Any paranormal process was thereby typified as a "conformance" (i.e., a disposition-serving outcome) respondent to the "need or other disposition" of an individual (p. 207). Stanford's 'conformance behavior' model is considered closely related to the observational theories (i.e., consciousness alone 'collapses' a probable state to an actual state—see Chapter 5). However, psi under this model does not need feedback so it is not generally classified as observational (see Stokes, 1987).

A second point in Stanford's (1978) modelling of the psi process is that conformance behavior theory regards both ESP and PK as "goal-oriented rather than information-based" (pp. 203, 208). Kennedy (1995) argued:

> The basic goal-oriented psi hypothesis assumes that psi phenomena (a) depend on a person's motivation for or benefit from the outcome of a random event, and (b) do not depend on the complexity or information-processing aspects of the random process.
>
> (p. 47)

Irwin and Watt (2007) described goal-orientation as non-mediational (i.e., not requiring a flow of information by various means which is not the case in the "cybernetic" theories which require some kind of mechanical transference, or processing of information, for an effect to take place). In other words, goal-orientation is sufficient in itself for an effect under PMIR, thus accounting for the sudden unexplained decision to take a different route home only to discover later that the usual route was blocked or had become a danger in some way. A similar example is given of the desire to avoid a laborious task (like mowing the lawn), only to discover that the lawn-mower conveniently will not start. While Stanford does discuss at length the many factors that can impede the goal (1990, pp. 62-153), he never did offer a reason "*how*" the organism brings about a favourable change of circumstances, but only stated that it "*does* occur" (Stanford, 1978, p. 208).

At a later date, Stanford (1990) was "less than fully convinced about the goal-oriented character of psi processes" (pp. 58–59), but maintained it for the most part in his resurrected PMIR model, which saw the abandonment of the conformance behavior (CB) model. Palmer (2008) still sees virtue in CB, and parallels it with synchronicity, noting points of departure:

> In my view, the closest fit to Jung's theory of synchronicity is Stanford's CB model. Without doing too much injustice to Jung's thought, I think one could describe Jungian synchronicities as the brain of a person coming into conformance with an external event in order to fulfil the person's needs and disposition. Of course, Jung's theory makes additional stipulations that go beyond the CB model or any of the other parapsychological theories. However, Stanford (1978) considers conformance to be a causal process.
>
> (p. 188)

As things stand, the primary underlying factor of the PMIR model is the "disposed" system (see next paragraph), and although Stanford still discusses ESP and PK as discernibly different processes (cf. Stanford, 1990, on ESP, with Stanford, 1974b, on PK),[18] he does hold that "implicit extrasensory guidance" is "part and parcel" (Stanford, 1974b, pp. 326–328) of many PK events and that "active-agent telepathy" (p. 344) may really be a special form of PK. Like Rhine (1947), Stanford thus appears to identify qualitative differences, but also compatibility between ESP and PK, while still suggesting that the one may be mistaken for the other. We see similar problems when attempts are made to force ESP and PK labels on synchronicity.

Stanford describes situations that are similar to synchronicity, in which "intriguing spontaneous occurrences, while they provide no compelling evidence that they are anything other than 'coincidences', might be instances of psi-mediated responses working in the service of the individual's needs" (1978, p. 201). In an earlier paper, he very clearly sees PMIR experiences as meaningful: "Odd coincidences of everyday life … seem to have meaning and importance for persons involved in them" (Stanford, 1977, pp. 840–841). Stanford regards such "fortuitous coincidences" as "psi mediated" (p. 841); hence the term "psi mediated instrumental response".

In summary, Stanford proposes two main aspects of PMIR specific to the "disposed" system: (i) psi can be brought about unintentionally; and (ii) psi is (provisionally) goal-oriented. For Jung (1952/1969, para. 912) too, unconscious agency ('nonintentionality') is self-evident in synchronicity, but where Jung saw synchronicity as goal-oriented (teleological), Stanford holds an "each-way" bet. Another parallel of PMIR with synchronicity is that effects can be meaningful: In fact, Stanford (1977) even makes the bold claim that PMIR would explain "synchronistic" events (p. 851).

Meaningful Information Creation

Biologist and evolutionary theorist, Lila Gatlin (2008),[19] proposed a theory-based model of paranormal process that is both intriguing and straight-forward; perhaps deceptively so for it is at first conceptually simple, but does get weighed down with the principles of information theory and a few statistical exercises to illustrate the process. Gatlin's Meaningful Information Creation (MIC) theory is different from PMIR, and theories yet to be featured in this chapter, in actually trying to explain synchronicity in terms of information creation as the linchpin of meaningfulness. She notes, however, that: "It is not necessary that every coincidence create information, but it is clear that coincidences are fertile ground for potential information creation" (p. 199). This point recalls certain *caveats* made earlier that apply in the case of meaningless chance groupings and individuation.

All around us we see information being created, but we also see entropy (the destruction of information). Even in the latter case, however, Gatlin (2008) argues that information is constantly changing (mutating), and despite the entropy change amounts to continuity at the root of evolutionary processes. From these assumptions, a living organism can be regarded as a *source line* (i.e., it is an information source that follows a certain path) where the '*if* A, *then* B rule' is not always true (i.e., it is probable; not predictable) so that an effect may only sometimes eventuate, as opposed to a *causal line* where '*if* A, *then* B' is always true. Source lines sit somewhere between absolute randomness and absolute certainty. Thus, Gatlin (2008) defines meaningful coincidence as

> the intersection of two or more independent source lines where identical or similar states occur. Clearly these similar states are not causally related. Such intersections may be located by aligning the source lines from the independent sources in the same time register and searching for identical or nearly identical states or "hits".
>
> (p. 201)

Gatlin (2008) goes on to argue that psi experiments follow this basic format, where the target sequence and the guess sequence are two intersecting sources. What interests the parapsychologist, however, is not outcomes (as chance-hits) that merely indicate mean chance expectation (MCE), but the process (usually referred to as psi) that raises the number of hits above MCE. Gatlin sees this process as non-random due to critical biases in the system (in relevant individuals, in evolution, in nature). Although Gatlin also sees the process as acausal at (say) the experimental level, she goes on to explain causality as being localizable somewhere in the so-called 'holon hierarchy'—by analogy, "atoms are parts of molecules, but wholes of elementary particles; molecules are parts of cells, but wholes of atoms …" (p. 205), with the word 'holon' standing for the unit:

> If the rise of hits above mean chance expectation in psi experiments is due to matching bias or pattern in target and guess sources, this makes the first level holon, the individual hit, acausal; and causality is displaced, so to speak, to the next higher level in the hierarchy.
>
> (p. 206)

These ideas align with Tart's (2008) *being-specific synchronistic causality* which "goes beyond the limits of our sensory and cognitive capacities, and the limits of our being (including whatever technological aids our minds produce)" (p. 119), but our intelligence might develop along evolutionary lines so that "observations which were formerly being-specific synchronistic to us would seem intelligible, becoming reduced to well understood or presumed physical or psychological causality or paranormal causality" (p. 121). Since Gatlin sees causality as existing at possibly other 'higher' levels, even if there is no evidence of causality at a 'lower' level, she might argue that synchronicity has a causal dimension, but one that clearly exists outside our purview. This argument over causality may be largely semantic as causality is actually a fluid concept difficult to demonstrate and usually only intuitively grasped, as Hume would remind us (this issue was discussed earlier in Chapter 3 under 'The Trick of the Cause in Parapsychology').

Gatlin (2008) sees synchronicity and psi unified under the principles of information theory. Seeing psi as a case of 'evolutionary synchronicity' at work, she classes psi as information creation; not information transmission that implies a causal process (from a cause to an effect). She argues that biological entities, which are inherently biased, can attune themselves to the rhythm of a random sequence of trials (a run), and these alignments are the result of evolutionary synchronicity—they are not random (e.g., a selection bias is involved), so they can be studied scientifically. Information sources can cross paths in a biased (non-random) and seemingly acausal way, yet they create meaningful coincidences in the process.

It should also be noted that Gatlin rules out precognition *per se*: "It follows that if a message has meaningful information content, it cannot be transmitted backwards in time regardless of what the nature of the carrier might be" (p. 206). In fact, it would seem that Gatlin's model readily accommodates effects that merely *look like* precognition (or *look like* psychokinesis) by appeal to information *creation* (not information *transmission*), and Gatlin claims no scientific laws are being broken.

Gatlin (2008) also points out that synchronistic connections do not simply come to an end, even after a psi experiment is finished, or even when a synchronistic experience seems to be over; nor, for that matter, do synchronistic connections necessarily start just at the moment we make our observations:

> The synchronous source lines continue to resonate or experience the same state at the same time without a causal connection; and this is misinterpreted

> as information transmission independent of space and time.... When we try to pinpoint the source of this apparent incoming information, it is indefinite in time because there is no signal. The information involved has not been transmitted, but rather *created* via the mechanism of synchronicity.
>
> (p. 208)

The principle of meaningful coincidence is given 'technical' support by Gatlin's model, which sees psi as a synchronistic process, but it is difficult to determine how intention fits in, if indeed there is a place for it—that is, the theory seems teleological or fatalistic. Arguably, that may be so for the greater number of synchronicities that are nonintentional, but there is a case for intentional synchronicity, as in the use of divinatory systems such as the *I Ching* and Tarot (see also Storm, 2025), and it is difficult to explain some synchronicities without assuming that intention was involved (i.e., contingent). The same applies to psi; the very idea of experimentation depends on it.

If Gatlin is saying those events we perceive as future psi effects and synchronistic outcomes have been preset, or at least evolved since time immemorial by the attunement of biased sources, then it seems the participant (irrespective of the experimenter's input, and the task at hand) is a mere actor playing out a role driven by evolutionary forces and principles. Ordinarily, we are given to think that 'disposition-serving' needs of the organism (to borrow from Rex Stanford) and, more generally, freewill (the freedom to choose), would seem essential in any schema that models the behaviour of organisms. No doubt Gatlin would agree, but it is difficult to imagine her defense, unless she would suggest that the occasional choice (as an act of freewill) that does deviate from that inbuilt bias may undermine the outcome—many parapsychologists would have observed this phenomenon in their experimental participants who confess an intuitive or instinctive feeling that they were unsure or were 'going against the grain' in their choices, only to 'psi miss' as a result. It would then seem that errors in judgement, like the chance factor, cannot be completely undermined (much less eradicated), entering as they do into so many situations (experimental or otherwise), helping to make outcomes sporadic and unrepeatable. Again, we see how psi mirrors intentional synchronicity in effects potentially made weaker by causes common to both.

Finally, while Gatlin's model mostly accommodates synchronicity's basic precepts, Gatlin does not speak to another key issue; archetypes. She does not mention archetypes as possible sources of the biases of which she speaks that would make *evolutionary synchronicity* a viable concept. In fact, she seems painfully close to the idea of the ubiquitous archetype, and its 'transgressivity' (i.e., its constellation beyond the individual psyche). With adjustments, Gatlin's model could recognise archetypes as somehow built into evolution as an ordering process, adding particular colourings and meanings to the outcomes (whether in real life or laboratory settings), in keeping with Jung's (1952/1969, para. 841, 845, 847, 912) definition of the archetype.

In summary, Gatlin's theory from a synchronistic perspective seems incomplete as long as there is no place for archetypes. She may beg to differ, being well aware of Jung's writings on the concept, but she may have felt that evolution incorporates archetypal principles which are a small part of a much bigger process—we simply do not know. I suggest we do see archetypal forces played out in exaggerated form in people like Ted Owens. As a rare type of individual, Gatlin would probably describe Owens as "psychically gifted" (p. 207), and primed for synchronicity/psi as may apply in the case of James Pike (see Chapter 4 in Storm, 2025).

Psychopraxia

The theory of psychopraxia first came to light in the late-1970s, effectively as an addendum to Thalbourne's Ph.D. dissertation (Thalbourne, 1981). The definition then entered Thalbourne's *Glossary* (1982, 2003), after which the construct and basic 'psychopractic' concepts were expanded into a monograph (Thalbourne, 2004). The term "psychopraxia" is derived from two Greek words: *psyche*, which means "soul", "mind", or "self", and *praxia*, from which we get our word "practice" (derived from *prattein*, meaning "to accomplish" or "bring about"). Psychopraxia theory is an attempt to achieve unification

> across both normal and *paranormal* psychology, and across action and *cognition*: in order to eliminate the conceptual distinction between (i) *extrasensory perception* and *psychokinesis* and (ii) normal information-acquisition and normal motor control.
>
> (Thalbourne, 2003, p. 99)

The theory emphasizes four fundamental aspects of action, whether action occurs endosomatically (within the body) or exosomatically (outside the body):

1 "The self, not defined further than that it is inclusive of the 'I' the common denominator of all experience and the co-agent of all action (this description allows for additional agency of the unconscious component of the self);
2 "The 'pro attitude': A person may be said to have a pro attitude towards state S when they would prefer S rather than -S (not S) if those two alternatives were to be brought to their attention. Under this heading fall goals, desires, wishes, intentions, needs, preferences, and dispositions, be they conscious or unconscious. Psi missing is also postulated to be the result of a pro attitude, perhaps unconscious, toward obtaining low scores. It is postulated that there is a hierarchy of pro attitudes, and the most potent one wins out. The self is said to 'adopt' a pro attitude;
3 "The goal-state S that is to be brought about (whether in the so-called 'mental' sphere or in the 'physical' sphere, is irrelevant);
4 "The set of intervening necessary conditions mediating between the self and its pro attitude and the goal-state S" (Storm & Thalbourne, 2000, p. 280).

Both the *endosomatic* and *exosomatic* aspects of our being speak to one fundamental ontological process, but the terms merely locate psi inside and outside the body of the experient, respectively. *Exosomatic psychopraxia* is effectively paranormal in the eyes of the casual observer: It is the self/psyche 'accomplishing' something *outside* the body, referring specifically to actions and cognitions beyond the normal compass of the sensory modalities or motor functions. *Endosomatic psychopraxia* (endo-psychopraxia) is no less a mystery than exosomatic psychopraxia (exo-psychopraxia) for, as is implied by Thalbourne (2004), the fundamental organic processes (e.g., of life) are still not understood—a comparatively broader knowledge (very often theoretical or modelled) of endosomatic (internal) functions is merely born of a cultural/historical advantage—these functions received greater attention from anatomists, physicians, neuroscientists, etc., especially in recent centuries. Therefore, whatever 'mysteries' do obtain or apply in the case of endosomatic psychopraxia, these processes I would call psychophysiological; they are generally explained in normal terms (e.g., as functions of the organs), but are not psychophysical, and are thus not paranormal. Less is known of the exosomatic functions (e.g., paranormal influences), but that is primarily because researchers find themselves epistemologically disadvantaged due to cultural and historical prejudices (Griffin, 1997, makes similar points).

Exo-psychopraxia embraces both ESP and PK, but the unification continues with ESP and PK being merged into a single construct which Thalbourne (2004) calls psychopraxia because ESP and PK are indeterminable in any instance where psi is discernible (even experimentally). The reason for the ambiguity comes from the fact that ESP and PK are discourse-dependent concepts that have emerged out of a fundamentally dualistic framework—any kind of paranormal cognition is automatically labelled ESP because it largely manifests mentally, and any kind of paranormal action is automatically labelled PK because it largely manifests physically. Researchers tend to avoid any attempt at disambiguation or clarification because there seems no way out of the impasse. As Radin (2006b) has noted, psychopraxia is a unitary phenomenon that "manifests in different ways according to context" (p. 376).

In continuing with his argument, Thalbourne (2004) points out that philosophical systems or paradigms necessarily and subjectively have psi effects labelled according to their ontological assumptions about reality. In Central-State Materialism, for example, all psi would be PK—since mental activity is reducible to brain function, ESP (nominally mental) can actually be seen as paranormal interaction between brains, or between a brain and any sufficiently displaced inanimate element in the environment, so that ESP = PK. In Idealism (Dogmatic, Critical, etc.), all psi would be ESP—since brain activities and apparently external events exist only as perceptions in the mind, PK (nominally physical) can actually be seen as paranormal interactions of mental perceptions, so that PK = ESP. It could be argued that it would be possible to differentiate two types of psi from *within* a philosophical doctrine (say, Dualism) on the basis that each has a mutually exclusive explanation, but note again the theoretical positions of Marwaha and May (2016), and Millar (2015), and others, described in Chapter 1 (see also the 'Multiphasic Model of Precognition' described shortly).

Thalbourne (2004) makes clear that the pro attitude can be held consciously, which compares with the individual's aim in intentional synchronicity. However, nonintentional synchronicity (the standard form), would not necessarily be the result of an unconscious pro attitude, though that could be inferred from the nature of the effect itself, or deduced from the outcome of in-depth analysis. The difference between unconscious psychopraxia and nonintentional synchronicity is that the latter supposedly results from the way the world is structured, and (importantly) how one *is*, or how one finds oneself in that world, with the self-system circumstantially involved, whereas psychopraxia is all about the 'self accomplishing' in an objectively separate world upon which the self can act in isolation (even if it happens to be outside the egoic framework; hence, unconscious). Like psi, psychopraxia then is more the result of an ability than a principle of nature. Though the self figures strongly in psychopraxia, as it does in synchronicity (we can assume Thalbourne's self parallels to some degree the Jungian Self), Thalbourne does not go into the analytical or clinical issues that may pertain, such as the meaningfulness of the experience, beyond its need-serving aspects (as in his personal 'library angel' experience; see Thalbourne, 2006a).

To date, Thalbourne's (2004) theory of psychopraxia has received only minor commentary from researchers in the field of parapsychology (e.g., Alvarado, 1983b; Beloff, 1985, 1988; Braud, 1983; McBeath, 1985; Roe et al., 2003). The major studies on psychopraxia, while often supportive of the theory, are not those of a broad range of investigators (e.g., Storm, 2003a, 2003b, 2005; Storm & Thalbourne, 2000, 2003, 2005a, 2005b). Results have not always been supportive of the theory (see Chapter 3 in Storm, 2025). And while there have been attempts to prove, for example, the ESP/PK distinction, results were inconclusive (e.g., see the series of studies by Roe et al. [2003, 2004, 2005, 2006] in *The Psi Process and Parapsychological Nomenclature* in Chapter 1). The major reason for neglect of the theory may be to do with the fact that the psychopraxia monograph (Thalbourne, 2004) has never fallen into a sufficient number of hands since its release (that is still the case), but lack of exposure is common for most of the theories presented here. It is also possible that, since 2004, researchers are still grappling with the theoretical and practical implications of psychopraxia, which are a challenge to conventional understandings in parapsychology, and a good reason to simply avoid the issue. Note too, as mentioned, endosomatic psychopraxia is essentially psychophysiological (not psychophysical), so the parapsychologist's main concern is only with exosomatic psychopraxia. These problems can only be resolved with time. Thalbourne's primary point, however, was not to settle the theoretical, practical, and philosophical debates, but merely to provide a terminology that does not try to reflect reality, but provides an ontology-free or neutral framework by which all researchers can work.

Decision Augmentation Theory

May, Utts, and Spottiswoode (1995a) proposed decision augmentation theory (DAT) as a "phenomenological, … logical and formal extension of Stanford's elegant PMIR model" (p. 456). Guided by the PMIR model, they proposed that "humans integrate information obtained by anomalous cognition [e.g., precognition] into the usual decision process" (May, Utts, & Spottiswoode, 1995b, p. 195). DAT is efficacious information acquisition from the past, present, and future, incorporated unconsciously into the mind continuously so as to influence the organism's mental and behavioural decisions—hence, *decision augmentation*. The RNG participant, for example, using anomalous cognition, opportunistically scans the environment for information in order to determine the appropriate moment to "press the button" (p. 195). The scanning component even extends to 'choosing' *anomalously* a preferred experimenter, or the most opportune day and time to attend a test session, and so on (May, Utts, & Spottiswoode, 1995b, p. 200). This idea of knowing when to act is supported by RNG data that shows no general mechanical deviations outside chance, yet participants' button presses show significant preponderances for one outcome over the other (e.g., significantly more 1's than 0's). May et al. (1995a) have effectively explained a conventional PK effect in the RNG case as an ESP effect (viz., anomalous cognition).

The governing principle in DAT, therefore, is information; not causal influence or interaction by force. DAT, however, does not explain all PK effects as ESP: For example, May et al. (1995b) concede they "would not invoke DAT … as an explanation of levitation" (p. 200).[20] One might tentatively exclude recurrent spontaneous psychokinesis (RSPK) from the DAT hypothesis, insofar as some examples of RSPK are attributable to human agency (not poltergeists). And we may exclude psychokinetic metal-bending (PKMB), and psychic healing, as it is difficult to see how DAT might be applicable.

While the tabled effects in Cardeña's (2018) study for 'anomalous perturbation' (i.e., PK) and 'anomalous cognition' (i.e., ESP) have similar ranges, DAT does not explain the dismally weak effect sizes on RNG devices—*if they were produced by ESP*, they should not be that weak compared to all other psi effects that are orders of magnitude stronger (see Cardeña's Tables 1 & 2, pp. 667-668). Furthermore, Dobyns and Nelson (1998) found empirical evidence that the process in RNG experiments involved

> an actual change in the operation of the experimental devices, taking place at the level of elementary binary decisions … [which] are inconsistent with the process of biased sampling required by the DAT model.
>
> (p. 256; see also Dobyns, 2006)

Other studies that may indicate distinct PK effects include Stevens (1998-1999) and any of the more recent studies led by Dean Radin (reviewed in Chapter 5). DAT, then, is not yet able to eliminate the need for the PK category, or psi modelling based on PK assumptions.

As another example, psychic healing (just mentioned) brings to mind bio-PK; a psychokinetic effect on a biological system. May et al. (1995b) even made the statement: "perhaps there is something unique about biological systems that allows force-like interactions, whereas physical systems such as RNGs do not" (p. 235).

They were referring to the DMILS study by Braud and Schlitz (1989)—those findings undermined the "intuitive data sorting model"; the predecessor of DAT (May, Radin, Hubbard, Humphrey, & Utts, 1985). However, as we have seen in regard to Bengston's own thoughts about so-called energy healing (see *Psychokinesis* in Chapter 1), bio-PK may involve the transfer of a specific kind of information that triggers self-healing, and thus may not be a force-like (PK) effect at all. That would put DAT in a good light, and the more general finding for human and nonhuman noncontact healing does not undermine Bengston's claim (see Roe, Sonnex, & Roxburgh, 2015).

Nevertheless, DAT is not out of the woods yet. And more to the point of this chapter, DAT is hardly comparable to synchronicity, conceptually, theoretically, or phenomenologically, except in one detail to do with intentionality of effect, which happens to create a problem for DAT as it would for any theory that reduces all psi effects to a single category (e.g., ESP or PK) or sub-category (i.e., to a modality or composite of modalities). For argument's sake, let us take a Rhinean view: An RNG experiment that neutral theoreticians might say is *prima facie* a test of PK, but is formally (by design) a test of DAT, will test for psi in a specific way (i.e., as ESP rather than PK). We can imagine then that what would be required of a sufficient number of informed participants is a honing of their intentions in a sufficient number of trials in such a way that they *do not detectably influence the apparatus with a PK force* (or that is what they think they would need to do and think they are doing). When a significant effect resulted, they (and the experimenter) would explain the hit-rate deviation as informationally facilitated via (say) precognition. The effect would actually be the result of a surreptitious 'bespoke intention' that accords with DAT—a kind of self-fulfilling prophecy. And the DAT theorist can safely argue that PK was never demonstrated.

All very well for participants who are 'in the know'. However, the 'right' intention could be unconsciously planted in participants' minds telepathically if they *are* blind to the experimenter's sole aim and intention, which is to seek support for the 'cherished (DAT) hypothesis'. And if the experimenter is also 'blind', the aim can still be 'discovered' psychically because there must be someone on the experimental team who knows what is sought. Albeit nonintentional this time, the psi effect could again be expressed as ESP. In other words, a so-called *demand characteristic* can be set up in DAT experiments (the same argument would apply to PMIR, and an effect to be discussed shortly; namely, MMPC). What we might expect in the long-run is that DAT pundits will generally find support for DAT, while those opposed may find evidence for PK, and a noncommittal cohort of experimenters may get chance results, or a mix of results for and against DAT. The flaw in theories that take sides (i.e., an ESP-stance or PK-stance) is that participants can be steered, consciously or otherwise, towards producing ESP-type effects or PK-type effects. These effects really only indicate a selection bias based on methodological criteria that includes experimental demands and expectations—the very outcomes Rhine (1946a, 1947) warned us about, and Roe et al. (2003, 2004, 2005, 2006) tried to demonstrate.

On the basis of what is intended and how it is envisioned that the intention should subsequently manifest, one can easily gain the impression that the phenomenon is extra-sensory or psychokinetic according to intention, but demonstration of a cause (or process, or mechanism) can be a matter of convenience, or purpose, or theoretical position, and may therefore be illusory. Philosophically, Thalbourne (2004) already argued this point. A single effect that seems like (and is argued to be) real-time PK on one occasion could be seen as (or argued to be) clairvoyance or precognition on another, and *vice versa*; it is similarly the case for precognition vs. retro-PK. We can stand outside this conditioned framework, not by making a choice between a 'force-like influence' *or* an 'informational mechanism', but instead by reframing the various scenarios, and see that the psychological dispositions of participants can be subjected to moulding by instructions and other aspects of the experimental methodology. These diverse treatments (coming from the protocols themselves and from the experimenter's aims and intentions) evoke archetypal responses, and even prohibit a range of opposing archetypal constellations. Rhine (1947) came close to this realization when he said "PK implies ESP, and ESP implies PK" (p. 129). Under synchronicity theory, there is only one *psychophysical* effect. Very likely, Rhine did not know how close he was to endorsing this key synchronistic principle. Synchronicity ultimately offers a complementary viewpoint. Some theorists even argue that we can accurately and informatively speak of psi as a complementarity involving correlations but no causal exchanges, as we shall see next.

Model of Pragmatic Information

As we have seen, some of the non-Jungian parapsychological theories and models that have been advanced thus far have a synchronistic thread running through them, but to varying degrees. Synchronicity theory has had considerable influence on German parapsychologist Walter von Lucadou (1987, 1995, 2015) in his Model of Pragmatic Information (MPI). While synchronicity is considered a "noncybernetic" process (Irwin & Watt, 2007, pp. 132–133), given that it does not involve the processing or transmission of information (Gatlin's theory follows the same principle), von Lucadou's MPI similarly implies synchronistic process in that "psi effects represent meaningful non-local correlations between a person and a target system" (Irwin & Watt, p. 129). But as von Lucadou (2001) states, "psi is no classical signal" *per se*; it is a "correlation in an entangled psychophysical system" (p. 13). The physical part of the system could be, for instance, an RNG, while the psychological part would be associated with the mind (psyche) of the participant in a laboratory study.

Entanglement implies complementarity. MPI even borrows these two key concepts from QM under Weak or Generalized Quantum Theory (see von Lucadou, Römer, & Walach, 2007). The reference to 'correlation' implies coincidence, suggesting that synchronicity theory is a guiding principle of MPI. But even more pertinent: MPI stresses that the entanglement correlations are created by the "meaning" (pragmatic information) of the situation (von Lucadou, 2015, p. 224)—a "message of vital relevance" (von Lucadou et al., 2007, p. 51)—quite the reverse of Gatlin's MIC, which holds that information is created out of the coincidence. One might argue that the two seemingly contrary positions are not irreconcilable if we rid ourselves of the causal language implied in both—meaning is both inherent and manifested.

This 'solution' seems not entirely accommodated by Gatlin's theory which, as far as it is discernable, does not consider the psychodynamics of the individual as MPI does—that is, MPI considers the unconscious state as a crucial element in RSPK (PK attributed to focus persons in poltergeist disturbances; see Pratt & Roll, 1958), describing RSPK as (say) the result of an "unconscious cry for help" (Lucadou & Zahradnik, 2004, p. 103). Roll (2006) concedes RSPK may also suggest post-mortem survival; meaning the poltergeist may be a causal factor in itself. In their investigations of haunt and poltergeist cases, Storm and Tilley (2020) suggest "psychically sensitive" persons may be the "focus of the disturbances", but "[s]ometimes there is no individual focus" (p. 22). And Alvarado (1983a) argues that "we have no right to accept the psychopathological model of the poltergeist agent without serious qualms" (p. 118)—there are many millions of people who could be diagnosed as "psychopathological", yet the number of poltergeist cases is extremely low. Whichever is the case, Gatlin does note that a certain type of individual is primed for synchronicity/psi.

Due to their complexity and irrelevance here, one can dispense with the details of von Lucadou's formal references to quantum theory and systems theory, the latter of which von Lucadou states is key to MPI, involving "events, behaviors, and experiences in complex systems" (2015, p. 222), but we cannot avoid mentioning the importance placed upon the "interface between the psychological and the physical description of the system" (von Lucadou, 1995, p. 13). This 'psychophysical system', in which occurs these 'entangled psychophysical correlations', is reminiscent of the concept of psychophysical parallelism, which has been compared to (and contrasted with) synchronicity.[21]

Von Lucadou (2015) makes two assumptions: (i) "any description of nature must have structure"; and (ii) "there must be an exchange of a minimal amount of pragmatic [meaningful] information or interaction with another system to enable information exchange and a measurement of it" (p. 223). A "system" is regarded as any part of reality that can be observed and investigated independently in the world (p. 224). An observer can be inside the system or outside the system.

Von Lucadou (1995) lists key concepts in the MPI, including "pragmatic information", "novelty", "confirmation", "autonomy", and "reliability" (p. 61), and two decades later, re-stated the same key concepts (von Lucadou, 2015, p. 225):

- "Pragmatic information (I): The meaning of given information measured by its action on a system;
- "Novelty (E): Aspect of pragmatic information which is completely new for the receiving system;
- "Confirmation (B): Aspect of pragmatic information which is already known by the receiving system;

- "Autonomy (A): Behavior of a system which cannot be predicted;
- "Reliability (R): Behavior of a system which is expected."

The various dynamics of these concepts in a given system can be described formulaically:

$$I = E*B = A*R$$

In a case of RSPK, for example, a poltergeist victim, who feels neglected, may at first experience Novelty (E; a series of unexpected events), but this goes into decline when Confirmation (B; recognition, acknowledgement) is gained from family members. At the same time, Reliability (R; stability, control) of the system gains the ascendancy as Autonomy (A; unpredictability) goes into decline.

To summarize the two fundamental theorems of MPI in von Lucadou's (1997, p. 162, as cited in Etzold, 2006, p. 45) own words:

1. Psi phenomena are non-local correlations in psycho-physical systems that are induced through pragmatic information which is generated by the (organisationally closed) system;
2. Each attempt at using non-local correlations for the purposes of signal transmission causes these [psi phenomena] to disappear, or converts them [in] an unpredictable manner.

As is evident, one may find MPI becomes increasingly difficult to grasp the deeper one delves into the theory, and most attempts to explain it are schematic to say the least (Etzold, 2006; Radin, 2006a). Etzold (2006) does, however, state that the first of the above two theorems is supported by the findings of paranormal belief research—psi believers tend to produce psi-hitting; whereas nonbelievers tend to produce psi-missing, and the belief of the experimenter also figures highly in these arrangements. Thus, a parapsychological (psi) experiment, as an 'organisationally closed' system, is constituted of participants, plus (probably) a tight-knit bunch of researchers/experimenters, and while their individual "expectations, hopes, fears, beliefs, and disbeliefs are self-referential, they act as self-fulfilling prophecies" (p. 52). That is the point I made above about DAT—that is, wittingly or unwittingly, those involved can distort the experimental parameters, compromising the experimental design and its outcomes with their intentions, whether these are from believers or skeptics.

According to the second theorem, psi cannot be a signal because the meaning in the information only serves a purpose to those within the system. This understanding leads to the conclusion that psi experiments (intentional synchronicity) might produce paranormal phenomena initially, but replication attempts will end in failure, decline, or displacement, if novelty and/or autonomy are effectively zero. Thus, MPI rules out any kind of systematic and profitable use of psi/synchronicity. However, experimenters would need to test the limits of novelty and autonomy to know for certain. Thus far, the theory does not explain the fact that standardization (as opposed to autonomy) in the ganzfeld technique is exactly the factor that explains its success and reliability. For example, in the meta-analysis by Bem, Palmer, and Broughton (2001), the standard ganzfeld design produced a significantly stronger proportion of hits (31%) compared to nonstandard (novel) designs (24%).

MPI also holds that high levels of novelty and autonomy are originally present in spontaneous psi (nonintentional synchronicity). Subsequent synchronicities for the same person will differ and therefore also show high levels of novelty and autonomy, so much so that prediction must be ruled out because, for example, displacement being unpredictable, offers no identifiable patterns from which one could make predictions from one event to another. It is possible to predict from MPI, but only in a prognostic and normal (non-precognitive) sense that describes four phases of a run of (say) RSPK events—these are "Surprise", "Displacement", "Decline", and "Suppression" (von Lucadou & Zahradnik, 2004, pp. 103–105). Similarly, these phases have been applied to other paranormal encounters—see Ouellet (2011) on the Washington UFO wave, and Ouellet (2014) on the Enfield Case.

I suggest, however, that we can find exceptions where prediction might be possible, as instanced in Jung's birds case, unless we call it prognosis, but certainly we do not need to suppose that a signal was involved (Jung, 1952/1969, para. 844-845). The woman was visited by a flock of birds no less than three times: First, we have novelty (e.g., the fated victim keeps changing—first, her grandmother, then her mother, and finally, her husband), and second, in spite of the continued autonomy and novelty (displacement), the woman was able to anticipate (predict) the third event (the death of her husband). This third correlation may not have had an embedded signal *per se*, since an induction (not a deduction) was made, but certainly, in a colloquial or vernacular sense, we can speak of a *sign*; if not, a *symbol*. It therefore does seem that autonomy and novelty do not prohibit prediction, even if a hint of repetition is in the air suggesting prognosis—it is not clear, one way or the other, that MPI makes that allowance. Nevertheless, any repetition should have resulted in increased reliability (stability), and loss of pragmatic information, which was not the case. Perhaps von Lucadou (2001) might argue that the paranormal effect, and its correlated meaning, must appear in some other form (i.e., as "a displacement in such a way that instead of the expected something else … happens"; p. 12). That does not seem true of the ganzfeld, and in Jung's birds case we have seen that displacement is not entirely undecipherable. Perhaps for displacement, von Lucadou might suggest grandmother → mother → husband.

As for declines, my experimental *I Ching* series of studies (see Appendix A), with its variable results (suggesting declines), might prove von Lucadou's second theorem correct. These declines do seem to dissipate (i.e., effects improve) with the introduction of novelty (see Storm & Rock, 2014a, 2014b), which is in direct proportion to pragmatic information and psi. Other examples can be found (see von Lucadou, 1995, pp. 64–65; 2015, p. 234; von Lucadou & Zahradnik, 2004,

p. 105). More generally, however, declines in the parapsychological literature are not as frequent as MPI suggests; declines simply do not manifest across large groups of investigators across great time spans (as the meta-analyses reveal; see Chapter 2). The only way MPI can cover for these long-term consistent psi effects is to propose that any given experimental design has constantly been modified over the years so that sufficient novelty keeps psi effects significant (however, as already argued, that is not the case for most psi domains), or a constant stream of confirmation-seeking experimenters (e.g., novice research assistants) are appointed to take over laboratory testing and, of course, the participants keep changing. While this latter assumption can be investigated, it seems unlikely that all implicated laboratories are refreshing their teams, and it must be noted that there is no significant inter-laboratory effect-size difference that might raise eyebrows (taking the ganzfeld paradigm as an example, see Storm & Tressoldi, 2020; Storm et al., 2010). What I must concede, however, is that my interest in the Melbourne Cup exercise is now virtually nonexistent (see again Appendix A), source material has been difficult to find and does not come easily (certainly not spontaneously), and the gains (meaningfulness) in the exercise have all but diminished.

To close, MPI seems to describe synchronicity in everything but name, only the formalisms are quite complex. Indeed, it is surprising that much of von Lucadou's relevant literature is bereft of references to Jung generally, and synchronicity specifically—only casual references are made to Jung in passing (e.g., von Lucadou, 2015; however, see also von Lucadou et al., 2007). Other scholars, however, have not let it go unnoticed (e.g., Roesler, 2014). Yet for such an obvious influence, one must wonder why archetypes and other synchronistic possibilities (e.g., prediction of outcomes) are overlooked.

Archetypal Synchronistic Resonance

Mishlove and Engen (2007) propose a "new theory"—Archetypal Synchronistic Resonance (ASR)—that is essentially a restatement of Jung's synchronicity: "We postulate that archetypes … serve as the central organizing components of a given paranormal experience" (p. 227). Mishlove and Engen parallel psi with reincarnation and rebirth, stating that "alleged rebirth or reincarnation experiences" are "emblematic of all ostensible paranormal experiences" (p. 229). Further, the authors

> regard alleged reincarnation experiences as signs of archetypal-synchronistic activation, manifesting in, for example, uncanny impressions of a kinship, resonance, or identification with a long-deceased individual.
>
> (p. 229)

By way of example, Mishlove reports that under hypnotic trance, "he encountered a man wearing a toga who identified himself as the Roman Seneca" (p. 230)—two psychics even proclaimed independently that Mishlove was Seneca in a past life. Similarly, Engen (after a 'past-life' reading with a trance-medium) states that he was a student of Seneca in a past life. Interestingly, Engen had an "abiding interest" in Seneca's writings. These two experiences are typed as ASR.

Two more synchronicities followed: first, an email sent by Engen to Mishlove at the very time Mishlove was heading for Seneca's birthplace in Cordoba for a vacation, and second, Engen's chance purchase of a book previously owned by Mishlove. The authors feel that the resonance is embodied in the inspiring and deeply personal connection they have for Seneca which induced a kind of rebirth experience for them both. The rest of the article develops synchronistically related ideas pertaining to meaningfulness, but not to the extent that it may be considered theoretically novel.

In ASR, we can see how a highly specific archetype may manifest or constellate in a person that predisposes that person to exhibit certain historically familiar characteristics and affinities in their personality, so we do not have to assume reincarnation—at best, it is implied in ASR. Personality traits may replicate with frequency, contemporaneously and/or down through the ages, but the recurrence of a specific archetype that stands behind those traits adequately explains the occurrence, and can even be expected. Crucially, however, and in principle, all human archetypal behaviours (inherited, human-wide modes of apprehension that can express in the personality) originate at some time in history, so questions that need answering in this regard will centre on the original sources of those archetypal behaviours.

Mishlove's and Engen's focus on alternatives to rebirth/reincarnation, albeit somewhat restrictive in terms of the usual extent and range of synchronistic expression, indicates a connectivity between Mishlove's and Engen's accounts that is insightful in a way that most coincidences (not always synchronistic), presented in collections such as Vaughan's (1979) *Incredible Coincidence*, are not. As a theory, or more accurately a theoretical position, ASR expands the range of synchronistic experience into the domain of the so-called 'retrocognitive' (which is rare in the synchronicity literature). Also, in ASR, the central place held by the archetype indicates a crucial component that is conspicuously absent in the other theories so far discussed.

Multiphasic Model of Precognition

As noted in a previous chapter, Marwaha and May (2015, 2016) introduced their Multiphasic Model of Precognition (MMPC) as a means by which all psi may be explained as precognition. This model seems to be the natural next step from May et al.'s (1995a, 1995b) Decision Augmentation Theory (DAT), but the 'scanning component' of DAT, which would include GESP, can now function without GESP—as the authors say, precognition need be "the only form of ESP" (Marwaha & May, 2015, p. 2; see also Shoup, 2015). However, the problem pointed out above for DAT (psi as a shifting form governed by intention), applies equally to MMPC, but Marwaha and May (2016) are focussed on an altogether different problem—specifically, the nature of clairvoyance and telepathy. They say information about the target could have come from any time, even the future: the "*when* and *where*" of an event are virtual unknowns (p. 90). Hence, the door is open for precognition to subsume clairvoyance and telepathy.

MMPC identifies two distinct phases:

> The first is the physics domain, which addresses the question of retrocausation [backward causation] and how it is possible for information to traverse from one spacetime point to another.... [and the] second is the neuroscience domain, which addresses the acquisition and interpretation of retrocausal signals.
>
> (Marwaha & May, 2015, p. 1)

Marwaha and May (2015) go through the various crucial steps to arrive at a workable theory. In Phase I, they describe what must transpire in the 'physics domain' to explain how information can be carried from future to present. They do this by referring to changes in entropy in the target system, where precognition seems to be in proportion to entropic change (Marwaha and May take entropy to be a "measure of chaos ... or lack of information"; p. 4). As entropy increases, the informational content goes into decline (its quality degrades). In real-time situations our sensory modalities are capable of picking up bursts of radiation—e.g., as light or heat—but the possibility of retrocausation (the future affecting the present), is justified by modern physics, where it is found that "all fundamental questions in physics are time-symmetric ... admitting both time-forward and time-reverse solutions; thus, retrocausation is mathematically allowable" (Marwaha & May, 2016, p. 79).[22]

In Phase II, Marwaha and May (2015) describe what must transpire in the 'neuroscience domain' (i.e., in the brain and CNS) to bring precognition into effect. And so we come to the experiential aspects (how the information is perceived, processed, and comprehended in the brain). The two theorists explain that "retrocausal signals emerging from a distant spacetime point impinge on an atypical sensory process, and are then cognized in the manner of other sensory inputs" (Marwaha & May, 2016, p. 80). However, Marwaha and May (2015) point out that the relevant literature reveals there are "no *stable* concomitant neural activities that seemed to occur *during* the point of time when precognition was supposed to have occurred" (p. 8). Also, they are not sure about the form of the energy carrier of the signal. Nevertheless, they are still prompted to state that "normal processing [of the future signal] occurs as it does for any other sensory input" (p. 8).

As we can see, Marwaha and May are vague on crucial points to do with the physics and neuroscience domains, but at least they bring attention to these problems (see the "challenges" to MMPC in Marwaha & May, 2015, p. 12). That is a brave step not tackled by other researchers and theorists, reason being the task is perhaps too foreboding. MMPC nevertheless comes across as over-ambitious, but *at least* it raises issues not covered by, or indeed not relevant to, other theories (some of these other theories are described in this chapter—e.g., MPI, described previously, and First Sight Theory, described next). For example, most models focus on cognitive processes only (how psi is experienced in the mind/brain complex), but they do not describe or explain psi as it originates in the physics domain; nor detail the various psychophysical and cortical processes.

Having just described Gatlin's (2008) MIC theory, the first point of interest, when one compares the two theories, is the fundamental clash that occurs; not once, but twice. Gatlin does not see how "meaningful information content" can be logically "transmitted backwards in time regardless of what the nature of the carrier might be" (p. 206). Griffin (1997) has made a similar point by arguing that retrocausation is self-contradictory (p. 91; see also Braude, 1986). Although writing in the 1970s, Gatlin (1977) may well have known about time symmetry back then (the theoretical possibility of backward causation), but that would not have made a difference to her because she sees information as being *created*, not *transmitted*—that is the second clash. For Gatlin, the "*when* and *where*" are irrelevant. It follows, that she would not see why an impossible effect (i.e., precognition) would need to be postulated when the simple notion of coincidence would suffice. The "*when* and *where*" of an event, even in the so-called future *and* at a remote location, becomes a non-issue for any kind of theory that does not depend on information transmission.

Marwaha and May (2015) follow the conventional view that precognitive (retrocausal) information is somehow transmitted backwards in time because the physics allows it ("the equations of motion are all symmetric in time.... time could move forward or backward"; p. 6). However, what may be stated in physics as 'allowable' is not a proof that psi can or must be retrocausal just because a theoretical premise seems to fit the bill. There may be many phenomena in the world (even human neurophysiological processes such as some kinds of cognition) that will not be properly understood until these fringe ideas in physics are grasped and applied, but psi does not have to be one of them. We can see that what has led Marwaha and May to propose MMPC in the first place is, in part, a Rhinean interpretation of 30+ years of parapsychological research (Millar, 2019, describes the "basis structure" of MMPC as "neo-Rhinean"), which suggests "the existence of *information transfer* [emphasis added] through processes that we are only now beginning to understand" (p. 2). A confident claim, but are we beginning to understand?

For similar reasons, I also note that Marwaha and May (2019a) subjected MMPC to a name-change due to their dislike of the term 'precognition'. Since they regard all perception as 'local' from the person-centric perspective, they now refer to MMPC as the Multiphasic Model of Informational Psi (MMIΨ). Other than that, there appear to be no other changes to the "basic structure and content", writes Nahm (2019, p. 57), who wonders why questions to do with "percipient selection and timing" (p. 58) still remain unanswered (that is "open for investigation" say Marwaha & May, 2019b, p. 99). Synchronicity does not require a spacetime-transcendent physical carrier for the information. As for percipient (experient) selection and timing of the unique experience, the former is given in the psychology of the individual, whereas there is nothing particularly special about the latter—the effect of interest has everything to do with why individuals volunteer for psi studies, and want to be tested in the first place.

First Sight Theory

In First Sight Theory (FST), psychologist James Carpenter (2012) renames the old 'folk' term *second sight* and calls it "first sight" because it is not secondary (i.e., not supplementary) to the other sensory modalities (seeing, hearing, etc.). He says of *first sight* that "psychic experience is actually going on all the time" (p. 3), albeit unconsciously; "all organisms are preconsciously engaged with reality beyond their physical, sensory boundaries", and those "distal engagements are termed *psi*" (p. 40). By way of a number of propositions or 'corollaries', the *first-sight* process is refined and clarified. I will not list and define all of them, but I will mention two that are key here: First is the "intentionality corollary" (p. 24)—if an individual finds an "element of potential meaning" useful, it is assimilated ('added') and that can result in psi hitting; if, however, the individual does not find an 'element' useful, it is dis-assimilated ('subtracted') and that can result in psi missing (incorrectly guessing an unknown target). The other example is the "liminality corollary" (p. 32)—this corollary refers to conscious experiences that are liminal (e.g., dreams, impulses, vague impressions) that are on the boundary between consciousness and the unconscious; these can be indicators of psi at work below and on the threshold of consciousness.

Carpenter (2012) states that "the First Sight model makes it explicit that psi events are not about … conscious experiences [of knowing or doing]" (p. 79). Elsewhere he is "not claiming that anyone gains explicit knowledge via psi but only inadvertently expresses implicit references to it" (p. 352). He means that the most parapsychologists can hope for is that so-called psi always and only ever starts in the unconscious as intuitions, stirrings, feelings, vague notions, or even "almost knowing" (p. 352), etc., that are then (or may be), in many cases, processed cognitively (i.e., made sense of) in consciousness, resulting in ideas that have to be verified (and if they are verified, they are called 'psi'), say as a direct hit of the target in a laboratory experiment, or say as a medium's best guess. I doubt this is completely true, although remote viewers would agree, as they vehemently rebut so-called *analytical overlay*—"Conscious subjective interpretation of signal line data, which may or may not be relevant to the site" (Smith, 1998, p. 17). However, my experience in free-response laboratory studies, and with psychics, confirms over and over again that in many instances, the psi product is specifically *known in consciousness*, and with a high degree of confidence; it can arrive in consciousness fully formed as an intelligible coherent datum of knowledge no different than recalling one's phone number or one's middle name—it is nothing like a best guess, or salient element that has to be drawn out from a stream of mentation, then analysed and judged, or ranked, or whatever. Of course, in many cases, Carpenter is quite right—most parapsychologists know, when they do their hit-counts to determine a p value, that real psi is indeterminable from a host of pure chance guesses that contribute to the count. But I do not feel that Carpenter has done his theory any favours by making the above absolute claim against "explicit knowledge via psi", which he lists as one of a number of "implicit assumptions that need to be changed", although his assumption about the redundancy of psi "abilities" *per se* is not out of place (pp. 75-91).

As noted, FST covers intentionality (e.g., "the intentions *of the experimenter* [emphasis added] might be adopted by the participant during the period of the experiment"; p. 290), but Carpenter expresses no concern about what this implies for psi as a mechanism beyond psi hitting. Perhaps that is because, generally speaking, parapsychologists take it on advisement that psi-conducive lab-etiquette is good lab-etiquette. I have covered the issue of the malleable nature of intention when I critiqued DAT—there I called it 'bespoke intention'.

FST is very much about keeping the whole psi phenomenon nested within subliminal psychological constructs, and not opening up a debate over the possibly unbounded limits of current physical (e.g., QM) paradigms. While Carpenter (2012) acknowledges many theoretical sources, which do, to varying degrees, inspire him and/or influence FST, synchronicity is not one of them (not overtly anyway). While Carpenter does cite Jung many times, the omission is almost inexcusable for an author who also happens to be a psychotherapist making claims about his own psychic experiences, one of which screams synchronicity, and involved a client of his (pp. 353-354). I make this point because synchronicity in the psychotherapeutic situation is not infrequent (see Connolly, 2015; Jung, 1952/1969; Schwartz, 2008). The omission is even more striking when we consider that Carpenter found it pertinent to include a section on "Freud and psi" (p. 350), but ignores Jung's input on psi.

My feeling is that Carpenter must hold that synchronicity goes against the grain of FST, for synchronicity has come down to us as a phenomenon that only happens sporadically and unpredictably in the everyday world, as though we have no control over it. It is not surprising that these ideas are maintained, as it was Jung who had us think that way, or if Jung meant otherwise, he did not make himself clear. However, a number of researchers (as we have seen) now see synchronicity as an *ongoing* and *common*, but mostly *undetected* process, and they agree with Jung that psi can be subsumed as synchronicity insofar as both have detectable *meaningful outcomes* (for converging viewpoints on synchronicity, see Storm, 2008c). All these conceptualisations (those just italicized) accord with FST. Perhaps the sticking point for Carpenter is that synchronicity is seen as a 'principle of nature' which is not how Carpenter sees FST, given first sight is a process confined to the individual.

Finally, Carpenter goes to protracted efforts to make clear just what is, and what is not explained by FST. This approach calls to mind Stanford's (1990, pp. 62–153) lengthy explication of PMIR that similarly sought to clarify how psi-mediation does, and does not, come about. In fact, Carpenter acknowledges PMIR quite often (e.g., pp. 108–114), and details its influences, and its points of departure from FST. Given the parallels between PMIR and FST, and PMIR and synchronicity, one may wonder still why synchronicity does not warrant a mention, unless we concede its 'holism' and coincidentiality are sticking points.

Synchronicity Theory Revisited: The Question of Psi

On numerous occasions throughout Jung's treatise (1952/1969; para. 840, 847-848, 863, 977-979), Jung drew psi (ESP and PK) into the domain of synchronicity, and even made comparisons between them. In Chapter 1, I questioned attempts by

Eisenbud (1980, 1983) to reduce the complex phenomenon of synchronicity to a variety of simpler psi forms. In this section, I will first draw formal parallels between synchronicity and psi based on their definitions, and I will then discuss the phenomenological overlap of the two.

Synchronicity Suggests Psi; Psi Equals Synchronicity

To justify the claim that synchronicity suggests psi, the following points are proposed:

1 In synchronicity, a physical event may occur *at the same time* as a parallel experience in the psyche at a distance outside the range of the normal sensory modalities (cf. clairvoyance, defined in the Introduction; includes clairaudience and clairsentience);
2 In synchronicity, a mental event may occur *at the same time* as a parallel experience in the psyche of someone else at a distance outside the range of the normal sensory modalities (cf. telepathy, defined in the Introduction);
3 Synchronicity is time-independent (cf. precognition, defined in the Introduction; premonition, retrocognition, and divination are also time-independent);
4 Synchronicity is independent of spatial/physical determinants (cf. psychokinesis, defined in the Preface; including micro-PK discussed in Chapter 1);
5 Synchronicity appears as a chance-like effect, and rather than being 'sporadic' and 'nonrepeatable', can be the subject of experimentation, as shown in a number of studies, which can also be regarded as tests of psi in principle—e.g., Jung (1952/1969) on astrology; Braud (1983) on meaningful coincidences; and Storm (1998-1999, 2008b, 2009, 2016) on the *I Ching* (see also Houran & Lange, 2012; Roe et al., 2014). (Some of these studies are reviewed in Appendix A).

Alternatively, it may be said that psi equals synchronicity.

It might also be thought that mere hints of synchronicity in psi processes imply a unidirectional resolution to the dichotomy that leans towards psi as the leading concept. As argued previously, this approach fails (again see Chapter 1), though we cannot say that the above definitional approach equates synchronicity with psi, or equates psi with synchronicity—perhaps we can only assume an *equivalence* (at least at this stage). However, there is also the case where they are phenomenologically similar. Jung (1952/1969) stated that psi is a form of synchronicity because it can be shown or argued that essential synchronistic criteria are met in psi (namely, meaningfulness, transcendence of conventional causality, and archetypal contingency):

1 Meaningfulness: Psi can be meaningful: "an affective expectation is present in one form or another [in an ESP experiment] even though it may be denied" (Jung, 1952/1969, para. 848). At the core of that arousal may be the anticipation of an outcome that is helpful, useful, pertinent, fortuitous, compensatory (i.e., generally meaningful) beyond the satisfaction of merely guessing right.

Seldom addressed by parapsychologists is the possibility that a psi experience can be meaningful, or even that meaning may be embedded in the psi experience, though some have been trying to make a similar point for decades now (e.g., Broughton, 1988; Eisenbud, 1963). Another exception is von Lucadou (1995, 2001) who does recognise psi in a more natural and holistic sense in his MPI theory. As just described, in MPI the 'pragmatic' component of psi is *meaning*. Mansfield et al. (1998) make the claim that parapsychological experiments that show paranormal effects do not present the quality of meaningfulness concomitant with their significant results. That may be largely due to the fact that many so-called 'hits' are merely those that arise by chance, which we must expect. Procedurally, synchronistic hits are not sought in psi experiments; an oversight that ignores the possibility that participants may be having meaningful experiences. The concession has been made, however, that "an acausal parapsychological occurrence might be a numinous experience providing an important unconscious compensation, one deeply meaningful for that individual" (Mansfield et al., p. 17). In Rhine's experiments, there is opportunity for meaningfulness to arise from the perceived "impossibility of the task that ultimately fixes the subject's attention on the process going on inside him, and thus gives the unconscious a chance to manifest itself" (Jung, 1952/1969, para. 848).

2 Acausality: Psi cannot be explained in terms of energy transmission, although some parapsychologists are of the opinion that information is transmissible, and their theories accord with that understanding, as given by some of the above theories. Subjective accounts of psi usually include reference to an inexplicable or 'unthinkable' causality (i.e., acausality) whereby the experience *seems* outside spacetime. In discussing Rhine's findings, Jung (1952/1969) refers to a psychic function or condition that can 'eliminate' the time factor and can even 'abolish' the spatial factor. Similarly, Jung claims the simultaneity of synchronistic events (i.e., synchronistic events "falling together in time") comes about because "synchronicity [is] a psychically conditioned relativity of space and time" (para. 840). Here we see parallels with psi and synchronicity. Whereas so-called normal phenomena supposedly follow causal rules, and function *within* spacetime, psi and synchronicity *characteristically and phenomenologically* appear to infringe those precepts. I suggest that synchronicity does not function causally, and functions *within* spacetime, and does not 'violate' it, which will therefore be true of psi if we are free to equate the two (see *Psychophysical Reality (the Unus Mundus)* in this chapter).

3 Archetypes: It might be suggested that some "anomalous correspondences" (which can be read as psi) may not be synchronistic because "an archetypal interpretation is sufficiently implausible to be ruled out *a priori*" (Palmer, 2008, p. 183). As was just mentioned, a similar claim is made against meaningfulness when, in fact, the literature itself demonstrates a severe short-coming—virtually no parapsychologist measures or tests for meaningfulness (though the principles are evident but only in a general sense in studies that looked at targets with an emotional charge). The same point applies here in that it may not suffice to make

a priori rulings on archetypes. Empirical observations need to be made to establish notable degrees of certainty that archetypes were not constellated. However, proving a negative is impossible outside a closed system. It might be best to demonstrate the *presence* (rather than absence) of archetypes, with the best chances of that in dream-ESP and Remote Viewing sessions, where the archetypal ground is more fecund compared to other psi designs. And given that activated archetypes are said to often correspond or align with emotional (affective) states, the researcher might gain from considering the psychophysiological correlates of psi in a new light (more on this point in a later subsection). Palmer also says some anomalous correspondences suggesting synchronicity may not involve psi. In such hypothetical cases, he claims "an archetypal interpretation is plausible" (p. 183), though statistical significance may not be demonstrated. Palmer gives the example of 'Barnum statements' (generalized readings made by psychics and mediums, not thought to involve psi). These readings are often given when "nothing 'good' seems to be coming through" (p. 183). But any archetypal gleanings from these spurious episodes could be as much the contrivance of an astute psychic or medium as the cold reading itself, and where that is found to be the case, neither the archetypal nor the synchronistic interpretation would hold validity. Palmer's point does, however, recall Browne's (2017) claim that a chance-like effect (not appearing to be psi) could be synchronicity (see "Alternative Explanations of Synchronicity: I. Chance" in Storm, 2025). However, Browne was referring to the single case of meaningful coincidence which is statistically indeterminable as synchronicity and therefore only *appears* chance-like. But a sufficient number of these, tested in the appropriate manner, could be significant.

Is Laboratory Psi Research Eliciting Synchronicity?

The previous subsection considered whether psi and synchronicity might be one and the same from definitional and phenomenological perspectives. In this subsection, I will look at laboratory psi research to see if key synchronistic elements may be evident and are coming through in the findings. First, however, I need to make a few crucial points about conventional parapsychological thinking. If modern-day psi research started with the work done by Rhine (Pratt et al., 1940/1966), then for over 80 years most psi experiments have depended on participants making *guesses* about concealed or future targets, though terms like *identifying*, *seeking*, or *detecting*, should be preferred rather than 'guessing' *per se*. I should mention that the blunt terms 'guess' and 'guessing' do go back earlier than Rhine's era, to the late 1800s, and the use of those terms persists.[23] It is as though *guessing* (assuming, presuming, or asserting without sufficient information *available to consciousness*) can sometimes be taken as a euphemism for *using psi*. But, on the one hand, *guessing* also implies one selection is as good as any other, since there is nothing overt and substantive to base the choices on, regardless of the fact that experimenters hypothesize that guessing can be subverted by occasional psi, and there can be levels of confidence in calling. On the other hand, however, even a hesitant attempt at *identifying* or *detecting* a concealed or future target implies a psi-related decision-making process (largely unconscious) idling away in the background, seeming to function intuitively, facilitating or causing the psi effect (see the previous section 'First Sight Theory'), with the chance result *partly* being a default outcome when the process is not optimal. This second scenario does not completely eliminate guessing *in principle*, and nor do I expect that to be possible, but that is not entirely my point. I am suggesting the very use of the word 'guess' in formal psi instructions, and encouragement to guess in psi studies, is counter-productive, and not the only process that transpires in those studies.

Given these two scenarios, two contradictory theoretical perspectives about psi can emerge—either (a) psi comes in and out of the picture (an all-or-none response) to yield hitting (because psi subverts guessing) or missing (due to pure guesswork); or (b) psi is ever-ready and constantly operative and never dissolves, though it may weaken, so that we have hitting due to strong psi or near-hitting due to weak psi (echoes of FST). The former we can call the ON/OFF perspective, and the latter we can call the STRONG/WEAK perspective. This latter understanding should be preferred as it makes more sense, and even accords with observation: First and foremost, psi never 'sleeps' (as we know from dream-ESP) even though our five sensory modalities do 'knock-off'; second, as just stated, missing could really be near-hitting (i.e., almost-hitting) leading the parapsychologist to consider the causes of weak psi; third, psi-hitting cannot come from *pure* guesswork alone because there is no OFF phase (the ostensible explanation for MCE); and fourth, expressions on the faces of ideal participants suggest they are not guessing, but are thinking about (pondering, or musing over) the stimuli before them, suggesting they personally involve themselves with the stimuli, trial after trial—it is a kind of *connective effort* or *engagement* with the stimuli.

I suggest that instructional words like *identify*, *seek*, or *detect*, would put the typical psi participant in a completely different frame of mind compared to the limited mental effort that *guessing* might invoke. In essence, then, if we adopt the ON/OFF perspective, we assume that *only* guessing (as a *pure* effect) is operative during the OFF phase, whereas if we take the STRONG/WEAK perspective, guesswork cannot be seen as a pure effect acting alone because psi is always operative, even when it may be weak and have only minimal influence. This latter understanding aligns with the current thinking in cognitive psychology whereby a genuine psychological effect in say a sample cannot be thought of as the result of guesswork (unless of course the research is on 'guessing' *per se*). This viewpoint is also more accommodating of synchronicity theory.

Now to my main aim in this subsection: To determine whether laboratory psi research is eliciting synchronicity. To do that, let us start by considering what correct targeting (hitting) means in the forced-choice and free-response domains. It will be seen that we cannot simply depend on quantitative outcomes, mere hit counts, to tell us much about the synchronistic process. In forced-choice studies, the *qualitative* aspects of the hits may help because judgements about quality (archetypally speaking) leave no room for interpretation (e.g., star for star; circle for circle), but they are attributable to only a select few participants who find the symbols (shapes, number, etc.) meaningful. That is, there is too little opportunity for archetypes to constellate due to the limited range of stimuli in forced-choice target sets. Palmer (2008) salvages the synchronistic notion by noting that circle = mandala; cross = crucifix. These would be archetypally relevant, but again only for those, say, of a religious or spiritual persuasion, providing the archetypes that correspond to the symbols will resonate and constellate at the time of testing, and as Palmer says those symbols are not meaningfully "rich" and not as open to "psychodynamic interpretations"; p. 182). It is perhaps for this reason that effect sizes are amongst the smallest in the forced-choice domain—the set of stimuli, being limited, resonate archetypally with very few participants, and therefore do not evoke general interest. Of course, constant testing in very long runs of trials are de-motivating and that can discourage psi performance (see Blackmore, 1991; Storm, 2006; see also the next subsection *Towards a Synchronistic Understanding of Psi*, where motivation is discussed). Similar arguments can be made about micro-PK experiments—binary (zero/one) scenarios have limited archetypal appeal, and psi performance is not helped by the tedium of seemingly endless runs.

In free-response studies, however, 'matching' depends on approximation, though I prefer the word 'correspondence' to 'matching', as do many others (e.g., Houtkooper, 2002; Jung, 1952/1969; Palmer, 2008; Rawlette, 2019a). Drawing from the mentation, the experimenter, judge, or participant, spots the similarities in the target, but ideally finds few or none in the so-called decoys. So, for example, a circle in a person's mentation (e.g., a *hula-hoop*) ought to correspond conceptually to the circular-shaped target in the array (even if it is, say, a *donut*), since it would stand out from the non-circular decoys. The problem is that such a 'direct hit' has only quantitative value (i.e., it contributes to the count of hits)—qualitatively, there is nothing at all *direct* about it (i.e., *hula-hoop* ≠ *donut*).[24] Yet while it is not exactly a qualitative 'hit', it is a 'good fit' because of the *equivalence*—it is a 'hit' at a superordinate (archetypal) level. In this sense, the pertinence of the synchronistic interpretation is clear—it ameliorates (if not, vanquishes) the strict assertion that 'close-fitting' should not count as psi, but the effect is more than that for it can be viewed as a meaningful coincidence. On the premise that it *is* a direct hit, some researchers feel confident that psi *was* effected, thus making acceptable or adequate blunt (fuzzy) approximations to images. (Of course, for argument's sake, in the examples presented thus far, we are ruling out these hits as chance outcomes, and assuming they contribute to success rates that exceed MCE.) This is to say, most researchers pay little heed to *qualitative* inaccuracies, and might argue that a stronger signal (or more concentration from the participant) would have furnished a mental image of a *donut*. The mistake in this thinking is that the synchronistic moment was not about hula-hoops or donuts which, in this case, concerns the archetype of 'circularity', since an archetype can only be represented as a found image in memory—that is, the participant did nothing wrong. A real problem may have resulted had there been more than one circular image amidst the decoys.

We draw closer to a major procedural flaw in standard free-response designs to do with target sets and the 'orthogonality' (independence) of images in picture arrays (worthwhile steps have been taken to rectify the selection problem; see May et al., 2012). While in one sense little can be done to convince the parapsychologist that there is a problem here, psi testing becomes counter-productive when target-missing *not attributable to chance* is the result of undesired archetypes constellating. Experiments are not designed with the participant's psychology in mind. Instead, the experimenter takes pot-shots with randomly generated (arguably meaningless) stimuli and targets (i.e., there is no consideration as to what these may mean to participants as perceivers and agents). Small wonder that minds wander and there is little interest in the stimuli (for one solution, see the next subsection, *Towards a Synchronistic Understanding of Psi*).

These assertions need to be unpacked: Under the principle of synchronicity, a paranormal hit can never be the result of information transmission,[25] or energy transfer—any kind of paranormal 'perceiving' is theoretically inapplicable in relation to the effect—a psi hit (e.g., 'equivalence' in synchronicity) is only ever an approximate *correspondence*, not to a target, but to archetypal content *represented* in the target (or even from some other source such as a decoy). From the Rhinean perspective, *because* psi is an unconscious process, the individual is thought of as one who processes incoming data (a target signal) to the best of their psi ability, whereupon they will likely recognise a perfect match, or settle for the closest fit—all by sheer impulse, intuition, hunch, and (some might say) guesswork. Note, for example, how Katz et al. (2021) make those same assumptions when they say remote viewers "access their intuitive-based *perceptual* and *sensory abilities* [emphasis added]" (p. 66). In truth, individuals cannot always be so certain (if ever) about what they are doing when they *select* to the best of their "abilities" *per se*, so we cannot exclude the possibility that correct selection is the direct result of responding to a fortuitous archetypal impulse that just happens to be present and letting the archetype have its say, so to speak.

This distinction is not based on mere semantic word-play for two very different processes are described here. Starting in the individual, the archetype (having been activated, or constellated), as a superordinate factor, works as a 'categorical imperative' that limits the number of meaningful correspondences between stimulus and target since they must fall into that archetypal category. When presented with choices (e.g., target + decoys), the individual's 'archetypal situation' is one which ideally *facilitates an appropriate choice*; interpreted as an 'effect'—a 'hit' (psi in the conventional sense). That is, the archetype behind the 'outer' component (the hit) in the synchronistic event (the trial) is the same archetype behind the 'inner' component (the image in the participant's mind). The two must come together for the joint effect to be a meaningful coincidence; the synchronistic outcome comes to be called a hit.

It is a fact that the modern-day parapsychologist labours under the apprehension that *psi ability* (precise and accurate psi targeting) is enabled by anomalous information transmission, anomalous (or extra-sensory) signal perception, or energy transfer, or some other comparable mechanism or cause. The problem here lies in the fact that 'signalling' or transmission models lack explanatory power—the idea of a signal only coming through *on occasion* and its possible distortion is put down to an undesirable imbalance in the signal-to-noise ratio. When we think like that, the proposition that we are often dealing with weak signals automatically has skeptics thinking that ESP is problematized by concepts like 'fuzzy' relations or 'close fitting', or "counting of 'close' or nearly alike events as if they were identical" (Diaconis & Mosteller, 1989, p. 853). But there is no problem. This so-called 'problem' arises because the situational (relative) restrictions of psi that must ideally be identified and controlled are in fact the natural limits of synchronicity. Synchronistic enhancement can never be a matter of strengthening a signal, or filtering out noise to reduce fuzziness. Either an archetype constellates or it does not.

However, archetypes are not like "separate particles" manifesting in their own unique way, for they can constellate together, and can even be "contaminated with one another", with consequent effects on perceived meaning (see von Franz, 1992, p. 9). We must simply accept that the archetype(s), as over-arching superordinate structure(s), can manifest as *representation(s)* in a target, *and even manifest elsewhere* (i.e., in decoys). Fortunately, the stream of significant findings in the meta-analyses suggests that archetypal representations in any of the decoys must be minimal—those types of archetypes are expected to constellate but rarely, and will show up as 'misses' (actually a form of displacement). Such outcomes could occur, for instance, if some number of participants have more than one complex leading to the constellation of competing archetypes. All this is to say that even good-quality target sets like those devised by May et al. (2012) might be good for testing psi under the premise that anomalous information transmission is the operative factor, but they are not necessarily good for testing synchronicity under the premise that meaningfulness is the operative factor. When meaningfulness is seen by the participant as embedded elsewhere (i.e., in the decoy), then a form of displacement will arise not because information was misread, but because an inappropriate archetype had constellated.

Displacement issues aside, these other points lead us to more recent developments in psi research: In the evolution of experimental designs, we can trace a shift from limited, static, simple tests of psi, to broad, dynamic, complex tests—a move to real-world (ecologically true) scenarios that align with the way psi best manifests, though the same claim is made for synchronicity. We can include experimental paradigms like dream-ESP and RV that have a built-in synchronistic sensibility, given the way their effects are elicited and the considerations that have gone into their design, though the influence of synchronicity theory tends not to be mentioned. Crucially, the finest experimental designs are meaningfully structured and offer a sense of purpose to participants and practitioners. Not surprisingly these designs also produce the largest effect sizes (see Baptista, Derakhshani, & Tressoldi, 2015; Storm, Sherwood et al., 2017; for a review, see Cardeña, 2018). Given that this kind of evidence results from designs that have a high degree of ecological validity, coupled with the fact that the more impressive cases of psi are of the spontaneous kind, the psi laboratory could become the ultimate proving ground for synchronicity provided that a somewhat artificial environment can be made to feel natural and encourage spontaneity.

Currently though, the majority of psi effects do not stand out as synchronicity. Partly, the reason for that oversight comes down to the unique phenomenology of synchronicity—at one end of the spectrum, its subtlety is not detected so it is interpreted as psi, whereas those not-so-subtle unfathomable scenarios at the other end of the spectrum help maintain the psi/synchronicity distinction, even though it is not entirely warranted as I will argue below. To illustrate the latter, I give the example of a distressed woman receiving a phone call from another distressed woman who had *accidentally dialled the wrong number* (see Beitman, Celebi, & Coleman, 2010).[26] The first woman was naïvely prepared to re-unite with her unreformed husband, but the conversation with the caller changed her mind when the caller revealed that she had divorced her similarly unrepentant husband. How does one even begin to create in the laboratory such a coincidence? Given that kind of complexity in terms of operationalization, the psi/synchronicity distinction seems justified, but I suggest it is not justified, for psi and synchronicity are different in *degree* only, not in *kind*. After all, the correspondence could be described as merely a psychic situation with strong telepathic overtones. Note also, for example, how real-world examples of psi (e.g., remote viewing) tend to trump low-key lab-based parallels (e.g., card-guessing) in terms of scale (numinosity or 'wow' factor), yet parapsychologists do not automatically see them as two different psi modalities.

In fact, I suggest that no self-respecting parapsychologist (of a Rhinean persuasion) could resist the opportunity of pointing out the possibility of a telepathic connection initiating the phone call in the two-women case (i.e., a desperate, emotional woman put out a mental call to a like-minded soul, even to the point of her necessarily dialling an ostensibly 'wrong' number). Beitman et al. (2010) refer to the "personal relevance" in this two-women encounter, and therein lies the meaningfulness, whereas many might assume laboratory psi testing is deficient in such meaningfulness. While the idea of testing telepathy is not new in parapsychology, experimenters need to start thinking in terms of connecting factors, which in the above case *was* 'personal relevance' (from which springs forth meaningfulness), and that too can be addressed in the laboratory. (For an example, see the study by Silberstein & Bigelow, 2024, discussed in the next subsection.) Using a little imagination, problems with operationalization can be overcome.

Experimenters often test participants on the basis of closeness or relatedness (genetic or otherwise), and examples of such studies abound (e.g., Alexander & Broughton, 2001; Broughton & Alexander, 1997; Sheldrake & Smart, 2003a, 2003b). I suggest these approaches are sound and represent good parapsychological practice, but as the above case shows, the so-called 'relatedness' referred to a single archetype alone that constellated in *two complete strangers*: The women were united in the same archetypal experience they had with their respective husbands—namely, the 'conflict of opposites' as represented in gender issues (e.g., the *anima*/*animus* conflict; see Jung, 1925; Wall, 2014). Interestingly, just as a free-response match is *coincidental*, we must presume that the naïve woman's change of heart (in favour of divorce) may be *convenient* if *appropriate* is too much to claim, given the whole encounter was also *coincidental*! How anyone goes about interpreting the meaningfulness in their encounters (natural or artificial) is their own business, and it is certainly not the business of the experimenter. What we can say, however, is that any subtle distinctions between psi and synchronicity are the mere products of situational contingencies, but the parallels remain. For more on experimental designs, see the next subsection, and for similar real-world cases that have synchronistic overtones, see Playfair (2002).

So while parapsychological studies are not generally designed to identify archetypal elements, it would be possible to revisit some of the free-response studies and conduct analyses aimed at identifying these elements, trial by trial (Jungian scholars might possibly be best suited to the task). Certainly, however, dream-ESP and RV studies often contain images that could be considered archetypal (numinous) in that they are graphic, emotionally powerful, and evocative, and may be meaningful to participants—these are often self-evident and need no elaboration, even for laypersons who have had only a rudimentary exposure to the literature (see McMoneagle, 1997, 2000; Targ & Puthoff, 1977; Ullman, Krippner, with Vaughan, 1973).

RV research has thus far focused on numinosity and intention (see Storm, 2025; see also Schwartz, 2007, 2014), as well as a third factor, entropy (the breaking down of structure with the concomitant release of energy). More generally, studies seem to suggest that high-energy systems make better targets than low-energy systems (May, Hawley, & Marwaha, 2017; May, Spottiswoode, & James, 1994). I draw a parallel between high-energy systems and archetypes, which have often been equated with sources of great power and energy, not just in psychological, religious, and mythological terms: Consider Johnson's electricity analogy described in Chapter 1 (Segaller, 1989). Earlier, Jung noted the "specific charge" of archetypes and their inherent numinous effects, and subsequent affectivity (para. 841). By the same criterion, we can understand why a ganzfeld meta-analysis by Bem and Honorton (1994) showed dynamic targets (e.g., movie film) elicited significantly stronger psi effects than static targets (e.g., photographs; see also Storm & Ertel, 2001). It is important to understand that it is the inherent dynamism (not the energy) in the stimuli that resonate with the individual. We can thus dispense with the notion that energy *per se* is somehow tapped, or syphoned off, to produce a paranormal effect—that idea merely resurrects the causality conundrum implied in the transfer of energy.

Related to this energy issue, studies by Thalbourne (2006b, 2008) on the relationship between Kundalini (ostensible body-energy) and psi have proved worthwhile in that it can be argued that affectivity is very closely related to subjectively identified Kundalini states. For example, in a re-assessment of past results from a series of Kundalini studies, with M. A. Thalbourne (M.A.T.) as self-experimenter, it was shown that M.A.T. favoured psi in the self-determined Kundalini condition *over* the self-determined non-Kundalini condition across no less than seven studies in which he tried to raise the counts on an RNG beyond chance: There were

(i) *directional* effects (i.e., sign-counts, or deviations from zero) 64% of the time; (ii) *magnitudinal* effects (Kundalini produced stronger psi 75% of the time); and (iii) *significant* effects in the direction hypothesized, four times out of five. The results indicated a tendency for psi to be "relatively *stronger* in the Kundalini condition, and generally *behave* (directionally speaking) as M.A.T. intended in that condition" (Thalbourne & Storm, 2015, p. 86). Of course, there is again no suggestion that psi is energy-related for reasons just given. The main point here is Jung (1952/1969) associates archetypes with *emotional* 'energy' and affectivity (para. 846). It is possible that Kundalini was M.A.T.'s best way of describing affectivity (manifesting in any number of ways including emotional surges, psychophysiological arousal, or even abreaction), but with the associated archetype came the corresponding psychophysical (synchronistic) parallels in the RNG. While RNGs are extremely limited in outcomes, and these provide very little in the way of meaning since they yield only binary (zero/one) outcomes, Thalbourne's intention was dichotomous (Kundalini vs. non-Kundalini) so outcomes were meaningful for him.

While some psi studies (e.g., free response) do look for matches of participants' inner images with randomly generated outer targets, there is no attempt at making these correspondences meaningful to the participant (see Storm, 2008c, for a fuller treatment of this topic). In truth, any experimenter with some sympathy for synchronicity has to hope meaningfulness will emerge, if they believe it is facilitative of psi. But a mere hope is about as far away from a controlling factor as one can get insofar as meaningfulness is unequivocally operative in synchronicity, which may stand as no less than the whole point behind testing a participant in the first place—as Broughton (1988) once said, "If you want to know how it works, first find out what it's for" (p. 187). Broughton specifically noted that psi is not particularly good at accomplishing what we think is its purpose, which means we may be mistaken in how we have conceptualized it, and have not defined it accurately (for details, see Broughton, 1988, pp. 191–194).

In seeking an answer to the purpose of psi, Broughton's (1988) analysis raises the 'need-serving' aspect of psi, which ultimately led to his conjecturing about the so-called *experimenter effect*—it is possible the experimenter has the greatest need, followed by the participants, and then anyone else tangentially involved in the study (see Chapter 2 for a consideration of this problem). Of course, the need-serving aspect to psi can be at the base of an outright instinct for self-preservation, or at least some relatively lesser benefit or advantage, which is surely fed by the same urge. This assumption is appropriate in the case of synchronicity, which is understood to be survival-linked insofar as it concerns transformation of personality leading to psychic wellbeing and wholeness—only an optimally functioning organism has an optimal survival advantage. Of course, attempts to achieve transformation by, for example, psychic training (via yogic or shamanic practices) for the sake of a survival advantage, can create a false hope from the synchronistic perspective—one does not 'transform' just because one has become more psychic, although 'psychic opening' may be concomitant with transformation (a.k.a. spiritual emergence) born of a spiritual emergency (see Storm & Goretzki, 2020, 2021; see also Grof & Grof, 1990).

Critically, one does have the option of training oneself to be more receptive and sensitive to the occurrence of synchronicity, which may facilitate a synchronistic atmosphere. This sensitivity, however, is often shown not simply to be optimized through concerted effort, but is more likely heightened through extreme personal crisis (e.g., spiritual emergency as just mentioned). A very likely, cogent example of someone who underwent such a crisis was 16th-century French physician and seer Michel de Nostredame (a.k.a. Nostradamus; 1503-1566). Nostradamus lost his first wife and their two children through plague, which would have been acutely anguishing for him given that he was a physician who healed many plague victims, yet could not save his own family. To make matters worse, his reputation suffered greatly, his patients abandoned him, he was shunned by even his closest friends, and he entered a kind of fugue-state (a kind of self-imposed exile). It is a matter of historical record that only after many years spent dealing with his crisis (from at least 1538 to 1544), which included much study, did his predictive skills (i.e., his synchronistic sensitivity) emerge to full effect, culminating in many paranormal prognostications and predictions, as embodied in his major work *Les Prophéties* (*The Prophecies*), which preoccupied the last years of his life (Cheetham, 1989; Hogue, 1987; see also Chapter 5 in Storm, 2025).

In summary, it can be said that parapsychologists elicit synchronicity in their laboratories, but not deliberately. As the short list shows in the previous subsection, there are very few studies where synchronicity was the intended effect in laboratory experiments. This subsection is a cursory attempt at pointing out the failure to acknowledge the synchronistic aspects and underpinnings in psi research (for other examples, see Beitman et al., 2010, pp. 458–463). Generally, parapsychologists do not go looking for synchronistic effects, and they overlook the qualitative aspects of their hits, so they do not design psi studies which try to show meaningful parallels that have numinous archetypal depths to them, and they certainly do not interpret psi in that way. While mainstream interests indicate their focus is primarily on variables such as paranormal belief, personality types, and run-of-the-mill cognitive processes, under the hypothesis that these will correlate with (i.e., predict) psi, parapsychologists seem to have been extraordinarily adept at steering clear of synchronistic variables. It could be said that they only look for synchronism; not synchronicity.

Towards a Synchronistic Understanding of Psi

Following from the previous subsection, and an earlier subsection (see *Rethinking Psi as Synchronicity* in Chapter 1), it is necessary to expand our understanding of psi, and synchronicity theory may help. If experimenters are to look into synchronicity, they must start with well-planned experimental designs based on adequate knowledge of the roles of meaningfulness (we must find out what psi stimuli and task outcomes actually mean to participants, and why). We must also consider affectivity (emotion), numinosity, and archetypes—the last of these is perhaps the most challenging concept to understand and operationalize in experiments. The roles of all four are pivotal, as indeed Palmer (2008) acknowledges, as are more conventional factors that muster interest from psi experimenters such as intention, compliance, paranormal belief, relaxation, mood, enthusiasm, expectation, individual differences such as prior psi experience and/or psi-training, and a panoply of personality factors. Jung makes this quite clear (1951/1969, para. 980-981; 1952/1969, para. 838, 841, 846). All these are thought to be psi causes, or more conservatively are thought to be psi-conducive. As I said before, there are other viewpoints: Greatrex (1999) notes that studying synchronicity would impel researchers to go beyond issues related to freewill "in certain contexts"[27] and "consciousness and the mind-body problem" because synchronicity, as a broader construct, is more holistic, so that the "nature and relationship" of physical and mental events "remains a separate issue" (pp. 5-6). In the subsection *Rethinking Psi as Synchronicity* in Chapter 1, I expanded on Greatrex's thoughts by saying there was no critical need to come from the standpoint that psi ability, extended consciousness, unlimited mind, and untethered freewill (intention and volition) are causal in any absolute sense.

As long as psi is not equated with synchronicity, our current understanding of psi gives an incomplete picture of processes currently referred to as paranormal. Recall my comparison of the Rhinean (psi) model with the Jungian (synchronistic) model in the previous chapter using Owens as a test case. From statements made in the previous subsection, we can see that one of the overarching problems in modern psi research is the fact that experimenters have differentiated psi from synchronicity on the basis of decades of findings that do not address the combined issues of the personal meaningfulness to participants of the stimuli and the test outcomes (the coincidences), especially the successful trial outcomes. This naïveté has given psi a unique but unjustified phenomenology (i.e., psi expresses a supposed ability and therefore is caused, and the effect is merely wanted or desired) that demarcates it from synchronicity (which supposedly just happens to people with impeccable timing who just happen to be in the right or wrong place at the right or wrong time).

Palmer (2016b) attempted to address the apparent conceptual differences between psi and synchronicity by conducting an experiment that tested meaningfulness (Palmer's study is also reviewed in the subsection *Ted Owens: The Synchronicity Man?* in Chapter 1, but here I only consider the stimulus material). In a counter-balanced design, target messages had to be identified in two tasks: A psi task (where an array of four messages were invisible and, under the psi hypothesis, a randomly pre-selected target would be chosen to the exclusion of the decoys), and a synchronicity task (where the four messages were visible, but one had to be designated 'most meaningful' which, under the synchronicity hypothesis, would be the randomly pre-selected target). Each task consisted of 40 trials. Palmer belatedly discovered the problem inherent in getting the balance right for all participants in terms of the meaningfulness in the messages (the stimulus material), couching the problem in terms of "feelings of frustration" on the participant's part (p. 211). I suggest a possible source of frustration stemmed from participants seeming to gain very little personal benefit (e.g., as opportunities for growth or inspiration) from diffuse Taoistic statements (e.g., "the more you give, the more you will have"; p. 199), or fortune-cookie-type platitudes ("soon you will be sitting on top of the world"; p. 199).[28] When it comes to meaningfulness, it is likely the ancient divinatory systems (*I Ching*, Tarot) are better suited in providing synchronistic targets as centuries, if not millennia, have been spent refining and isolating pivotal archetypal situations that tune in meaningfully to participants' affective states. Experiments have been designed that accommodate these individual differences in participants (see Blackmore, 1983; Storm, 2008b; these two studies will be discussed shortly).

Tests on meaningfulness are a good place to start for experimenters since psi studies do not centre their attentions sufficiently (if at all) on both the quality and nature of the stimuli themselves (since affect starts here) *and* the associated responses (since these are the subsequent effects). The same reasoning applies to archetypes, given everything that has been said of them thus far. Developing ways to operationalize experiments that feature archetypes can pose serious challenges to researchers, and little research has been done on archetypes in psychology (for a review, see Bradshaw & Storm, 2013). The same may apply to parapsychology, though perhaps unbeknownst to psi experimenters, presentiment research touches on archetypal themes in the context of arousing stimuli that feature sexuality and violence (e.g., Mossbridge et al., 2012). Palmer (2008) proposes that archetypes (drawn from an approved list) could be activated before a psi task to improve psi scoring, but choices of archetypes, and their representational forms, both need consideration involving consultation with participants—the stimuli to be targeted that are hidden amongst decoys must be archetypally and meaningfully relevant (shortly, I discuss modification to the basic ganzfeld design that would accommodate synchronicity).

While there are no pragmatic reasons not to equate psi and synchronicity (i.e., to test psi as synchronicity), we do need to look at both concepts a little more closely because it seems there are discrepancies in the way Jung described their processes, even though he drew many parallels. Indeed, experimental work on psi as synchronicity may be impeded without a clear theoretical understanding. Of the Rhinean ESP process, Jung (1952/1969) assumes an "*already existing, correct, but unconscious image of the result* [emphasis added] enables … [the subject's] conscious mind to score a more than chance number of hits" (para. 857). Crucially, the subject is described as having a correlated "tense expectation or emotional state". To make the point that the processes of psi and synchronicity are effectively the same, Jung directly follows up on the Rhinean example (where he notes that ESP is measured in "hits") by referring again to the scarab case as though his client's *response* (the dream) effectively indicated precognition upon the imminent pairing (matching) of content in that response to the subsequent target (rose-chafer = *stimulus*).

Our first concern with this parallel is that the Rhinean example demonstrates intentional psi, whereas the scarab case demonstrates nonintentional synchronicity (i.e., no intention at the conscious or egoic level of Jung's client). The scarab case is more like spontaneous psi (e.g., telephone telepathy; see Sheldrake, 2014) where intention can be the furthest thing from the percipient's conscious thoughts. Albeit not known to Jung in his day, other (better) parallels exist since not all laboratory psi tests require intention from participants, and some studies show that it is not the participant's conscious intention, but their emotional system that is under scrutiny, as in presentiment research or (at a stretch) Rex Stanford's PMIR (see Hitchman, Roe, & Sherwood, 2015; Hitchman, Sherwood, & Roe, 2015). Indeed, what is more critical here is that in the scarab case, the client appeared to be in an 'emotional state' (she was in a 'critical' phase under treatment and in an "impossible" situation—she was "stuck" with "no way out of the impasse"; Jung, 1952/1969, para. 847). Jung paints her as an intellectually inclined, rationally minded skeptic, and that is why the rose-chafer had such an impact on her. While she may have been in an emotional state, it is arguably unlikely that she had 'tense expectation' for a specific outcome because, as already stated, she was not intending any specific effect. With intention (as in Rhine's ESP experiments or intentional synchronicity), there can be an 'emotional state' and 'tense expectation', but when a psi or synchronistic effect is not intended and is unexpected, the most the observer might presume to be present is an emotional state (i.e., physiological arousal), albeit barely perceived or dimly perceived, but not a fully conscious state of tense expectation.

Experimenters *do* recognize that the individual can unconsciously respond to emotionally charged stimuli (as in presentiment), but our second concern is that they have yet to consider (and investigate the possibility) that stimulus, emotional component, and ESP (physiological) response *are all keyed into archetypal processes*. In order to elicit psi, Jung (1952/1969) tells us "the emotional factor plays an important role", and he notes how the "formal aspect [of affectivity] is the archetype" (para. 846). Archetypes have a "specific charge" and "develop numinous effects which express themselves as *affects*" (para. 841). And since Jung notes how synchronistic phenomena also require "necessary emotional and archetypal conditions" (para. 905), the psi/synchronicity parallel is clear.

Our third (possibly more important) concern is with the standard Rhinean thinking of the day, which holds that information transfer explains the effect—after all, Rhine was opposed to psi processes being classed as acausal, opining that "necessary energetics" were involved (Rhine, 1954, as cited in Mansfield et al., 2008, p. 132). Jung's paralleling synchronicity with Rhinean psi does not imply synchronicity might involve information transfer; in fact, Jung (1952/1969, para. 840) disputes the assumption. However, some might argue that Jung speaks of certain information (an 'image') having an effect in a causal (even paradoxical) way when he refers to the scarab dream as

> a conscious representation arising from an unconscious, *already existing image of the situation* [emphasis added] that will occur on the following day, i.e., *the recounting of the dream* [emphasis added] and the appearance of the rose-chafer.
> (Jung, 1952/1969, para. 857)[29]

Taking the text as it is, we might be led to think (falsely) that the 'already existing image' must hail from some external source, but the next part (recounting of the dream) is exactly the kind of paradox that Griffin (1997) and Braude (1986) warned against if the 'recounting' is meant to have causal (actually retrocausal) properties suggesting the dream cannot happen *unless and until it is recalled* (hence the paradox). As an aside, parapsychologists are not often bothered by such minutiae. Retrocausal paradoxes are only occasionally addressed; usually by parapsychologists with a background in physics (e.g., Bierman, 2010; Sheehan, 2015; Walker, 1984). For example, physicist Evan Harris Walker (1984), arguing from QM principles, justifies such paradoxes under the assumption that two events (the observation and the quantum state collapse) displaced in time are to be treated as a single event. However, even under QM principles, this explanation will not do for some situations such as the drilling scenario described earlier (see *Laboratory Psi and Parapsychological Nomenclature* in Chapter 1). And it will not do here. Even though Jung links the two (the recalled dream + rose-chafer), we need not think the *recalled dream* has causality independent of the rose-chafer. We should understand Jung to mean the two are merely contingent. However, it makes better sense to break the coupling, assume Jung was more interested in the role of the rose-chafer, and put the clumsy telling down to a lapse in judgement on Jung's part (or his intent was lost in translation).

Still we have a problem—the rose-chafer now appears *instrumental*, given the way Jung speaks of it, forcing us to regard that element as *influential* (e.g., retrocausal). In synchronicity, that cannot be. The events that combine to make up a coincidence are not connected (causally or retrocausally), and if they are in some way connected that way (other than through *meaning* in the case of synchronicity), they are not coincidences. Truly Jung (perhaps inadvertently and certainly suggestively) presents the scarab case as *mechanistically* precognitive, and in so doing, we end up thinking our way through the problem as a Rhinean might if we are not careful. All this is quite vexing, and made worse when we consider the following:

> Among the subliminal contents we must distinguish perceptions from what I would call an inexplicable "knowledge," or an "immediacy" of psychic images.... [T]his "knowledge," or the "immediacy" of unconscious images, either has no recognizable foundation *or else we find that there are recognizable causal connections with certain already existing, and often archetypal, contents* [emphasis added]. But these images ... stand in an analogous or equivalent (i.e., meaningful) relationship to objective occurrences which have no recognizable or even conceivable causal relationship with them.
>
> (Jung, 1952/1969, para. 856)

Jung seems to be allowing for the possibility of a so-far 'unrecognizable foundation' underpinning (responsible for) the relevant 'knowledge' or 'images'. Is he allowing for some other paranormal process? When there *is* a 'recognizable foundation', the unconscious Self sifts through its inventory (so to speak), finds a match to the 'objective occurrence', takes that image *because it is representative of* ('analogous' or meaningfully equivalent to) an "already existing … archetypal" content, and throws it up to consciousness in (say) a dream. This intracerebral or endopsychic sequence would unfold thus: Due to the particular psychology of Jung's client, a pre-existing archetypal image was constellated in her mind (viz., the golden scarab which, it must be noted, trumps the rose-chafer archetypally speaking), and this image seeded her dream in the guise (representation) of a piece of jewellery (for reasons best known to, or to be unearthed by, the dreamer with Jung's help). The "situation" of the "following day" is contingent upon the activated archetypal element which already made its presence known in the dream and, given that the archetype has been constellated, we can dispense with retrocausal notions. That would be the ideal (synchronistic) interpretation, but Jung has invited criticism due to his indecisiveness about the source of that 'inexplicable knowledge' and the relevant 'unconscious psychic images'. In those critical paragraphs (para. 856-858), he comes over as flummoxed by his own (seemingly) inevitable conclusion that the external sources (the "objective occurrences") somehow render the vital information *acausally*. Jung has also courted doubt by saying of the 'pre-existing image' that it is "often archetypal" (para. 856). Often? If there is no archetype, there is no contingent factor, and we have to speak of chance relations, which is of no help to us—the same problem is already known to us in psi experiments (i.e., false positives, as mentioned previously; see also Chapter 3). Perhaps his use of the word 'often' was just his scientific conservatism.

There would be those who would push for an alternative Rhinean solution by arguing that a bio-psychokinetic (bio-PK) causal solution is preferable (i.e., the dream coupled with its retelling by the dreamer, act as an invocation that 'summons' the rose-chafer). This version might be preferred by Braude (1986), given his criticisms of retrocausation (see also Eisenbud, 1983). This latter rationalization, however, assumes there was a 'summoning' for a rose-chafer (and surprisingly no other flying insect—a pretty tall order), which again implies causality (rejected by Greatrex, 1999, *et alia*), whereas synchronicity is a linked series of events meaningfully nested in the constellated archetype, which includes the external physical elements, enabling observation and the subsequent recognition of a correspondence.

We see that the various Rhinean analyses conflict with a synchronistic interpretation, and since interpretations always have implications on the fundamental premises and status of parapsychology, as it does for any science, it is important that ambiguity be avoided. The experimenter may have to see the arrow of time as irrelevant and misleading, even when it is tempting to fall back on traditional stimulus/response or cause/effect sequences, or their reversal.[30] In the past, assumptions about these associations (what is thought to have transpired in a given experiment) have created understandings that are not questioned, and are instead constantly defended despite their ambiguity (these problems have also been covered in Chapter 1).

To continue this synchronistic approach to psi research, we can measure a number of psychological functions from the perspective that they are synchronicity correlates, including the aforementioned affectivity (emotionality) which has been so cogently tied in with synchronicity. Even measuring meaningfulness and numinosity, subjectively and objectively (as will be seen), will not prove difficult. Numinosity ties directly into emotion and research has been conducted on emotional correlates of psi (for a review, see Broughton, 2015)—particularly, presentiment research (Mossbridge et al., 2012)—though thus far research on numinosity is limited mainly to remote viewing (Schwartz, 2007, 2018). In studies like these, experimenters can use the various instruments available that measure physiological responses as possible correlates of feeling-toned emotional responses (affects).

On that point, for parapsychologists using ganzfeld and other free-response techniques, one way of testing synchronicity would be to use target images that trigger (say) the emotional responses of the agent (sender), but not the percipient (receiver). The aim here is to determine if an agent can 'activate' a meaningful and/or emotionally-charged image and a percipient can be drawn into it. One could describe these targets as 'bespoke' in nature, and one would expect them to be archetypal or at least meaningful, which in the latter case means the images should be tailored to the idiosyncrasies of the individual (as agent) so as to create an environment with meaningful options (see Storm, 2008c).[31] Pre-selection of targets can be done subjectively (i.e., by personal choice) and/or objectively during pre-screenings (using GSR, EEG, and EMG measures). Pre-selected decoys should be neutral to the agent (to minimize distractions) though this protocol may not be critical, but certainly *all* pre-selected images, decoys *and* targets, must be neutral to the percipient (to avoid a selection bias). From that point on, standard randomisation procedures would follow so there can be no collusion, but the difference in this design is that *meaningfulness* is potentially operative in an experimental design where the agent's reactions to the target image may trigger a selection-response in the blinded (ganzfeld) percipient, resulting in target identification.[32] If such designs yield stronger effects than the conventional ganzfeld design, the upshot might be that conventional ganzfeld targets had not been sufficiently meaningful.

A possible forerunner of this design is the neuropsychological study by Richard Silberstein and Felicity Bigelow (2024) using five pairs of sensorially isolated monozygotic twins. As stimuli, Silberstein and Bigelow used 50 general (neutral) photographs (landscape, natural scenery) and 50 personally or emotionally relevant (meaningful) photographs actually provided by the twins (e.g., birthday parties, childhood pets), interspersed among each other and randomly presented and viewed by one twin while the other twin passively viewed a static image in another room (roles were also reversed). Functional connectivity (i.e., brain-region interaction) was recorded using Steady State Topography (an evoked potential methodology developed in Silberstein's laboratory at Swinburne University in Melbourne). The agent's and perceiver's brain activities during the one-second presentation periods of meaningful images were synchronized and then analyzed. Silberstein and Bigelow found significant changes in perceiver functional connectivity when the measure of event-related connectivity was determined using agent viewing times. Also, significant increases in functional connectivity were found seven times during presentations of meaningful images compared to only three during presentations of neutral images. Such studies demonstrate the important role of meaningfulness.

Beitman et al. (2010) recognised the psi/synchronicity overlap: For example, "knowing who is calling before picking up the phone can be considered a telepathic experience … [but] context … can make it synchronistic" (p. 457). But the authors also differentiated synchronicity from psi on the basis of information validation. They suggest this can be done by considering the *verifiability* and *meaningfulness* of a given anomalous event: While the psi event is easy enough to verify, synchronicity "gains its relevance by rendering an ambiguous experience personally *meaningful*" (p. 457). So context *is* critical. On the one hand, the pedestrian nature of many laboratory psi-tasks is evident if it is shown they are bereft of meaning-making. On the other hand, some designs lend themselves to synchronicity by setting up ecologically valid contexts and scenarios, and in those cases participants can be quizzed on the meaningfulness of their hits outcomes, which can help researchers draw a distinction between chance hits and synchronistic hits. For that purpose, only hits data should be analyzed, and participants should rate their selections before they know whether they hit or miss. Some hits may be rated very low on meaningfulness (possibly indicating chance hits), while other hits may be highly rated (possibly indicating synchronicity).

Preliminary work in this area has been conducted using *I Ching* hexagram readings which were rated for meaningfulness by the participants who generated them (Storm, 2008b). In that study, meaningfulness was rated significantly high by participants who scored a hit for the hexagrams they generated that matched one of the 16 preselected 'descriptor pairs' associated with those hexagrams (for details, see Appendix A). I made specific reference to synchronicity in that study, by noting that "the effect was interpreted as fulfilling a theoretical condition that defines 'meaningful coincidence' or synchronicity" (p. 103).

We have seen that procedures in some forms of divination, like the *I Ching* and Tarot, can be modified to accommodate the demands of laboratory testing. By design, all forms of divination draw on the universal themes that underpin human nature, and these are depicted as archetypal scenarios and/or images that resonate philosophically, psychologically, and emotionally with users. The first set of *I Ching* studies (see Appendix A) allowed participants multiple choices based on their own (meaningful) frames of mind that were thought to be represented archetypally in the 64 readings (for example, see Storm, 2006, 2008b). The *I Ching* is amongst the few mantic arts that give users the opportunity to focus on a specific, immediate issue of concern which invariably brings in affect, numinosity, and meaningfulness. In the case of Tarot, professional readings derived from picture-card arrays can easily be generated with little or no deviation from standard (traditional) procedures. For example, parapsychologist Susan Blackmore (1983) conducted a few Tarot experiments designed to give participants a genuine experience. Both types of studies (*I Ching* and Tarot) initially produced significant results, but further studies saw the effects tailing off. In both cases, the two experimenters reported evidence that emotional and motivational factors played pivotal roles in the declines (Blackmore, 1991; Storm, 2006).

As suggested here, there may be a certain elusiveness to synchronicity; it seems nature dictates that the element of surprise must be preserved. In that respect, and as I said above, nonintentional synchronicity is not unlike spontaneous cases of psi, but where loss of enthusiasm, motivation, or emotional drive is evident in those all-too-subtle (nuanced) intentional cases, individuals may have to find ways to crank up whatever innate cognitive resources they have (including their ability to detect patterns), if synchronicity detection is to work optimally. For example, divination produces a more rewarding result when used during times of emotional pique (e.g., during crisis), which ties in with numinosity (the charge or dynamism of the experience) as a correlative factor (see von Franz, 1980), and in experimental situations, experimenters have known for some time that they must take steps to ensure interest is maintained during laboratory testing (see Pratt et al., 1940/1966). Clearly, there are no ethical violations involved in creating numinosity *per se* (albeit cloaked as emotional pique) as the work in 'feeling the future' (Bem, 2011; Bem et al., 2016) and presentiment (Mossbridge & Radin, 2018b; Mossbridge et al., 2012) has already demonstrated.

Unfortunately, participant enthusiasm is not easy to maintain—for example, a study by Krippner et al. (2019) had a more than 50% drop-out rate because those participants felt the target pictures were not "engaging," "interesting," or "emotionally involving" (p. 34). However, Krippner et al. also made appreciable (*post hoc*) attempts at demonstrating the very big role played by numinosity in ameliorating these sorts of problems because numinosity is tied in directly with affect/emotion. They hypothesized that "correspondence between the target and participant responses would be significantly correlated with the degree of numinosity ["pleasant or unpleasant emotionality"] of the target" (p. 34). Their study used concealed full-colour slide images of various locations, and participants were given the option of using the corresponding geographical coordinates to help them remote view the target. Judging was based on scoring the target and the decoy using the mentation as a guide. Once all trials were completed and responses were judged, targets were then rated for numinosity by parapsychologist Stephan Schwartz. Remote viewers' self-rated hits were found to be significantly more numinous than their self-rated misses, but there was no significant difference when the independent judges' ratings were tested, suggesting that participants see something crucial in the targets that judges cannot gauge from the mentations alone. Emotional response is ultimately part of a participant's subjective experience, but it is possible the subtlety of an emotional state or response can escape verbal expression.

Admittedly, only one person (Schwartz) rated the targets for numinosity—ranging from 1 ('no numinosity') to 100 ('full numinosity')—so there was a high degree of subjectivity in these ratings, but the study still has internal validity. Worth noting is the fact that control participants (not under the RV protocol) produced no hit/miss difference ratings on numinosity. I would attribute this to the disadvantage of not having the benefits of the remote-viewing protocol to aid image formation (the protocol is clearly suitable for activating archetypal processes even if it is not 100% reliable—for examples, see the brief review of Associational Remote Viewing studies in Storm, 2025). Again, the similarities between psi and synchronicity become evident, but the twist here is that this study (as we might expect) fails to make explicit reference to synchronistic principles.

A final word on this topic; this time on individuation—psi studies and perhaps even some spontaneous cases of synchronicity do not seem to be about individuation (*pace* Mansfield, 1995). Yet we often see a biological (evolutionary) need being served by synchronicity in much the same way proposed of psi by Broughton (1988). It is suggested that Jung's bias as a psychiatrist explains his over-emphasis on the psychotherapeutic aspects of synchronicity. Pauli's comment is fitting here:

> the further development of the ideas of the unconscious will not take place within the narrow framework of their therapeutic applications, but will be determined by their assimilation to the main stream of natural science.
>
> (Pauli, 1994, p. 164)

I do not propose we dispense with the individuating needs of the psyche, which evidence shows can be achieved through synchronicity, but it might be wise to make exceptions when situations call for it.

***

In this chapter, synchronicity theory was explained in detail, and the theory was compared to eight other parapsychological models/theories that bear some similarities, at least in principle. Five theories all count meaning/meaningfulness as a crucial element of psi: PMIR (Stanford, 1990), MIC (Gatlin, 2008), MPI (von Lucadou, 2015), ASR (Mishlove & Engen, 2007), and FST (Carpenter, 2012). Only Mishlove and Engen (ASR) gave credence to the possibility that archetypal dynamics play a part in psychic functioning—these may contribute to the numinosity of the experience. None of the models/theories effectively proposes an actual mechanism that crucially models how consciousness, the mind/brain complex, and the world interact beyond normal (understood) mediations, although Marwaha and May (2015) make a worthy attempt with MMPC. Gatlin ventured into the territory of our evolutionary past and history spanning eons by proposing that the psi bias of our species is the result of non-random selection, though that still does not explain the mechanism—it only suggests how we came by it.

Though it was found that there appears to be an evolution in parapsychological thought, from personal desires and needs-focused notions to broader viewpoints bordering on the holistic (i.e., concerned with the whole system; the macrocosm and our place in it), the essence of the modern parapsychological model/theory is still ability-focused, with the exceptions of FST and a question mark over MPI.

A number of features that psi and synchronicity share were listed to drive home earlier points about the psi/synchronicity parallel. Presented for the reader's consideration were a number of experiments where synchronicity (not just psi) was arguably investigated in the laboratory, which is suggested in the designs. In those experimental environments, it seems synchronicity *as psi* is barely person-focused (therapeutically speaking), but paradoxically, psi seems weakened (is never made stronger) due to a failure to consider the personal quotient (e.g., why a participant wants to be in a psi study in the first place, and what the outcome might mean to them). Thus we see a lack of influence of synchronistic ideas on researchers, which may account for the bevy of standard protocols that invariably deliver modest (low-yield) demonstrations of paranormal effects characterized as psi.

It is argued that parapsychology needs to make room for synchronistic ideas. It is time for experimenters to consider how the individual is placed in the *world*—not just in the *laboratory*—so that the broader ramifications of the psi hypothesis can be teased out and modified where necessary. The next chapter considers various views concerning quantum mechanical processes in order to gauge whether a 'hard' scientific approach can explain how the individual might interact with the world.

Notes

1 I have not come across this term 'event stream' in any texts on synchronicity. The term does come up occasionally in other fields (Artificial Intelligence, Mathematics, Information Science), but not in the sense I use it.
2 These archetypal ideas are explored in Storm (2008g).
3 The alchemical *Unus Mundus* = 'One World' or *unus mundus* refers to an all-encompassing unity back to which psyche and matter can be traced.
4 For an alternative to dualism in parapsychology, see Dommeyer's (1982, pp. 122-123) views on Rhine's position.
5 This overall assumption and understanding changes very little if we view the standard synchronistic effect as two physical events; an inner (cerebral) event and an outer physical (environmental) event.
6 Broader discussions of these issues can be found in Atmanspacher (2014a, 2014b) and Seager (2014).
7 See footnote 5 in the Introduction.
8 It needs pointing out, however, that off-shoots of these holistic and holographic ideas may become over-extended, resulting in exaggerated views of reality that not only lack viability or plausibility, but are too bound up in speculative and/or socio-political factors (Marshall, 2002; McLaughlin, 2013).
9 For a modern psychodynamic perspective on the relationship between synchronicity and expanded consciousness, see Gildersleeve and Crowden (2019).
10 We might suppose that an outsider from another tribe, prior to assimilation, may find it difficult at first to synchronize with that party.
11 It is therefore not surprising to learn that belief in ESP (telepathy) can range anywhere from 30% (C. Roe, personal communication, 2023) to 41% (Moore, 2005), and even up to a staggering 60% of people (Irwin, 2009; Rice, 2003) depending on the population sampled and the year of the study.
12 Note that inter-brain neural synchronization is distinct from a form of so-called "brain-to-brain interface" (Rao et al., 2004) that is actually "synthetic telepathy" (Miller, 2001), or even hailed as a "first step towards thought communication" (Warwick et al., 2004, p. 185). Signals/messages are transmitted and/or induced via microwaves, EEG, TMS,

the Internet, and so on. The major difference in these studies is that actual information is induced or transmitted to a recipient indirectly by technological means, whereas in neural synchronization, percipients are directly linked in consciousness.

13 Henry and Thompson (2011) use the word "psychophysical" (p. 247) in a casual sense to describe how the stimuli of the physical environment lead to subjective psychological responses, and a subsequent awareness of self in two spaces (body and world). There is another use of the term *psychophysical*, seemingly adopted by Wolfgang Pauli who preferred the term 'unified psychophysical reality' as a more scientifically suitable variant of Jung's term *unus mundus*, which Jung borrowed from Dorn (Roth, 2022, p. 6).

14 Progoff (1973) directly references the macrocosm in this instance, and takes it to mean the *unus mundus*. I will stay with Jung's preferred term *unus mundus* because his few references to the macrocosm tend to be restricted to philosophical principles.

15 The Jungian 'Self' construct is not comparable to the 'self' (as 'I') proposed by Henry and Thompson (2011). The Self equates with "the unity of the personality as a whole" (para. 789), thus differing from the exclusively aware/conscious 'self' of Henry and Thompson and, for that matter, the Freudian 'ego'.

16 In Storm (2025), I argue that the capacity to visualize with specific intention, using the deep imagination (interfacing with archetypal processes), brings innate unconscious 'knowing' to consciousness.

17 Bierman (2010) states that time symmetry applies to some of the 'formalisms' (e.g., electromagnetic theories), but as he points out: "… in physical systems time symmetry is not observed" (p. 274). However, Bierman also proposes that conscious observation can partly lift the "constraints that prohibit time symmetry to occur" (p. 274). Synchronicity does not require this proviso.

18 Stanford (1990, p. 57) regards his earlier paper (i.e., Stanford, 1974b) as the definitive reference for PMIR in terms of psychokinetic effects (see especially Stanford, 1974b, pp. 348-351).

19 Gatlin's article was originally published in 1977.

20 For impressive examples of levitation, see Braude's (1986) reports on St. Joseph of Copertino and D. D. Home.

21 Psychophysical parallelism "excludes all causal interaction between mind and body inasmuch as it seems inconceivable that two substances as radically different in nature could influence one another in any way" (see Encyclopedia Britannica: www.britannica.com/science/psychophysical-parallelism). See also Jung (1952/1969, para. 968).

22 However, see again, footnote 17 in this chapter.

23 See 'Experimental Psi' in the SPR Encyclopedia (https://www.spr.ac.uk/3-experimental-psi).

24 Stimulus/response discrepancies have been noted for some time in parapsychology's history (e.g., Warcollier, 1938).

25 As mentioned earlier, Irwin and Watt (2007) describe Jung's theory of synchronicity as "noncybernetic"—that is, it abandons "the notion of information flow" (p. 132).

26 Browne (2017) gives a similar example of a rabbi suffering heart pains, who incorrectly dialled the emergency number for his doctor, only to find that he'd made contact with his doctor on that incorrectly dialled number.

27 It seems Greatrex (1999) means 'volition' or 'intention' in his use of the term "freewill" (p. 6). But intention is not infallible and is no guarantee of an effect as the Owens case shows (see Chapter 1).

28 For his target pool, Palmer (2016b) used Psyleron SyncTxt (Psyleron, 2008-2009), which is an online program that uses RNGs to generate SMS messages for "subscribers to explore the world of synchronicity and meaningful coincidence on their mobile phone".

29 This statement from Jung also raises the basic idea of so-called memory models of ESP, which hold that the ESP information source is effectively long-term memory (see

Chapter 3 in Storm, 2025; see also Irwin, 1979; Stevens, 2002). These models never explain how an unseen target triggers the memory.

30 Some psi theories depend on this premise (e.g., Bierman, 2010), but I see no need for it given a strict synchronistic interpretation.

31 Along similar lines, but due to different arousal levels in males and females, Bem (2011) showed that it is possible to conduct successful studies that tailor target sets according to individual differences and preferences. For example, males were exposed to "stronger and more explicit images" (p. 409) compared to target sets for females.

32 Though not necessary to test synchronicity *per se*, roles can be switched, with a new target set created for the former percipient now acting as agent. Also, both can be tested as percipients by a third person as agent. These variations help decide whether a person is better in one role or another.

Chapter 5

Quantum Mechanics, Consciousness, and Psychophysical Reality

> …there is real magic in QM. But, like all good tricks, QM relies to some extent on sleight of hand and misdirection.
>
> (Ron Garret, 2016)

Given the findings of Quantum Mechanics (QM), some parapsychologists see quantum theory as a doorway to understanding the basic principles of paranormal phenomena. The two fields, QM and parapsychology, are branches or subdisciplines of physics and psychology, respectively. The two fields are not held in equal regard in academia or mainstream society, but they are seen as domains of "weird science", and in both cases, their phenomena boggle the mind and are not adequately understood. What then, in terms of fundamental factors, can the two fields do for each other? That is a question asked by Jung and Pauli. Is consciousness the link to both? Perhaps the two irreducible principles, mind (*psyche*) and matter (*physis*), are two aspects of a single principle, forming a unitary 'psychophysical reality' where the two are essentially inseparable.

Quantum Mechanics

From where the academic world is currently positioned in its understanding of Quantum Mechanics (QM), and even for those with just a smattering of what QM is all about, the demonstrated phenomena (e.g., *collapse of the wave-function*, *entanglement*, *superposition*, *quantum tunnelling*, etc.)[1] must be seen as even weirder than psi. Still, very few parapsychologists dare associate paranormal phenomena with QM, and even fewer build QM into their theories (exceptions include Walter von Lucadou and a few of his colleagues). Some parapsychologists reframe precognition as a form of *retroaction* (a QM concept), with the general aim being to integrate parapsychological theory into mainstream physical science instead of having it viewed exclusively as psychological science (see Millar, 2015).

To gain a clearer picture of what QM is all about, and how it might have something to do with psi, synchronicity, or (as they tell us) consciousness, it would prove helpful to describe a couple of the more popular QM phenomena; namely,

DOI: 10.4324/9781003561323-6

wave-particle duality and entanglement (the former epitomized in the double-slit experiment that demonstrates the so-called *collapse of the wavefunction*). This illustration may serve to show how seemingly inexplicable effects are not exclusive to parapsychology, and that the discipline of physics, despite its recognition of QM phenomena, is not comfortable with them, ontologically speaking—that is to say, nobody really knows how or why the phenomena do what they do—as physicist Richard Feynman once said: "I think I can safely say that nobody understands quantum mechanics".[2] In fact, in spite of all the seemingly credible notions thrust upon us from the mainstream and fringe camps, it is more than likely that QM and parapsychology contain "mythic" elements that seriously need to be challenged.

So far, with synchronicity as my reference point, I have spent the major part of this book questioning conventions in parapsychology, but I have only briefly mentioned QM. For what it is worth, it is thought by some that QM may facilitate an understanding of psi because of the similarities between quantum effects and psi (for a representative account, see Roll, Alexander, Williams, & Persinger, 2021). Psi effects and quantum mechanical effects both seem to be independent of spacetime (nonlocal), but are not independent of consciousness, or so it is argued (Radin, 2006a). That proposition has been a guiding light for some theorists (e.g., von Lucadou, Römer, & Walach, 2007), but it must also be pointed out that even though quantum effects are not understood properly (if at all, as Feynman implies), the findings have been used to propagate an avalanche of dimly formed notions and hopes about the nature of reality, psi, and consciousness. Even Radin's (2012) brief review sufficiently exposes the views and opinions circulating within the physics community, showing just how deep the problem runs. More on the QM problems later (especially in relation to psi and synchronicity), but it would be better to start with a brief overview of the *science* of QM before I attempt to deal with the *spin* and *culture* of QM.

Quantum mechanics incorporates four classes of phenomena for which classical physics cannot account:

- *quantization of certain physical properties* (transition from a classical to a quantum understanding about physical phenomena—e.g., photons are referred to as 'field quanta' or 'light quanta');
- *the principle of uncertainty* (i.e., the position of a particle can be determined, but at the cost of determining its momentum, and *vice versa*);
- *quantum entanglement* (subatomic particles interacting in unison—e.g., a pair of particles may share the same space, but only the whole system can be described; not one particle independent of the other);
- *wave-particle duality* (i.e., a quantum entity may be described as either a particle or a wave depending on how it is observed).

All this is to say that the 'sacred cows' of our classical world, *causality*, *determinism*, *continuity*, *conservation of energy*, and *spacetime*, are all violated in quantum mechanics (at least under the Copenhagen Interpretation, of which more shortly).

Working backwards through these four dot-points, I will discuss the double-slit experiments (wave-particle duality) first, and then look at entanglement. The other two dot-points do not really apply in parapsychology. From there, I will endeavour to bring these ideas into alignment with consciousness, psi, and synchronicity, and consider whether a broader holistic view that incorporates the medieval *unus mundus* ("one world")—a.k.a. *psychophysical reality* (taken to mean a *psyche/physis* or mind/matter merger)—may be sufficient to our needs.

The Double-Slit Experiment

To appreciate the peculiarities of the typical double-slit experiment, we must first start with the conventional view that light travels in straight lines or rays which seem to be comprised of discrete particles. In 1905, Albert Einstein (1879-1955) provided evidence that such may be the case. He drew from the work of German physicist and Nobel Prize laureate Max Planck (1858-1947), who in 1901 expanded the understanding that light transmission was wave-like by showing that ultraviolet radiation consisted of discrete frequencies. Planck (1901) proposed that the energy in light was *quantized* (i.e., light came in discrete packets). These particles or packets were later called *photons* in 1929 (named by physicist Gilbert Lewis). Other findings confirmed the particle-like nature of light (e.g., Compton, 1923; Röntgen, 1895/1972).

Centuries earlier in 1704, Isaac Newton (1643-1727) had also thought of light as being composed of particles or corpuscles, and did not think of light as wave-like in nature, even though he had demonstrated that a beam of light could be split by a prism into various colours, indicated by different wave-lengths (Newton, 1704). Yet the idea of light having wave-like properties was not new: French philosopher René Descartes (1596-1650) had proposed a wave theory of light as early as 1637; Francisco Grimaldi (1618-1663) discovered coloured fringe patterns on shadows of sharp edges; English natural philosopher Robert Hooke (1635-1703) compared the spreading of light to waves in water; and a mathematical wave theory of light was proposed by Dutch physicist Christiaan Huygens (1629-1695) in 1678 (Huygens reputedly explained reflection and refraction better than Newton, basing his idea on the principle that light was propagated by a series of wavefronts; see Huygens, 1690/1912).

In the late 1800s, mathematical physicist James Clerk Maxwell (1831-1879) devised equations to describe the theory of electromagnetism (Maxwell, 1873), and these were based on equations for electricity, magnetism, and light, all of which are related. From his work, the modern electromagnetic spectrum was developed, starting with cosmic rays and gamma rays at the high-frequency, high-energy end (with the shortest wave-lengths), followed by the visible spectrum (bracketed by ultra-violet and infrared waves), and ending with radio-waves at the low-frequency, low-energy end (these have the longest wave-lengths).

However, the wave/particle paradox reared its head once it was discovered that even though a photon can be refracted in a lens just as a wave can be dispersed and diffracted, and can demonstrate wave-like interference with itself (described shortly), it also has no mass, and no electric charge, but can still have measurable position *and* momentum (though only one of these measures could be made at any one time, given the *uncertainty principle*). From these discoveries, the new science of QM emerged, and with it the wave-particle theory of light (a.k.a. wave-particle duality). It is worth noting that the *particle* referred to in the term "wave-particle duality" is not merely a particle *per se* (small portions of matter). The term implies that the so-called particle appears to exhibit *behaviour similar to a normal object* when it is not behaving like a wave (i.e., when a wavefunction does not appear to be manifested). In fact, when photons and electrons cause *detection events* the assumption should be that they only *act* like particles. This distinction will become clearer once the modern double-slit experiment is explained.

Wave-particle duality really took root when the first *low-intensity* double-slit experiments were conducted by Sir Geoffrey Ingram Taylor in 1909. Introducing Taylor at this juncture is to jump the gun slightly, and we must go back more than a century to British scientist Thomas Young (1773-1829), who proved the wave theory of light to his satisfaction in 1801. But there was more to light than Young could possibly have known, though he did discover that a light source fired at a single slit forms a characteristic wave pattern (a so-called Fraunhofer interference pattern) that has a central maximum and a number of smaller and dimmer maxima on both sides, as shown in Figure 5.1. These maxima occur because (as Huygens had explained) a single wave front provides multiple sources for other waves (not shown in Figure 5.1), resulting in constructive interference (bright bands) and destructive interference (dark bands).

Young discovered that two slits also produce constructive and destructive interference, but unlike the single-slit experiment, the bright bands are of equal intensity. Enter Taylor: When the light source is refined or narrowed so that we have a *coherent*[3] stream of photons fired off *one by one* in single file at both slits, an interference pattern results (see Figure 5.2), instead of the photons clumping (collapsing) into two bands as we might expect of particles. However, if only one slit

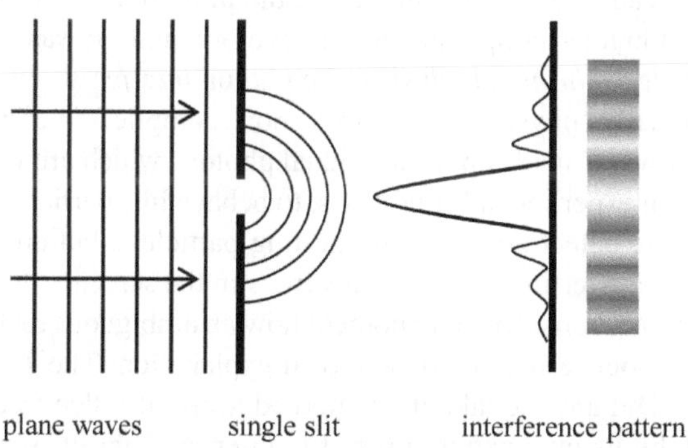

Figure 5.1 Young's single-slit experiment: Photons (like electrons) produce a wave (interference) pattern when one slit is used. (*Source:* © 2024, L. Storm)

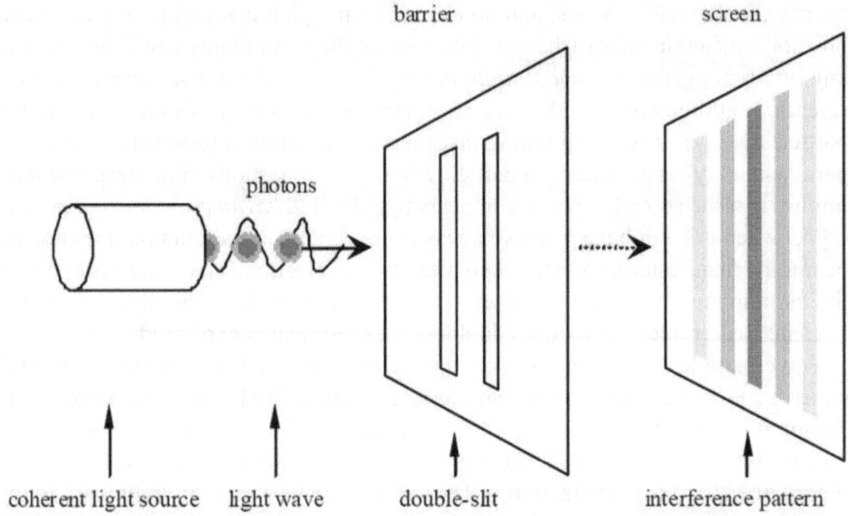

Figure 5.2 The double-slit experiment: Photons (like electrons) produce a wave (interference) pattern when two slits are used. (*Source:* © 2024, L. Storm)

is used, there is no banding; the pattern is bright in the middle, and evenly spreads across the screen on both sides with no dark bands. These observations proved that photons, thought to be small portions of matter, have wave-like properties when they are confronted with two slits. In fact, the general consensus is that light is *always a wave*, and when it is shown to behave like a particle (i.e., like an object), that really only means its energy manifests in a particle-like way as energy quanta.

By 1927, the quantization of the electromagnetic field was widely accepted, and Taylor's 1909 paper describing the above experiment became a key reference work. Not until 1986, was Taylor's experiment confirmed using a more sophisticated apparatus. Thus, it came to be understood that the interference effect had nothing to do with one photon interfering with another photon; rather it was proposed that *the single photon travels through both slits*; the photon *interferes with itself.* This 'explanation' is actually 'physics-speak' for a more complicated conception of light as a 'probability wave' made up of individual photons which are wave packets that seem, under given experimental conditions, to behave like particles (e.g., as dots on a screen which are detection events suggesting particles), but are actually caused by wave energy transferring to atomic electrons in the screen.

Before I continue, consider for a moment how an ambiguous real-world problem was resolved without resort to a paradoxical explanation: The Tunguska event in Russia in 1908. Did anyone take the patterned array of fallen trees to mean each tree was struck by its own extraterrestrial high-energy object (see Plate 5.1)? We know the event was not likely to be a conglomerate of unique detection events because even a rudimentary understanding of the effects of a single explosive force

Plate 5.1 The Tunguska Event: Fallen trees radiate out from the impact focus. Vast areas of forest are now thought to have been flattened by a meteorite in Tunguska (Russia) in 1908 (Kvasnytsya et al., 2013). [*Source:* © 1927, Leonid Kulik; Public Domain]

informs us to the contrary. Therefore the general consensus about the Tunguska event is that a single source of energy irradiated outward in a wave-like fashion, thus felling all the trees at once.

Now consider the exact opposite of this situation at the microphysical level: Upon the so-called collapse of the wave function, where we have a unique scenario of multiple events on a detection plate (clumping), we are told we are looking at many independent events so the conclusion is reached that transformations have taken place (wave → particle). Suddenly, erroneously, many individual wave fronts are thought to no longer explain the multiple effects; each individual event has to be caused by a particle! That is only half-right, but the distinguishing difference is that many photons, even in their wave-like capacity, are responsible for many individual events that only look like particle action.

Physicists thought differently; if there was a transition, how did it happen? They hypothesized that detectors could record the photons going through the slits and reveal whether or not they could actually behave like particles and clump instead of forming an interference pattern (see Figure 5.3). Described as a "which-way" experiment, the reasoning behind the hypothesis comes from the claim that "measuring devices for the measurement of a particle (the path) and for the measurement of a wave (the interference pattern) are mutually exclusive" (Mittelstaedt, Prieur, & Schieder, 1987, p. 891). Thus, a modified double-slit experiment should prove

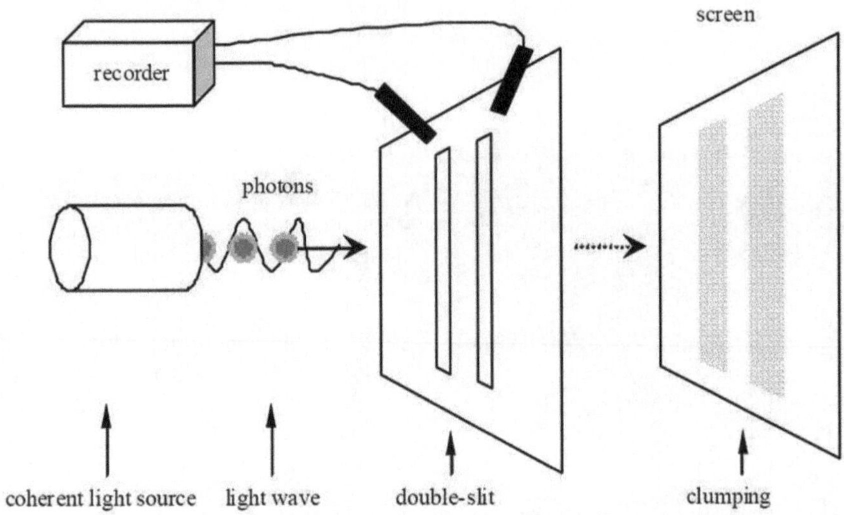

Figure 5.3 One popularized (but impossible) scenario of how the "which-way" experiment is schematized: Photons or particles of matter (like electrons) would clump (i.e., there would be collapse of the wavefunction) *under the assumption they could be seen going through the slits.* (*Source:* © 2024, L. Storm)

wave-particle duality (complementarity), as formalized in the Copenhagen Interpretation, which argues that probable states in a system are reduced to a specific state by measurement. This interpretation was devised in the 1920s and 1930s, mainly by Danish physicist Niels Bohr (1885-1962) and German physicist Werner Heisenberg (1901-1976), to account not only for wave-particle duality, but also for superposition, collapse of the wave function, the uncertainty principle, and the observer's role in the so-called measurement problem (for definitions, see footnote 1 in this chapter). The Copenhagen Interpretation is not without its detractors.

In the late-20th century, only rudimentary attempts were made at proving complementarity. For example, Wootters and Zurek (1979) showed that determining which beam the electron was in, did not destroy all wave knowledge. Taking a pragmatic view, Zeilinger (1999) argued that "*the essential criterion* for quantum interference to appear" is that there be no which-path information, so logically, if one could access path information, it would be "sufficient to destroy the interference pattern" (p. 289). However, it is suggested that no actual double-slit experiment has been conducted that measured one photon at a time with detectors at the slits:

> As strange as it may be to hear, the double-slit experiment conducted one photon at-a-time with "detectors at the slits" is *nothing short of a myth*. No such experiment has been reported in a peer-reviewed journal or any reputable book or publication. Talk of this supposed experiment, and even figures illustrating

> it, can be found throughout the internet, but these refer to no actual experiment being performed. The origin of the myth is a poor popularization of the quantum eraser experiment, which though "marking" the photons traveling through each of the two slits with which-way information and destroying the interference pattern, involves no detectors or recorders in front of or behind the slits except for the main CCD [charge-coupled device] backplate.
>
> (Reishi, 2016)

Where observation and measurement have been made at the slits, the experimenters have used polarizing filters or thin layers of material over the slits. These methods change the way the wave propagates, the light source loses its coherence, and the collapse pattern results. Thus, a method had to be developed that would eliminate this decoherence problem.

Kim, Yu, Kulik, Shih, and Scully (2000) conducted an experiment using a delayed choice quantum eraser (DCQE). They used a beta-barium-borate (β–BaB_2O_4) optical crystal (BBO) that converted the photon coming from a single slit into an orthogonally polarized signal-idler photon pair (each in the pair having half the energy of the original photon). Importantly, this crystal preserves the coherence of the light source. If a photon came from slit A, it fell on detector D_0 *before* its twin reached detector D_3; if a photon came from slit B, it fell on detector D_0 *before* its twin reached detector D_4. The time-lag was eight nanoseconds. As long as it was possible to determine (from D_3 and D_4 data) which slits the photons went through, there was no interference pattern and clumping was shown upon analysis of the data. Note too that the DCQE does not detect photons until *after* they clump (hence, delayed choice). It is *as if* the photons had to follow the same clumping rule no matter when the detection was made—even if it was in the future (although this proposition was experimentally refuted by Peruzzo et al., 2012). The idea behind this part of the design was (a) to show that measurement collapses the wavefunction (thus supporting the Copenhagen Interpretation), and (b) to discern where it was in the photon's trajectory that either particle or wave behaviour emerged (as suggested in the delay component).

The DCQE had two additional detectors D_1 and D_2 (the quantum eraser) which collected photons that had by-passed detectors D_3 and D_4. The role of the quantum eraser was to destroy source-information about the photons by mixing photons from both sources (slits A & B) together. At this point, clumping ceased, and the interference pattern returned (which is to say the earlier registering was not lost; merely obscured by newer data); once again, this result supported the Copenhagen Interpretation. Kim et al. (2000) concluded:

> The experimental results demonstrate the possibility of observing both particle-like and wave-like behavior of a light quantum via quantum mechanical entanglement.[4] The which-path or both-path information of a quantum can be erased or marked by its entangled twin even after the registration of the quantum.
>
> (p. 3)

Are these conclusions correct? Dennis F. Polis (2014) regards interpretations of the delayed choice *and* quantum erasure experiment as misleading and incorrect (see also Sabine Hossenfelder, 2022). First, he starts with the premise that light is never two kinds of things (i.e., sometimes a wave; sometimes a particle), but is always a wave, and to propose particle-like behaviour is to misinterpret the data (which equally applies in the case of Young's double-slit experiment). The wave remains a wave, even without interference; the error lies in the assumption about what a detector detects. What really happens is that the amount of energy the detector absorbs is *quantized*, which can give the impression that a wave is a particle. The photons are not forced to choose collapse just because the paths will be identified micro-seconds later by the observer (at D_3 and D_4). Wave behaviour has merely been disguised by the fact that the photon's energy has been split between two detectors so that less than a photon's worth of energy is enough to trigger one detector and, due to conservation of energy, the other detector will not register the same photon. Polis comments: "Classically, each detector is a separate entity, but quantum mechanically, all of the electrons in all the atoms of all the detectors are part of one system." This conceptualization is tantamount to saying that there is no way of distinguishing the appearance of a single photon on a plate from a similar excited atom caused by an electromagnetic wave (recall the Tunguska analogy). This point will be become clearer in the next paragraph.

Second, Polis (2014) points out that Kim et al. (2000) described each outcome at Detector D_1 and D_2 (the eraser) as "a standard Young's double-slit interference pattern" (p. 2). In fact, Young's pattern is symmetrical whereas Kim et al.'s two graphs are asymmetrical because they are coincidence plots (D_0 signal photon impingements correlated with idler photons at D_1 and D_2); not interference patterns (see Figure 5.4). Kim et al. have graphed the data from D_1 and D_2, *but presented them separately*, so as to suggest no "which path" information (thus, falsely assuming interference). Polis notes that the two graphs are out of phase by half a wavelength (one π radian; noted also by Kim et al.), but if one goes further than Kim et al., and combines the two datasets, a single graph results that demonstrates *no interference* (see the top graph in Figure 5.5). The same effect is shown graphically from data collected at Detectors D_3 and D_4 (see the bottom graph in Figure 5.5, which shows D_3 data only).

Problems with the interpretations put forward by Kim et al. (2000) have been noted by others (Cockshott, 2018; Ellerman, 2015; Garret, 2016; Gidney, 2016). Ellerman argues against retrocausality in multiple cases of QM phenomena. Garret agrees with Polis that the quantum eraser does not erase 'which-path' information (i.e., the eraser does not restore interference) because there was no collapse in the first place. In agreement with Garret, Cockshott argues against the Copenhagen Interpretation for DCQE outcomes. Gidney runs the same argument as Polis. That light is presumed to have a 'particulate nature' is a misinterpretation of wave behaviour, how detectors detect, and partial data sets. Crucially, in exactly the same double-slit set-up (Reiter, 2014), quantum effects have not been demonstrated for gamma rays, which are high-energy photons.

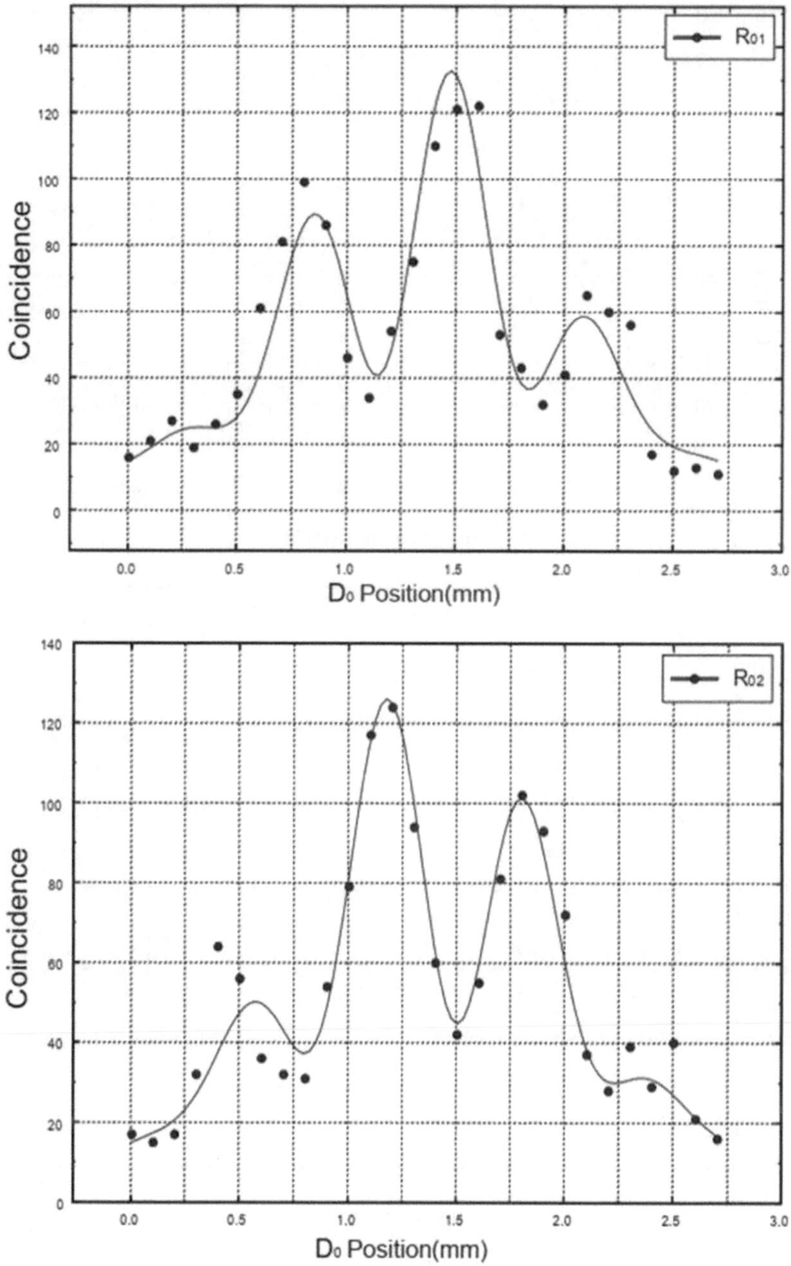

Figure 5.4 On the top, joint detection rate (D_0 and D_1) against *x* coordinates of D_0. On the bottom, joint detection rate (D_0 and D_2) against *x* coordinates of D_0. (Note the π phase shift between the two plots.) (*Source:* © Kim et al., 2000, p. 4; Used with permission.)

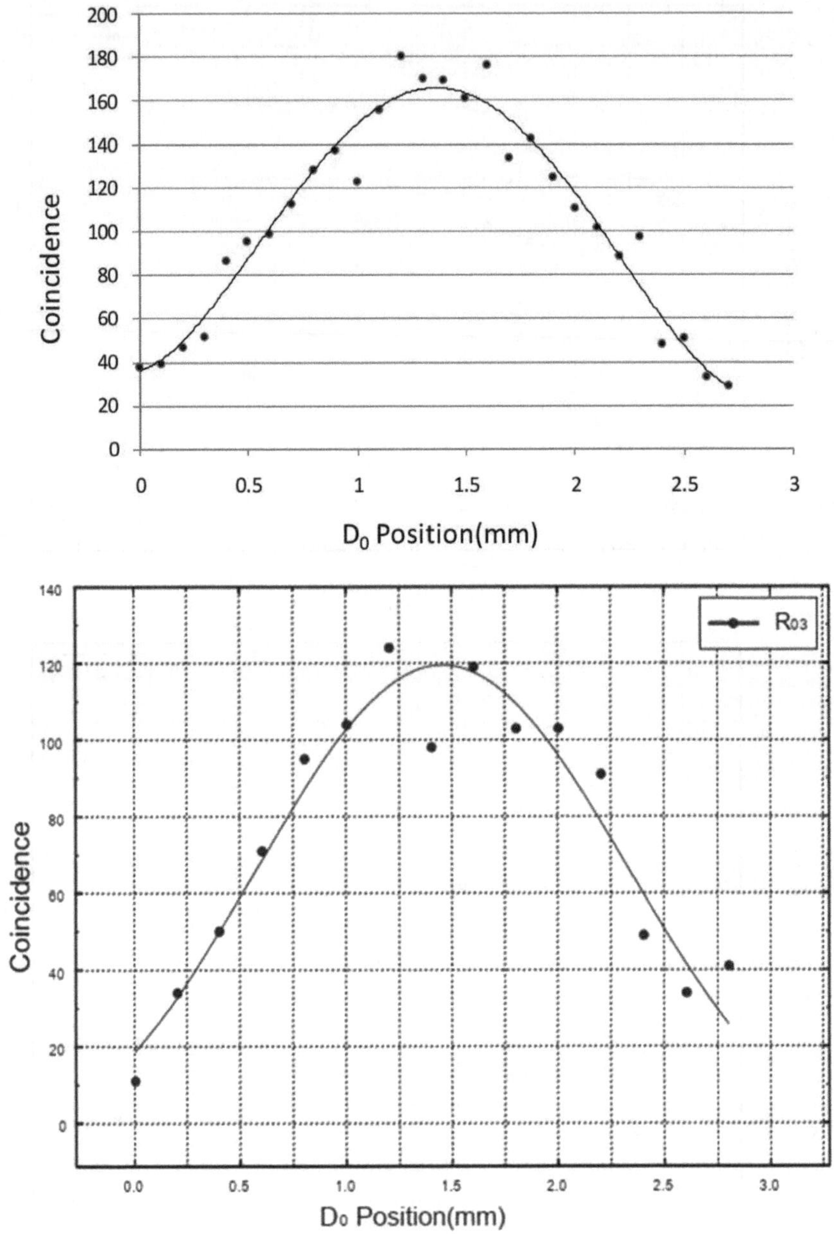

Figure 5.5 On the top, joint detection rate (D_1 and D_2). No interference demonstrated (data taken from graphs in Kim et al., 2000, p. 4) (*Source:* © 2024, L. Storm); On the bottom, joint detection rate (D_0 and D_3). No interference demonstrated. (*Source:* © Kim et al., 2000, p. 4; Used with permission.)

Polis (2014) not only critiques the work of Kim et al. (2000); he claims that the argument from the interferometer findings of Jacques et al. (2007), that tested Wheeler's (1984) original thought experiment, are also flawed in the assumption that photons are particles: "an assumption that turns a simple experiment confirming quantum theory, into a baseless myth about magical happenings." Once again, delayed choice is not demonstrated; there can be no choice if light is only ever a wave. Jacques et al. merely showed how photons impinge on detectors as waves: If there is interference it is because two waves constructively and destructively interfere with each other; when there is no interference, it is because photons, as waves on only one path carrying energy quanta, impinge on the detector. The following quote from Cerf and Adami (1997) is relevant:

> … as we unmask the particle-like behavior of quantum systems to be an illusion created by the incomplete observation of a quantum (entangled) system with a macroscopic number of degrees of freedom, we are led to conclude once more that the wave-nature of quantum systems is fundamental, and that there is no particle-wave duality, only an apparent one.
>
> (Cerf & Adami, 1997, p. 15)

The modern double-slit experiment really proves a single behaviour for the photon (that of a wave), with wave-particle duality merely being a physics construct to help explain two apparently different effects, with the particle-like effect being a conclusion reached by making an "incomplete observation" of an 'entangled' system. Ellerman (2015) notes that it is a misinterpretation to claim that the particle was detected going through one slit or the other:

> If the detector is suddenly removed after the particle has passed the slits, then the superposition state continues to evolve and shows interference on the far wall … in which case people say "the particle went through both slits." Thus the "bad talk" makes it seem that by removing or inserting the detector after the particle is beyond the slits, one can retrocause the particle to go through "both slits" or one slit only.
>
> (p. 186)[5]

If we can conclude that the conventional wave-particle narrative propagates an oft-repeated 'misinterpretation' of what really happens, the same mistake has been demonstrated with other particles such as electrons (Davisson & Germer, 1928), and so-called 'buckyball' (fullerine) molecules 60 carbon atoms in size (large enough to be seen under an electron microscope; Nairz, Arndt, & Zeilinger, 2003). The size of particles that can produce interference effects is growing all the time, from 810 atoms (Eibenberger et al., 2013) up to molecules 2000 atoms in size (Fein et al., 2019). However, there is an upper size limit for particles in these sorts of experiments. Every particle, every object, has a wavelength (even people), which governs slit size. Since wavelength decreases with object size, and slit size must approximate wavelength, the slits would ultimately be far too small for objects on the macro-scale to pass through.

More importantly, growing alongside the findings and the particles is a cluster of interpretations that have accrued myth-like proportions, and these have been championed by a handful of philosophers, a few physicists, and (needless to say) some parapsychologists—many of whom propose variations on the theme of reality-does-not-exist-until-it-is-observed, or retrocausation has been demonstrated in the physics lab. For example, Mossbridge and Radin (2018a) give the two papers discussed above (Jacques et al., 2007; Kim et al., 2000) as evidence of effects coming before their causes. These conceptions are being taken as gospel under the assumption of wave-particle duality. Some go so far as to say we create reality just through observation, willing into being a universe of things, as we wish, as we see fit. While this understanding is more conservatively expressed—that is, reality exists *in potentia* as probable states, and the choice of state resides with the observer (see Stapp, 2009)—we may wonder if there is any evidence to support even this claim. In the next section, I explore the role of consciousness and its relationship with QM processes.

The Role of Consciousness

Two of the studies just mentioned have other problems: Nairz et al. (2003) noted that "which-path" information cannot be determined in their study because photon emissions from the energized fullerines are not of a measurable magnitude. Although they make a virtue of a disadvantage (because it helps ensure an interference effect), their study only demonstrates the wave-like property of matter; not collapse. In the best-case scenario, it seems consciousness as a collapsing mechanism is confined to micro systems (under the assumption that consciousness plays such a role at all). Also, the study by Eibenberger et al. (2013) suggests a problem at a whole other level since experimenters are now moving away from the standard double-slit design to any kind of laboratory setup that will demonstrate coherent states only (i.e., superposition). An additional consideration for these new designs is particle temperatures, necessarily extreme to avoid potential environmental interactions; needed are either very cold temperatures (near absolute zero; see O"Connell et al., 2010), or relatively high temperatures (see Eibenberger et al.).

It seems the new wave of experimental aims of physicists is not convergent with the aims of those who have hopes for consciousness as a non-passive player that extends to the physical (macro) world beyond the mental and physical self. Also, a range of related problems has arisen that applies specifically to biological systems, leading some researchers to conclude that QM processes in the brain are extremely unlikely, and therefore not related to consciousness; the mean operating temperature of the brain and CNS cannot prevent environmental decoherence, and if a coherence state was achievable, it would be too short-lived to enable such processes as neuronal firing (see Tegmark, 2000). However, Stapp (2000) disagrees, stating that "the particular quantum effects that allow a person's thoughts to influence his brain are not affected by environmental decoherence" (p. 1). Similar ideas to Stapp's have been proposed (e.g., Hameroff & Penrose, 1996). Indeed, literally hundreds of papers find that the "laws of quantum physics may operate in warm-wet-noisy biological structures" (Tarlacı & Pregnolato, 2015, p. 161). It is this body of evidence that allows Tarlacı and Pregnolato to state:

> These days quantum photochemical reactions are seen as normal, … quantum mechanics forms the base of the senses of sight and smell, photosynthesis, and magnetic direction finding in animals.
>
> (p. 162)

Putting aside the conflicting opinions for the moment, a variation of the broader 'observation' hypothesis is still worthy of investigation; namely, that consciousness collapses the wavefunction (a.k.a. the *consciousness collapse hypothesis*; CCH). This idea idled away in the background of the previous section, but it is apropos to this section that the issue now be covered more fully. It should be noted that a number of proposed experiments that would support the CCH (given the appropriate results), have never actually been conducted (e.g., Rosenblum & Kuttner, 2011; Schrödinger, 1935/1980;[6] Wheeler, as cited in Davies & Brown, 1991). However, Bohr never considered observer-induced collapse of the wave packet to be viable. What mattered most in the quantum event was the *interaction between the object (e.g., photons) and the measurement apparatus*: "the state of the object and the state of the instrument are dynamically inseparable during the interaction" (Faye, 2019). And the event was completely objective, and not at all the outcome of a subjective (observing) consciousness. Indeed, rather than it being a *consensus omnium*, only a contingent of speculative individuals, like Heisenberg, emphasized the "privileged role for the observer and observer-induced wave packet collapse" (Faye, 2019). Niels Bohr, however, explicitly rejected the idea that the observer is instrumental in the experimental outcome.

Arguably the reality-creating factor of consciousness first came to light in philosophical circles dating back to the solipsistic Subjective Idealism of Bishop Berkeley (1685-1753), or further back if we admit ancient Greek sophistry. In parapsychology, an expanded definition of consciousness is thought by some theorists to be a helpful new construct in explaining, for example, nonlocal effects and violations of causality, which were thought true of QM processes. However, conjecture is one thing; proof is another. How we should go about providing such proofs is debatable. What follows is a description of a series of studies illustrating one approach. Whether the various conclusions are valid or not, remains to be seen. Certainly, the situation is not helped if the very idea of collapse, and whether it can be brought about by consciousness (observation) or not, contributes to a parcel of myths that need challenging (Polis, 2014).

Dean Radin and his team conducted a series of studies designed to test whether consciousness can collapse the wavefunction (Radin et al., 2012, 2013, 2015, 2016).[7] Participants were instructed to perturb the photon path in a double-slit optical system using attention/intention only (tests were conducted with participants near to, and far away from the apparatus). Participants were tasked to alternate between two conditions: attention-toward ("concentrate") periods, and attention-away ("relax") periods, with the focus being on the two slits inside the optical system. Technically, this method is an ideal way to study the pure effect of consciousness only.

While Radin's team satisfactorily showed that interference patterns (represented graphically as spectral power) can be significantly changed by concentration (attention/intention), Radin's team never demonstrated actual wave collapse, though they did *suggest* at one stage that four of their experiments "*appeared to confirm* [emphasis added] the consciousness collapse hypothesis" (Radin et al., 2012, p. 164). Indeed, statements such as the following are open to interpretation:

- "the results of the present experiments appear to be consistent with a consciousness-related interpretation of the QMP [quantum measurement problem]" (Radin et al., 2012, p. 170);[8]
- "the experiments found evidence supportive of an interaction that appears to "steer" the wavefunction to either reduce or to sharpen interference fringes" (Radin et al., 2015, p. 82);
- "these results do not support a *strong* role for the mind, as in consciousness literally causing a collapse of the quantum wavefunction" (Radin et al., 2016, p. 21).

The newer the statement, the more conservative it is. Certainly it appears attention/intention can have demonstrably real psychokinetic (PK) effects on optical systems, even at the quantum level, but that does not imply collapse of the wavefunction—the more accurate description of the outcome is an "attention-modulated mind-matter interaction effect" (Radin et al., 2013, p. 566), which is PK by any other name. Figure 5.6 illustrates one possible scenario *suggesting* collapse.

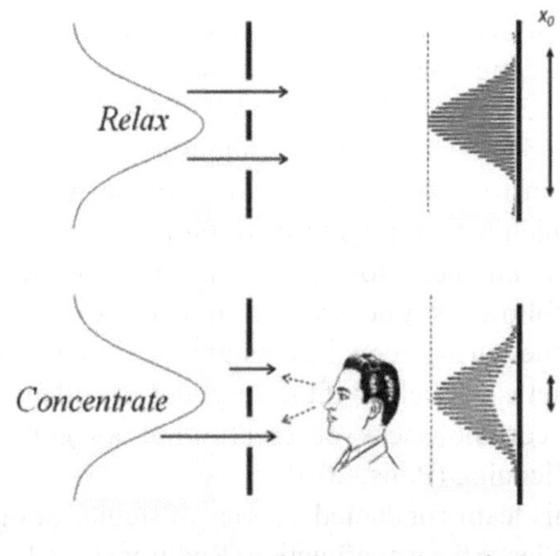

Figure 5.6 Speculative interpretation of the results of the modelling effort by Radin, Michel, Johnston, and Delorme (2013). (*Source:* © Radin et al., 2013, p. 561; Used with permission.)

Another issue with the Radin series concerns *attention* vs. *intention*: Testing the *observer effect* (i.e., attention), under the assumption that collapse can occur because a conscious observer witnesses or observes or measures the optical system, is different from testing actual conscious intention as a requirement for collapse which is less widely accepted in mainstream QM. Specifically, as part of the procedure, participants were instructed "to direct their attention toward two tiny slits located inside a sealed black box (the double-slit optical system)" with the added instruction to "Please influence the beam now" (Radin et al., 2012, p. 159). To rectify the ambiguity, instruction was expanded, thus

> … try to mentally block one of the slits, or to "become one with" the optical system in a contemplative way, or to mentally push the laser beam to cause it to go through one of the two slits rather than both.
>
> (p. 160)

The problem here is that the "focussed attention" kind of consciousness Radin was encouraging (i.e., to "*Concentrate*"; see again Figure 5.6) is not the ordinary consciousness of a physicist during mere observation/measurement, so that the protocols in most of the Radin studies only encourage PK. But do these various aims test the CCH? Radin et al. (2015) pointed out that the CCH assumes a "*passive*" role for consciousness (p. 84), yet an alternative view, embodied in the consciousness-influence hypothesis (CIH), sprang into being in that 2015 paper. As I see it, that new hypothesis was there all along in the earlier studies, but Radin et al. were now acknowledging a goal-oriented ("steering") role for consciousness; not just an observer role. Fast forward a few years and the protocol had not changed: "participants were invited to … mentally intend for the signal to increase", which they call an "attention condition" (Radin, Bancel, & Delorme, 2021, p. 16). Again, we can speak of a PK task not necessarily interpretable as collapsing the wave function.

To drive the message home, attention means attending to an event by *passively observing it* (i.e., determining some properties of an object without altering that object), whereas intention implies a little more—either *mentally picturing a change of state of an external object, or even mentally trying to change the state of an external object.* Indeed, an intention is not unlike a wish in that there is an aim or goal. All along, it seemed the Radin series had been testing a conflation of observation and intention. Radin et al. (2015) now suggested that support for the CCH would manifest as "a rise in photon counts at a fringe minimum", thus showing a "decline in interference", whereas support for the CIH would manifest as "a shift [in interference] in accordance with the context of the interaction, as operationally defined by the feedback [i.e., tone, graph, Buddha-doll illumination during trials]", thus showing "deviations in interference" (p. 84).

It might seem a minor point, but the conventional understanding is that *observation only* (or the observer making a *measurement*) is supposed to be the operative element that underpins the QM effect of interest, whereas in psi studies, the effect of interest results from intention (even if the intention is sometimes assumed to be at an unconscious level, as in PMIR). As such, the Radin studies test for a hybrid quantum/PK effect insofar as intention was involved, at least up until 2015 when the CCH *and* the CIH were independently tested. Not long after I wrote this section, Radin said: "What we're seeing in these experiments might "simply" be a PK effect (as though we knew what that was) rather than a quantum observer effect (as though we knew what that was too!)" (D. I. Radin, personal communication, March 2, 2019). What we do know is PK requires intention; the observer effect does not. Perhaps not surprisingly, the 2015 results using a single-photon double-slit apparatus supported the CIH (that a PK effect took place); not the CCH.

A follow-up study (Radin et al., 2016) led the authors to state that "the mind has the capacity to modulate probabilities associated with the transition from quantum to classical behavior" (p. 21). It is moot whether such a "transition" was demonstrated. Tremblay (2021) confirmed there were "shifts in fringe visibility in the direction expected by the mind-matter interaction hypothesis" (p. 1), but the shifts were not significant and he concluded there was no evidence for the hypothesis. Tremblay also made reference to "human intention" (p. 1), but he did not take issue with the fact that the experimenters had not looked *exclusively* for passive observational effects *per se* as we expect when a conscious observer merely takes a measurement.

There were other criticisms of the experiments by Radin's team (Walleczek & von Stillfried, 2019), but these were not grounded in solid statistical knowledge or argument, and they do not consider all the Radin experiments, as pointed out by Radin et al. (2020). To account for possible 'mind-wandering' and 'other distractions' that might have produced unpredictable fluctuations in the data, Radin and Delorme (2022) then developed a "variance-based analysis", which tested for a "bidirectional effect (i.e., a shift in variance)" instead of a "unidirectional effect (a shift in mean)" (p. 362). Significant effects were found in two sets of data. Effects were still described as the result of "attention or intention".[9]

Given Radin's experiments, we learn two very important things: First, the general conclusion from Radin's team (e.g., Radin et al., 2016) is that PK on at least one quantum system (the double-slit apparatus) may be possible requiring an organism with intention. But it was not shown that collapse of the wavefunction could be caused by an unbiased conscious observer taking a measurement. Atmanspacher (2014a) expresses a similar point: "I think it is deceptive and will not be viable to look for a *direct* influence of consciousness on physical matter via the not-yet-fully understood measurement process in quantum physics" (p. 285). Indeed, earlier studies go further: May and Spottiswoode (1989) found consciousness was not a "*necessary* component of state vector collapse [i.e., wavefunction collapse]" (p. 63). Yu and Nikolić (2011) allegedly proved that "the suggested link between human consciousness and collapse of wavefunction does not seem viable" (p. 931), though both Reason (2017), and De Barros and Oas (2017), dispute their approach. Of course, all this is to assume that the wavefunction could collapse under certain conditions, which is to perpetuate the supposed myth that Polis (2014) and others are out to bust.

Second, and related to this previous point, quantum 'entities' only seem to be defined by circumstance, but in fact, they never truly can *become* 'objects' that behave like normal everyday (classical) objects. Certainly, the double-slit experiment does not tell us that quantum entities behave in two different ways. Properly considered, the experiment should challenge our notion of what we think behaviour should be at the quantum level. In fact, quantum entities are always waves, and if they behave differently, that is because that is what they appear to do when certain interactions with detectors are made possible. Might it be possible that attempts to collapse the wavefunction (i.e., prove wave-particle duality) are as much doomed to failure as attempting to throw tails using a two-headed coin? But we have the added burden of deciding what the PK effect is, and what it means. We might not dispute the evidence that something seemingly anomalous occurred in the apparatus, and we have seen the term "mind-matter interaction" used on a number of occasions to describe the effects, but that term too is misleading. From a dualist perspective, there might be phenomenological grounds for making that claim, but under dual-aspect monism there is no *interaction*—the aspects do not interact; there is only one reality in which events occur and we see but two aspects of a single process (Atmanspacher, 2014a).

Many other questions can be raised in relation to QM, but the main task of this chapter was to come to some conclusions about QM and its relation to consciousness and psi. In that regard, not all relevant QM phenomena have been discussed thus far, and in the interest of fairness, one baffling phenomenon mentioned above (namely, entanglement) is featured further, though space permits only a brief rundown. Einstein, Podolsky, and Rosen (1935) theorized, and Bell (1964) showed, that two particles (and I use the term 'particles' loosely) from the same source, in a state of superposition (overlapping without interference), are entangled at any distance: "two measurements will give random but highly correlated … results, despite [the entangled particles] being unable to communicate with each other in the conventional sense" (Shoup, 2015, p. 65; for similar views, see Walach et al., 2009, pp. 292*ff*). For example if the 'spin' of an electron (i.e., the magnetic field orientation of the charged particle) is measured to be 'up', the spin of its entangled but distant twin will be measured to be 'down'. Einstein regarded this effect as "spooky-action-at-a-distance", though his use of the word "action" is inappropriate in the case of entanglement. Critically, this effect is regarded as a *correlation*; not *information transmission* via a *signal*. Von Lucadou, Römer, and Walach (2007) apply the same reasoning to psi effects (for a formal proof, see pp. 69-72 of their paper).

It is tempting to appeal to quantum entanglement to explain ESP, and physicist Daniel P. Sheehan (2015) argues that psi effects like precognition (retrocausation) are "permitted within the time-symmetric laws of physics [but] it is not known if or whether life can or does exploit quantum processes on a macroscopic scale such as to incorporate them into precognition" (pp. 104-105).

While it seems though that some QM processes may be evident at biological levels in certain organisms (Ball, 2011), these still do not establish a link between psi and QM beyond analogy. Could we iron out these problems in our understanding of QM if we had a better handle on psi and consciousness? As we have seen, it is not for lack of trying—indeed, it is a noteworthy and land-mark effort on the part of Dean Radin and his collaborators, regardless of their findings, that the hypothesized role of consciousness in QM was tested *parapsychologically*. Interestingly, physicist and parapsychologist Evan Harris Walker speaks to this need for further knowledge:

> an understanding of psi phenomena and of consciousness must provide the basis of an improved understanding of [quantum mechanics].
>
> (1985, p. 26)

These days, many parapsychological theorists hold a conception of psi as something that depends on nonlocal factors, and it is this conception that draws interest in QM phenomena. It is plain to see when we consider how (a) *thoughts* or *images* of others and things may manifest in ways that defy the capacities of the normal sensory modalities (as in ESP), or (b) matter may respond to *mental influence* alone (as in PK). However, these ideas should not necessarily give rise to the notion that a transcendent consciousness, thought to be fundamental to psi, is pivotal in deciding a QM outcome. In truth, we have evidence that we do not fully know what QM outcomes entail, or even mean. Nevertheless, it seems we are talking about two different constructs: One being an *objective consciousness* that knows no bounds when it comes to what we regard as paranormal situations; the other arguably being more about *awareness* (that which is behind observation and measurement) in QM situations. How did these two ever get mixed up? One answer is that they easily stand in for each other (Koch, 2019), even on the back of disparate musings in a field where there is very little agreement on the fundamentals,[10] and indeed the study of these fundamentals has been anathema to the field for too long (Becker, 2019).

CCH has not been demonstrated, and entanglement just seems to be what 'particles' *from the same source* have always been free to do. I find attempts to merge ideas from the two fields, parapsychology and physics, optimistic but they appear largely speculative, at least as far as I can determine given their general lack of clarity (for examples, see Roll et al., 2021). What is clear is that an improved understanding of QM might aid our understanding of consciousness (or awareness) and psi, which is to reformulate Walker's statement. This turn-around logically and necessarily must be made for two main reasons: First, current psi theories are not advancing the cause, and second, many statements made by physicists are more than ambiguous; they are misleading—take the following from John von Neumann who supposed that

> it is a fundamental requirement of the scientific viewpoint—the so-called principle of psycho-physical parallelism—that it must be possible so to describe the extra-physical process of the subjective perception as if it were in reality in the physical world—i.e., to assign to its parts equivalent processes in the objective environment, in physical space.
>
> (von Neumann, 1955, pp. 418–419)

Lon Becker (2004) alerts his readers to the astounding fact that that there has been no agreement amongst physicists as to what von Neumann meant by these words! Becker takes von Neumann to mean:

> The extra-physical process of the subjective perception here is the observer noting the unique measurement result of the experiment.... The physical state of the observer's brain will correspond to what is seen.
>
> (pp. 123-124)

This way, there is no violation of psycho-physical parallelism, and the role of the mind cannot be "causal" though it is "essential" (Becker, 2004, p. 128). Becker concludes that his interpretation draws us *away* from the conventional view that von Neumann believed the psyche had an instrumental role to play in QM collapse.

Around the same time, physicist Eugene Wigner (1961) said

> it is the entering of an impression into our consciousness which alters the wave function.... It is at this point that consciousness enters the theory unavoidably and unalterably.
>
> (p. 289)

Like all of us, Wigner has the prerogative to change his mind, and he later retracted all such remarks by saying we "will not embrace solipsism" and "will let us admit that the world really exists" (Wigner, 1995, p. 593). Which is to say human consciousness does not have god-like powers; it certainly does not create anything except in the mind. To borrow from Becker (2004), the physical state of the observer's brain will correspond to what is observed. Whether or not a primary physics myth (if it is a myth) must play itself out to exhaustion before more reasonable prospects can be pursued unimpeded, some key scholars (listed in the previous section) have tried to cut the 'Gordian Knot' that is the mystery (if not the myth) of QM. The next section looks at other opinions that also contribute to the debate.

Psychophysical Reality Revisited

We may conservatively concede that the court is still out on the CCH, but it is looking like extending the role of consciousness to a world-creating factor writ large is too much to claim at this juncture, and certainly not supported by scaled-down variants conjectured to take place in the laboratory. When Jung (1989) noted that a "world-creating quality attaches to human consciousness" (para. 129), he implied something altogether different from the assumption that *consciousness collapses the wavefunction*. He was referring to the *realization* that the world exists simply because it comes into conscious awareness. Before that, we have "nameless happenings" (para. 129).

Yet, unlike classical physics, QM may move us closer to a holistic (nonlocal) picture of reality—Ismael and Schaffer (2020) seem to think so (more on their ideas shortly). But if consciousness (i.e., the observer) has no *direct* role to play in QM, then QM gives us a narrower view of reality than was first thought. Indeed, a recent poll showed that only 6% of attendees at a conference on the foundations of QM believe that the observer plays a "distinguished physical role … through a consciousness-induced collapse of the wave-function" whereas 55% thought not (Schlosshauer, Kofler, & Zeilinger, 2013, p. 7). But when asked if "physical objects have their properties well defined prior to and independent of measurement" (Sivasundaram & Nielsen, 2016, p. 4), 47% of 149 physicists answered "No" and 11% said "Yes in all cases" (p. 4). Sivasundaram and Nielsen explained that the "intention of the question was to ascertain the participants' view of wave function collapse" (p. 4).

These figures are not surprising for the "Copenhagen interpretation [endorsed by 42%] does not necessarily imply a belief in a fundamental role for consciousness" (Schlosshauer et al., 2013, p. 7). A more recent figure is 39% endorsement (Sivasundaram & Nielsen, 2016, p. 11). Schlosshauer et al. go on to say:

> Popular accounts have sometimes suggested that the Copenhagen interpretation attributes such a role to consciousness. In our view, this is to misunderstand the Copenhagen interpretation.
>
> (p. 7)

Nevertheless, a large minority endorse the Copenhagen interpretation—somewhere between 39% and 42%—and that minority is in fact the predominant view. And because of the misunderstanding, it is no wonder many philosophers and parapsychologists go with that "popular" interpretation that observation collapses the wavefunction. And when we consider the hypothetical, vastly more extended "role the observer plays in nature" (Sivasundaram & Nielsen, 2016, p. 5), the authors reported that 22% of physicists say the observer "Plays a distinguished physical role" (p. 5). Radin and Delorme (2022) understood this to mean "a sizeable minority of physicists today agree that the formation of physical reality involves some sort of mind-matter interaction" (p. 365). This is a much broader view, but it is extrapolated from the dubious CCH which is not endorsed by a majority of physicists; nor is it proved. Sivasundaram and Nielsen (2016, p. 5) also tell us 41% thought the observer plays either no "fundamental role" (10%) or no "distinguished physical role" (31%). It is little wonder physicists are rethinking the role played by consciousness and are producing revised or new theories that have no role for it (Ananthaswamy, 2018):

> we cannot yet make any claims about the nature of reality, even if the claims are well-motivated mathematically or philosophically. And given that neuroscientists and philosophers of mind don't agree on the nature of consciousness, claims that it collapses wave functions are premature at best and misleading and wrong at worst.

Arguments for quantum holism do come in new guises. For example, in their theory, called simply "Quantum Holism", Ismael and Schaffer (2020) say: "Quantum mechanics seems to portray nature as nonseparable, positing non-identical but modally connected events" (p. 4131). For example, two subatomic particles emitted from the same source are nonseparable (i.e., entangled). They argue for the construct of 'quantum nonseparability', and propose a 'common source' or 'common ground' between 'nonseparable entities'. I suggest this common ground works in the same way as the archetype, and the two may in fact share phenomenological similarities. The theory is best understood via analogy:

> quantum mechanics seems to allow two entities—call them Alice and Bob—to be in separate places, while being in states that cannot be fully specified without reference to each other. Alice herself thus seems incomplete (and likewise Bob), not an independent building block of reality, but perhaps at best a fragment of the more complete composite Alice+Bob system (and ultimately a fragment of the whole interconnected universe).
>
> (p. 4132)

Ismael and Schaffer identify the composite "Alice+Bob" system as 'holistic' in that it seems to be "more than the sum of its parts" (p. 4145). As will be seen, the psychophysical reality of the *unus mundus* suggests the "Alice+Bob" *correlation* is something "more", where "more" could be *meaningful* (archetypal) connections that are only there because of their nonseparability, if we are free to assume the theory could work for psychic (synchronistic) connections between people. However, Ismael and Schaffer do not raise parapsychological issues, and nor do they posit a role for consciousness in this quantum process. I note again the related point raised by Beitman et al. (2010) that the quantum connection "lacks the meaningful quality that defines synchronicity" (p. 453). Beitman et al. are, however, referring to particles, not people, and quantum mechanical processes are observed in biological structures (Tarlacı &Pregnolato, 2015).

While the "nonlocal connection between Alice and Bob arises from their spatially spread-out common ground" (p. 4149) quantum entanglement is characterized by its instantaneity, so once again that "ground" would probably be archetypal in nature and not involve the transfer of information or energy and therefore not involve any causal process. Many a parapsychologist might find Quantum Holism supportive of the psi hypothesis, and I have already pointed out that some theorists are sympathetic to the idea that entanglement in physics could be used to model the psi function (Filk, 2014), even though others have doubts (Sheehan, 2015).

Decades earlier, Stokes (1987) commented on these sorts of issues. He noted that parapsychologists were "quick to realize the implications of nonlocality for a theory of psi" (p. 138), and they jumped on the notion of nonlocal consciousness. Why is the idea of nonlocal consciousness seen as such a critical factor in parapsychology? For one thing, nonlocality validates the extended role of mind in psi; it is the necessary coordinating factor that provides the informational link between the experient and the target. This understanding gave consciousness a potency it never had before, although some of the early quantum physicists beat parapsychologists to the punch. Only now, both camps have their detractors.

Consciousness—that ethereal, diaphanous, nebulous, indefinable, paradoxical aspect of our being—is even hailed as fundamental, sharing that status with something else fundamental; namely, those virtual nothings that spin and jump and bind and tunnel. These virtual nothings build up, quark by quark, atom by atom, molecule by molecule, to make something substantial, organic, and living, like *Homo sapiens*. But we acknowledge that, as simple forms lead to more complex forms, many *emergent* phenomena arise—as examples, molecules have properties that cannot be anticipated from their atoms; the organizational aspects and cultures of the many species cannot be anticipated in single specimens (which recalls Gatlin's [1977] "holon hierarchy", as discussed in "Meaningful Information Creation" in Chapter 4). To borrow from Gatlin, who proposed that causality may only be found somewhere further up the holon chain, we may say, the kind of consciousness we enjoy is not found when we go down through the holon chain. Then, if we have no sense of consciousness being 'atomic', or better, 'particulate' or 'granular', that is because it is something altogether so different to the point we cannot understand or appreciate it as consciousness *per se*; or it cannot even pass as consciousness and does not exist (like Gatlin's causality) at lower holon levels. So-called "constitutive panpsychism" disagrees with the latter position; our consciousness is constituted of irreducible mental parts found in everything. Though that may befit its nature, we are then faced with the unanswered question of how something non-physical can affect something physical, which has had repercussions throughout the ages, and throughout academia in disciplines such as philosophy, psychology, and parapsychology.

If we can convince ourselves that this ontological dichotomy is easily surmounted (with many ways of doing that philosophically—for example, see Robinson, 2020), and so we stick to the idea that consciousness is able to function nonlocally (e.g., all minds are entangled with the universe; see Radin, 2006a, pp. 263–267), then our search for an answer to the psi process is redundant; we no longer need the psi construct. But there will still be this 'paranormal' aspect to consciousness that is far from explained, even if we no longer need to concern ourselves with understanding the psi mechanism; though psi will probably retain its descriptive status. In whatever way the dichotomy is resolved, the idea of a *transcendent* psi ability working through (or with) extended consciousness or extended mind must be abandoned, and the idea of 'extension' is more a term of convenience. A quantum view aids us further still: We only need "Alice+Bob" connections and coincidences from which new information emerges—in some situations (e.g., the laboratory) these may even be correctly interpreted as successful targeting due to archetypal resonance, recalling Gatlin's (1977) idea of meaningful information creation (reviewed in Chapter 4).

The upshot though is that the 'psi process', and 'consciousness', and its 'nonlocal' capacity, are convenience terms describing a broader *awareness system*, but then we also need a filtering system to handle the anomalous content. Otherwise, what will do the job of retaining just that anomalous 'information' (experience) we need while filtering out all else given the arguably unlimited (nonlocal) 'extension' (so-called)? Or do we give this *awareness system* a filtering role as well that appears to function unconsciously? Apart from holding an optimistic intention for a psi effect, all the theories reviewed above (see Chapter 4) have not explained how psi information is filtered. For example, note the complete uncertainty concerning Phase II (the "neuroscience domain"—i.e., brain and CNS) in the MMPC theory (Marwaha & May, 2015) that supposedly brings precognition into effect. Probably for evolutionary reasons, this filter *largely* (but not exclusively) does not filter *per se*, but we would be limited to a necessary (crucial) 'paranormal' experience, possibly governed by affectivity and numinosity, and in those factors we come back to archetypes—they will serve as components of our 'filtering system' (if we must give it such a name). Openness to those experiences *from time to time* may be intended or unintended (by agent or perceiver), but that openness will still depend on belief and a range of inner and outer *conducive* and necessarily *inhibitive* circumstances and variables (many already specified in a vast body of literature).

I suggest the ostensibly paranormal function is basically synchronistic and intrinsically linked to those creative properties of the "deep imagination" (for details, see Storm, 2025), which means the 'mechanism' *per se* underpinning that function (an archetypal system) is psychological (mind-based) *and* neurobiological (brain-based), but ultimately psychophysical.[11] Indeed, as a species we may assume the brain seems to cooperate to varying degrees (depending on the person; for ideas as to how the brain acts as a filter, see Freedman et al., 2018), and psychic/synchronistic experiences do appear to be objectively detectible, not just as successful psi targeting. To back up my points, Williams (2015) has reviewed the neuropsychological correlates of psi. He concludes that "real-time ESP (i.e., telepathy and clairvoyance) performance appears to be correlated with brainwave activity in the alpha frequency range" (p. 103). Williams adds precognition and PK performance to that list, and notes the dominant involvement of the right hemisphere in ESP and micro-PK tests. Similar conclusions were reached decades earlier by Stokes (1987) whose review suggested "right hemisphere activity may be conducive to the reception of telepathic information", as well as PK (pp. 178-179). Note that we may speak in terms of correlates, not causes, without any threat to the synchronistic model.

To describe this notion of an archetypal filtering system another way, we know that psi effects are not strong, and successful demonstrations on demand are rare, so a filter is a fair postulate, but any block to an experience may be endopsychic (i.e., occurring within the Self system which includes the ego). That means an archetype was not activated internally because any of those numerous circumstances and variables were not sufficiently controlled or optimized. If and when there is no block *per se*, or a block is lifted (i.e., negative circumstances are ameliorated or eliminated), the experience may seem to have an extrapsychic source, but it does not involve (and does not need to be thought of as involving) transmitted information—again, it comes down to a shared experience within the field (so to speak) of the constellated archetype. Under synchronicity theory, the process would be defined by, and limited to, archetypal constellations, which in themselves would constitute a filtering system of sorts that limits the experient to specific (affective and/or numinous) content. This system, by analogy, would function like rods and cones in the retina that have designated and mutually exclusive roles, or the tongue which can discern one taste from another.

I find Radin (2006a) talks in a similar way: As is the case with synchronicity, he does not speak of "information transfer" but of "correlations" (p. 264). However, he regards *all* "events distributed throughout space and time" as knowable (p. 266), provided one can find a parallel in memory. In synchronicity, however, the "knowable" is limited to those external events that parallel archetypal patterns in the psyche and can be represented in consciousness. To that extent, we can see why failure is built into synchronicity and therefore psi. We may say these phenomena are not as rare as skeptics might think, but nor are they completely at our disposal, just as we see in the laboratory.

As we have seen, Radin et al. (2015) posited an ultimate 'sameness' for mind and matter. Jung and Pauli suggested that this mystery is embodied in the *unus mundus* concept or (what is the same thing) *psychophysical reality*—a unified deeper order of reality from which all things mental and physical emanate. Strangely, Jung's *Synchronicity* essay makes no overt mention of the concept of the *unus mundus*,[12] and only later does Jung state that synchronicity is the "parapsychological equivalent" of the *unus mundus*: "events must possess an *a priori* aspect of unity" since everything happens in the same "one world" (Jung, 1963/1970, para. 662). In fact, had Jung covered this ancient concept in his essay in more depth, his problem with acausality would have been well and truly resolved in dual-aspect monism (of which more detail can be found in Storm, 2025).

The closest Jung gets to this ontological outlook is when he talks of "getting rid of the incommensurability between the observed and the observer. The result, in that case, would be a unity of being" (1952/1969, para. 960), where the "observed" is the outer world that the "observer" experiences mentally. That blunt statement might not satisfy at first because it could be read as stating what we already know—that our experience is an inner interpretation of the outer (physical) world—recall Becker's (2004) words above. But what Jung means by "incommensurability" is surely that we cannot ordinarily heal the split that gives us this *illusion* of two worlds, inner and outer. It would seem, however, the split is necessary for it implies two crucial factors for survival: namely, autonomy of being, *and* ultimately the birth of consciousness, or 'awareness', or that 'awareness system' I mentioned above. Thus, for mundane existence, there is no need to 'heal the split' *per se*, but in a sense, synchronicity does briefly merge and dissolve the illusion. In the words of von Franz (1992): "Synchronistic events are 'singularities' in which the oneness of psyche and matter, the *unus mundus*, becomes sporadically manifest" (p. 101). Browne (2015) puts this quite succinctly:

> synchronistic occurrences … are, in Jung's conceptualisation, a manifestation *in* time of 'the transcendental *unus mundus*, the potential world outside of time' [Jung, 1963/1970, para. 718], which von Franz further describes as the 'cosmic

> background which is neither matter nor psyche … [where] all opposites are still unified' [1992, p. 217]. By definition, therefore, the *unus mundus* does *not* act selectively or intrude, rather it is *revealed* under the specific conditions of a synchronistic event.
>
> (p. 118)

The idea of the *unus mundus* came late for Jung (albeit only a few years after publication of his synchronicity essay),[13] but it caught on fast, and von Franz expresses it quite clearly—indeed, the two scholars both help round out an understanding of the synchronicity concept in terms of the *unus mundus*.

With those ideas in place, we can move towards a worldview where words like 'complementarity', 'interaction', 'observation', and 'measurement' are relative concepts. Not only do those words hold no place in a unifying or unitary framework (because they suggest separation), they mislead us into thinking that relationships must always pertain (i.e., there is only us and the world and how each relates to the other), when it may not always be appropriate, helpful, or even scientific, to think so. Where does that leave consciousness? To borrow from Feynman, I think I can safely say that nobody understands consciousness, but it certainly partakes in that above-mentioned illusion which it cannot dissolve by sheer act of will. In synchronicity, we do seem to be able to overcome the limitations of our everyday consciousness and see that *mental experience* (metacognition) is not to be reified as consciousness, as it is only ever a representation (i.e., a content in consciousness), whereas consciousness *per se* is an ineffable other part of our being that the philosophers muse over *ad libitum*.

Intellectual limitation puts the *unus mundus* (admittedly a 'metaphysical speculation' says Jung) beyond the reach of normal experience, but it is said to be experienced *psychologically* in those borderline states of the imagination such as dreaming and synchronicity (Atmanspacher, 2014a). Those moments described as altered states of consciousness (ASCs) and synchronicity (and psi, if we must call it that) offer a temporary healing of the split between subject and object, mind and matter, where we intuit and glimpse that deeper reality beyond mind or matter. The words of Jungian-influenced artist, designer and out-of-body experiencer, Jurgen Ziewe are quite illustrative of that moment:

> It appears that when consciousness is released from the tether to its exclusive physical focus it enters its home territory of non-physicality where it may broaden and accentuate its self-awareness into new frontiers. That which consciousness then experiences in its home world are the infinite and myriad things that can be perceived, encountered, processed, imagined, fantasised about, projected into and reinterpreted in waking life, in addition to all the former unseen subconscious elements which are no longer subconscious, but rather an open book for the experiencer not just to see, but wander through and experience.
>
> (Ziewe, 2016, p. 121)

As an aside, I have raised the issue of extended consciousness previously (see *Expanded and Extended Consciousness* in the subsection *On Model Building* in Chapter 4), and I do so again because it is relevant here: What we experience as extended consciousness *seemingly* transcends spacetime and conjures up in the mind the image or idea that any number of meaningful, archetypally-defined and dependent interconnections (correspondences) are possible throughout the world. Actually the transcendent experience would be the bounded ego linking to the collective unconscious that gives an impression of an unbounded self, thus exposing the naïve ego to a greater experience with its numinous and transcendent aspects. These correspondences are links to the archetypal world and therefore other psyches at the psychoid level. Such experiences might be said to break that twofold spell of causality and paranormality for we would crack through the veil, as did Flammarion's 'missionary' (see Plate 5.2).

Plate 5.2 UNIVERSUM [THE UNIVERSE]. The alchemical *Unus Mundus* (One World) is embodied in the synchronistic experience of the "medieval missionary [who] tells that he has found the point where heaven and Earth meet ..." This dazzling image is known as the Flammarion Woodcut (unknown artist), from Camille Flammarion's *L'atmosphère: Météorologie Populaire* (Paris, 1888), a meteorological work meant for the lay public. [*Source:* Wikimedia Commons]

These kinds of experiences do not reduce to an overly creative imagination; an epiphenomenal outcrop unique to (say) paranormal believers nursing a range of cognitive deficits (see Irwin & Watt, 2007, pp. 231–232). On the contrary, such experiences refer to a mental 'world', or realm, or inner *topos* that opens up before those individuals who, with natural capacity or advanced training, discover a psychic aspect to matter. This "home territory" or "home world" is a place Jung rather limitedly referred to as a unique aspect of matter, and by that he specifically means a cerebral process that he extends to the psyche generally. Jung made such comment in his second interview with Richard Evans in *The Houston Films*:

> the psyche … is a quality of matter, just as our body consists of matter. We discover that this matter has another aspect, namely a psychic aspect. It is simply the world seen from within.
>
> (1977, p. 303)

As Ziewe implies, this world can be accessed via ASCs and paranormal experiences. Jung (1960/1969) has even stated that "synchronistic phenomena can be evoked by putting subjects in an unconscious (trance) state" (para. 440).

It is necessary to take a 'quantum' leap to the idea that our conceptual spaces can be barriers to understanding. Our classical understanding is hard to escape, with its precepts even being imposed on QM 'behaviours'. It seems that to a very large extent interpretation is an artifact of methodology (a problem already noted in parapsychology). A broader understanding of the causes and relations inherent in the world, at all levels, requires pluralistic and holistic thinking: Clearly an approach lacking in modern parapsychological theory-making. Each of eight theories covered in Chapter 4 almost stands on its own. In point of fact, the astute reader will spot similarities in the various theories. It is as if the *theories* as much as the *phenomena* await unification—there would only be a chance of the former ever seeing the light of day. But why pursue that course of action when the theory of synchronicity does the job, and more likely offers a broader perspective than any hybrid theory could offer? Truly, none of these theories incorporate the macrocosm, of which humble *Homo sapiens* is a small part. By exploring the nature of the archetypes, one can get an idea of the relationship between microcosm and macrocosm. Thus far, parapsychology, like the social sciences generally, looks at how humans may be responsible (i.e., it takes interest in human abilities) whenever it *looks like* humans are at the centre of what they do. This view is somewhat limited as was demonstrated in my analysis of Ted Owens—clearly not a man in total control of events around him; and deep down he knew it (see Chapter 1). The time is ripe for a science of the transpersonal that truly reaches outward and is not a flashy New-Age misappropriation of a term that could and should mean so much more than is currently understood by that term *trans*-personal.

In the main, the imaginal world is surely the key to a fuller understanding of synchronicity that is bound to the idea of the *unus mundus*, and goes well beyond that which mainstream scientists and philosophers have in mind when they wish to *reduce* all ASCs to something occurring exclusively in, and not beyond, the mind/brain complex, though that notion is not altogether wrong; but it is incomplete. They overlook our archetypal connections *that parallel external reality*. Hence, synchronicity relativizes our experience through the meaningful coincidence of the 'inner' and the so-called 'outer'—that meaningfulness can be seen when the two invariably mirror each other because the two are one.

Notes

1 'Collapse of the wave-function' is a sub-atomic particle reducing or transforming from a wave-like state to a localized particle due to interaction with the external world; 'nonlocality' refers to entanglement between spatially separated systems; 'superposition' refers to the overlapping of two wave forms without interference; 'quantum tunnelling' refers to a particle's motion through a barrier that it 'classically' could not penetrate.

2 See https://www.youtube.com/watch?v=w3ZRLlIWgHI

3 A coherent source of light means the waves have the same wavelength and amplitude, and are in phase.

4 In the double-slit scenario, the term *entanglement* is widely used, though arguably it does not apply since the relevant effects involve a single photon that is split and therefore only in *superposition* (see https://physics.stackexchange.com/questions/21009/entanglement-and-the-double-slit-experiment).

5 For an alternative (relativistic) explanation, see Nagy and Scully (2011).

6 Nobel Prize winning physicist Erwin Schrödinger (1887-1961) described a thought experiment involving the survival (or not) of a cat in a box (theoretically in superposition), based on whether (or not) a radioactive atom would decay and cause the release of a deadly gas. Schrödinger tried to expose the "ridiculousness" (cited Penney, 2020, p. 24) of the idea that the cat could be considered neither dead nor alive until it was observed. The Copenhagen interpretation does not propose collapse by observation—the wavefunction is a statistical tool with no real physicality, so observer-induced collapse of the wavefunction was out of the question, and superposition has nothing to do with the cat's fate: "The cat would be dead or alive long before we open the box to find out" (Faye, 2019).

7 I focus on the research by Radin's team because it is the only long-running and thorough series of studies available that feature principles and aims pertinent to the issues addressed in this chapter.

8 Radin et al. (2012) refers to the quantum measurement problem as a "curious effect whereby quantum objects appear to behave differently when observed than when unobserved" (p. 157).

9 Radin explains "… we found that people got bored pretty fast if they were just passively attending to that feedback, so we added an intentional task to keep them focused …." (D. I. Radin, personal communication, July 6, 2024).

10 As an example of the flexibility of QM fundamentals, Garret (2016) offers a mathematical proof that entanglement and measurement are the same phenomenon (i.e., entanglement is a measurement that destroys interference).

11 I realize some philosophers may conceptualize the 'brain' as a construct—a complex arrangement or manifestation of ethereal mental elements that give rise to (or depict) the complexities of consciousness—rather than a physical structure with causal properties. This conceptualization is irrelevant. I am saying it is likely that a necessarily complex system (mental/cerebral/archetypal) takes on a filtering role to avoid the unmanageable

inundation of unlimited content (e.g., see Freedman et al., 2018). Intention alone will not suffice.

12 Jung (1952/1969) seems to be heading towards a unifying principle when he agrees with Renaissance philosopher Pico della Mirandola: "omnes mundi partes unus sunt mundus [all parts of the world constitute one world]" (para. 927, n20).

13 One of the earliest in-depth considerations of the *unus mundus* by Jung is in 1958 in *Flying Saucers* in which he argues that "parapsychological phenomena … do away with the awkward hypothesis of psychophysical parallelism, and afford us an opportunity to construct a new world model closer to the idea of the *unus mundus*" (Jung, 1964/1970, para. 780).

Appendix A

Experiments on Meaningful Coincidence

Braud's Experiments with Meaningful Key Words

Braud (1983) conducted two experiments to assess meaningful coincidence quantitatively, and in both cases he achieved significant results. In the first experiment, Braud selected ten *key* words on the basis of a "special feeling" or "anomalous attention". Ten *control* words were selected from a compilation of spoken English frequency norms. Both key and control word-pairs were matched on frequency. The experiment was run over a 24-hour period for each pair. Occurrences of the key words were found in the environment, casual conversation, radio dialogue, etc.

Braud did not count the occurrences of the key word in its initial context, since it was over-represented there. Braud (1983) also conducted his day-to-day routine as per usual, so as to avoid seeking out "confirmatory contexts" where the key word might appear with greater than usual frequency. Upon statistical analysis, the "key (synchronistic) instances occurred significantly sooner than the matched control instances" (p. 6).

In a second experiment, Braud (1983) used a "limited newspaper record" (p. 7) to source his key and control words (selection was as per the first experiment). Again ten trials were run. The newspaper, the *San Antonio Express*, was pre-selected, as was the issue for the day if "a possible meaningful coincidence was identified on a particular day" (p. 7). Braud read the articles column by column, and readings were timed. The two words were timed from the moment they appeared in the text. Again there was a significant result. The key words were encountered sooner than the matched controls. These results suggested that not only does "a *tool* for the study of synchronicity" exist (p. 8), but also that synchronicity is at least as regular and predictable as parapsychological phenomena.

Experiments with the I Ching

The *I Ching* is an ancient Chinese system of divination, consisting of a book of 64 hexagrams (six-line symbols) and their corresponding readings that supposedly enlighten in practical and philosophical ways, and even provide forecasts of future events in response to questions posed by the user. The *I Ching* then, as the so-called

'Book of Changes', was both didactic and oracular. The 64 hexagrams symbolize human, social, and cosmic 'situations'. Hellmut Wilhelm (1905–1990)—son of Richard Wilhelm (1873–1930), both of whom were noted German sinologists—argued in his book *Changes* that these situations addressed "primary needs", "evolution of personality", "character traits", "social life", and "images of suprapersonal significance" (Wilhelm, 1960, pp. 4–5).

Storm and Thalbourne (1998-1999) conducted an initial study using the *I Ching* in a somewhat unorthodox manner, though one of the traditional techniques (i.e., coin-throwing) was used as the means by which hexagram lines were generated (there were six studies using this design up to 2014). Participants were required to pre-select 16 'descriptors pairs' out of the complete set of 64 descriptors that corresponded to 64 *I Ching* readings. The divinatory process kicks in when three coins are tossed six times to produce a so-called hexagram (a symbol comprised of six lines that is linked to a reading that gives a forecast). Though seemingly chosen at random, the forecast is argued by Jung to be derived as part of a process that is synchronistic—"the psychic process itself is just as much 'arranged' as the coinciding representation which anticipates the external physical process" (Jung, as cited in Greatrex, 1999, p. 6). In other words, in these early studies up to 2014, it was reasoned that some of the 16 choices—if not all of them—may resonate for the participant at various emotional levels and this inner (psychological) process would meaningfully connect with the physical (outer) arrangement of the coin outcomes that determine the symbol and subsequent reading.

In the first two studies, Storm and Thalbourne (1998-1999, 2001) found significant effects—outcome hexagrams were matched to descriptor-pairs more often than could be explained by chance (32% and then 35%, where chance is only 25%). Although other *I Ching* studies have produced mixed results on the hexagram outcome variables (fluctuating around chance), the overall trend has been towards above-chance hitting at 27% (see Storm, 2001, 2002, 2006, 2008b; Thalbourne & Storm, 2014). Besides the aggregate effect being weak (though weak does not mean unimportant), the effects have been inconsistent from study to study.

Storm (2008b) conducted a follow-up study to test perceptions of meaningfulness of hexagram readings (these were rated on scale of '0% meaningful' to '100% meaningful'). He found significant differences between (i) believers (77.24%) and nonbelievers (53.26%), and (ii) 'hitters' (participants who correctly preselected the outcome hexagram; meaningfulness score = 72.53%) and 'missers' (participants who failed to preselect the outcome hexagram; meaningfulness score = 64.70%). Also, the believer/nonbeliever difference on hitting was also significant (30.1% vs. 19.4%, respectively, where MCE = 25%), which is also known as a sheep-goat effect (for a definition of sheep-goat effect, see footnote 10 in Chapter 2).

Palmer (2016b) pointed out that the hitting/missing meaningfulness difference is "most likely an artifact" (p. 194) given that some participants could tie their outcome readings to one of their 16 pre-selected descriptor pairs and therefore possibly rate the readings high on meaningfulness, while others with no relevant pre-selections could therefore possibly rate their readings low. Ordinarily, when we have an artifact, we withdraw the claim for a genuine effect but, in this case, that would be unreasonable. For a start, whether or not *some* participants might refer back to their pre-selections (assuming the parallel even dawned on them), nothing will stop *all* participants reviewing their genuine mental (psychological) states as they read, so the content has every chance of resonating meaningfully, and with integrity in either case. Note too that "Participants were not told whether their hexagram was a hit or not" (Storm, 2008b, p. 112). This fact adds emphasis to my previous point. Also, the sheep/goat × hitting/missing interaction effect was not significant, so it is unlikely that (a) getting a hit resulted in disproportionately high meaningfulness ratings given by some hitters who were sheep, *OR* (b) getting a miss resulted in disproportionately low meaningfulness ratings given by some missers who were goats. Since sheep scored significantly more hits than goats, either of these two, (a) or (b), would only have been a likely scenario *if there was a significant interaction effect.*

Roe, Martin, and Drennan (2014) used cards with short statements (synopses) to paraphrase the hexagram readings, and these cards were slotted into a triangular grid-like framework (a Q-Sort grid) of 64 cells, which amounts to a rating or ranking process. The *I Ching* methodology was computerized so that the entire procedure involved no manual steps (i.e., no ticking off 16 of 64 descriptor pairs, and no coin-throwing). Participants were guided by on-screen instructions and electronic read-outs, with all data-entry by keyboard, and an RNG was used to generate hexagram lines. Graphically and statistically, an ostensible psi effect in a sample is indicated by a significant shift from a mean score of zero to some higher mean score. In two randomization methods (*pseudo* and *true*), Roe et al. reported positive mean shifts in the hypothesized direction, and one negative mean shift (method: random number tables)—all shifts were small and nonsignificant. The major problem with the study was that the small sample of only 33 participants did not have sufficient power for the small effects to reach significance.

In 2014, Storm and Rock (2014a) borrowed the Q-Sort protocol designed by Roe et al. (2014), but modified it, thus giving participants the chance to rank all 64 two-word descriptor-pairs (ranging from –7 to +7; with a mean of zero), instead of selecting only 16 from the pool of 64. This procedure also dispensed with the 64 lengthy statements Roe et al. used. Some significant effects were found for paranormal believers with believers producing stronger *I Ching* effects than nonbelievers.

Houran and Lange (2012) investigated combinations of Paranormal Belief (high-scoring vs. low-scoring as measured on Tobacyk's, 1988, Revised Paranormal Belief Scale) and Transliminality (high-scoring vs. low-scoring) in the context of an *I Ching* task. The authors reported a statistically significant hexagram hit rate of 45% for the overall sample, where MCE = 25%. As hypothesized, the high/high group produced the highest hit rate. In a follow-up study, Lange and Houran (2013) again hypothesized that experimenters and participants scoring high on both Paranormal Belief *and* Transliminality (i.e., high-participant/high-experimenter) would produce a higher hexagram hit rate than their low scoring participant/experimenter counterparts (i.e., low-participant/high-experimenter; high-participant/

low-experimenter, and low-participant/low-experimenter). The "First Hexagram" hit rate for both the overall sample and the high-high group was statistically significant, but at chance level for the other three groups.

Gedankenexperiment: Imagery Cultivation vs. I Ching

In relation to points raised in the section 'False Positives and False Negatives' in Chapter 3, I offer the following *Gedankenexperiment* (German: 'thought experiment') to illustrate how hits might be qualitatively assessed, which would also be a way to estimate false positives which inflate the psi hit rate. It will be seen that experimenters should weigh up the importance of meaningfulness and not put so much stock in significance. Imagine a researcher conducting two experiments—an Imagery Cultivation experiment (Study #1) and an *I Ching* experiment (Study #2)—who wants to check the hit content (pictures, readings) on meaningfulness ratings since a Meaningfulness Scale (MS) is to be administered to participants in both experiments (photos and readings are rated on the MS, respectively). The experimenter is only interested in analysing the hit data.

In Study #1 (Imagery Cultivation; $N = 500$), the experimenter finds a significant total hit count of 170 participants (34%, $p < .001$), and of those 34%, 10% ($n = 17$) rated Meaningfulness ≥ 95%. Note that the hit-rate of 34% is 9% above MCE (MCE = 25%). But in Study #2 (*I Ching*; $N = 500$), the experimenter finds a non-significant total hit rate of only 125 participants, with scoring therefore exactly at chance (i.e., 25%, where MCE = 25%), which compares rather poorly with the 34% hit rate in Study #1 that was 9% above MCE. However, a high 20% of hitters (25 participants) rated Meaningfulness ≥ 95%.

An experimenter who thinks like Jung would seek support for the synchronicity hypothesis, and so on a case-by-case basis, 17 of 170 hitters (10%) in Study #1 and 25 of 125 hitters (20%) in Study #2 are good outcomes. Yet for the conventional parapsychologist, only Study #1 gives a significant p value, and therefore supports the psi hypothesis. But the experimenter can make some pertinent claims: those 17 participants (3.4%) in Study #1 probably did not produce false positives because they had high MS scores; arguably, by the same token, the impressive rate of 25 participants (5%) in Study #2 probably did not produce false positives either because they too had high MS scores. The experimenter is thinking in terms of synchronicity and the importance of meaningful outcomes. Of course, the scenario given above is idealistic. The above *Gedankenexperiment* is only presented to contrast significance (to determine psi) against meaningfulness (to determine synchronicity).

The Author's Synchronicity Tests on the Melbourne Cup

The Melbourne Cup, Australia's biggest horse race, held in Melbourne, Victoria, every year on the first Tuesday of November, has a long and illustrious history going back to 1861. It has achieved worldwide fame, and Alice Johnson (1899) noted how it was not surprising that there have been many dream-ESP cases that describe successful predictions of Melbourne Cup winners. She does appeal to the Law of Truly Large Numbers ("… as the dreams must be numbered by thousands, one or two of the dreams occasionally come true"; p. 317), but she gives one example that is out of the ordinary: Some four months before the Melbourne Cup of 1895, a Redfern resident dreamed of the horse *Auraria* winning, but he also dreamed he would die before the race was run. He backed the horse for a £200 win, and gave the ticket to his wife. Although he enjoyed good health at the time of the dream, he took ill and died (as predicted) some weeks before the race, but *Auraria* did win (as also predicted). His wife collected the winnings. Johnson makes light of the win on statistical grounds giving odds against dreaming of a winning horse at "not more than about 100 to 1" (p. 319), and she presumes that the dreamer may have been aware (even subliminally) that a life-threatening malady was imminent, but she was never able to prove her theory.

The following four studies do not depend on the arbitrary and effectively nonintentional nature of dreams, but were conducted to test the proposition that synchronicity can be intentional.

Study One (2013). On the Monday night before the Melbourne Cup race, I attempted intentional synchronicity to see if it might yield the Cup winner (reported in Storm, 2014). It happened to be the case that I wanted to watch a classic Japanese movie *Gate of Hell* (Nagata & Kinugasa, 1953) that I had never seen, and had been putting off for almost a week. Monday night before the big day Tuesday, I finally did watch the film, which was set in feudal Japan. Two rivals were out to prove themselves in an annual horse race, and I found it most intriguing that the horse of one rival was draped in a bright purple sash, for I wondered if the horse and colour purple were clues to the identity of the Cup winner. The other rival's horse sported an orange sash. The horse in purple won. Come Tuesday morning, before the main race at 2:30 p.m., I checked the newspaper for information about the horses. The Cup was running three horses with jockeys in purple (*Fiorente*, *Hawkspur*, and *Simenon*). Come Tuesday morning, I put *win and place* bets (i.e., each-way bets) on three horses: *Fiorente* (a favourite), *Hawkspur*, and *Voleuse de Coeurs* (based on a tip from a self-proclaimed psychic friend). For reasons not clear to me, I did not bet on *Simenon*, which ultimately came fourth. *Fiorente* was the winner, and I made a small profit.

Study Two (2014). I set about my evening (Monday night before the race on Tuesday) in the usual way—by sitting down to an evening in front of the TV (reported in Storm, 2015). I watched a re-run of *Agatha Christie's Marple* (an episode called 'Murder Is Easy'). I was looking for a 'sign', but the only thing that jumped out at me repeatedly were blue wild flowers. I kept blue in mind. Interestingly, I had a dream the day before (early Sunday morning) about my riding a brown horse, but there are many brown and brownish (i.e., bay, chestnut) horses in the Melbourne Cup, so the colour brown was of little help. My clues thus far: blue flower, and brown (or chestnut, or bay!) horse. As was the case in 2013, I expected the blue to associate with the jockey's silks (in particular, one jockey riding the favourite,

Protectionist, which was to win), but there were at least six other jockeys in blue silks—I had no exclusion criteria to get a reasonable shortlist of (say) three or four horses to bet on. But I was in the ball-park. In fact, I found an online ABC NEWS article confirming that (a) bays win the Cup most often, and (b) "runners with predominantly blue jockey silks" also win most often.[1] This outcome could therefore be regarded as synchronistic. As it happened, I did not have time nor inclination to make an official bet anyway—without some additional criteria, and extra time for a little more homework on colour combinations, I did not fancy my chances.

Study Three (2015). On the Monday night before the Melbourne Cup race, I watched an episode of *The Saint* (Charteris et al., 1964), which happened to feature a horse race. Unfortunately, this episode was in black and white, and only a brief scene of the horse race was shown, so I could not make out any distinguishing features (colours or numbers) that would be of help to me in preparing a short list of jockeys/horses.

Study Four (2018). I did not follow the Melbourne Cup in 2016 and 2017, and had very nearly ignored the race in 2018. In fact, I had forgotten about the race up until the Tuesday morning of race day, having been preoccupied with more pressing matters. At around 12:30 p.m. (two hours before the race, Adelaide time), I wondered what activity I could engage in that might create an opportunity for intentional synchronicity. I was actually driving to the beach intending to have lunch on the foreshore, and on the way I thought to play some music in the car, and listen for clues in the lyrics of whatever song came up, though I cannot say why I thought that might create the first half of the synchronicity (the corresponding second half being the future target—i.e., the winning jockey/horse). In the car, I *thought* of playing some music by Swedish pop group ABBA (which I did not do), but at that moment a particular album cover of theirs, Voulez-Vous, came to mind which features a mainly blue cover, with Agnetha Fältskog wearing a blue dress—note point (b) in *Study Two* above about jockeys wearing "predominantly blue jockey silks" winning most often *as of 2015*. However, only later that day (after the race) did I discover that the website Races.com.au noted that more "winning jockeys have worn black as their main colour than any other colour", followed by "navy blue and royal blue" as the next more popular colour in recent Melbourne Cup history.[2] So, I was to go against the trend for when I arrived back home at 2:00 p.m., I did not play any ABBA music, but (with so little time left) I decided instead to check a list of all 24 jockeys and single out those jockeys wearing purely blue silks for my shortlist. I found three jockeys who wore only blue silks—their horses were *Best Solution*, *Avilius*, and *Cross Counter*. The winning horse was *Cross Counter*. There was no time for betting, but my usual strategy (when there are not too many horses on my shortlist) would have been to bet *each-way* (i.e., bet for a win and a place) on all short-listed horses. The odds (win, 9:1; place, 3:1) would have assured a profit.

Study Five (2019). Going about my usual routine on the night prior to the race, I felt somewhat compromised as I was working my way through the 1960s TV drama series *Peyton Place*, and did not think any particular episode could produce much that was reliable in the way of colour clues (the series ran from 1964 to 1969, and went to colour in 1966). Very old videotape copies of the episodes were obviously recorded directly from television, and years later were converted to digital format, and then uploaded to YouTube channel 'SoapsNthings', but with much colour degradation and/or alteration (some of the worst copies were awash in shades of grey and purple, with only occasional splashes of colour here and there). On the Monday night before the race, I had nearly completed watching the entire five seasons on YouTube. That night, I viewed a few of the remaining episodes, including episode #490, although all that came to my attention in that episode was the elderly widow, Maggie Riggs, wearing a woollen scarf alternately coloured red and black (or perhaps *orange* and black, given the colour distortion). There were no jockeys wearing red and black, or orange and black, although three jockeys did feature orange in their silks—they rode *Il Paradiso*, *Vow and Declare*, and *Magic Wand*. The winner was *Vow and Declare* whose jockey wore mainly orange (much more orange than the other two). Only two jockeys wore red: *Prince of Arran*'s jockey wore red and blue silk; *Steel Prince*'s jockey wore silk featuring a red cross—these two ran second and third, respectively. With five horses on the shortlist, and not knowing which to eliminate, the best gambling option would have been to make *each-way* or *place* bets on all five horses.

Discussion and Conclusions

William Braud's successful experiments were simple, straight-forward attempts to see if his unique selection of key words would pop up externally somewhere (e.g., in media), thus forming matched pairs with greater than chance frequency. Braud called these matches 'meaningful coincidences', but he also deferred to the word 'synchronicity'. It was never clear to me whether he thought the two were different somehow, perhaps with meaningful coincidence, in his mind, being a lesser form of synchronicity. It would seem so, as the coincidence factor is definitely there, but his examples do not seem to express any great level of meaning for him personally—at least, not beyond that 'first level' described by Aziz (1990).

The author's experiments with the *I Ching* tried to overcome that limitation by making possible a meaningful experience for participants, which is the crux of the *I Ching* philosophy. The ancient Chinese were interested in how and why things in nature and human experience that occur together might be related, and whether there was some way of deliberately capturing that in a humanly devised process or system. The development of the *I Ching* came to be particularly focused on higher principles not dependent on temporal or spatial parameters, but were universal and forever true. Ideally, these 'truths' could or would be addressed and presented in philosophical contexts, manifesting as meanings generated and represented in pertinent readings. The author's studies were encouraging in that respect—it seemed that chance could not explain how some participants were able to produce readings that anticipated or spoke to their feelings *a priori*. Two different approaches to testing the *I Ching* were taken, but outcomes bore similarities that supported (though only somewhat) the general assumption that the *I Ching* system can offer perspectives on, or solutions to unanswerable or unresolvable questions, without the outcome necessarily being wholly attributable to chance factors.

Generally, the results of a series of Melbourne Cup races suggest that intentional synchronicity may be a viable means of predicting future outcomes in a gambling scenario, and could even prove lucrative (as in *Study One*). However, questions relating to source (or better, priming) material, especially its quality, need addressing (as was the case in *Study Three* and *Study Five*). Basically, good-quality source material is not always available, though that will depend on the practitioner's lifestyle (e.g., his/her media and entertainment preferences and interests). That is to say, clues do not always appear in the stimulus material, but that is due to choices and capacity to spot clues if they are there in the material (which is hopefully of good quality), so various natural limits come into play. On the one hand, a major part of the protocol (i.e., identifying and evaluating the cogency of the stimuli) seems more like art than science requiring training (as in remote viewing) to filter out nonessential details. On the other hand, it may be that essential details are lacking so that a shortlist cannot be prepared as was evident in *Study Two* and *Study Four*.

Many more trials are needed that test a range of participants (e.g., both amateur and professional gamblers), to see how well the protocol performs in the long run, and for whom. In the meantime, strategic betting is advised, although opinion is divided as to which form of betting is going to be more fruitful and/or profitable when shortlists do result from the protocol—e.g., *place betting* or *each-way betting*. That may depend on the odds, as every race is different. Of course, the author's run of Melbourne Cup studies were tests of synchronistic intention; not betting strategies (if the former is consistent, the latter will have to be devised by those with a basic understanding of statistics, and/or a good knowledge of the betting world).

Notes

1 https://www.abc.net.au/news/2015-11-02/melbourne-cup-2015-how-the-runners-compare-to-past-champions/6891238
2 http://www.races.com.au/melbourne-cup/melbourne-cup-history/facts-and-statistics/

Appendix B

Synchronistic Confirmation?

By Charles T. Tart[1]

One of the most interesting things about apparently synchronistic events is that they change apparently unrelated, meaningless events into importantly meaningful ones; they illuminate the humdrum aspects of life. I shall now describe an apparently synchronistic series of events accompanying an earlier presentation of these ideas which I interpret as a synchronistic "confirmation" of the usefulness of thinking about synchronicity in this way. The text of the presentation was run off on a ditto machine on Thursday, January 29, 1976, and a dozen copies were ready for me to take back to my home in Berkeley that evening so I could distribute them at a meeting the next evening of a group of local California scientists interested in parapsychology. The meeting was the first in a planned series for these scientists, who were to meet at my home once a month to discuss their current research and interests. Those attending this first meeting, in addition to me, were John Palmer, Arthur Hastings, Russell Targ, Elizabeth Rauscher, John Jungerman, and Lila Gatlin. A series of events happened in connection with our going to dinner before we began our formal meeting that were synchronistic in the way this term is usually used. These events were so apropos to my presentation on synchronicity and to the formal purpose of the meeting, Targ's description of the latest SRI research on remote viewing, that I shall interpret them as a synchronistic confirmation of the usefulness of presenting my paper.

First, background information about some of the participants in the meeting will be necessary to show why the synchronistic events were so appropriate. Although the meeting had not been called specifically to discuss out-of-body experiences (OBEs), several parapsychologists active in OBE research were present. My first contribution (Tart, 1968) to OBE research was a study on the physiological correlates of OBEs in a subject identified as Miss Z in the original report. This research attracted considerable attention among parapsychologists, and is generally considered to have stimulated further laboratory investigations in this area. Palmer is one of the most active investigators of OBEs, having published several articles (Palmer & Lieberman, 1975; Palmer & Vassar, 1974) on the subject in the last few years. He was working with me on the analysis of a large case collection of OBEs at the time of the meetings, and we hoped to do physiological research with talented OBE subjects in the future. Hastings was an old friend of Miss Z, and had assisted me in carrying out the research with her more than a dozen years ago. Targ also was acquainted with Miss Z at the time the original research with her was done, and he has had a long-term interest in OBEs. His remote viewing experiments with Harold Puthoff (Puthoff & Targ, 1976; Targ & Puthoff, 1977) represent a phenomenon that is similar to an aspect of some OBEs—the acquisition of information at a distance from the physical body. Although I think the OBE is a different phenomenon from remote viewing when we look at both closely, Targ and I have often discussed just what the similarities and differences are. Rauscher, a physicist at the University of California, Berkeley, had done some pilot work on remote viewing, and she planned to carry out a more complete experiment later that year.

Before the meeting was to begin, we had to decide where to go for dinner. I named several restaurants within a five-minute drive from my home, and the group chose Shakey's Pizza Parlor on Solano Avenue in Berkeley. We drove there in two cars. Those who arrived in the first car picked seats at one of the long tables to hold a place for the group while the others ordered the pizza. I was among the latter, and while I was standing at the counter Hastings came up to me and announced that Miss Z was sitting at the opposite end of our group's long table! After completing my research with Miss Z more than a decade ago, she moved to Southern California and I lost track of her; then I heard indirectly that she had emigrated to Israel. I eventually learned that she had returned to California, and I ran across her in San Francisco a couple of years before the date of our meeting. We had chatted for a while about whether she was still having OBEs (they were very rare with her now). The only other occasion that I had run into her since then was about a year and a half earlier, when Hastings and I met her in the ticket line for a San Francisco show. She said she very rarely visited Berkeley. It struck me as a remarkable "coincidence" that Miss Z should show up at the same table as a group of people comprising several of the most active researchers on OBEs. Hastings, Palmer, and I spoke with Miss Z only briefly, and she left not long after we arrived. The other members of our group were too engrossed in conversation at the time to be aware of what was happening.

Moreover, two other events that seemed to reinforce this synchronicity occurred while Miss Z was still at the other end of the table. Shakey's Pizza Parlor showed old movies and various selected shorts continuously. While we were talking about Miss Z being there, a short came on telling the story of Mary Poppins: Miss Z was the well known parapsychological subject who had apparently left her body to "float around" the ceiling. Now it was Mary Poppins floating around in the air with her umbrella and doing various other "magical" things. This was not only appropriate for the specific OBE parallelism, but also for the paranormal theme of the meeting in general. Further, I had been in a small store selling miscellaneous used goods that afternoon and had noticed a woman looking at and handling a rather old umbrella. This struck me as odd at the time, as we had been having a drought, and umbrellas were not needed. Following the Mary Poppins film after one intervening film was a cartoon version of Alice in Wonderland, called "Alice and the White Rabbit," showing a variety of "magical" changes underscoring of parapsychological events. Further, the intervening film comprised something of a minor personal synchronicity for me, as it was a cartoon of "Brer Rabbit and the Tar Baby," a story that my daughter had read aloud to our family just the previous weekend while we were on a camping trip. It is very rare for my family to read this sort of story, aloud or to ourselves. I chose to interpret these events as an example of either being-specific or synchronistic causality. Paranormal causality does not seem particularly plausible as there were so many events to arrange to give the final happening its full flavor.

It seems rather cumbersome to imagine someone's unconscious mind using psi to make sure that some active OBE researchers were at just that place, influencing Miss Z's activity to send her from San Francisco to Berkeley at just the right time, and affecting the showing of just those particular films. What this amounts to saying is that the pattern of events seems so meaningful that I cannot dismiss them as nothing but coincidence, or merely projected meaning or projected causality on my part; but neither do I feel comfortable trying to fit them into a paranormal causality framework. I am inclined to think that this pattern of events was an instance of being-specific synchronistic causality because my own desire a week earlier for an example of synchronicity had only been partially met by my colleague's phone call from the East Coast.[2] That was interesting, but not entirely convincing. While this very lack of "overconvincingness" was quite useful to me in illustrating the difficulties in distinguishing categories of synchronicity, some part of me still hoped for something better.

Notes

1 Excerpt taken from Tart (2008, pp. 123–125; reprinted with permission).

2 Tart (2008) states that being-specific synchronistic causality is "an anthropomorphic projection of our belief that everything is caused, even though we recognize that we will never be able to prove it" (p. 119).

Appendix C

Optional Stopping and Optional Extension

Rounding Out *Ns*

Original Database (Storm, Tressoldi, and Di Risio, 2010)

The homogeneous database consists of 102 studies: mean $z = 0.81$ ($SD = 1.23$; range: −2.30 to 4.32), mean ES = 0.135 ($SD = 0.20$; range: −0.44 to 0.65), and Stouffer $Z = 8.13$ ($p < 10^{-16}$). CIs (95%) are as follows: *z* scores, [0.56, 1.07]; ES values, [0.10, 0.17]. Note that neither of these includes mean chance expectation (MCE)—that is, zero—which means there is no statistical likelihood that the results fall within chance parameters. Of the 102 studies, 74 (72.5%) had positive *z* scores. Twenty-seven (26.5%) of the 102 studies are independently significant ($\alpha \leq .05$).

Rounded Database ("Nonround *Ns*" Removed)

The database consists of 52 studies: mean $z = 0.71$ ($SD = 1.21$; range: −1.97 to 3.41), mean ES = 0.130 ($SD = 0.22$; range: −0.44 to 0.65), and Stouffer $Z = 5.08$ ($p = 1.89 \times 10^{-7}$). CIs (95%) are as follows: *z* scores, [0.37, 1.04]; ES values, [0.07, 0.19]. Note that neither of these includes MCE—that is, zero. Of the 52 studies, 34 (65.4%) had positive *z* scores. Thirteen (25.0%) of the 52 studies are independently significant ($\alpha \leq .05$).

The difference between the two mean *z* values is not significant, using the $Z_{\text{diff.}}$ (*Z*-difference) formula, $Z_{\text{diff.}} = [Z_1 - Z_2]/\sqrt{2} = [0.81 - 0.71]/\sqrt{2} = 0.07$ ($p = .472$).

It is worth mentioning that Bierman, Spottiswoode, and Bijl (2016) provide a link to their own set of 79 ganzfeld studies which they label the "S1 Dataset" (p. 4). These 79 are all the post-1985 studies they deemed suitable for analysis, having excluded the questionable studies that had "procedural weaknesses" (p. 3). Bierman et al. produced a Cohen's effect size $d = 0.14$. If we take out all nonround *Ns* from their database, the dataset reduces to 37 studies, with corresponding $d = 0.12$. Again, we see little change. There is no evidence of optional stopping or optional extension.

References[1]

Akers, C. (1987). Parapsychology is science, but its findings are inconclusive. *Behavioral and Brain Sciences, 10*, 566–568.

Alcock, J. E. (1981). *Parapsychology: Science or magic? A psychological perspective*. Pergamon Press.

Alcock, J. E. (2003). Give The null hypothesis a chance: Reasons to remain doubtful about the existence of psi. In J. Alcock, J. Burns, & A. Freeman (Eds.), *Psi wars: Getting to grips with the paranormal* (29–50). Imprint Academic.

Alexander, C. H., & Broughton, R. S. (2001). Cerebral hemisphere dominance and ESP performance in the autoganzfeld. *Journal of Parapsychology, 65*, 397–416.

Alvarado, C. S. (2011). Prescribing for parapsychology: Note on J. B. Rhine's writings in the Journal of Parapsychology. *Australian Journal of Parapsychology, 11*, 89–99.

Alvarado, C. S. (1983a). Psychological evaluations of poltergeist agents: A critique. In R. A. White, & R. S. Broughton (Eds.), *Research in parapsychology 1983* (117–118). Scarecrow Press.

Alvarado, C. S. (1983b). [Review of the book *a glossary of terms used in parapsychology*, by M. A. Thalbourne]. *Journal of the American Society for Psychical Research, 77*, 347–349.

Ananthaswamy, A. (2018, September 13). What does quantum theory actually tell us about reality? *Different Impulse: Tech News*. https://differentimpulse.com/what-does-quantum-theory-actually-tell-us-about-reality/

Armonk, N. Y. (2004). MOCKINGBIRD, project. *Encyclopedia of intelligence and counter-intelligence* (1st ed.). Routledge.

Atmanspacher, H. (2014a). 20th century variants of dual-aspect thinking. *Mind and Matter, 12*(2), 245–288.

Atmanspacher, H. (2014b). Notes on psychophysical phenomena. In H. Atmanspacher, & C. A. Fuchs (Eds.), *The Pauli-Jung conjecture and its impact today* (181–199). Imprint Academic.

Atmanspacher, H., & Fuchs, C. A. (Eds.). (2014). *The Pauli-Jung conjecture and its impact today*. Imprint Academic.

Australian Institute of Parapsychological Research. (2022, September 25). *Turning the unconventional into the conventional: Some experiments capturing healing intention (Bill Bengston)* [Video]. YouTube. https://www.youtube.com/watch?v=V5CRau19mhw

Aziz, R. (1990). *C. G. Jung's psychology of religion and synchronicity*. State University of New York Press.

Ball, P. (2011). The dawn of quantum biology. *Nature, 474*, 272–274.

Ballard, J. A. (1986). Adequacy of some parapsychological terms. In D. H. Weiner, & D. I. Radin (Eds.), *Research in parapsychology 1985* (144–148). Scarecrow Press.

Bancel, P. A. (2018). Simulating questionable research practices. *Proceedings of the presented papers of the Parapsychological Association 61st annual conference* (105–115). Parapsychological Association.

Bancel, P. A. (2017a). Response to Nelson's weighing the parameters. *Explore: The Journal of Science and Healing*, *13*(2), 106–107.
Bancel, P. A. (2017b). Searching for global consciousness: A 17-year exploration. *Explore: The Journal of Science and Healing*, *13*(2), 94–101.
Bancel, P. A., & Nelson, R. (2008). The GCP event experiment: Design, analytical methods, results. *Journal of Scientific Exploration*, *22*(3), 309–333.
Baptista, J., Derakhshani, M., & Tressoldi, P. (2015). Explicit anomalous cognition: A review of the best evidence in ganzfeld, forced-choice, remote viewing and dream studies. In E. Cardeña, J. Palmer, & D. Marcusson-Clavertz (Eds.), *Parapsychology. A handbook for the 21st century* (192–214). McFarland.
Basterfield, K. (2001). Paranormal aspects of the UFO phenomenon. *Australian Journal of Parapsychology*, *1*, 30–55.
Basterfield, K., & Thalbourne, M. A. (2002). Belief in, and alleged experience of, the paranormal in ostensible UFO abductees. *Australian Journal of Parapsychology*, *2*, 2–18.
Bauer, E. (1984). Criticism and controversy in parapsychology: An overview. *European Journal of Parapsychology*, *5*, 141–166.
Becker, A. (2019). *What is reality? The unfinished quest for the meaning of quantum physics*. John Murray.
Becker, L. (2004). That von Neumann did not believe in a physical collapse. *British Journal for the Philosophy of Science*, *55*(1), 121–135.
Beitman, B. (2022). *Meaningful coincidence: How and why synchronicity and serendipity happen*. Park Street Press.
Beitman, B. D., Celebi, E., & Coleman, S. L. (2010). Synchronicity and healing. In D. A. Monti, & B. D. Beitman (Eds.), *Integrative psychiatry* (445–483). Oxford University Press.
Bell, J. (1964).On the Einstein Podolsky Rosen paradox. *Physics*, *1*(3), 195–200.
Beloff, J. (1977). Psi phenomena: Causal versus acausal interpretation. *Journal of the Society for Psychical Research*, *49*, 573–582.
Beloff, J. (1978). The inevitability of dualism. *Behavioral and Brain Sciences*, *1*(3), 347–347.
Beloff, J. (1985). Robert Henry Thouless 1894-1984: An appreciation. *Journal of Parapsychology*, *49*, 221–227.
Beloff, J. (1988). Parapsychology and physics: Can they be reconciled? *Theoretical Parapsychology*, *6*, 23–29.
Beloff, J. (1990). *The relentless question: Reflections on the paranormal*. McFarland.
Beloff, J. (1994). Lessons of history. *Journal of the American Society for Psychical Research*, *88*, 7–22.
Beloff, J. (2008). Psi phenomena: Causal versus acausal interpretation. In L. Storm (Ed.), *Synchronicity: Multiple perspectives on meaningful coincidence* (99–108). Pari Publishing.
Bem, D. J. (2011). Feeling the future: Experimental evidence for anomalous retroactive influences on cognition and affect. *Journal of Personality and Social Psychology*, *100*(3), 407–425.
Bem, D. J., & Honorton, C. (1994). Does psi exist? Replicable evidence for an anomalous process of information transfer. *Psychological Bulletin*, *115*, 4–18.
Bem, D. J., Palmer, J., & Broughton, R. S. (2001). Updating the ganzfeld database: A victim of its own success? *Journal of Parapsychology*, *65*, 207–218.
Bem, D., Tressoldi, P. E., Rabeyron, T., & Duggan, M. (2016). Feeling the future: A meta-analysis of 90 experiments on the anomalous anticipation of random future events. *F1000Research*, *4*, 1188.
Bierman, D. J. (2001). On the nature of anomalous phenomena: Another reality between the world of subjective consciousness and the objective world of physics? In P. Van Loocke (Ed.), *The physical nature of consciousness* (269–292). Benjamins.
Bierman, D. J. (2010). Consciousness induced restoration of time symmetry (CIRTS): A psychophysical theoretical perspective. *Journal of Parapsychology*, *74*, 273–299.

Bierman, D. J., Spottiswoode, S. J. P., & Bijl, A. (2016). Testing for questionable research practices in a meta-analysis: An example from experimental parapsychology. *PLoS ONE, 11*(5), 1–18.

Birge, W. R. (1948). A new method and an experiment in pure telepathy. *Journal of Parapsychology, 12*(4), 272–288.

Blackmore, S. J. (1983). Divination with tarot cards: An empirical study. *Journal of the Society for Psychical Research, 52*, 97–101.

Blackmore, S. J. (1991). Correspondence regarding "probability and the psyche". *Journal of the Society for Psychical Research, 58*, 116–177.

Blackmore, S. J. (1985). Unrepeatability: Parapsychology's only finding. In B. Shapin & L. Coly (Ed.), *The repeatability problem on parapsychology: Proceedings of an international conference* (183–206). Parapsychology Foundation.

Blackstone, W. (1978). *Commentaries on the laws of England* (9th ed.). Garland Publishers. (Original work published in 1783)

Boerenkamp, H. G., & Schouten, S. A. (1983). Estimating the potential paranormal value of verbal statements. *Journal of Parapsychology, 47*, 121–130.

Bohm, D. (1986). A new theory of the relationship of mind and matter. *Journal of the American Society for Psychical Research, 80*, 113–135.

Bohm, D. (1996). *Unfolding meaning: A weekend of dialogue with David Bohm*. Routledge.

Bond, N. W., & McConkey, K. M. (2001). *Psychological science: An introduction*. McGraw-Hill.

Bösch, H., Steinkamp, F., & Boller, E. (2006). Examining psychokinesis: The interaction of human intention with random number generators—A meta-analysis. *Psychological Bulletin, 132*, 497–523.

Boswell, J. (1799). *The life of Samuel Johnson*. Bigelow, Brown & Company. (Published by Baldwin & Son).

Bradshaw, S., & Storm, L. (2013). Archetypes, symbols, and the apprehension of meaning. *International Journal of Jungian Studies*, *5*(2), 154–176.

Braud, W. G. (1983). Toward the quantitative assessment of "meaningful coincidence." *Parapsychological Review, 14*(4), 5–10.

Braud, W. G. (1985). ESP, PK and sympathetic nervous system activity. *Parapsychology Review, 16*, 6–16.

Braud, W. G., & Schlitz, M. A. (1989). Possible role of intuitive data sorting in electrodermal biological psychokinesis (bio-PK). *Journal of the American Society for Psychical Research, 83*, 289–302.

Braud, W. G., & Schlitz, M. A. (1991). Consciousness interactions with remote biological systems: Anomalous intentionality effects. *Subtle Energies, 2*, 1–46.

Braude, S. E. (1979). *ESP and psychokinesis: A philosophical examination*. Temple University Press.

Braude, S. E. (1986). *The limits of influence: Psychokinesis and the philosophy of science*. Routledge & Kegan Paul.

Braude, S. E. (1998). Terminological reform in parapsychology: A giant step backwards. *Journal of Scientific Exploration, 12*(1), 141–150.

Braude, S. E. (2001). [Review of the book *the PK man: A true story of mind over matter*, by J. Mishlove]. *Journal of Parapsychology, 65*, 183–188.

Braude, S. E. (2003). *Immortal remains: The evidence for life after death*. Rowman & Littlefield.

Braude, S. E. (2007). *The gold leaf lady and other parapsychological investigations*. University of Chicago Press.

Braude, S. E. (2008). The fear of psi: It's the thought that counts. In G. Taylor (Ed.), *Darklore* (Vol. 2, 99–111). Daily Grail.

Braude, S. E. (2015). Macro-psychokinesis. In E. Cardeña, J. Palmer, & D. Marcusson-Clavertz (Eds.), *Parapsychology. A handbook for the 21st century* (258–265). McFarland.

Braude, S. E. (2017). Jule Eisenbud. *Psi Encyclopedia.* https://psi-encyclopedia.spr.ac.uk/articles/jule-eisenbud

Braude, S. E. (2020). *Dangerous pursuits: Mediumship, mind, and music.* Anomalist Books.

Broad, C. D. (2011). *Lectures on psychical research: Incorporating the Perrott lectures given in Cambridge University in 1959 and 1960.* Routledge. (Original work published in 1962)

Broad, C. D. (1949). The relevance of psychical research to philosophy. *Philosophy, 24,* 291–301.

Broughton, R. (2018). Foreword. In E. C. May, & S. B. Marwaha (Eds.), *The star gate archives: Reports of the United States government sponsored psi program, 1972-1995. Volume 1: Remote viewing, 1972-1984* (2–4). McFarland.

Broughton, R. S. (2015). Psi and biology: An evolutionary perspective. In E. Cardeña, J. Palmer, & D. Marcusson-Clavertz (Eds.), *Parapsychology. A handbook for the 21st century* (139–148). McFarland.

Broughton, R. S. (1988). If you want to know how it works, first find out what it's for (Presidential Address to the Parapsychological Association). In D. H. Weiner, & R. L. Morris (Eds.), *Research in parapsychology 1987* (187–202). Scarecrow Press.

Broughton, R. S., &Alexander, C. H. (1997). Autoganzfeld II: An attempted replication of the PRL autoganzfeld research. *Journal of Parapsychology, 61,* 209–226.

Brown, D. E. (1991). *Human universals.* McGraw-Hill.

Browne, L. (2015). Some difficulties in coincidence analysis. *Australian Journal of Parapsychology, 15,* 53–79.

Browne, L. (2017). *The many faces of coincidence.* Imprint Academic.

Burri, M. (2005). Der "Pauli-Effekt". *ETHistory.* http://www.ethistory.ethz.ch/besichtigungen/objekte/paulieffekt/

Cambray, J. (2009). *Synchronicity: Nature and psyche in an interconnected universe.* Texas A&M University Press.

Campbell, J. (2008).*The hero with a thousand faces* (3rd ed.). New World Library.

Campbell, T. (2007). *My big TOE: Awakening, discovery, inner workings.* Lightning Strike Books.

Cardeña, E. (2014). A call for an open, informed study of all aspects of consciousness. [Opinion*]. Frontiers in Human Neuroscience, 8*(17), 1–4. doi: 10.3389/fnhum.2014.00017.

Cardeña, E. (2015). The unbearable fear of psi: On scientific censorship in the 21st century. *Journal of Scientific Exploration, 2*(4), 601–620.

Cardeña, E. (2018). The experimental evidence for parapsychological phenomena: A review. *American Psychologist, 73*(5), 663–677.

Cardeña, E. (2019). Abracadabra psi? [Review of the book *real magic,* by D. Radin]. *Journal of Parapsychology, 83*(1), 93–96.

Cardeña, E., Palmer, J., & Marcusson-Clavertz, D. (2015). *Parapsychology: A handbook for the 21st century.* McFarland.

Carpenter, J. C. (2012). *First sight: ESP and parapsychology in everyday life.* Rowman & Littleman Publishers.

Carpenter, L., Cannard, C., Wahbeh, H., & Radin, D. (2021). Psychophysical interactions with photons: Three exploratory studies with unexpected results. *Journal of the Society for Psychical Research, 85,* 31–48.

Carroll, P. J. (1987). *Liber null & psychonaut: An introduction to chaos magic.* Weiser Books.

Carroll, S. (1990). *Something deeply hidden: Quantum worlds and the emergence of spacetime.* Dutton Books.

Carter, C. (2012). *Science and psychic phenomena: The fall of the house of skeptics.* Inner Traditions.

Cella, M., Vellante, M., & Preti, A. (2012). How psychotic-like are paranormal beliefs? *Journal of Behavior Therapy and Experimental Psychiatry, 43,* 897–900.

Cerf, N. J., & Adami, C. H. (1997). Quantum mechanics of measurement. *Physical Review A*, 1–18.

Chandler, K. (2001). *PSI – What it is and how it works: A central model for parapsychology*. Authors Choice.

Charteris, L., Forrester, L. (Writers), & Carstairs, J. P. (Director). (1964). The romantic matron [Television series episode]. In R. S. Baker & M. Berman (Producers), *The Saint*. ITC/Granada Television Network.

Cheetham, E. (1976). *The prophecies of Nostradamus*. Corgi Books.

Cheetham, E. (1989). *The final prophecies of Nostradamus*. Bramley Books.

Church Committee Reports. (2014). Church Committee reports. *Assassination Archives and Research Center (AARC) Public Library*. http://www.aarclibrary.org/publib/church/reports/contents.htm

Cockshott, P. (2018, July 25). Materialism and delayed choice quantum eraser experiments. *Paul Cockshott's Blog*. https://paulcockshott.wordpress.com/2018/07/25/materialism-and-delayed-choice-quantum-eraser-experiments/

Colborn, M. (2007). The decline effect in spontaneous and experimental psychical research. *Journal of the Society for Psychical Research*, *71*, 1–21.

Colquhoun, D. (2017). An investigation of the false discovery rate and the misinterpretation of *p*-values. *Royal Society Open Science*, *1*, 140216.

Combs, A., & Holland, M. (1996). *Synchronicity: Through the eyes of science, myth, and the trickster*. Marlowe & Company.

Compton, A. H. (1923). A quantum theory of the scattering of x-rays by light elements. *Physical Review*, *21*(5), 483–502.

Connolly, A. (2015). Bridging the reductive and the synthetic: Some reflections on the clinical importance of synchronicity. *Journal of Analytical Psychology*, *60*, 159–178.

Crosby, P. B. (1996). *Quality is still free: Making quality certain in uncertain times*. McGraw-Hill.

Crosby, P. B. (1999). *Quality and me: Lessons from an evolving life*. Jossey-Bass.

d'Espagnat, B. (2006). *On physics and philosophy*. Princeton University Press.

Daher, J. C., Jr., Damiano, R. F., Lucchetti, A. L. G., Moreira-Almeida, A., & Lucchetti, G. (2017). Research on experiences related to the possibility of consciousness beyond the brain: A bibliometric analysis of global scientific output. *Journal of Nervous and Mental Disease*, *205*(1), 37–47.

Darwin, C. (2004). *On the origin of species*. Collector's Library. (Original work published in 1859)

Davey, G. C. (Ed.). (2011). *Applied psychology* (1st ed.). Wiley-Blackwell.

Davies, P., & Brown, J. (1991). *The ghost in the atom: A discussion of the mysteries of quantum physics*. Cambridge University Press.

Davisson, C. J., & Germer, L. H. (1928). Reflection of electrons by a crystal of nickel. *Proceedings of the National Academy of Sciences of the United States of America*, *14(*4), 317–322.

De Barros, J. A., & Oas, G. (2017). Can we falsify the consciousness-causes-collapse hypothesis in quantum mechanics? *Foundations of Physics*, *47*, 1294–1308. doi: 10.1007/S10701-017-0110-7

Delin, P. (2002). Scepticism and credulity. *Australian Journal of Parapsychology*, *2*, 28–36. (Reprinted from *Search*, Vol. 3, No. 7, July 1972)

DeMets, D. L., Hardy, R., Friedman, L. M., & Lan, K. K. G. (1984). Statistical aspects of early termination in the Beta-blocker heart attack trial. *Control Clinical Trials*, *5*, 362–372.

Deutsch, D. (2011). *The fabric of reality*. Penguin.

Diaconis, P., & Mosteller, F. (1989). Methods for studying coincidences. *Journal of the American Statistical Association*, *84*, 853–861.

Dias, B. G., & Ressler, K. J. (2014). Parental olfactory experience influences behavior and neural structure in subsequent generations. *Nature Neuroscience*, *17*, 89–96.
Dobyns, Y. H. (2006). Retrocausal information flow: What are the consequences of knowing the future? In D. P. Sheehan (Ed.), *Frontiers of time: Retrocausation—Experiment and theory*. AIP Conference Proceedings, *863*. American Institute of Physics.
Dobyns, Y. H., & Nelson, R. D. (1998). Empirical evidence against decision augmentation theory. *Journal of Scientific Exploration*, *12*(2), 231–258.
Dommeyer, F. (1982). J. B. Rhine and philosophy. In K. R. Rao (Ed.), *J. B. Rhine: On the frontiers of science* (117–133). McFarland.
Donati, M. (2008). Beyond synchronicity: The worldview of Carl Gustav Jung and Wolfgang Pauli. In L. Storm (Ed.), *Synchronicity: Multiple perspectives on meaningful coincidence* (42–63). Pari Publishing.
Dudley, R. T. (1999). Effect of restriction of working memory on reported paranormal belief. *Psychological Reports*, *84*, 313–316.
Dunne, J. W. (1927). *An experiment with time*. Faber & Faber.
Edwards, T. (Producer & Writer). (1983). *The case of ESP* [Television documentary]. British Broadcasting Corporation.
Ehrenwald, J. (1947). *Telepathy and medical psychology*. Allen & Unwin.
Ehrenwald, J. (1975). Cerebral localization and the psi syndrome. *Journal of Nervous and Mental Disease*, *161*(6), 393–398.
Eibenberger, S., Gerlich, S., Arndt, M., Mayor, M., & Tüxen, J. (2013). Matter-wave interference of particles selected from a molecular library with masses exceeding 10000 amu. *Physical Chemistry Chemical Physics*, *15*, 14696–14700.
Einstein, A., Podolsky, B., & Rosen, N. (1935). Can quantum-mechanical description of physical reality be considered complete? *Physical Review*, *47*, 777–780.
Eisenbud, J. (1963). Psi and the nature of things. *International Journal of Parapsychology*, *5*, 245–268.
Eisenbud, J. (1980). Synchronicity, psychodynamics and psi. In W. G. Roll (Ed.), *Research in parapsychology 1979* (25–26). Scarecrow Press.
Eisenbud, J. (1982). *Paranormal foreknowledge: Problems and perplexities*. Human Sciences Press.
Eisenbud, J. (1983). *Parapsychology and the unconscious*. North Atlantic Books.
Ellerman, D. (2015). Why delayed choice experiments do not imply retrocausality. *Quantum Studies: Mathematics and Foundations*, *2*, 183–199.
Emerson, R. W. (1957). *Selections from Ralph Waldo Emerson*. Houghton Mifflin.
Etzold, E. (2006). Does psi exist and can we prove it? Belief and disbelief in parapsychological research. *European Journal of Parapsychology*, *21*(1), 38–57.
Faye, J. (2019, December 6). Copenhagen interpretation of quantum mechanics. *Stanford Encyclopedia of Philosophy*. https://plato.stanford.edu/entries/qm-copenhagen/
Felser, J. M. (2001). Philosophical sensitives and sensitive philosophers: Gazing into the future of parapsychology. *International Journal of Parapsychology*, *12*, 53–82.
Filk, T. (2014). Quantum entanglement, hidden variables, and acausal correlations. In H. Atmanspacher, & C. A. Fuchs (Eds.), *The Pauli-Jung conjecture and its impact today* (109–123). Imprint Academic.
Fisher, J., &Allen, W. H. (1964). *My darling Clementine*. Pan.
Flegstein, D., Barabasz, A., Barabasz, M., Trevisan, M. S., & Warner, D. (1998). Hypnosis enhances recall memory: A test of forced and non-forced conditions. *American Journal of Clinical Hypnosis*, *40*(4), 297–305.
Flew, A. (1953). Coincidence and synchronicity. *Journal of the Society for Psychical Research*, *37*, 198–201.
Frazer, J. G. (1922). *The golden bough: A study of magic and religion*. Bartleby. (Original work published in 1889)

Freedman, M., Binns, M., Gao, F., Holmes, M., Roseborough, A., Strother, S., Vallesi, A., Jeffers, S., Alain, C., Whitehouse, P., Ryan, J. D., Chen, R., Cusimano, M. D., & Black, S. E. (2018). Mind–matter interactions and the frontal lobes of the brain: A novel neurobiological model of psi inhibition. *Explore: The Journal of Science and Healing*, *14*(1), 76–85.

Gardner, M. (1981). *Science: Good, bad, and bogus*. Prometheus Press.

Garret, R. (2016). *Quantum mysteries disentangled.* [Unpublished manuscript]. http://www.flownet.com/ron/QM.pdf

Gatlin, L. L. (1977). Meaningful information creation: An alternative interpretation of the psi phenomenon. *Journal of the American Society for Psychical Research*, *71*, 1–18.

Gatlin, L. L. (2008). Meaningful information creation: An alternative interpretation of the psi phenomenon. In L. Storm (Ed.), *Synchronicity: Multiple perspectives on meaningful coincidence* (195–211). Pari Publishing.

Gidney, C. (2016, January 7). Deflating delayed choice quantum erasure. *Algorithmic Assertions*. https://algassert.com/quantum/2016/01/07/Delayed-Choice-Quantum-Erasure.html

Gildersleeve, M., & Crowden, A. (2019). Spiritual synchronicity and place: I. A psychoanalytic perspective. *Australian Journal of Parapsychology*, *19*, 121–142.

Grattan-Guinness, I. (1978). What are coincidences? *Journal of the Society for Psychical Research*, *49*, 949–955.

Greatrex, D. (1999). A note on synchronicity and seriality. *Paranormal Review*, *9*, 5–7.

Griffin, D. R. (1997). *Parapsychology, philosophy, and spirituality: A postmodern exploration*. State University of New York Press.

Grof, C., & Grof, S. (1990). *The stormy search for the self.* Jeremy Tarcher.

Hameroff, S., & Penrose, R. (1996). Orchestrated reduction of quantum coherence in brain microtubules: A model for consciousness. In S. R. Hameroff, A. W. Kaszniak, & A. C. Scott (Eds.), *Toward a science of consciousness: The first Tucson discussions and debates* (507–540). MIT Press.

Hansel, C. E. M. (1980). *ESP and parapsychology: A scientific reevaluation*. Prometheus.

Hansen, G. P. (2001). *The trickster and the paranormal*. Xlibris Corporation.

Haraldsson, E. (2011). A perfect case? Emil Jensen in the mediumship of Indridi Indridason, the fire in Copenhagen on November 24th 1905 and the discovery of Jensen's identity. *Proceedings of the Society for Psychical Research*, *59*, 195–223.

Harary, K., & Targ, R. (1985). A new approach to forecasting commodity futures. *PSI Research*, *4*(3–4), 79–88.

Hardy, C. H. (2011). *The sacred network: Megaliths, cathedrals, ley lines, and the power of shared consciousness*. Inner Tradition.

Haule, J. R. (2011). *Jung in the 21st century. Volume 2: Synchronicity and science*. Routledge.

Heilprin, A. (1903). *Mont Pelée and the tragedy of Martinique: A study of the great catastrophes of 1902, with observations and experiences in the field*. Cambridge University Press.

Heisenberg, W. (1949). *The physical principles of the quantum theory* (C. Eckart & F. C. Hoyt, Trans.). Dover.

Henry, A., & Thompson, E. (2011). Witnessing from here: Self-awareness from a bodily versus embodied perspective. In S. Gallagher (Ed.), *The Oxford handbook of the self* (228–249). Oxford University Press.

Hergovich, A., Schott, R., & Arendasy, M. (2008). On the relationship between paranormal belief and schizotypy among adolescents. *Personality and Individual Differences*, *45*(2), 119–125.

Hermann, A., von Meyenn, K., & Weisskopf, V. F. (Eds.). (1984). *Scientific correspondence with Bohr, Einstein, Heisenberg and Others. Volume II: 1930–1939*. Springer-Verlag.

Hine, P. (1993). *Prime chaos: Adventures in chaos magic*. New Falcon Publications.

Hitchman, G. A., Roe, C. A., & Sherwood, S. J. (2015). The relationship between lability and performance at intentional and non-intentional versions of a PMIR-type psi task. *Journal of Parapsychology*, *79*, 65–86.

Hitchman, G. A., Sherwood, S. J., & Roe, C. A. (2015). The relationship between latent inhibition and performance at a non-intentional precognition task. *Explore: The Journal of Science and Healing*, *11*(2), 118–126.

Hocoy, D. (2012). Sixty years later: The enduring allure of synchronicity. *Journal of Humanistic Psychology*, *52*(4), 467–478.

Hogue, J. H. (1987). *Nostradamus and the millennium. Predictions of the future*. Bloomsbury.

Honorton, C. (1985). Meta-analysis of psi ganzfeld research: A response to Hyman. *Journal of Parapsychology*, *49*, 51–91.

Honorton, C. (1993). Rhetoric over substance: The impoverished state of skepticism. *Journal of Parapsychology*, *57*, 191–214.

Honorton, C., & Ferrari, D. C. (1989). "Future telling": A meta-analysis of forced-choice precognition experiments, 1935-1987. *Journal of Parapsychology*, *53*, 281–308.

Honorton, C., Ferrari, D. C., & Bem, D. J. (1998). Extraversion and ESP performance: A meta-analysis and a new confirmation. *Journal of Parapsychology*, *62*, 255–276.

Houran, J., & Lange, R. (2004). Redefining delusion based on studies of subjective paranormal ideation. *Psychological Reports*, *94*, 501–513.

Houran, J., & Lange, R. (2012). *I Ching* outcomes from experimental manipulations of transliminality and paranormal belief. *Australian Journal of Parapsychology*, *12*, 39–58.

Houtkooper, J. M. (2002). Arguing for an observational theory of paranormal phenomena. *Journal of Scientific Exploration*, *16*(2), 171–185.

Hövelmann, G. H. (2015). On the usefulness of parapsychology for science at large. In E. Cardeña, J. Palmer, & D. Marcusson-Clavertz (Eds.), *Parapsychology. A handbook for the 21st century* (389–398). McFarland.

Howard, M. C. (2018). A meta-reanalysis of dream-ESP studies: Comment on Storm et al. (2017). *International Journal of Dream Research*, *11*(2), 224–229.

Huston, H. L. (1992). *Direct and indirect tests of archetypal memory*. [Unpublished master's thesis]. Texas A&M University.

Huygens, C. (1690). *Treatise on light* (Silvanus P. Thompson, Trans.). Macmillan. (Original work published in 1912)

Hyman, R., & Honorton, C. (1986). Joint communiqué: The psi ganzfeld controversy. *Journal of Parapsychology*, *50*, 351–364.

Inglis, B. (1990). *Coincidence: A matter of chance – Or synchronicity?* Hutchinson.

Irwin, H. J. (1979). *Psi and the mind: An information processing approach*. Scarecrow Press.

Irwin, H. J. (1985). Is psi a unitary domain? Analysis in terms of performance patterns. *Parapsychological Journal of South Africa*, *6*, 34–46.

Irwin, H. J. (1993). Belief in the paranormal: A review of the empirical literature. *Journal of the American Society for Psychical Research*, *87*, 1–39.

Irwin, H. J. (2009). *The psychology of paranormal belief: A researcher's handbook*. Hertfordshire, UK: University of Hertfordshire Press.

Irwin, H. J. (2014). The major problems faced by parapsychology today: A survey of members of the Parapsychological Association. *Australian Journal of Parapsychology*, *14*, 143–162.

Irwin, H. J., Dagnall, N., & Drinkwater, K. (2012). Paranormal beliefs and cognitive processes underlying the formation of delusions. *Australian Journal of Parapsychology*, *12*, 107–126.

Irwin, H. J., Dagnall, N., & Drinkwater, K. (2017). Tweedledum and Tweedledee: Are paranormal disbelievers a mirror image of believers? *Journal of the Society for Psychical Research*, *81*, 161–179.

Irwin, H. J., & Watt, C. A. (2007). *An introduction to parapsychology* (5th ed.). McFarland.

Ismael, J., & Schaffer, J. (2020). Quantum holism: Nonseparability as common ground. *Synthese, 197*, 4131–4160.https://doi.org/10.1007/s11229-016-1201-2

Ivonin, L., Chang, H.-M., Diaz, M., Catala, A., Chen, W., & Rauterberg, M. (2015). Traces of unconscious mental processes in introspective reports and physiological responses. *PLoS ONE, 10*(4), 1–31.

Jacques, V., Wu, E., Grosshans, F., Treussart, F., Grangier, P., Aspect, A., & Roch, J.-F. (2007). Experimental realization of Wheeler's delayed-choicegedanken experiment. *Science, 315*(5814), 966–968.

Jaffé, A. (1967). C. G. Jung and parapsychology. In J. R. Smythies (Ed.), *Science and ESP* (263–280). Routledge & Kegan-Paul.

James, W. (1897). *The will to believe and other essays in populist philosophy*. Longmans, Green & Company.

Jenkins, H. (2017). Dowsing. *Psi Encyclopedia*. https://psi-encyclopedia.spr.ac.uk/articles/dowsing

Jinks, A. L. (2012). Paranormal and alternative health beliefs as quasi-beliefs: Implications for item content in paranormal belief questionnaires. *Australian Journal of Parapsychology, 12*, 127–158.

Johansen, M. K., & Osman, M. (2015). Coincidences: A fundamental consequence of rational cognition. *New Ideas in Psychology, 39*, 34–44.

John, L. K., Loewenstein, G., & Prelec, D. (2012a). Measuring the prevalence of questionable research practices with incentives for truth telling. *Psychological Science, 23*(5), 524–532.

John, L. K., Loewenstein, G., & Prelec, D. (2012b). Measuring the prevalence of questionable research practices with incentives for truth telling (supplemental materials (1–17). https://journals.sagepub.com/page/pss/suppl/data-supplements

Johnson, A. (1899). Coincidences. *Proceedings of the Society for Psychical Research, 14*, 158–330.

Jung, C. G. (1925). Marriage as a psychological relationship. *CW17* (187–202).

Jung, C. G. (1954). Transformation symbolism in the mass. *CW11* (203–296). (Original work published in 1942)

Jung, C. G. (1968). *The archetypes and the collective unconscious* (2d. ed.). *CW9i*. (Original work published in 1959)

Jung, C. G. (1968). Letters on synchronicity. *CW18* (502–509).

Jung, C. G. (1969). Appendix: On synchronicity. *CW8* (520–531). (Original work published in 1951)

Jung, C. G. (1969). Synchronicity: An acausal connecting principle. *CW8* (417–519). (Original work published in 1952)

Jung, C. G. (1969). The structure and dynamics of the psyche (2nd ed.). *CW8*. (Original work published in 1960)

Jung, C. G. (1970). Civilization in transition. *CW10*. (Original work published in 1964)

Jung, C. G. (1970). Mysterium coniunctionis: An inquiry into the separation and synthesis of psychic opposites in alchemy (2nd ed.). *CW14*. (Original work published in 1963)

Jung, C. G. (1975). *C. G. Jung letters 2: 1951–1961* (R. F. C. Hull, Trans.). Routledge & Kegan Paul.

Jung, C. G. (1979). The practice of psychotherapy. *CW16*. (Original work published in 1946)

Jung, C. G. (1989). *Foreword to the I Ching or book of changes*. In R. Wilhelm, C. F. Baynes. *I Ching or book of changes* (xxi–xxxix). Princeton University Press.

Jung, C. G., & Pauli, W. (1955). *The interpretation of nature and the psyche*. Pantheon Books.

Kalat, J. W. (2011). *Introduction to psychology* (9th ed.). Wadsworth.

Katz, D. L., Grgić, I., Tressoldi, P., & Fendley, T. W. (2021). Associative remote viewing projects: Assessing rater reliability and factors affecting successful predictions. *Journal of the Society for Psychical Research, 85*, 65–90.

Keel, J. A. (1978). *The cosmic question*. Granada/Panther.

Kelly, E. W., & Tucker, J. B. (2015). Research methods with spontaneous case studies. In E. Cardeña, J. Palmer, & D. Marcusson-Clavertz (Eds.), *Parapsychology. A handbook for the 21st century* (63–76). McFarland.

Kennedy, J. E. (1995). Methods for investigating goal-oriented psi. *Journal of Parapsychology, 59*, 47–62.

Kennedy, J. E. (2000). Do people guide psi or does psi guide people? Evidence and implications from life and lab. *Journal of the American Society for Psychical Research, 94*, 130–150.

Kennedy, J. E. (2003). The capricious, actively evasive, unsustainable nature of psi: A summary and hypotheses. *Journal of Parapsychology, 67*, 53–74.

Kennedy, J. E., & Taddonio, J. L. (1976). Experimenter effects in parapsychological research. *Journal of Parapsychology, 40*, 1–33.

Kim, Y.-H., Yu, R., Kulik, S. P., Shih, Y. H., & Scully, M. (2000). A delayed choice quantum eraser. *Physical Review Letters, 84*, 1–5.

Koch, C. (2019). *The feeling of life itself: Why consciousness is widespread but can't be computed*. Cambridge/The MIT Press.

Koestler, A. (1974). *The roots of coincidence*. Picador.

Kolata, G. B. (1981). Drug found to help heart attack survivors. *Science, 214*, 774–775.

Krippner, S., Rock, A. J., Friedman, H. L., & Zingrone, N. L. (2021). Introduction: Criticism, proof, process and practical applications. In S. Krippner, A. J. Rock, H. L. Friedman, & N. L. Zingrone (Eds.), *Advances in parapsychological research 10* (1–13). McFarland.

Krippner, S., Saunders, D. T., Morgan, A., & Quan, A. (2019). Remote viewing of concealed target pictures under light and dark conditions. *Explore: The Journal of Science and Healing, 15*(1), 27–37.

Kuhn, T. S. (1962). *The structure of scientific revolutions*. University of Chicago Press.

Kvasnytsya, V., Wirth, R., Dobrzhinetskaya, L., Matzel, J., Jacobsen, B., Hutcheon, I., Tappero, R., & Kovalyukh, M. (2013). New evidence of meteoritic origin of the Tunguska cosmic body. *Planetary and Space Science, 84*, 131–140.

Lange, R., & Houran, J. (2013). Towards a replicable formula for significant *IChing*outcomes. *Australian Journal of Parapsychology, 13*, 9–25.

Langmuir, I. (2002). *Pathological science*. Langmuir's Talk on Pathological Science. http://www.cs.princeton.edu/~ken/Langmuir/langmuir.htm (Original work published in 1953)

Lawrence, T. R. (1993). Gathering in the sheep and goats: A meta-analysis of forced-choice sheep-goat ESP studies, 1947-1993. In *Proceedings of the 36th Annual Convention of the Parapsychological Association* (75–86). Parapsychological Association.

Lilienfeld, S. O., Ammirati, R., & David, M. (2012). Distinguishing science from pseudoscience in school psychology: Science and scientific thinking as safeguards against human error. *Journal of School Psychology, 50*(1), 7–36.

Ljunquist, K. (2002). The poet as critic. In K. J. Hayes (Ed.), *The Cambridge companion to Edgar Allan Poe* (p. 15). Cambridge University Press.

Lufityanto, G., Donkin, C., & Pearson, J. (2016). Measuring intuition: Nonconscious emotional information boosts decision accuracy and confidence. *Psychological Science, 27*(5), 622–634.

Main, R. (2004). *The rupture of time: Synchronicity and Jung's critique of modern western culture*. Routledge.

Mangan, G. L. (1955). Evidence of displacement in a precognition test. *Journal of Parapsychology, 19*, 35–44.

Mansfield, V. (1995). *Synchronicity, science, and soul-making: Understanding Jungian synchronicity through physics, Buddhism, and philosophy*. Open Court.
Mansfield, V., Rhine-Feather, S., & Hall, J. (1998). The Rhine-Jung letters: Distinguishing parapsychological from synchronistic events. *Journal of Parapsychology, 62*, 3–25.
Mansfield, V., Rhine-Feather, S., & Hall, J. (2008). The Rhine-Jung letters: Distinguishing parapsychological from synchronistic events. In L. Storm (Ed.), *Synchronicity: Multiple perspectives on meaningful coincidence* (129–151). Pari Publishing.
Maraldi, E. O. (2017). The scientific investigation of anomalous self and identity experiences. *Journal of Nervous and Mental Disease, 205*(11), 900.
Marshall, A. (2002). *The unity of nature: Wholeness and disintegration in ecology and science*. Imperial College Press.
Marwaha, S. B., & May, E. C. (2015). Rethinking extrasensory perception: Toward a multiphasic model of precognition. *SAGE Open*, January/March, 1–17.
Marwaha, S. B., & May, E. C. (2016). Precognition: The only form of psi? *Journal of Consciousness Studies, 23*(3–4), 76–100.
Marwaha, S. B., & May, E. C. (2019a). Informational psi: Collapsing the problem space of psi phenomena. *ZeitschriftFürAnomalistik [Journal of Anomalistics], 19*, 12–51.
Marwaha, S. B., & May, E. C. (2019b). Signals: A mechanism to understand psi phenomena. *ZeitschriftFürAnomalistik [Journal of Anomalistics], 19*, 73–112.
Maxwell, J. C. (1873). *A treatise on electricity and magnetism*. Macmillan and Co.
May, E. (2014). Anomalous cognition: A replication and correlation with the gradient of Shannon entropy. In E. May, & S. B. Marwaha (Eds.), *Anomalous cognition. Remote viewing research and theory* (314–326). McFarland.
May, E. C., Faith, L. V., Blackman, M., Bourgeois, B., Kerr, N., & Woods, L. (2012). A target pool and database for anomalous cognition experiments. *Journal of the Society for Psychical Research, 76*, 94–103.
May, E. C., Hawley, L., & Marwaha, S. B. (2017). Do changes of thermodynamic entropy at a remote site enhance the quality of anomalous cognition? Paper presented at the 60th Annual Parapsychological Association Convention, Athens, Greece.
May, E. C., Lantz, N. D., & Piantineda, J. (1994). *Feedback considerations in anomalous cognition experiments*. Technical Report, 29 November 1994. SAIC.
May, E. C., & Marwaha, S. B. (2015a). *Extrasensory perception: Support, skepticism, and science, volume 1 – History, controversy, and research*. Praeger.
May, E. C., & Marwaha, S. B. (2015b). *Extrasensory perception: Support, skepticism, and science, volume 2 – Theories of psi*. Praeger.
May, E. C., Radin, D. I., Hubbard, G. S., Humphrey, B. S., & Utts, J. (1985). Psi experiments with random number generators: An informational model. In *Proceedings of the 28th Annual Convention of the Parapsychological Association* (237–266). Parapsychological Association.
May, E. C., & Spottiswoode, S. J. C. (1989). A Michelson-interferometer Schrödinger cat: The death of the observation theories. In L. A. Henkel, & R. E. Berger (Eds.), *Research in parapsychology 1988* (p. 63). Scarecrow Press.
May, E. C., & Spottiswoode, S. J. P. (2011a). The global consciousness project: Identifying the source of psi. *Journal of Scientific Exploration, 25(*4), 663–682.
May, E. C., & Spottiswoode, S. J. P. (2011b). The global consciousness project: Identifying the source of psi. A response to Nelson and Bancel. *Journal of Scientific Exploration, 25*(4), 695–698.
May, E. C., Spottiswoode, S. J. P., & James, C. L. (1994). *Managing the target pool bandwidth: Noise reduction for anomalous cognition experiments*. Paper presented at the 37th Annual Parapsychological Association Convention, Netherlands: University of Amsterdam.

May, E. C., Utts, J. M., & Spottiswoode, S. J. P. (1995a). Decision augmentation theory: Applications to the random number generator database. *Journal of Scientific Exploration*, *9*(4), 453–488.

May, E. C., Utts, J. M., & Spottiswoode, S. J. P. (1995b). Decision augmentation theory: Toward a model of anomalous mental phenomena. *Journal of Parapsychology*, *59*, 195–220.

Mayer, E. L. (2007). *Extraordinary knowing: Science, skepticism, and the inexplicable powers of the human mind*. Bantam Books.

Mayer, G. (2018). A walk through the manifold world of coincidences [review of the book *The many faces of coincidence*, by Laurence Browne]. *Journal of Parapsychology*, *82*, 204–207.

McBeath, M. K. (1985). Psi and sexuality. *Journal of the Society for Psychical Research*, *53*, 65–77.

McGilchrist, I. (2009). *The master and his emissary: The divided brain and the making of the western world*. Yale University Press.

McLaughlin, T. J. (2013). *Holistic universe*. Thoughtware Press.

McLean, C. P., & Miller, N. A. (2010). Changes in critical thinking skills following a course on science and pseudoscience: A quasi-experimental study. *Teaching of Psychology*, *37*(2), 85–90.

McMahan, E. A. (1946). An experiment in pure telepathy. *Journal of Parapsychology*, *10*(4), 224–242.

McMoneagle, J. (1997). *Mind trek: Exploring consciousness, time, and space through remote viewing*. Hampton Roads.

McMoneagle, J. (2000). *Remote viewing secrets*. Hampton Roads.

Meier, C. A. (Ed.) (2001). *Atom and archetype: The Pauli/Jung letters, 1932-1958*. Routledge.

Millar, B. (2015). Quantum theory and parapsychology. In E. Cardeña, J. Palmer, & D. Marcusson-Clavertz (Eds.), *Parapsychology. A handbook for the 21st century* (165–180). McFarland.

Millar, B. (2019, June 25). Observational theories of psi. *Psi Encyclopedia*. https://psi-encyclopedia.spr.ac.uk/articles/observational-theories-psi

Millar, B. (2012a). From warehouse to temple: Science axioms and the frameworks they build. *Journal of Nonlocality*, *1*, http://journals.sfu.ca/jnonlocality/index.php/jnonlocality/article/viewFile/10/9

Millar, B. (2012b). Towards a forensic parapsychology in the OT paradigm. *Journal of Nonlocality*, *1*(1), 1–23.

Miller, R. A. (2001). Synthetic telepathy and the early mind wars. Presented at the Consciousness Technologies Conference, Sisters, Oregon, USA (July 19-21, 2001).

Milton, J. (1997). A meta-analytic comparison of the sensitivity of direct hits and sums of ranks as outcome measures for free-response studies. *Journal of Parapsychology*, *61*, 227–237.

Milton, J., & Wiseman, R. (1999). Does psi exist? Lack of replication of an anomalous process of information transfer. *Psychological Bulletin*, *125*(4), 387–391. doi: 10.1037/0033-2909.125.4.387.

Mishlove, J. (2000). *The PK man: A true story of mind over matter*. Hampton Roads.

Mishlove, J. (2021). Beyond the brain: The survival of human consciousness after permanent bodily death. *Bigelow Institute*. https://www.nonlocalmind.org/wp-content/uploads/2021/11/Jeff-Mishlove-Essay-for-Bigelow-Institute.pdf

Mishlove, J., & Engen, B. C. (2007). Archetypal synchronistic resonance: A new theory of paranormal experience. *Journal of Humanistic Psychology*, *47*(2), 223–242.

Mittelstaedt, P., Prieur, A., & Schieder, R. (1987). Unsharp particle-wave duality in a photon split-beam experiment. *Foundations of Physics*, *17*(9), 891–892.

Moore, D. W. (2005, June 16). Three in four Americans believe in paranormal: Little change from similar results in 2001. *Gallup*. https://news.gallup.com/poll/16915/Three-Four-Americans-Believe-Paranormal.aspx

Moreman, C. M. (2003). A re-examination of the possibility of chance coincidence as an alternative explanation for mediumistic communication in the cross-correspondences. *Journal of the Society for Psychical Research*, *67*, 225–242.

Morris, R. L. (1968). Obtaining non-random entry points: A complex psi task. In J. B. Rhine, & R. Brier (Eds.), *Parapsychology today* (75–86). Citadel Press.

Morris, R. L. (1982). Assessing experimental support for pure precognition. *Journal of Parapsychology*, *46*, 321–336.

Morris, R. L. (1975). Tacit communication and experimental theology. In J. D. Morris, W. G. Roll, & R. L. Morris (Eds.), *Research in parapsychology 1974* (179–198). Scarecrow Press.

Mossbridge, J. A. (2023). Precognition at the boundaries: An empirical reviews and theoretical discussion. *Journal of Anomalous Experience and Cognition*, *3*(1), 5–41.

Mossbridge, J. A., & Radin, D. (2018a). Plausibility, statistical interpretations, physical mechanisms and a new outlook: Response to commentaries on a precognition review. *Psychology of Consciousness: Theory, Research, and Practice*, *5*(1), 110–116.

Mossbridge, J. A., & Radin, D. (2018b). Precognition as a form of prospection: A review of the evidence. *Psychology of Consciousness: Theory, Research, and Practice*, *5*(1), 78–93.

Mossbridge, J., Tressoldi, P., & Utts, J. (2012). Predictive physiological anticipation preceding seemingly unpredictable stimuli: A meta-analysis. *Frontiers in Psychology*, *3*, 1–18.

Müller, M., & Wittmann, M. (2021). Anomalous cognition in the context of time: Does the viewer describe a deterministic or a probabilistic future? *Journal of Scientific Exploration*, *35*(3), 542–569.

Mundle, C. W. K. (1964). Does the concept of precognition make sense? *International Journal of Parapsychology*, *6*, 179–198.

Mundle, C. W. K. (1967). The explanation of *ESP*. In J. R. Smythies (Ed.), *Science and ESP* (197–208). Routledge & Kegan-Paul.

Nachman, G. (2010). [Review of the book *Synchronicity: Multiple perspectives on meaningful coincidence*, by L. Storm (Ed.)]. *Journal of Parapsychology*, *74*, 387–391.

Nagata, M. (Producer), & Kinugasa, T. (Director). (1953). *Gate of hell* [Motion picture]. Daiei Film.

Nagy, G. A., & Scully, M. (2011). Causal and relativistic loopholes in a delayed-choice quantum eraser experiment. *Semantic Scholar*, Corpus ID: 52107095; https://www.semanticscholar.org/paper/Causal-and-relativistic-loopholes-in-a-Quantum-A.Nagy-Nagy/120d1b09acadf9043f2a4d6578d547a88d7393c8

Nahm, N. (2019). Assessing the problem space of precognition: Can it be the only form of psi? A commentary on the multiphasic model of informational psi. *ZeitschriftFürAnomalistik [Journal of Anomallstics]*, *19*, 57–67.

Nairz, O., Arndt, M., & Zeilinger, A. (2003). Quantum interference experiments with large molecules. *American Journal of Physics*, *71*(4), 319–325.

Nelson, R. D. (2011). Reply to May and Spottiswoode on experimenter effect as an explanation for GCP results. *Journal of Scientific Exploration*, *25*(4), 683–689.

Nelson, R. D. (2015). Implicit physical psi: The global consciousness project. In E. Cardeña, J. Palmer, & D. Marcusson-Clavertz (Eds.), *Parapsychology: A handbook for the 21st century* (282–292). McFarland.

Nelson, R. D. (2022, November 19). Global consciousness project. *Psi Encyclopedia*. https://psi-encyclopedia.spr.ac.uk/articles/global-consciousness-project

Nelson, R. D., & Bancel, P. A. (2011). Effects of mass consciousness: Changes in random data during global events. *Explore: The Journal of Science and Healing*, *7*(16), 373–383.

Newton, I. (1704). *Opticks: A treatise of the reflexions, refractions, inflexions and colours of light*. Smith and Walford.

Newton, R. G. (1967). Causality effects of particles that travel faster than light. *Physical Review*, *162*, 1274.

Newton, R. G. (1970). Particles that travel faster than light? *Science*, *167*, 1569–1574.

Nickerson, R. S. (2000). Null hypothesis significance testing: A review of an old and continuing controversy. *Psychological Methods*, *5*(2), 241–301.

O'Connell, A. D., Hofheinz, M., Ansmann, M., Bialczak, R. C., Lenander, M., Lucero, E., Neeley, M., Sank, D., Wang, H., Weides, M., Wenner, J., Martinis, J. M., & Cleland, A. N. (2010). Quantum ground state and single-phonon control of a mechanical resonator. *Nature*, *464*(7289), 697–703. doi: 10.1038/nature08967.

O'Neill, M. (2001). "The world's largest ESP experiment ever": Wiseman's 'experimenter effect' examined. *Paranormal Review*, *17*, 5–8.

Osis, K. (1953). A test of the relationship between ESP and PK. *Journal of Parapsychology*, *17*, 298–309.

Osis, K., & McCormick, D. (1980). Kinetic effects at the ostensible location of an out-of-body projection during perceptual testing. *Journal of the American Society for Psychical Research*, *74*, 319–329.

Ouellet, E. (2011). Extending von Lucadou's model of pragmatic information to UFOs: A case study of the 1952 Washington DC UFO wave. *Australian Journal of Parapsychology*, *11*, 116–137.

Ouellet, E. (2014).Social psi: A framework for understanding large scale anomalies. *Edge Science*, *18*, 5–11.

Owens, T. (1969). *How to contact space people*. New Saucerian Press.

Palmer, J. (2008). Synchronicity and psi: How are they related? In L. Storm (Ed.), *Synchronicity: Multiple perspectives on meaningful coincidence* (175–192). Pari Publishing.

Palmer, J. (2015). Implicit anomalous cognition. In E. Cardeña, J. Palmer, & D. Marcusson-Clavertz (Eds.), *Parapsychology. A handbook for the 21st century* (215–229). McFarland.

Palmer, J. (1986a). Comments on the "joint communique." *Journal of Parapsychology*, *50*, 377–381.

Palmer, J. (1986b). Terminological poverty in parapsychology: Two examples. In D. H. Weiner, & D. I. Radin (Eds.), *Research in parapsychology 1985* (138–141). Scarecrow Press.

Palmer, J. (2016a). Hansel's ghost: Resurrection of the experimenter fraud hypothesis in parapsychology [editorial]. *Journal of Parapsychology*, *80*, 5–16.

Palmer, J. (2016b). Psi and synchronicity: A controlled comparison. *Journal of the Society for Psychical Research*, *80*, 193–213.

Palmer, J. (2016c). Statistical issues in parapsychology: Hypothesis testing—Plus an addendum on Bierman et al. (2016) [Editorial]. *Journal of Parapsychology*, *80*, 141–143.

Palmer, J., & Lieberman, R. (1975). The influence of psychological set on ESP and out-of-body experiences. *Journal of the American Society for Psychical Research*, *69*, 193–213.

Palmer, J., & Millar, B. (2015). Experimenter effects in parapsychological research. In E. Cardeña, J. Palmer, & D. Marcusson-Clavertz (Eds.), *Parapsychology. A handbook for the 21st century* (293–300). McFarland.

Palmer, J., & Vassar, C. (1974). ESP and out-of-the-body experiences: An exploratory study. *Journal of the American Society for Psychical Research*, *68*, 257–280.

Parapsychological Association. (2022, April 22). *A tour d'horizon of mind matter interactions covering a plethora of various phenomena* [Video]. YouTube. https://www.youtube.com/watch?v=Sh57iVWf2Lc

Parker, A., & Millar, B. (2014). Revealing psi secrets: Successful experimenters seem to succeed by using their own psi. *Journal of Parapsychology*, *78*, 39–55.

Pauli, W. (1994). Ideas of the unconscious from the standpoint of natural science and epistemology. In C. Enz, & K. von Meyenn (Eds.), *Writings on physics and philosophy* (146–164). Springer.

Peat, F. D. (1987). *Synchronicity: The bridge between mind and matter*. Bantam.

Peat, F. D. (2008). Divine contenders: Wolfgang Pauli and the symmetry of the world. In L. Storm (Ed.), *Synchronicity: Multiple perspectives on meaningful coincidence* (15–24). Pari Publishing.

Penney, M. T. (2020). *Models, interpretations, and realism in quantum physics*. [Unpublished doctoral thesis]. Department of Philosophy, University of Bristol.

Peruzzo, A., Shadbolt, P., Brunner, N., Popescu, S., & O'Brien, J. L. (2012). A quantum delayed-choice experiment. *Science, 338*(6107), 634–637. doi: https://doi.org/10.1126/science.1226719.

Pinker, S. (2002). *The blank slate: The modern denial of human nature*. Viking.

Planck, M. (1901). Über das Gesetz der EnergieverteilungimNormalspektrum [On the law of the distribution of energy in the normal spectrum]. *Annalen der Physik [Annals of Physics], 309*, 553–563.

Playfair, G. L. (2002). *Twin telepathy*. Vega.

Playfair, G. L. (2015). Uri Geller. *Psi Encyclopedia*. https://psi-encyclopedia.spr.ac.uk/articles/uri-geller

Playfair, G. L. (2017). Monozygotic twins and macro-entanglement. *Journal of Nonlocality, 5*(1), 1–10.

Polis, D. [dfpolis]. (2014, November 9). *Demythologizing quantum theory 1a: Delays, erasures & other errors* [Video]. YouTube. https://www.youtube.com/watch?v=F-PAjJcRVCs

Pratt, J. G. (1978). Prologue to a debate: Some assumptions relevant to research in parapsychology. *Journal of the American Society for Psychical Research, 72*, 127–139.

Pratt, J. G., Rhine, J. B., Smith, B. M., Stuart, C. E., & Greenwood, J. A. (1966). *Extra-sensory perception after sixty years*. Bruce Humphries. (Original work published in 1940)

Pratt, J. G., & Roll, W. G. (1958). The Seaford disturbances. *Journal of Parapsychology, 22*, 79–124.

Progoff, I. (1973). *Jung, synchronicity, and human destiny: Noncausal dimensions of human experience*. Julian Press, Inc.

Puthoff, H. E., & Targ, R. (1976). A perceptual channel for information transfer over kilometer distances: Historical perspective and recent research. *Proceedings of the IEEE, 64*, 329–354.

Rabeyron, T. (2020). Why most research findings about psi are false: The replicability crisis, the psi paradox and the myth of Sisyphus. *Frontiers in Psychology, 11*: 562992. doi: 10.3389/fpsyg.2020.562992

Radin, D. I. (2018). *Real magic: Ancient wisdom, modern science, and a guide to the secret power of the universe*. Harmony.

Radin, D. I. (2006a). *Entangled minds: Extrasensory experiences in a quantum reality*. Paraview/Pocket Books.

Radin, D. I. (2006b). Experiments testing models of mind-matter interaction. *Journal of Scientific Exploration, 20*(3), 375–401.

Radin, D., Bancel, P. A., & Delorme, A. (2021). Psychophysical interactions with entangled photons: Five exploratory studies. *Journal of Anomalous Experience and Cognition, 1*(1-2), 9–54.

Radin, D., & Delorme, A. (2022). Psychophysical effects on an interference pattern in a double-slit optical system: An exploratory analysis of variance. *Journal of Anomalous Experience and Cognition, 2*(2), 362–388.

Radin, D. I., & Ferrari, D. C. (1991). Effects of consciousness on the fall of dice: A meta-analysis. *Journal of Scientific Exploration, 5*(1), 61–83.

Radin, D. I., Michel, L., & Delorme, A. (2016). Psychophysical modulation of fringe visibility in a distant double-slit optical system. *Physics Essays, 29*(1), 14–22.

Radin, D. I., Michel, L., Galdamez, K., Wendland, P., Rickenbach, R., & Delorme, A. (2012). Consciousness and the double-slit interference pattern: Six experiments. *Physics Essays, 25*(2), 157–171.

Radin, D. I., Michel, L., Johnston, J., & Delorme, A. (2013). Psychophysical interactions with a double-slit interference pattern. *Physics Essays, 26*(4), 553–566.

Radin, D., Michel, L., Pierce, A., & Delorme, A. (2015). Psychophysical interactions with a single-photon double-slit optical system. *Quantum Biosystems*, *6*(1), 82–98.

Radin, D. I., & Nelson, R. D. (1989). Evidence for consciousness-related anomalies in random physical systems. *Foundations of Physics*, *19*, 1499–1514.

Radin, D. I., & Nelson, R. D. (2003). Research on mind-matter interactions (MMI): Individual intention. In W. B. Jonas, & C. C. Crawford (Eds.), *Healing, intention and energy medicine: Research and clinical implications* (39–48). Churchill Livingstone.

Radin, D., Wahbeh, H., Michel, L., & Delorme, A. (2020). Commentary: False-positive effect in the Radin double-slit experiment on observer consciousness as determined with the advanced meta-experimental protocol. *Frontiers in Psychology*, *11*, 1–2.

Randi, J. (1980). *Flim-Flam! The truth about unicorns, parapsychology and other delusions*. Lippincott & Crowell.

Rao, K. R. (1968). Spontaneous ESP in laboratory tests: The error phenomenon. *Journal of the American Society for Psychical Research*, *62*, 63–72.

Rawlette, S. H. (2019a). Coincidence or psi? The epistemic import of spontaneous cases of purported psi identified post-verification. *Journal of Scientific Exploration*, *33*(1), 9–42.

Rawlette, S. H. (2019b). *The source and significance of coincidences: A hard look at the astonishing evidence*. Sharon Hewitt Rawlette.

Reason, C. M. (2017, July 5). Comment on the paper "Quantum mechanics needs no consciousness", by Yu and Nikolic (2011). arXiv:1707.01346v1

Reber, A. S., & Alcock, J. E. (2020). Searching for the impossible: Parapsychology's elusive quest. *American Psychologist*, *75*(3), 391–399.

Reishi, D. (2016, May 9). How does one detect a single photon? *Stack Exchange: Physics*. https://physics.stackexchange.com/questions/102313/how-does-one-detect-a-single-photon

Reiter, E. S. (2014). New experiments call for a continuous absorption alternative to quantum mechanics: The unquantum effect. *Progress in Physics: The Journal on Advanced Studies in Theoretical and Experimental Physics, Including Related Themes from Mathematics*, *10*(2), 82–88.

Rhine, J. B. (1934). *Extra-sensory perception*. Boston Society for Psychic Research.

Rhine, J. B. (1947). *The reach of the mind*. William Sloane Associates, Inc.

Rhine, J. B. (1950). *New frontiers of the mind*. Pelican/Penguin. (Original work published in 1937)

Rhine, J. B. (1953). *New world of the mind*. William Sloane Associates, Inc.

Rhine, J. B. (1969). Position effects in psi test results. *Journal of Parapsychology*, *33*, 136–157.

Rhine, J. B. (1974). Telepathy and other untestable hypotheses. *Journal of Parapsychology*, *38*, 137–152.

Rhine, J. B. (1946a). ESP and PK as "psi phenomena. *Journal of Parapsychology*, *10*, 74–75.

Rhine, J. B. (1946b). Hypnotic suggestion in PK tests. *Journal of Parapsychology*, *10*, 126–140.

Rhine, L. E. (1971). The establishment of basic concepts and terminology in parapsychology. *Journal of Parapsychology*, *35*, 34–56.

Rhine, J. B., & Pratt, J. G. (1974). *Parapsychology: Frontier science of the mind* (5th ed.). Charles C. Thomas. (Original work published in 1957)

Robbins, K., & Roe, C. A. (2010). An empirical test of the theory of morphic resonance by using recognition for Chinese symbols. *Explore: The Journal of Science and Healing*, *6*, 256–262.

Robinson, H. (2020, September 11). Dualism. *Stanford Encyclopedia of Philosophy*. https://plato.stanford.edu/entries/dualism/

Roe, C. A., Davey, R., & Stevens, P. (2003). Are ESP and PK aspects of a unitary phenomenon? A preliminary test of the relationship between ESP and PK. *Journal of Parapsychology*, *67*, 343–366.

Roe, C. A., Davey, R., & Stevens, P. (2004). Arousal and performance at ESP and PK tasks using a common protocol. *European Journal of Parapsychology*, *19*, 29–43.

Roe, C. A., Davey, R., & Stevens, P. (2005). Are ESP and PK aspects of a unitary phenomenon? The effects of deception when testing the relationship between ESP and PK. *Journal of the Society for Psychical Research, 69*, 18–32.

Roe, C. A., Davey, R., & Stevens, P. (2006). Experimenter effects in laboratory tests of ESP and PK using a common protocol. *Journal of Scientific Exploration, 20*(2), 239–253.

Roe, C. A., Martin, H., & Drennan, S. (2014). Effects of participant and target system lability upon PK performance using an IChing task. *Journal of the Society for Psychical Research, 78*, 219–238.

Roesler, C. (2014). Investigating synchronistic events in psychotherapy. In H. Atmanspacher, & C. A. Fuchs (Eds.), *The Pauli-Jung conjecture and its impact today* (242–254). Imprint Academic.

Roe, C. A., Sonnex, C., & Roxburgh, E. C. (2015). Two meta-analyses of noncontact healing studies. *Explore: The Journal of Science and Healing, 11*(1), 11–23.

Roll, W. (2006). A discussion of the evidence that personal consciousness persists after death with special reference to poltergeist phenomena. *Australian Journal of Parapsychology, 6*, 5–20.

Roll, W. G. (1966). The psi field. In W. G. Roll & J. G. Pratt (Eds.), *Proceedings of the Parapsychological Association, 1, 1957-1964* (32–65). Parapsychological Association.

Roll, W. G., Alexander, C. H., Williams, B. J., & Persinger, M. A. (2021). Parapsychology, quantum theory and neuroscience. In S. Krippner, A. J. Rock, H. L. Friedman, & N. L. Zingrone (Eds.), *Advances in parapsychological research 10* (70–166). McFarland.

Roney-Dougal, S. (2010). *Where science and magic meet* (3rd ed.). Dorchester, UK: Green Magic. (Original work published in 1991)

Röntgen, W. C. (1972). *Fundamental contributions to the X-ray: The three original communications on a new kind of ray* (Trans. Ernest Kraft). US National Library of Medicine. (Original work published in 1895)

Rosenblum, B., & Kuttner, F. (2011). *Quantum enigma: Physics encounters consciousness.* Duckworth Overlook.

Rosen, D. H., Smith, S. M., Huston, H. L., & Gonzalez, G. (1991). Empirical study of associations between symbols and their meanings: Evidence of collective and unconscious (archetypal) memory. *Journal of Analytical Psychology, 36*, 211–228.

Rosenthal, R. (1979). The 'File Drawer Problem' and tolerance for null results. *Psychological Bulletin, 86*(3), 638–641.

Roth, R. F. (2022). Wolfgang Pauli's magician and the problem of psychophysical reality (unus mundus): The dispute between Wolfgang Pauli, C. G. Jung and Marie-Louise von Franz, and a possible solution. [Unpublished manuscript].

Rubin, L., & Honorton, C. (1971). Separating the yins from the yangs: An experiment with the *I Ching*. *Journal of Parapsychology, 35*, 313–314.

Rubin, L., & Honorton, C. (1972). Separating the yins from the yangs: An experiment with the *I Ching*. In W. G. Roll, R. L. Morris, & J. D. Morris (Eds.), *Proceedings of the 15th Annual Convention Parapsychological Association* (6–7). Parapsychological Association.

Russell, B. (1953). *Mysticism and logic.* Pelican. (Original work published in 1917)

Sabine Hossenfelder. (2021, April 24). *Particle physics discoveries that disappeared* [Video]. YouTube. https://www.youtube.com/watch?v=kGggYZTK1ik

Sabine Hossenfelder. (2021, October, 30). *The Delayed Choice Quantum Eraser, Debunked* [Video]. YouTube. www.youtube.com/watch?v=RQv5CVELG3U

Saltmarsh, H. F. (1975). *Evidence of personal survival from cross correspondences.* Arno Press. (Original work published in 1938)

Scargle, J. D. (1999, September 17). Publication bias (The "File-Drawer Problem") in scientific inference. https://arxiv.org/pdf/physics/9909033

Schlitz, M. J. (2001). Boundless mind: Coming of age in parapsychology. *Journal of Parapsychology, 65*, 335–350.

Schlitz, M., Bem, D., Marcusson-Clavertz, D., Cardeña, E., Lyke, J., Grover, R., Blackmore, S., Tressoldi, P., Roney-Dougal, S., Bierman, D., Jolij, J., Lobach, E., Hartelius, G., &Delorme, A. (2021). Two replication studies of a time-reversed (psi) priming task and the role of expectancy in reaction times. *Journal of Scientific Exploration*, *35*(1), 69–94.

Schlosshauer, M., Kofler, J., & Zeilinger, A. (2013). A snapshot of foundational attitudes toward quantum mechanics. *Studies in History and Philosophy of Science Part B: Studies in History and Philosophy of Modern Physics*, *44*(3), 222–230.

Schmeidler, G. R. (1964). An experiment on precognitive clairvoyance. Part I. The Main Results. *Journal of Parapsychology*, *28*, 1–14.

Schmeidler, G. R. (1969). Introduction. In G. R. Schmeidler (Ed.), *Extrasensory perception* (1–29). Atherton Press.

Schmeidler, G. R. (1977). Methods for controlled research on ESP and PK. In B. B. Wolman (Ed.), *Handbook of parapsychology* (132–159). Van Nostrand Reinhold.

Schmeidler, G. R. (1988). *Parapsychology and psychology: Matches and mismatches*. McFarland.

Schmeidler, G. R. (1994). PK: Recent research reports and a comparison with ESP. In S. Krippner (Ed.), *Advances in parapsychological research 7* (198–237). McFarland.

Schmidt, S., Müller, S., & Walach, H. (2004). Do you know who is on the phone? Replication of an experiment on telephone telepathy. In *Proceedings of the 47th Annual Convention of the Parapsychological Association* (245–254). Parapsychological Association.

Schmidt, S., Schneider, R., Utts, J., & Walach, H. (2002). Remote intention on electrodermal activity: Two meta-analyses. *Proceedings of the 45th Annual Convention of the Parapsychological Association* (27–47). Parapsychological Association.

Schmidt, S., Schneider, R., Utts, J., & Walach, H. (2004). Distant intentionality and the feeling of being stared at: Two meta-analyses. *British Journal of Psychology*, *95*, 235–247.

Schouten, S. A. (1994). An overview of quantitatively evaluated studies with mediums and psychics. *Journal of the American Society for Psychical Research*, *88*, 221–254.

Schreiner, M. (2016, May 17). Fanaticism explained. *Existential Psychology*. https://evolutioncounseling.com/fanaticism-explained/

Schrödinger, E. (1980). The present situation in quantum mechanics: A translation of Schrödinger's "Cat Paradox" paper (J. D. Trimmer, Trans.). *Proceedings of the American Philosophical Society*, *124*, 323–228. (Original work published in 1935)

Schwartz, B. E. (2008). Synchronicity and telepathy. In L. Storm (Ed.), *Synchronicity: Multiple perspectives on meaningful coincidence* (67–77). Pari Publishing.

Schwartz, S. A. (2000). *The Alexandria project*. Author's Guild.

Schwartz, S. A. (2005). *The secret vaults of time*. Hampton Roads.

Schwartz, S. A. (2007). *Remote viewing conference 2006: Factors that impact on remote viewing success*. East Windsor Hill, CT: International Remote Viewing Association/CreateSpace.

Schwartz, S. A. (2009, Spring). The mist wolf. *Parabola*, 6–11.

Schwartz, S. A. (2014). Through time and space: The evidence for remote viewing. In D. Broderick, & B. Goertzel (Eds.), *Evidence for psi: Thirteen empirical research reports* (168–212). McFarland.

Schwartz, S. A. (2018). Nonlocal consciousness and the anthropology of religion. *Explore: The Journal of Science and Healing*, *14*(6), 402–404.

Schwartz, S. A. (2023). A reality based on consciousness. *Dialogo*, *8*(1), 205–217.

Seager, W. (2014). Dual support for Pauli's dual aspects. In H. Atmanspacher, & C. A. Fuchs (Eds.), *The Pauli-Jung conjecture and its impact today* (125–150). Imprint Academic.

Segaller, S. (Producer/Director). (1989). *The wisdom of the dream* [Television documentary]. British Broadcasting Corporation.

Shakespeare, W. (1993). Hamlet. *The Complete Works of William Shakespeare*. http://shakespeare.mit.edu/hamlet/hamlet.3.2.html (Original work published in 1601)

Sheehan, D. P. (2015). Remembrance of things future: A case for retrocausation and precognition. In E. C. May, & S. B. Marwaha (Eds.), *Extrasensory perception: Support, skepticism, and science, volume 2 – Theories of psi* (85–109). Praeger.

Sheldrake, R. (1981). *A new science of life: The hypothesis of morphic resonance*. J. P. Tarcher.

Sheldrake, R. (2014). Telepathy in connection with telephone calls, text messages, and emails. *Journal of the International Society of Life Information Science, 32*(1), 7–10.

Sheldrake, R., & Smart, P. (2003a). Experimental tests for telephone telepathy. *Journal of the Society for Psychical Research, 67*, 184–199.

Sheldrake, R., & Smart, P. (2003b). Videotaped experiments on telephone telepathy. *Journal of Parapsychology, 67*, 147–166.

Shermer, M., (2014, October 1). Anomalous events that can shake one's skepticism to the core. *Scientific American*. https://www.scientificamerican.com/article/anomalous-events-that-can-shake-one-s-skepticism-to-the-core/

Shoup, R. (2015). Physics beyond causality: Making sense of quantum mechanics and certain experimental anomalies. In E. C. May, & S. B. Marwaha (Eds.), *Extrasensory perception: Support, skepticism, and science, volume 2 – Theories of psi* (63–83). Praeger.

Silberstein, R., & Bigelow, F. J. (2024). Brain functional connectivity correlates of anomalous interaction between sensorily isolated monozygotic twins. *Frontiers in Human Neuroscience, 18*. doi: 10.3389/fnhum.2024.1388049

Singh, A. K. (2015). *Engineered nanoparticles: Structure, properties, and mechanism of toxicity*. Academic Press.

Sivasundaram, S., & Nielsen, K. H. (2016). Surveying the attitudes of physicists concerning foundational issues of quantum mechanics. *ArXiv*:1612.00676 [Physics, Physics:QuantPh]. http://arxiv.org/abs/1612.00676

Smith, P. H. (1998). *Coordinate remote viewing training manual*. SRI International.

Sotirova-Kohli, M., Opwis, K., Roesler, C., Smith, S. M., Rosen, D. H., Vaid, J., & Djonov, V. (2013). Symbol/Meaning paired-associate recall: An "Archetypal memory" advantage? *Behavioral Science, 3*, 541–561.

Sotirova-Kohli, M., Rosen, D. H., Smith, S. M., Henderson, P., & Taki-Reece, S. (2011). Empirical study of kanji as archetypal images: Understanding the collective unconscious as part of the Japanese language. *Journal of Analytical Psychology, 56*, 109–132.

Spencer, B. (1995). Correlations, sample size, and practical significance: A comparison of selected psychological and medical investigations. *Journal of Psychology, 129*, 469–475.

Stanford, R. G. (1977). Conceptual frameworks of contemporary psi research. In B. B. Wolman (Ed.), *Handbook of parapsychology* (823–858). Van Nostrand Reinhold.

Stanford, R. G. (1978). Towards reinterpreting psi events. *Journal of the American Society for Psychical Research, 72*, 197–214.

Stanford, R. G. (1990). An experimentally testable model for spontaneous psi events: A review of related evidence and concepts from parapsychology and other sciences. In S. Krippner (Ed.), *Advances in parapsychological research 6* (54–167). McFarland.

Stanford, R. G. (1974a). An experimentally testable model for spontaneous psi events: I. Extrasensory events. *Journal of the American Society for Psychical Research, 68*, 34–57.

Stanford, R. G. (1974b). An experimentally testable model for spontaneous psi events: II. Psychokinetic events. *Journal of the American Society for Psychical Research, 68*, 321–356.

Stapp, H. P. (2000). The importance of quantum decoherence in brain process. *Lawrence Berkeley National Laboratory Report LBNL-46871*. https://doi.org/10.48550/arXiv.quant-ph/0010029

Stapp, H. P. (2009). *Mind, matter, and quantum mechanics* (3rd ed.). Springer-Verlag.

Steinkamp, F. (2000). Does precognition foresee the future? A postal experiment to assess the possibility of true precognition. *Journal of Parapsychology, 64*, 3–18.

Steinkamp, F. (2001). Does precognition foresee the future? series 2, laboratory replication and series 3, a world wide web replication. *Journal of Parapsychology, 65*, 17–40.

Steinkamp, F., Milton, J., & Morris, R. L. (1998). A meta-analysis of forced-choice experiments comparing clairvoyance and precognition. *Journal of Parapsychology, 62*, 193–218.

Stevens, P. (1998-1999). Remote psychokinesis. *European Journal of Parapsychology, 14*, 68–79.

Stevens, P. (2002). Can we differentiate between ESP and imagination? *Journal of the Society for Psychical Research, 66*, 239–246.

Stokes, D. M. (1985). Parapsychology and its critics. In P. Kurtz (Ed.), *A skeptic's handbook of parapsychology* (379–423). Prometheus.

Stokes, D. M. (1987). Theoretical parapsychology. In S. Krippner (Ed.), *Advances in parapsychological research 5* (77–189). McFarland.

Stokes, D. M. (2007). *The conscious mind and the material world*. McFarland.

Stokes, D. M. (2015). The case against psi. In E. Cardeña, J. Palmer, & D. Marcusson-Clavetz (Eds.), *Parapsychology: A handbook for the 21st century* (42–48). McFarland.

Storm, L. (2001). Technical note: Effect size in 'The transliminal connection between paranormal effects and personality in an experiment with the *I Ching*' by Storm & Thalbourne (1998-1999). *European Journal of Parapsychology, 16*, 107–108.

Storm, L. (2002). A parapsychological investigation of the *I Ching*: Seeking psi in an ancient Chinese system of divination. *Australian Journal of Parapsychology, 2*, 44–62.

Storm, L. (2003a). Research note: The pro attitude and the 'sheep-goat' effect in the *I Ching* database. *Australian Journal of Parapsychology, 3*, 147–152.

Storm, L. (2003b). The *I Ching* and the Lotto game: Trying to beat the odds using an ancient Chinese system of divination. *Australian Journal of Parapsychology, 3*, 140–146.

Storm, L. (2005). A critique of the theory of psychopraxia. In M. A. Thalbourne, & L. Storm (Eds.), *Parapsychology in the twenty-first century: Essays on the future of psychical research* (205–219). McFarland.

Storm, L. (2006). A parapsychological investigation of the *I Ching*: The relationships between psi, intuition, and time perspective. *Journal of Parapsychology, 70*, 121–141.

Storm, L. (2008a). Archetypes, causality, and meaning. In L. Storm (Ed.), *Synchronicity: Multiple perspectives on meaningful coincidence* (259–272). Pari Publishing.

Storm, L. (2008b). Investigations of the *I Ching*: I. Relationships between psi, time perspective, paranormal belief and meaningfulness. *Australian Journal of Parapsychology, 8*, 103–127.

Storm, L. (2008c). Synchronicity and psi. In L. Storm (Ed.), *Synchronicity: Multiple perspectives on meaningful coincidence* (273–296). Pari Publishing.

Storm, L. (2008d). Synchronicity, causality, and acausality. In L. Storm (Ed.), *Synchronicity: Multiple perspectives on meaningful coincidence* (153–174). Pari Publishing.

Storm, L. (Ed.). (2008e). *Synchronicity: Multiple perspectives on meaningful coincidence*. Pari Publishing.

Storm, L. (2008g). *The enigma of numbers*. Pari Publishing.

Storm, L. (2009). Investigations of the *I Ching*: II. Reliability and validity studies. *Australian Journal of Parapsychology, 9*, 111–142.

Storm, L. (2014). At my desk. *THE A.I.P.R. NEWS, 8*(1), 2.

Storm, L. (2015). At my desk. *THE A.I.P.R. NEWS, 9*(1), 2.

Storm, L. (2016). Conformity and reactance in the *I Ching* using a Q-Sort/RNG-PK method: A pilot study. *Australian Journal of Parapsychology, 16*, 133–162.

Storm, L. (2022). The effects of imagery-cultivation on mood and psi performance. *Journal of the Society for Psychical Research, 86*, 95–113.

Storm, L. (2023a). The dark spirit of the trickster archetype in parapsychology. *Journal of Scientific Exploration, 37*(4), 665–682.

Storm, L. (2023b). The effects of imagery-cultivation on phenomenological and paranormal experience. *Journal of the Society for Psychical Research*, *87*(1), 1–21.

Storm, L. (2025). *A new approach to synchronicity: A re-appraisal of Jung's acausal connecting principle with a focus on psi*. Routledge.

Storm, L., Drinkwater, K., & Jinks, A. L. (2017). A question of belief: An analysis of item content in paranormal belief questionnaires. *Journal of Scientific Exploration*, *31*(2), 187–230.

Storm, L., & Ertel, S. (2001). Does psi exist? Comments on Milton and Wiseman's (1999) meta-analysis of ganzfeld research. *Psychological Bulletin*, *127*, 424–433. doi:10.1037/0033-2909.127.3.424

Storm, L., & Goretzki, M. (2020). Spiritual emergency and psi: Testing the psychic opening hypothesis. *The Journal of Transpersonal Psychology*, *52*(1), 142–162.

Storm, L., & Goretzki, M. (2021). The psychology and parapsychology of spiritual emergency. *Journal of Scientific Exploration*, *35*(1), 36–64.

Storm, L., & Rock, A. J. (2014a). An investigation of the *I Ching* using the Q-Sort Method and an RNG-PK design: I. Four possible psi predictors. *Australian Journal of Parapsychology*, *14*, 29–67.

Storm, L., & Rock, A. J. (2014b). An investigation of the *I Ching* using the Q-Sort Method and an RNG-PK design: II. The effect of reactance on psi. *Australian Journal of Parapsychology*, *12*, 163–190.

Storm, L., Sherwood, S. J., Roe, C. A., Tressoldi, P. E., Rock, A. J., & Di Risio, L. (2017). On the correspondence between dream content and target material under laboratory conditions: A meta-analysis of dream-ESP studies, 1966-2016. *International Journal of Dream Research: Psychological Aspects of Sleep and Dreaming*, *10*(2), 120–140.

Storm, L., & Thalbourne, M. A. (1998-1999). The transliminal connection between personality and paranormal effects in an experiment with the *I Ching*. *European Journal of Parapsychology*, *14*, 100–124.

Storm, L., & Thalbourne, M. A. (2000). A paradigm shift away from the ESP-PK dichotomy: The theory of psychopraxia. *Journal of Parapsychology*, *64*, 279–300.

Storm, L., & Thalbourne, M. A. (2003). Perceived complexity, perceived task difficulty, and other states of mind: The influence of mental states on psi outcomes. *Journal of the American Society for Psychical Research*, *97*, 155–174.

Storm, L., & Thalbourne, M. A. (2005a). The effect of a change in pro attitude on paranormal performance: A pilot study using naïve and sophisticated skeptics. *Journal of Scientific Exploration*, *19*(1), 11–29.

Storm, L., & Thalbourne, M. A. (2005b). The effects of intuition and attitudes towards gambling on ESP performance during a gambling task. *European Journal of Parapsychology*, *20*, 22–49.

Storm, L., & Thalbourne, M. A. (2018). Research note: Demonstrating the concurrent validity of two coincidence measures. *Australian Journal of Parapsychology*, *18*, 57–69.

Storm, L., & Tilley, R. (2020). Haunt and poltergeist clearing in Australian residences: A retrospective survey. *Australian Journal of Parapsychology*, *20*, 21–55.

Storm, L., & Tressoldi, P. E. (2017). Gathering in more sheep and goats: A meta-analysis of forced-choice sheep-goat studies, 1994-2015. *Journal of the Society for Psychical Research,81*, 79–107.

Storm, L., & Tressoldi, P. E. (2020). Meta-analysis of free-response studies 2009-2018: Assessing the noise-reduction model ten years on. *Journal of the Society for Psychical Research,84*, 193–219.

Storm, L., & Tressoldi, P. E. (2023). Assessing 36 years of the forced-choice design in extrasensory perception research: A meta-analysis, 1987 to 2022. *Journal of Scientific Exploration*, *37*(3), 517–535.

Storm, L., Tressoldi, P. E., & Di Risio, L. (2010). Meta-analyses of free-response studies 1992-2008: Assessing the noise reduction model in parapsychology. *Psychological Bulletin*, *136*(4), 471–485. doi: 10.1037/a0019457.

Storm, L., Tressoldi, P. E., & Di Risio, L. (2012). Meta-analyses of ESP studies 1987-2008: Assessing the success of the forced-choice design in parapsychology. *Journal of Parapsychology*, *76*, 243–273.

Tammet, D. (2007). *Born on a blue day: Inside the extraordinary mind of an autistic savant*. Free Press.

Targ, R. (2012). *The reality of ESP: A physicist's proof of psychic abilities*. Theosophical Publishing House.

Targ, R. (2019). What do we know about psi? The first decade of remote-viewing research and operations at Stanford Research Institute. *Journal of Scientific Exploration*, *33*(4), 569–592.

Targ, R., & Katra, J. (1998). *Miracles of mind: Exploring nonlocal consciousness and spiritual healing*. New World Library.

Targ, R., & Puthoff, H. E. (1977). *Mind-reach: Scientists look at psychic ability*. Hampton Roads.

Targ, E., Targ, R., & Lichtarge, O. (1985). Realtime clairvoyance: A study of remote viewing without feedback. *Journal of the American Society for Psychical Research*, *79*, 493–500.

Targ, R., & Tart, C. T. (1985). Pure clairvoyance and the necessity of feedback. *Journal of the American Society for Psychical Research*, *79*, 485–492.

Tarlacı, S., & Pregnolato, M. (2015). Quantum neurophysics: From non-living matter to quantum neurobiology and psychopathology. *International Journal of Psychophysiology*, *103*, 161–173.

Tarnas, R. (2007). *Cosmos and psyche: Intimations of a new world view*. Penguin/Plume.

Tart, C. T. (1968). A psychophysiological study of out-of-the-body experiences in a selected subject. *Journal of the American Society for Psychical Research*, *62*, 3–27.

Tart, C. T. (1984). Acknowledging and dealing with the fear of psi. *Journal of the American Society for Psychical Research*, *78*, 133–143.

Tart, C. T. (2008). Causality and synchronicity: Steps towards clarification. In L. Storm (Ed.), *Synchronicity: Multiple perspectives on meaningful coincidence* (109–126). Pari Publishing.

Taylor, J. (2019). A model for psi based on information transfer between brains. *Mindfield: The Bulletin of the Parapsychological Association*, *11*(1), 13–19.

Tegmark, M. (2000). The importance of quantum decoherence in brain processes. *Physical Review E*, *61*(4), 4194–4206.

Tennant, G. (2001). *SIX SIGMA: SPC and TQM in manufacturing and services*. Gower Publishing.

Thalbourne, M. A. (1981). *Some experiments on the paranormal cognition of drawings with special reference to personality and attitudinal variables* [Unpublished doctoral thesis]. Department of Parapsychology, University of Edinburgh.

Thalbourne, M. A. (1982). *A glossary of terms used in parapsychology*. Heinemann.

Thalbourne, M. A. (1995). Science versus showmanship: A history of the Randi hoax. *Journal of the American Society for Psychical Research*, *89*, 344–366.

Thalbourne, M. A. (2003). *A glossary of terms used in parapsychology*. Puente.

Thalbourne, M. A. (2004). *The common thread between ESP and PK*. The Parapsychology Foundation.

Thalbourne, M. A. (2008). A second experiment on the effect of kundalini on the output of a random number generator. *Journal of Parapsychology*, *72*, 155–168.

Thalbourne, M. A. (2006a). A statistical test of the 'library angel'. *Australian Journal of Parapsychology*, *6*, 186–191.

Thalbourne, M. A. (2006b). Kundalini and the output of a random number generator. *Journal of Parapsychology*, *70*, 303–333.

Thalbourne, M. A., Bartemucci, L., Delin, P. S., Fox, B., & Nofi, O. (1997). Transliminality: Its nature and correlates. *Journal of the American Society for Psychical Research*, *91*, 305–331.

Thalbourne, M. A., & Houran, J. (2000). Transliminality, the Mental Experience Inventory and tolerance of ambiguity. *Personality and Individual Differences*, *28*, 853–863.

Thalbourne, M. A., & Storm, L. (2014). A further study of psychopraxia using the *IChing. Australian Journal of Par apsychology, 14*, 115–142.

Thalbourne, M. A., & Storm, L. (2015). Debunking an alleged feedback artifact in Thalbourne's RNG studies. *Australian Journal of Parapsychology, 15*, 81–87.

Thalbourne, M. A., & Storm, L. (2019). The relationship between paranormal belief and psychopathology with special focus on magical ideation, psychosis, and schizotypy. *Australian Journal of Parapsychology, 19*, 181–211.

Thouless, R. H., & Wiesner, B. P. (1947). The psi process in normal and "paranormal" psychology. *Proceedings of the Society for Psychical Research, 48*, 177–196. [Abridged in *Journal of Parapsychology*, 1948, *12*, 192–212.]

Tierney, I. (2020). Dissonance, complementarity, and psi. *Journal of Parapsychology, 84*, 276–286.

Timm, U. (2000). The problem of finding an optimal measure of effect size for psi experiments. *Journal of Parapsychology, 64*, 253–254.

Tobacyk, J. J. (1988). *A revised paranormal belief scale*. [Unpublished manuscript]. Ruston, LA, USA: Louisiana Tech University.

Tom Campbell. (2014, September 28). *The key to understanding our reality* [Video]. YouTube. https://www.youtube.com/watch?v=BhMIz_iJtzQ&t

Tremblay, N. (2021). Correction: Independent re-analysis of alleged mind-matter interaction in double-slit experimental data. *PLoS ONE, 16*(6), 1–20.

Tressoldi, P. E., Storm, L., & Radin, D. (2010). Extrasensory perception and quantum models of cognition. *Neuroquantology: An Interdisciplinary Journal of Neuroscience and Quantum Physics, 8*(4), S81–87.

Tyrrell, G. N. M. (1936). Further research in extra-sensory perception. *Proceedings of the Society for Psychical Research, 44*, 99–167.

Tyrrell, G. N. M. (1946). Perspective in psychical research. *Journal of the American Society for Psychical Research, 40*, 229–240.

Ullman, M., Krippner, S., & with Vaughan, A. (1973). *Dream telepathy: Experiments in nocturnal ESP*. McFarland.

Utts, J. (1991). Replication and meta-analysis in parapsychology. *Statistical Science, 6*, 363–378.

Utts, J. (1996). An assessment of the evidence for psychic functioning. *Journal of Scientific Exploration, 10*(1), 3–30.

Utts, J. (1999). The significance of statistics in mind-matter research. *Journal of Scientific Exploration, 13*(4), 615–638.

Valencia, A. L., & Froese, T. (2020). What binds us? Inter-brain neural synchronization and its implications for theories of human consciousness. *Neuroscience of Consciousness, 20*(1), 1–12. doi: 10.1093/nc/niaa010.

Varvoglis, M., & Bancel, P. A. (2015). Micro-psychokinesis. In E. Cardeña, J. Palmer, & D. Marcusson-Clavertz (Eds.), *Parapsychology. A handbook for the 21st century* (266–281). McFarland.

Vaughan, A. (1979). *Incredible coincidence: The baffling world of synchronicity*. Ballantine.

Vaughan, A. (1980). Synchronicity, causality and consciousness as creator. In W. G. Roll (Ed.), *Research in parapsychology 1979* (21–23). Scarecrow Press.

Venning, T. (2019, June 5). Time's arrow: Albert Einstein's letters to Michele Besso. *Christie's*. https://www.christies.com/features/Einstein-letters-to-Michele-Besso-8422-1.aspx

Ventura, T. (2020, March 25). Dean Radin on Global Consciousness, Parapsychology, and Psychic Research. *Medium*. https://medium.com/predict/dean-radin-on-global-consciousness-parapsychology-and-psychic-research-685b4d3b7382

Von Franz, M.-L. (1980). *On divination and synchronicity*. Inner City.

Von Franz, M.-L. (1992). *Psyche and matter*. Shambhala.

Von Lucadou, W. (1987). The model of pragmatic information (MPI). *Proceedings of the 30th Annual Convention of the Parapsychological Association* (236–254). Parapsychological Association.

Von Lucadou, W. (1995). The model of pragmatic information (MPI). *European Journal of Parapsychology*, *11*, 58–75.
Von Lucadou, W. (2001). Hans in luck: The currency of evidence in parapsychology. *Journal of Parapsychology*, *65*, 3–16.
Von Lucadou, W. (2015). The model of pragmatic information. In E. C. May, & S. B. Marwaha (Eds.), *Extrasensory perception: Support, skepticism, and science, volume 2 – Theories of psi* (221–242). Praeger.
Von Lucadou, W. (2019). Causality and entanglement: Results of the correlation matrix method (CMM): The sheep hide on the banks of the river. Contribution to the Workshop on Psi Theories, Paris, France, July 2-3, 2019 to Wednesday July 3: Generalized Quantum Theory and Psi.
Von Lucadou, W., Römer, H., & Walach, H. (2007). Synchronistic phenomena as entanglement correlations in generalized quantum theory. *Journal of Consciousness Studies*, *14*(4), 50–74.
Von Lucadou, W., & Zahradnik, F. (2004). Predictions of the Model of Pragmatic Information about RSPK. In *Proceedings of the 47th Annual Convention of the Parapsychological Association* (99–112). Parapsychological Association.
Von Neumann, J. (1955). *Mathematical foundations of quantum mechanics*. Princeton University Press.
Walach, H., Kohls, N., von Stillfried, N., Hinterberger, T., & Schmidt, S. (2009). Spirituality: The legacy of parapsychology. *Archive for the Psychology of Religion*, *31*, 275–306.
Walach, H., Schmidt, S., Schneider, R., Seiter, C., & Bösch, H. (2002). Melting boundaries: Subjectivity and intersubjectivity in the light of parapsychological data. *European Journal of Parapsychology*, *17*, 72–96.
Walker, E. H. (1984). A review of criticisms of the quantum mechanical theory of psi phenomena. *Journal of Parapsychology*, *48*, 277–332.
Wall, K. E. (2014). *Romantic love, relationship, and the journey of individuation*. [Unpublished master's thesis]. Pacifica Graduate Institute.
Walleczek, J., & von Stillfried, N. (2019). False-positive effect in the Radin double-slit experiment on observer consciousness as determined with the advanced meta-experimental protocol. *Frontiers in Psychology*, *10*, 1–18.
Warcollier, R. (1938). *Experimental telepathy* (trans. by J. B. Gridley from *La telepathie*, 1921). Boston Society for Psychical Research.
Warwick, K., Gasson, M., Hutt, B., Goodhew, I., Kyberd, P., Schulzrinne, H., & Wu, X. (2004). Thought communication and control: A first step using radiotelegraphy. *IEE Proceedings on Communications*, *151*(3), 85–189.
Watt, C. (1988). Characteristics of successful free-response targets: Theoretical considerations. *Proceedings of the 31st Annual Convention of the Parapsychological Association* (17–21). Parapsychological Association.
West, D. J., & Fisk, G. W. (1953). A dual ESP experiment with clock cards. *Journal of the Society for Psychical Research*,*37*, 185–189.
Wheeler, J. A. (1984). Law without law. In J. A. Wheeler, &W. H. Zurek (Eds.), *Quantum theory and measurement* (182–213). Princeton University Press.
White, R. A. (1994). Seek ye first the kingdom of heaven: What are EHEs and what can we do about them? In R. A. White (Ed.), *Exceptional human experience: Background papers i* (34–46). Exceptional Human Experience Network.
Wigner, E. P. (1961). Remarks on the mind-body problem. In I. J. Good (Ed.), *The scientist speculates* (284–301). Heinemann.
Wigner, E. P. (1995). *Philosophical reflections and syntheses*. Berlin: Springer-Verlag.
Wilhelm, H. (1960). *Change: Eight lectures on the IChing* (C. F. Baynes, Trans.). Princeton University Press.
Williams, B. J. (2014). Revisiting the ganzfeld ESP debate: A basic review and assessment. In D. Broderick, & B. Goertzel (Eds.), *Evidence for psi: Thirteen empirical research reports* (77–92). McFarland.

Williams, B. J. (2015). *Psychic phenomena and the brain: Exploring the neuropsychology of psi*. Gladesville, NSW: Australian Institute of Parapsychological Research, Inc.
Williams, B. J. (2019). Reassessing the "impossible": A critical commentary on Reber and Alcock's "Why parapsychological claims cannot be true. *Journal of Scientific Exploration*, *33*(4), 599–616.
Window to the Soul. (2019, August 9). *Synchronicity is not just a coincidence: What is synchronicity & what does it mean?* [Video]. YouTube. https://www.youtube.com/watch?v=ptUfqs06oBU
Wiseman, R. (2001). A reply to O'Neill. *Paranormal Review*, *17*, 8–10.
Wiseman, R. (2009). Heads I win, tails you lose: How parapsychologists nullify null results. *Skeptical Inquirer*, *34*(1), 36–40.
Wiseman, R., & Schlitz, M. (1997). Experimenter effects and the remote detection of staring. *Journal of Parapsychology*, *61*, 197–207.
Wolman, B. B. (Ed.). (1977). *Handbook of parapsychology*. Van Nostrand Reinhold.
Wootters, W. K., & Zurek, W. H. (1979). Complementarity in the double-slit experiment: Quantum nonseparability and a quantitative statement of Bohr's principle. *Physical Review D*, *19*(2), 473–484.
Wyld, H. C., & Partridge, E. H. (Eds.). (1968). *Webster universal dictionary: Unabridged international edition*. Routledge & Kegan Paul.
Young, J. H. (2023). Synchronicity: A glimpse of the higher power? *Psychological Perspectives*, *66*(1), 106–129.
Yu, S., & Nikolić, D. (2011). Quantum mechanics needs no consciousness. *Annals of Physics*, *523*(11), 931–938. doi: 10.1002/andp.201100078.
Zeilinger, A. (1999). Experiment and the foundations of quantum physics. *Reviews of Modern Physics*, *71*(2), S288–S297.
Ziewe, J. (2016). Challenges in obtaining verifiable data during out-of-body-experiences. In A. De Foe (Ed.), *Consciousness beyond the body: Evidence and reflections* (116–128). Melbourne Centre for Exceptional Human Potential.
Zingrone, N. L. (2002). Controversy and the problems of parapsychology. *Journal of Parapsychology*, *66*, 3–30.
Zipes, J. (Ed.). (2017). *The sorcerer's apprentice: An anthology of magical tales*. Princeton University Press.

Notes

1 [*CW* = The Collected Works of C. G. Jung (20 volumes). Edited by Gerhard Adler, Michael Fordham, and Herbert Read; William McGuire, Executive Editor; translated by R. F. C. Hull. New York and Princeton (Bollingen Series XX) and London, 1953–1979.]

Index